PRECOLUMBIAN

PRECOLUMBIAN GOLD

Technology, Style and Iconography

EDITED BY COLIN McEWAN

Published for The Trustees of The British Museum by BRITISH MUSEUM PRESS

THE TRUSTEES OF THE BRITISH MUSEUM

GRATEFULLY ACKNOWLEDGE GENEROUS

ASSISTANCE TOWARDS THE PRODUCTION

OF THIS BOOK FROM BP AMOCO.

Published by British Museum Press
A division of The British Museum Company Ltd
46 Bloomsbury Street, London WC1B 3QQ

A catalogue record for this book is available
from the British Library

ISBN 0 7141 2534 2

Designed by Harry Green
Printed in Singapore

FRONTISPIECE
Hammered and embossed sheet *tumbaga* (gold-copper alloy)
ornament with depletion-gilt surface, Manteño, Ecuador,
AD 800–1500. The inset shows a false-colour SEM image of a
magnified cross-section through the thin sheet of the object,
which has been depletion gilt on both sides and the outer
surface then burnished. The sheet (false blue) is 0.15 mm thick
and the gilding (false yellow) is 10–15 microns thick. The
stripes in the sheet metal indicate elongation of the grain
structure produced by hammering.

Contents

Foreword

As this volume demonstrates, we have come to a turning point in our approach to the metal inventory of Precolumbian peoples. In the past ten years or so a small number of carefully controlled archaeological excavations, primarily of burial sites, have yielded metal artefacts in their original, undisturbed contexts. The availability of context frees us from having to study and interpret isolated, naked artefacts often removed from tombs without regard for their association with other burial furniture. The extraction of Precolumbian metal objects without proper archaeological control, and the consequent loss of potential information about what these objects meant for the people who made them, continue to be driven by the international antiquities market. Gold, silver and platinum artefacts are sought not only as prized collectors' items but often for nothing more than the commercial value of the metal. By contrast, copper and bronze artefacts are frequently discarded as essentially worthless, having little or no economic value. Consequently many objects are isolated from their cultural settings, or are destroyed and lost forever to scientific study.

The scientifically excavated sites that have had a dramatic impact on our ability to assess the role of metal and of metal objects among Precolumbian societies thus far are located primarily in the central Andean region, with a few in the south-central Andes. They include Sipán, the Moche elite tomb district on the lower Lambayeque River, north coastal Peru;[1] Batán Grande, a large, complex Sicán/Chimú metal production centre, and residential and burial site on the nearby Leche River drainage (see Shimada *et al.*, this volume); and several sites of Inca ritual offerings in the form of human burials, located on the high peaks of the Andean cordillera in Peru, Chile, and Argentina (see Dransart, this volume).

Metal objects figure prominently in the burials at all these sites. Equally prominent is their close association and even direct physical contact with objects made from a variety of other materials: among them shell, coloured minerals, gem quality stones, cloth, feathers. Often the metal objects themselves are composites of a range of materials, most notably feathers, coloured stones and even painted pigments. In these burial contexts metal plays a role as one part of a suite of materials, and we must suppose that there is a meaningful pattern to the way in which the suite is assembled: which materials are associated with others, how they are associated, whether in the fabrication of an object one material substitutes for another, and under what circumstances, and so forth. Other primary data obtained from these contexts include the organization of the contents of each burial, the placement of each object with respect to the interred individual or animal and in relation to other objects, and the kinds of objects selected for interment. So too are the choices of materials of which the objects are made and the assembly of those materials into coherent suites.

The opportunity to consider materials as suites or complexes offers invaluable advantages to scholarly study. It lessens the burden of having to determine meaning for any one subset of materials alone, such as metal, for example, or, within the category of metal, for gold or *tumbaga*. We can therefore document the persistence of specific assemblies of materials through time and over a considerable spread of geographic and cultural zones. The continuity in the assemblage of metal, shell and feathers as a minimum or primary set is striking, from Moche usage through Inca and into the contact period among Taino and other Caribbean groups (see Oliver, this volume). For the central Andean region, cloth ought probably to be added to the set (see Dransart, this volume).[2]

Once we recognize and delimit a functioning materials 'environment' that contributes culturally to the organization or association of specific groups of objects, it is easier to ask significant questions about any single category of materials because of the relationships between that category and others in the suite. In the case of metal – especially gold in the context of this volume, as well as silver and *tumbaga* – we would like to know whether and how the pure metals or their alloys were accorded gender: alone, in association with one another, or with other materials. Does gender change as context changes (see Dransart, and Oliver, this volume)?[3] Some students of native American value systems and cosmologies are exploring the extent to which metals and alloys were associated with celestial bodies, how early we have evidence for this association, and whether there is widespread cross-cultural continuity in such associations (see Shimada *et al.*, this volume). Oliver's study of *guanín* among Taino elites considers both these broad issues. He uses archaeological, ethnohistoric and ethnographic evidence to reconstruct an entire cultural schema embodied in the semantic field of *guanín*, in the materials that give *guanín* presence, and in the properties inherent in and bestowed by those materials. This work demonstrates impressively the usefulness of an approach that recognizes the materials environment of an artefact assemblage as fundamental to establishing its context and, ultimately, its cultural message.

This volume adds weight to a growing body of evidence that Precolumbian metallurgy was truly pan-American. The salient features of the metallurgy, wherever metal objects were made or used, are its emphasis on development of specific colours or colour ranges in metals and alloys; its stress on shinyness, reflectivity, iridescence of metallic surfaces; and the predominant use of a triad of metals – copper, silver, gold – and the alloys they formed in combination. That is not to say that arsenic bronze and tin bronze were of little consequence, especially in the Andean region, but it underscores the centrality of the three core metals and their alloys throughout a vast region, including Mesoamerica, and for millennia. As we track the continuities in traditions or styles of materials utilization through time, the overwhelming cultural commitment to the triad metals and their alloys and to the way these were worked to develop specific, inherent physical and sensual properties becomes clear. This commitment was transmitted and shared throughout much of ancient America. Far from visiting upon earlier Andean societies the values, choices, biases of the Inca, as best we understand them (see Shimada *et al.*, this volume), we continue to analyse what the Inca and other late prehispanic societies drew from the experiences of earlier or contemporary peoples in terms of culturally significant materials and materials technologies,[4] and whether and how they modified them. In helping to bound a cluster of associated materials, including metal, that appears to have maintained its integrity throughout large regions of the Americas, this volume substantially broadens the scope of our inquiry and refines the tools by which we proceed.

HEATHER LECHTMAN
Center for Archaeological Materials
Massachusetts Institute of Technology

Notes

1 Alva and Donnan 1993.

2 See also Lechtman 1996.

3 See also Alva and Donnan 1993; Lechtman 1999, in press.

4 Lechtman, in press.

References

Alva, Walter and Christopher B. Donnan
1993 *Royal Tombs of Sipán*. Fowler Museum of Cultural History, Los Angeles.

Lechtman, Heather
1996 Cloth and Metal: The Culture of Technology. In *Andean Art at Dumbarton Oaks*, ed. Elizabeth Hill Boone. Dumbarton Oaks, Washington, DC, pp. 33–43.
1999 Afterword. In *The Social Dynamics of Technology*, ed. Marcia-Anne Dobres and Christopher R. Hoffman. Smithsonian Institution Press, Washington, DC, pp. 223–32.
2000 The Inka and Andean Metallurgical Tradition. In *Variations in the Expression of Inka Power*, ed. Ramiro Matos, Richard Burger and Craig Morris. Dumbarton Oaks, Washington, DC.

Introduction

This volume is the outcome of a conference held at the Museum of Mankind,[1] London, in 1996 to mark the opening of the exhibition *The Gilded Image: Precolumbian Gold from South and Central America*. Initially it was proposed that the exhibition should simply feature a selection of outstanding objects, following a 'treasures from the collections' approach. This, I felt, would have served little real purpose, for the Precolumbian gold collections held by the British Museum, in common with those of other major museums, comprise an eclectic and rather arbitrary assemblage of objects. Moreover, there has been no lack of such exhibitions over the years. Each, in its own way, has attempted to transcend the inherent limitations posed by individual museum collections, often by drawing together a wider range of material from further afield.

One approach has been to weave the objects into a story that tells something of particular sites and finds. This is what the *Gold of El Dorado* exhibition in its various guises succeeded admirably in doing.[2] By unearthing the facts underlying this enduringly popular legend, the exhibition explored some of the lore surrounding the use of gold among the indigenous cultures of Colombia. Like other similar but smaller exhibitions both before and since, it served to define and reinforce our sense of the principal regional gold-working styles in Precolumbian America and to portray the range of variation within each. Another approach has been to focus on a cohering theme that cuts across a range of regional cultures and styles. A well-conceived organizing theme can not only serve as a rationale for display, but also provides an opportunity to disseminate new information and insights to a wider audience. The breadth and depth of the collections in the Museo del Oro, Bogotá, for example, have been used to great effect to develop themes such as shamanistic transformation that undoubtedly inspired the creation of many objects and help explain their significance and ritual use.[3] Yet a third rationale for display has been to present the excavated contexts in which important assemblages of gold and other metals have been found. *River of Gold* set out to do this for one of a series of rich tombs excavated many decades ago at Sitio Conte in the Coclé province of Panama.[4] More recently the Sipán exhibition curated by Walter Alva and Chris Donnan set a new standard for exhibition display as a means to communicate the results of scientific excavation.[5] Izumi Shimada has also incorporated the results of a sustained programme of analytical study into exhibitions which offer unprecedented insights into the contexts and interpretation of Precolumbian metallurgical production and consumption.[6]

These advances in the range and quality of information presented to an increasingly sophisticated public audience pointedly underscore the question of what can best be done with significant museum collections that are often bereft of contextual information. Many of the collections include types of objects that have not yet been recovered from scientifically excavated contexts. Nevertheless, they are often of particular historical interest, and may also represent an invaluable point of reference for comparative purposes and for analytical study.[7] In the British Museum's case, before preparations for *The Gilded Image* began, only a fraction of the objects had ever been on public view. To have adopted the 'treasures' approach to the exhibition would have meant leaving the bulk of the collection to languish unseen and unstudied. A fortuitous informal conversation with Susan La Niece and Nigel Meeks (both metallurgists in the British Museum's Department of Scientific Research) led to a constructive solution. Although their particular expertise lay in the study of ancient 'Old World' goldworking traditions, they welcomed the invitation to begin a comprehensive programme of analytical work on objects drawn from the Museum's Precolumbian collections. The collaborative initiative forged between curator and metallurgists focused on revealing the sophisticated technical accomplishments of native metallurgical traditions in the Americas. The exhibition title, *The Gilded Image*, was itself devised to reflect an important and widespread technique, and to intimate what all students of Precolumbian metallurgy know: that beauty is indeed often skin deep. Although the exhibition occupied a modest space in the Museum of Mankind, the range of the Museum's gold collections was, nevertheless, sufficient to illustrate most of the principal goldworking styles and techniques deployed by cultures spanning Central America and the length of the Andes. The illustrations and explanations of the different techniques provided a unifying theme running through the exhibition, and this was complemented by interpretations of the iconography and symbolism.

Technology, style and iconography

The most productive insights into Precolumbian goldworking emerge at the intersection of technological studies, the recognition and definition of style and the interpretation of iconography. As Heather Lechtman observes in the Foreword to this book, our insights into the production, use and deposition of objects worked in gold are immeasurably enhanced when we have an accurate recording of the excavated contexts from which they came. The reason for convening the scholars' conference to mark the exhibition opening was precisely to draw together the range of interests and expertise represented by archaeologists, art historians, metallurgists and museum curators. Many of the participants could fairly claim to wear more than one hat. This volume represents the fruits of that gathering and its interdisciplinary character is reflected in the contents. It offers a cross-section of current research into Precolumbian metallurgy, especially goldworking.

As 'Old World' specialists, Susan La Niece and Nigel Meeks present a comparative perspective on the technology of gold production that is not often available to scholars on both sides of the Atlantic. Their venture into the metalwork of the Precolumbian Americas demonstrates that it compares well with such traditions elsewhere in the world at that time. Moreover, the solutions to particular technical problems arrived at by Precolumbian artisans challenged many of La Niece and Meeks's own underlying assumptions.

Precolumbian gold from the Caribbean is hard to come by: here the conquistadors' demands for the precious metal were most ruthless. Notwithstanding the small sample of actual objects, José Oliver skilfully combs the ethnohistoric sources to reconstitute the significance of *guanín*. Later in the colonial period other collections of gold were removed but not destroyed, and Jeffrey Quilter offers an example of a significant collection from Costa Rica that can now be provenanced to a site. In Panama Richard Cooke's irrepressible appetite for dirt archaeology yields cultural contexts and fine-grained chronological control for which there is no substitute. Ana-María Falchetti's essay on Zenú goldwork likewise represents the fruits of a lifetime's work combining field excavation and study of museum collections. She brings new insights to the stylistic groups that can be recognised within a regional tradition, the identification of motifs in different media and opens up some intriguing iconographic leads. Roberto Lleras-Pérez's methodical study of Muisca figurines yields thematic patterning that can only be revealed by this sort of comprehensive overview. Warwick Bray, having been immersed for much of his professional life in Colombia, can be relied on to recognize a good thing when he sees it. His assessment of the new-found Malagana site and style traces its far-reaching connections and influences.

Some of the most spectacular recent tomb finds have been made in Peru. Although an intact Chimú tomb has yet to be scientifically excavated, Karen O'Day's description of the distinctive aesthetics of Chimú metallurgical production and its antecedents in earlier North Coast traditions offers a useful synthesis of our current state of knowledge. Izumi Shimada's campaign of excavations over the last two decades are quite remarkable for their scope, rigorous excavation methodology and meticulous recording, which together have yielded an astounding wealth of information. Joerg Haeberli and I joined forces to pursue the trail of a previously undescribed corpus of hammered gold diadems, some of which surfaced unexpectedly in the British Museum's collections. Each contribution combines a distinctive blend of technical, stylistic and iconographic data and shows how inextricably linked these lines of investigation must be if we are to gain a fuller understanding of the cultural matrix within which the objects were created.

It goes without saying that by focusing on gold, the volume carries an in-built bias. Its powers of resistance to corrosion mean that gold endures in archaeological contexts far longer than other precious metals. While gold may have been privi-

General map of South and
Central America with key to
more detailed regional maps
to be found later in the book.

Opposite: Cast gold pectoral,
Popayan, Colombia,
AD 1100–1500, with (inset)
a magnified detail of the
striking plumed headdress
worn by the central figure,
which was cast using the
lost-wax method. Although
the headdress might appear
at first sight to have been
made with wire filigree, the
magnified image shows that
the grooves were in fact
carved into the original wax
model. The small gold
sphere on the surface reveals
where a drop of molten wax
fell on the model before it
was moulded in clay.

leged above other metals among Andean cultures
themselves, it is rarely found alone (silver is usually associated in a naturally occurring admixture),
worked alone (when alloyed with copper, it is
immediately rendered much more malleable) or
deposited in the form of isolated cultural artefacts.
Directly or indirectly, its cultural role is closely
bound up with all other metals. Although this

volume focuses first and foremost on gold as the
most highly valued of all precious metals, I hope
that it will avoid simply reinforcing existing
biases, but rather help stimulate continued
research into the other metals, in order to add to
what we know about the individual objects, the
contexts in which they were used and the people
who made them.

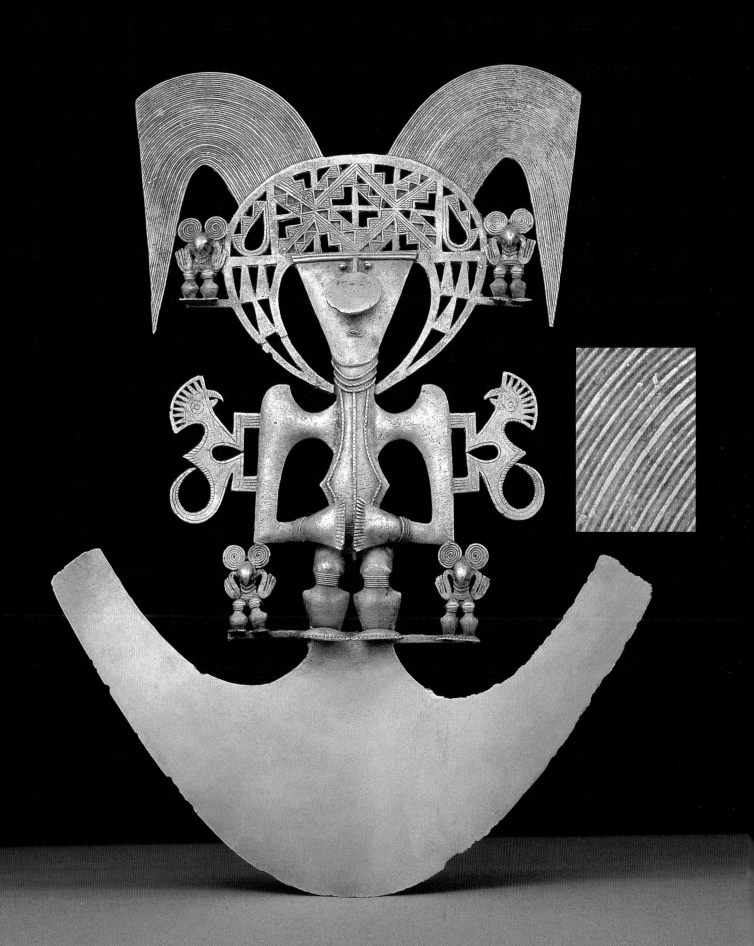

Acknowledgements

The exhibition *The Gilded Image: Precolumbian Gold from South and Central America* at the Museum of Mankind (May 1996–December 1997) was generously supported by British Petroleum (now BP Amoco). The Scholar's Conference that took place in May 1996 soon after the opening was one of those happy occasions when a combination of hard work and good will spiced with happenstance brought about an unexpectedly rich and representative gathering of scholars and friends. I would particularly like to thank Carmen Azurin (then Cultural Attaché with the Peruvian Embassy in London) who helped secure support from the Peruvian Embassy in Washington to enable Walter Alva and Izumi Shimada to come to London. The Colombian Embassy provided accommodation for Ana-María Falchetti during her visit, Alexandra Morgan generously hosted Walter Alva during his stay and John Merkel (Institute of Archaeology, UCL) kindly hosted Izumi Shimada. Clara Bezanilla (British Museum) and Joanne Harwood (University of Essex) ably assisted with planning and running the conference. The original gathering was intended to offer scope for established figures in the field to mix with younger scholars and I have endeavoured to adhere to that spirit in preparing this publication. Unfortunately, not all the conference presentations could be included in the final volume.

In addition to sponsoring the original exhibition, BP Amoco have also supported the publication of this book with a substantial subvention. The British Museum approved support for a special assistant to help prepare the volume for publication. Marcia Arcuri contributed valuable assistance before passing the baton on to Isabel Anderton, who undertook a workmanlike job of assembling the graphic materials and liaising with the contributing authors. I thank both Marcia and Isabel for their respective contributions, and also Isabel Shackell who helped tie up some of the remaining loose ends. I am grateful to Robin Kiang for the great care he took to ensure the high quality of the maps, chronologies and site plans. A grant from the British Museum Publications Support Fund helped defray the costs of acquiring and preparing the graphic materials, and I greatly appreciate the fact that Director Dr Robert Anderson approved my request for this support in the face of increasing financial strictures. Valuable support from the British Museum Townley Group has also enabled us to deploy essential colour imagery. I would like to add a personal note of thanks to Heather Lechtman for agreeing to write the Foreword amid many other exacting demands. Finally, for producing the book I am most appreciative of the skills and expertise supplied by the British Museum Press staff, especially Joanna Champness, Teresa Francis, Colin Grant, Harry Green and Susan Walby. The consistent backing provided by Emma Way (Head of Publishing at the Press) has also been a source of encouragement and inspiration.

Notes

1 The Museum of Mankind at Burlington Gardens formerly housed the Department of Ethnography of the British Museum. In late 1997 the building was closed to prepare for the Department's move to a new Study Centre close to the main British Museum building in Bloomsbury.

2 Bray 1978

3 Reichel-Dolmatoff 1988; Pineda 2000.

4 Hearne and Sharer 1992.

5 Alva and Donnan 1993.

6 Ono and Shimada 1994; Rickenbach 1997.

7 Cantwell, Griffin and Rothchild 1981.

References

Alva, Walter and Christopher B. Donnan
1993 *Royal Tombs of Sipán*. Fowler Museum of Cultural History, Los Angeles.

Bray, Warwick
1978 *The Gold of El Dorado*. Times Books, London.

Cantwell, Anne-Marie, James B. Griffiths and Nan A. Rothchild (eds)
1981 The Research Potential of Anthropological Museum Collections. In *Annals of the New York Academy of Sciences*, vol. 376: 77–121.

Hearne, Pamela and Robert J. Sharer (eds)
1992 *River of Gold: Precolumbian Treasures from Sitio Conte*. The University Museum, University of Pennsylvania, Philadelphia.

Ono, Masahiro and Izumi Shimada (eds)
1994 *Sicán: Excavations at the Pre-Inca Golden Capital*, exh. cat. Tokyo Broadcasting System, Tokyo.

Pineda, Roberto
2000 *Les Esprits, l'Or et le Chamane*, exh. cat. Réunion des Musées Nationaux, Paris.

Reichel-Dolmatoff, Gerardo
1988 *Goldwork and Shamanism: An Iconographic Study of the Gold Museum*. Editorial Colina, Medellin.

Rickenbach, Judith (ed.)
1997 *Sicán – ein Fürstengrab in Alt-Peru: eine Ausstellung in Zusammenarbeit mit dem peruanischen Kulturministerium*. Museum Rietberg, Zürich.

Contributors

WARWICK BRAY recently retired as Professor of Latin American Archaeology at the Institute of Archaeology, University College London. He has conducted extensive fieldwork in Colombia and Ecuador and is a specialist in the study of Precolumbian metalwork. He authored *The Gold of El Dorado* (1977) and co-edited *The Archaeology of Mesoamerica: Mexican and European Perspectives* (1999).

RICHARD COOKE is staff scientist in Archaeology and Palaeoecology at the Smithsonian Tropical Research Institute in Panama. His research interests include marine ecology and reconstructing adaptive strategies in Lower Central America, and he is currently directing excavations at the site of Cerro Juan Díaz, Panama. He has contributed to *The Art of Precolumbian Gold: The Jan Mitchell Collection* (1985) and *Icons of Power: Felid Symbolism in the Americas* (1998).

PENNY DRANSART is Lecturer in Archaeology at the University of Wales, Lampeter. Her research focuses on the herding of llamas and alpacas in the Andes, and issues related to textiles, dress and gender. She was co-editor of *Basketmakers: Meaning and Form in Native American Baskets* (1992) and editor of *Andean Art* (1995).

ANA MARÍA FALCHETTI was Deputy Director of the Gold Museum in Bogotá, Colombia, until she retired in 1993. Her research has centred on the eastern cordillera and the Caribbean lowlands of Colombia. She is currently working on symbolism in prehispanic metallurgy, combining mythology, ethnohistory and archaeology. The results of her work are presented in *El Oro del Gran Zenú* (1995) and other books published by the Gold Museum.

JOERG HAEBERLI is an organic chemist (retired 1993) and his interests include Andean archaeology and ethnohistory. In recent years he has identified three early Siguas textile traditions from the far south coast of Peru. His publications include *Twelve Nasca Panpipes: A Study* (1979) and *The Brooklyn Museum Textile No. 38.121: A Mnemonic and Calendrical Device, a Huaca* (1995).

SUSAN LA NIECE is a metallurgist and archaeologist in the Department of Scientific Research at the British Museum. She has contributed to publications on a wide range of archaeo-metallurgical research, including medieval European metalwork, niello, coins, the history of gilding and silvering, Arab metalwork and Precolumbian gold. She was co-editor of *Metal Plating and Platination* (1993) and currently edits the journal *Jewellery Studies*.

ROBERTO LLERAS-PÉREZ is Deputy Director at the Gold Museum in Bogotá, Colombia, where he is engaged in a five-year research programme with the Museum. Recent publications include *Muisca Offerings in Lake Guatavita* (1998) and *Structures of Dualistic Thought among the Indigenous Societies of the Eastern Andes* (1998).

COLIN MCEWAN is Curator of the Latin American collections at the British Museum, London. He has excavated extensively in South America and has published on Inca state rituals and on northern Andean archaeology and iconography. He is the author of *Ancient Mexico in the British Museum* (1994) and a co-editor of *Patagonia: Natural History, Prehistory and Ethnography at the Uttermost End of the Earth* (1997).

NIGEL MEEKS is a metallurgist with silversmithing experience who specializes in the application of scanning electron microscopy and microanalysis to the investigation of a variety of ancient metal technologies. Particular research interests and publications include the fabrication processes of European, Mediterranean and Central and South American goldwork, the classical use of high-tin bronze and tinning and early gold refining at Sardis.

KAREN O'DAY is a doctoral candidate in the Art History department at Emory University, Atlanta, and is researching the art of Sitio Conte in Panama for her Ph.D dissertation.

JOSÉ OLIVER is Lecturer in Latin American Archaeology at the Institute of Archaeology, University College London. He has directed excavations in the southeastern United States, the Virgin Islands, Puerto Rico and western Venezuela. His research focuses on the development of chiefdom polities in the circum-Caribbean region. Recent publications are *The Taíno Cosmos* (1997) and *El Centro Ceremonial de Caguana, Puerto Rico* (1998).

JEFFREY QUILTER is Director of Precolumbian studies and Curator of the Precolumbian Collection at Dumbarton Oaks, Washington DC. He has undertaken fieldwork at the sites of Paloma, Media Luna and El Paraíso, Peru, and Rivas in Costa Rica. He is the author of *Life and Death at Paloma* (1989)

IZUMI SHIMADA is Professor of Anthropology at Southern Illinois University, Carbondale. He is a specialist in Andean archaeology, and his interests include the technology and organization of craft production. For the past two decades, he has directed the Sicán Archaeological Project in the Batán Grande region of the north coast of Peru. Recent publications include *Pampa Grande and the Mochica* (1994), *Cultura Sicán* (1995), and *Andean Ceramics* (1998).

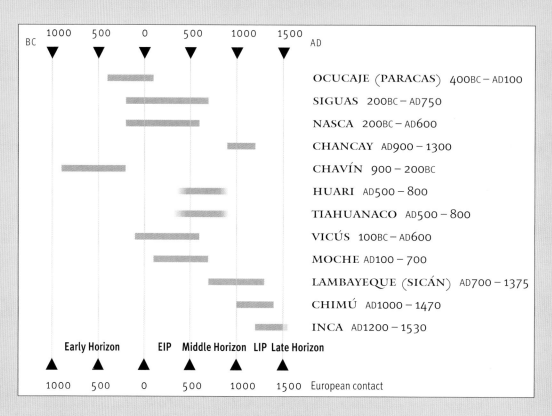

| BC | 1000 | 500 | 0 | 500 | 1000 | 1500 | AD |

OCUCAJE (PARACAS) 400BC – AD100

SIGUAS 200BC – AD750

NASCA 200BC – AD600

CHANCAY AD900 – 1300

CHAVÍN 900 – 200BC

HUARI AD500 – 800

TIAHUANACO AD500 – 800

VICÚS 100BC – AD600

MOCHE AD100 – 700

LAMBAYEQUE (SICÁN) AD700 – 1375

CHIMÚ AD1000 – 1470

INCA AD1200 – 1530

Early Horizon   EIP   Middle Horizon   LIP   Late Horizon

| 1000 | 500 | 0 | 500 | 1000 | 1500 | European contact |

Over and above specific cultural designations, the prehistory of the central Andes is conventionally divided into a sequence of alternating temporal units known as horizons and periods. The beginning of each of the three major horizons is marked by a widespread change in pottery style apparent across a large area of the Andes. The intervening Early Intermediate Period (EIP) and Late Intermediate Period (LIP) are each characterized by greater regional variation and the predominance of local styles. Since pottery styles evolve and spread gradually rather than instantaneously, the precise chronological placement of the horizons and periods varies from valley to valley and throughout north, central and southern Peru.

PERU, BOLIVIA AND CHILE

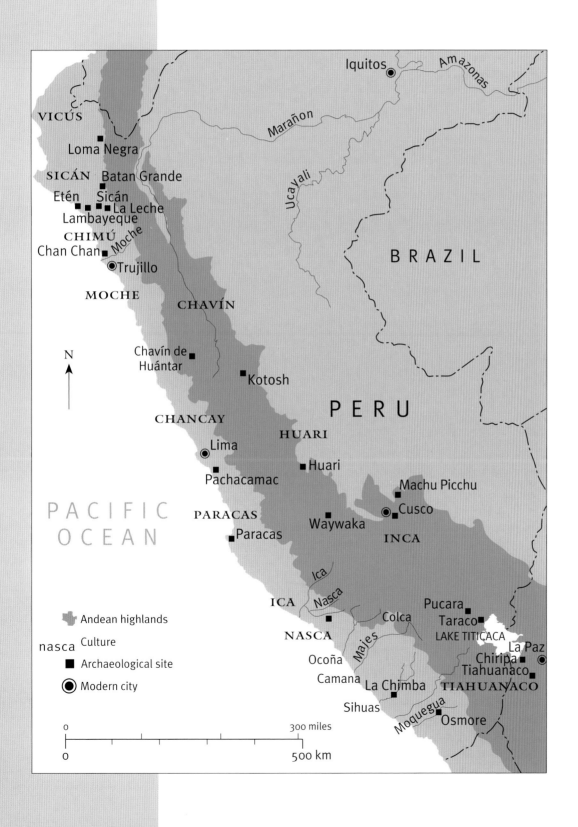

Iquitos

Amazonas

Marañon

Ucayali

VICÚS

Loma Negra

SICÁN   Batan Grande

Etén   Sicán
         La Leche
Lambayeque

CHIMÚ   Moche
Chan Chan   Moche

Trujillo

BRAZIL

MOCHE

CHAVÍN

Chavín de
Huántar

Kotosh

PERU

CHANCAY

HUARI

Lima

Huari

Machu Picchu

Pachacamac

PACIFIC
OCEAN

PARACAS

Waywaka

Cusco

Paracas

INCA

Ica

ICA   Nasca

Pucara

Colca   Taraco

NASCA   Majes   LAKE TITICACA

La Paz

Ocoña   Chiripa

Camana   Tiahuanaco

Sihuas   La Chimba   TIAHUANACO

Moquegua   Osmore

Andean highlands

nasca   Culture

■   Archaeological site

◉   Modern city

0   300 miles

0   500 km

Ancestors Past but Present

Gold Diadems from the Far South Coast of Peru

Colin McEwan and Joerg Haeberli

Introduction

This paper describes a corpus of hammered gold diadems from the far South Coast of Peru (see map on previous page). These are distinguished by their standardized form and by regularities in the structure and content of the iconography that they bear (Fig. 1.1).[1] There is little precise information presently available on the provenance of the objects and even less about the specific contexts in which they have been found. Nevertheless, at least one is known to have come from a tomb accidentally discovered in 1824 in the Camaná Valley.[2] Within the last twenty years or so a number of similar diadems, as well as many textiles from the far South Coast, have been appearing for sale on the international art market.[3] This material is generally ascribed to the Nasca culture, presumably as a matter of convenience to enhance its saleability. This assignation appears questionable and there is good reason to believe that much of it belongs instead to independent traditions embracing the lower reaches of the coastal valleys lying west of the Titicaca Basin.

Drainage systems such as the Ocoña, Colca-Majes-Camaná, Sihuas, Tambo and Osmore-Moquegua have long served as natural east–west conduits linking the mountains to the sea.[4] The polities that developed in these valleys from the Early Horizon Period (700 BC–AD 100) onwards engaged in regular contact with the nascent polities of the Andean highlands as well as with neighbouring valleys to the north, including those of the Nasca drainage. Such connections have always played a vital role in the genesis of Andean civilization and this wider context will help illuminate the use and interpretation of the diadems discussed here.

We will first offer a technical assessment of the diadems and describe their iconography. This enables us to propose a possible cultural affiliation and to assign a tentative chronological placement. We will then point to comparisons that can be made between the iconography on this material and that of other southern Andean regional traditions. Strong similarities and parallels suggest a core set of widely shared religious beliefs and the gradual emergence of a distinctively Andean iconic structure.

Technical description

While some gold in the form of placer deposits is found in the river valleys of southern Peru, it does not appear to be abundant. Some (or even most) of the gold deployed by coastal cultures may also have been procured from further afield, although at present there is no direct evidence to prove this. The relative scarcity of gold on the far South Coast may help to explain the rather limited repertoire and smaller overall volume of the metal invested in elite objects compared, for example, with the goldworking cultures of the Peruvian North Coast (see Shimada *et al.*, and O'Day, this volume). The diadems, mouth masks, arm bands and other ritual regalia that represent the principal categories of objects on the South Coast are all made from hammered gold sheet and are almost invariably of modest size.[5]

Three of the diadems featured in this paper belong to the British Museum's collections and have been examined by metallurgists in the Museum's Department of Scientific Research.[6] Each is approximately 0.15 mm thick although there is some variation.[7] They range from 20 to 25 cm high and 26 to 34 cm wide and, being made of thin sheet metal, they would once have swayed and trembled in sympathy with the

1.1. Line drawing of the diadem illustrated in Fig. 1.2. The face has large circular eyes and two cone-like elements project upwards from the head.

wearer's movements. The repoussé designs were executed by impressing the hammered gold sheet from the back with a suitable tool. The metal compositions of the three diadems are summarized below (see Table 1.1).

Although the silver content of two of the British Museum diadems is high, it falls within the range acceptable for naturally occurring placer gold from South America. The silver may not therefore have been deliberately added. The copper on the other hand, although only a minor component, is probably a deliberate alloying addition. The differences in metal compositions of the three diadems preclude any suggestion that they were made from the same melt or to the same alloy specifications. Furthermore, just as with other Precolumbian objects made from gold-copper alloys where the percentage of added copper is variable, the diadems range in colour from a 'pure' yellow to a strong reddish yellow hue. Together these observations suggest that production of the diadems was not rigidly standardized. The differences that can be detected may reflect variation in the output of an individual artisan or workshop, or perhaps some degree of

inter-valley variability. Our present analytical knowledge of southern Peruvian goldwork is quite limited so that the alloy composition reported here is insufficient in and of itself to propose any specific cultural affinities.[9]

Clearly one of the most distinctive features is the broadly consistent size and shape of the gold diadems. No obvious meaning can be read into this form.[10] The closest analogy that comes to mind, albeit at a much smaller scale, are the sets of zoomorphic components that make up the necklaces popular among a number of Precolumbian goldworking cultures.

There is some evidence to suggest how the diadems may have been worn. The three British Museum examples (see Figs 1.1–2, 1.5 and 1.7) have four perforations spaced about 8–10 cm apart at the corners of a hypothetical square in the middle of each. The holes were made by punching through the metal from front to back and seem likely to have served for sewing them onto a textile backing. The diadems do not have any other perforations, such as 'eye openings', which might have permitted the wearer to position the object over his face and still see where he was going. It seems unlikely (although not impossible) that they were used as pectorals. They were most probably worn as diadems affixed to a turban or headdress, although there is no direct evidence or any representation in other media that might help confirm this. Perhaps they were never intended to be worn at all in life, but rather reserved exclusively for affixing to burial shrouds or mummy bundles, which were then placed in tombs.

Iconography

We now turn to consider the distinctive corpus of iconography found embossed on the diadems. We will begin with the most straightforward representation and from there show how this image is either elaborated or simplified in various ways.

The central image is a bodiless frontal face with the eyes formed by large round circles (Figs 1.1 and 1.2). The mouth is shown with lips closed and no teeth visible. Beneath it a pattern of parallel vertical embellishments may represent a beard or allude to the idea of something issuing from the mouth or nostrils (Figs 1.3–5). Immediately below the lower half of the face a row of circles of various sizes may indicate a beaded collar or necklace. A band runs across the forehead and above this two cone-shaped projections point upwards. A line of smaller circles runs vertically up the centre of each cone, which terminates in a rounded tip at the top. The frontal face is flanked by flexed, raised

Table 1.1 Metal composition of the three diadems in the British Museum collections[8]

Reg. no.	BMRL no.	Sample no.	% Au (gold)	% Ag (silver)	% Cu (copper)
+7819	6723-101-K	J1262	68.5	24.2	7.5
+7820	6723-102-M	J1263	92.6	5.8	1.7
n/n	6723-103-R	J1264	68	28.8	3.6

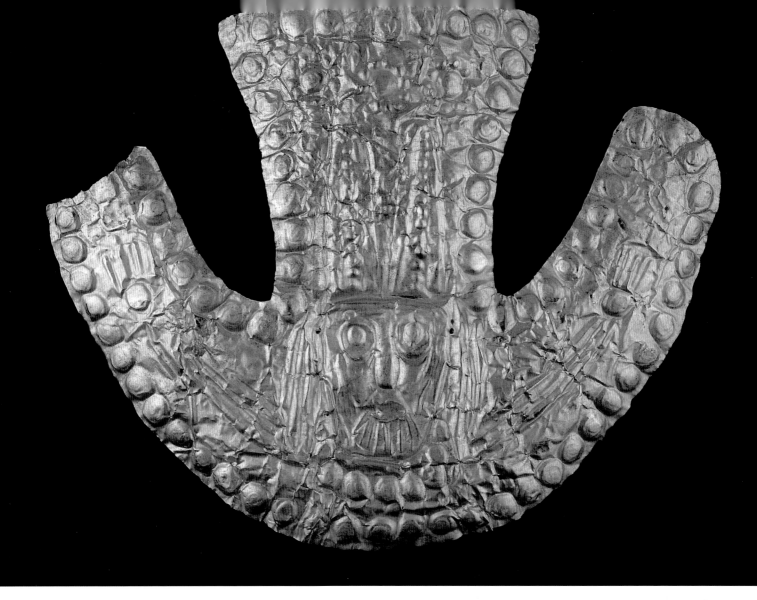

1.2. Hammered gold diadem bearing a single central image of a 'bearded', bodiless face with outstretched arms (height 23.5 cm, width 27.1 cm).

arms with the palms of the hands open and the fingers extended. An unusual impression is conveyed by the fact that no shoulders or torso are shown and that the arms begin on either side at the top of the head and then bend outward at the elbow at the level of the chin. The splayed, elongated forearms, help reinforce the visual relationship between the figure's pose and the form of the diadem itself. A continuous row of evenly sized, closely spaced circles runs around the entire border of the diadem. Above the head three further circles are positioned in a horizontal row, each in turn with smaller circles running around the circumference.

The 'bearded' frontal face with outstretched elongated arms is readily recognizable in more elaborate diadems with multiple representations (Figs 1.3–4). Here the cone-like projections are absent but an almost identical face of the same size is superimposed vertically above. The vertical elements of the 'beard' are emphasized to the exclusion of the mouth. Parallel horizontal cheek

markings are also now visible. The eyes may have a row of smaller circles around them. Subtle differences are apparent between the two superimposed faces. In one case the upper face is framed by a continuous undulating motif, while the lower one is bordered instead by a row of circles (Fig. 1.3). In another case the upper one is surrounded by a double border of smaller circles, while the lower one has a single row of larger circles (Fig. 1.4). The lower face is flanked by two smaller faces on either side positioned in the crook of the elbow of the flexed arms. Each faithfully replicates simplified versions of the eye, nose and 'beard' elements, as well as the horizontal cheek marks on the larger faces, and each is itself surrounded by a row of circles. The arms are outlined by a continuous row of small circles. The continuous undulating motif frames much of the overall design, running parallel to and inside the continuous border of circles around the edge of the diadem.

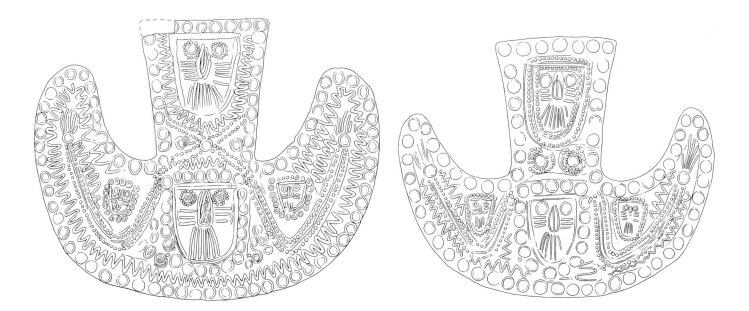

On the more elaborate diadems illustrated here, the two larger faces superimposed vertically one above the other contrast with the pair of smaller lateral faces. The space between the upper and lower principal head is filled in one instance by an extension of the rows of circles from the outstretched arms in the form of a St Andrew's Cross (Fig. 1.3) and in the other by a pair of circles each surrounded by concentric circles of smaller 'dots' (Fig. 1.4). Simplification and variations in the arrangement of the principal and secondary faces are found on other diadems. In one case the four faces are rendered more schematically (see Fig. 1.5). Interestingly, it is this diadem that is known to have come from the Camaná Valley. There are no arms visible

where they might be expected on either side of the largest (lower) face. The tendency to reduce and simplify the superimposed face as well as the two smaller flanking faces recalls the three abstract roundels placed above the head of Fig. 1.1. In Fig. 1.6 the features of the smaller flanking faces are similar to those of the larger principal face and the outstretched arms with extended digits can still be picked out. Likewise, the twin 'cones' above the head are similar to those described for Fig. 1.1, and above these are another pair of smaller faces. The larger principal faces of the diadems shown in Figs 1.5 and 1.6 both have straight or undulating vertical elements running down their cheeks. These are clearly analogous to the tearlines which are a recurring motif in other southern Andean traditions, and contrast with the horizontal cheek markings visible on Figs 1.3 and 1.4.

Further examples where simplification is apparent have a lower principal face flanked by a pair of similar smaller faces (see Fig. 1.7). All three faces have two sets of vertical elements below the mouth. Two have dotted markings on their cheeks and the third has a single line as a cheek marking. The outstretched arms are barely discernible. The design field above the principal face is devoid of additional figurative elements, although the vertical rows of small circles are interrupted by a row of horizontal impressions. In Fig. 1.8 a rather tentative rendering of the superimposed principal faces appears, the lower one with much abbreviated, outstretched arms but no smaller flanking faces. Although both the latter diadems offer substantially simplified versions of the full iconic structure, they nevertheless retain the pervasive

1.3 (above) Embossed decoration from a gold diadem showing two superimposed, 'bearded' frontal faces. The lower image is flanked by two smaller secondary faces placed in the crook of the outstretched arms.

1.4 (above right) The arrangement of the faces is the same as Fig. 1.3. Both have horizontal cheek markings, and are framed by undulating elements and a continuous row of circles running round the edge.

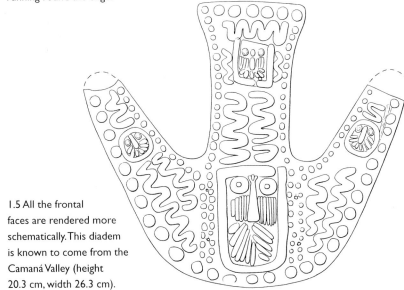

1.5 All the frontal faces are rendered more schematically. This diadem is known to come from the Camaná Valley (height 20.3 cm, width 26.3 cm).

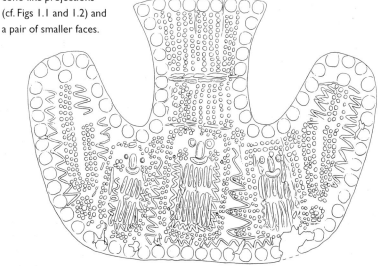

1.6 (above) The principal frontal face and the flanking secondary faces all have undulating or 'zigzag' tearlines. Above the central face are two cone-like projections (cf. Figs 1.1 and 1.2) and a pair of smaller faces.

1.7 (above) The principal 'bearded' face flanked by two similar secondary images can just be discerned. An overall reduction in detail and cursory execution is apparent in this example (height 24.7 cm, width 33.5 cm).

1.8 (below) A diminutive central figure lacks any flanking motifs but the superimposed face above is retained.

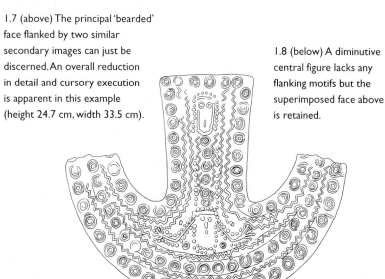

undulating motifs and small circle filler elements, as well as the continuous border of regularly spaced larger circles that characterize all the diadems described here.

Provenance and chronology

The range of archaeological work undertaken in the valleys of the far South Coast is meagre compared to other parts of Peru. From the Camaná Valley Early Intermediate Period early Nasca-style remains have been reported.[11] Otherwise the published reports of surface surveys undertaken in the Ocoña, Majes/Camaná and Sihuas valleys mention only Middle Horizon Huari and post-Huari material.[12] In the meantime looting of ancient cemeteries in these valleys has proceeded unabated. Many so-called 'Nasca-style' textiles have appeared on the art market along with new metalwork, and much of this material is said to come from the Ocoña, Majes and Sihuas valleys.

In 1997 discarded weaving fragments were collected by Haeberli, Rómulo Pari Flores and Marco Lopez at the looted burial ground of La Chimba in the Sihuas Valley. These include early Nasca pieces as well as a distinctive local tradition that has been designated 'Siguas'.[13] The earliest phase of this local tradition evidently develops parallel to, but largely independent of, other coastal cultures of the late Early Horizon (200 BC–AD 100) until Nasca influence becomes apparent during the succeeding Early Intermediate Period (see chronology in note 13). The principal motif on Early Horizon Siguas textiles is a bodiless, frontal face with tearlines and radiating appendages.[14] In one example the face has 'quartered' eyes, stepped tearlines and bared teeth with lateral markings projecting on either side of the mouth (see Fig. 1.9).[15] From around the face radiate stepped appendages with rectangular/circular filler elements. A shorthand 'eye with tearline' motif is framed in the rectangle at the extremity of each appendage. Other prominent motifs include a diamond with four pairs of recurving appendages, and undulating,[16] double-headed snakes.[17] This is typical of the range of motifs found on early Siguas textiles and they clearly share some elements in common with the diadem iconography.[18] The similarities (though not complete identity) suggest that the diadems can be tentatively assigned to the late Early Horizon or the early Early Intermediate Period (approximately AD 100–300), but this needs to be confirmed by finds of the diadems in secure excavated contexts with

1.9. Late Early Horizon, Siguas textile fragment, (length 56 cm, width 25 cm). The principal motif is a bodiless, frontal face with stepped 'tearlines', bared teeth and lateral 'whiskers'.

appendages as well as equilateral checkered crosses and rings. Perhaps the best known of these is the Taraco stela which features an archetypal 'ancestral' couple: a pair of frontal figures with elongated arms clasped against their chests (see Fig. 1.10).[20] Arranged around the figures are undulating double-headed serpentine and zoomorphic elements,[21] and bodiless heads with radiating appendages. Another, and possibly later, stela in this tradition from the sunken courtyard at the site of Tiahuanaco shows a single anthropomorphic figure with its arms similarly clasped across its chest (see Fig. 1.11).[22] It is also flanked by a pair of vertical, undulating serpentine elements and wears what is arguably a mouth mask. The figure lacks any explicit representation of the abdomen or lower limbs but a pair of opposed felines are placed beneath the image. Secondary figures, quadrupeds or perhaps amphibians surround the head.[23] To this day on the altiplano snakes and amphibians are associated with weather phenomena: the former with thunderbolts and rain, and the latter with rain and water in general. The Yaya-Mama figures and anthropomorphs found on other stelae may therefore be interpreted as representing supernaturals, analagous to the Andean thundergod Tunupa, who governed the weather and controlled the arrival of the rains that are so essential to life.

Among this constellation of motifs the bodiless frontal face or mask can be traced across a range of late Early horizon and early Early Intermediate Period cultures in the highlands and on the coast.[24] In addition to the Yaya-Mama tradition around the Titicaca Basin, it occurs in both Chiripa and Pucara iconography, and further north in the Cusco region it is found in what is probably a variation of the Marcavalle tradition. The same image makes its appearance on the South Coast in Paracas, Topará and Nasca iconography, and on the far South Coast in Siguas as discussed here. Painted cloth mummy masks from Paracas (Ocucaje), for example, bear representations of a bodiless face (see Fig. 1.12).[25] Some of these depictions have tearlines and sport lateral whiskers projecting on either side of the mouth or from the lower side of the head.[26] Additional elements including single and double-headed serpents and a pair of opposed felines parallel those just described for the Yaya-Mama tradition.[27] The fact that this iconography is applied to mummy bundles serves to underline the association with the ancestors. Later in the Ocucaje sequence the emphasis on large concentric eyes in many images has led to it being described as the 'Oculate Being'.[28] This later 'Oculate Being' is now represented mainly in full body and

the textiles. Further assessment of the dating may yet be necessary.

Comparisons and connections

Anthropologists who have studied the emergent art styles of the southern Andes point to a constellation of overlapping iconographic elements found among various regional traditions of both the highlands and the coast. In order to sketch some of these connections we will turn first to the Yaya-Mama religious tradition of the southern Titicaca Basin which fostered a distinctive iconographic corpus sculpted on stone monoliths.[19] Anthropomorphic representations on these monoliths are associated with single and double-headed undulating snakes, amphibians, quadrupeds, bodiless heads with radiating

1.10 (right) The Yaya-Mama stela from Taraco, Peru, depicts an archetypal 'ancestral' couple accompanied by undulating double-headed serpents, zoomorphic motifs and bodiless heads with radiating appendages.

1.12 (far right) Paracas (Ocucaje) painted cloth mummy mask bearing the image of a frontal, bodiless face with 'tearlines' and whiskers.

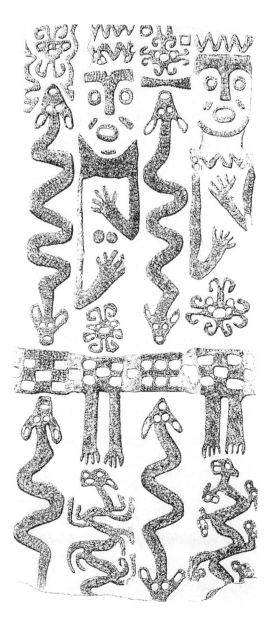

1.11 The Yaya-Mama tradition Stela 15 from the sunken courtyard at the great ceremonial centre of Tiahuanaco shows a single anthropomorphic figure with undulating snakes on each side and a pair of opposed felines beneath.

is associated with secondary figures including small humans, two types of small heads (one with and the other without appendages), felines, birds, and particularly snakes, which frequently emerge from its head.

Analogous elements are to be found embedded in the iconography of Middle Horizon hammered gold plaques (Figs 1.13–15).[29] While their form differs from the diadems of the far South Coast, nevertheless a number of iconographic details show interesting parallels.[30]

The form of the golden plaque illustrated in Fig. 1.13 suggests the outstretched wings and prominent tail feathers of a hovering raptorial bird. The wing-tips end in eight snake heads with the curling body and circular filler elements apparent in the uppermost pair. The tail feathers end in four skulls or trophy heads. The bird form is made quite

explicit in other plaques which have frontal faces with beaks (but no mouths) as well as talons (Fig. 1.14). Here, too, the outstretched wing-tips terminate in snakes' heads and the tail feathers in what appear to be death faces.

In Fig. 1.13 the right-facing profile head features bared teeth and prominent fangs. A pronounced tearline motif with circular filler elements issues from an oval shaped eye. In Fig. 1.15 a plaque of a different form bears two frontal faces, one superimposed above the other. The lower mask is framed in a rectangular cartouche and has clearly marked tearlines and bared teeth. The cartouche is surrounded by a continuous row of circles and flanked in turn by another pair of elongated undulating elements and additional details, which are unclear. Vertically above, a circular cartouche contains another frontal face with bared teeth but lacking tearlines. A row of small faces runs around the upper border of the object. Perforations are visible similar to those found on the diadems. The symbolism of the Middle Horizon gold plaques in the shape of birds associated with snake imagery (Figs 1.13–14) and showing frontal faces with bared teeth, tearlines and undulating motifs (Fig. 1.15) clearly also alludes to supernaturals representing weather phenomena. Similarly the 'death faces' or 'trophy heads' can be linked to notions of ancestral descent.

1.13 (above) Hammered gold plaque of a bird with outstretched wings (height 21.9 cm, width 15.8 cm). The profile head features a tearline motif, bared teeth and prominent fangs.

1.14 (right) Hammered gold plaque of a raptorial bird with snake motifs and 'death faces' (height 16.5 cm)

1.15 (far right) Hammered gold plaque (height 17.5 cm, width 19 cm). The lower rectangular cartouche shows a frontal face with tearlines and bared teeth. The face in the upper circular cartouche just has bared teeth.

Conclusions

The cultural histories of the Southern Highlands and the South and far South Coast of Peru have long been inextricably linked. While independent regional traditions are recognized by their individual styles, commonalities among these are revealed in the shared iconographic elements that recur in various guises. The consistent shape, general similarity in size and distinctive iconography of the hammered gold diadems from the far South Coast all combine to confer a sense of uniformity and coherence on this material. The principal image on the diadems is a 'bearded' frontal face with large round eyes and outstretched arms often depicted with a similar image superimposed above and with flanking secondary faces.[31] These are paralleled by the iconography on: (i) Siguas (late Early Horizon) textiles of a bodiless frontal face with tearlines and appendages, and human figures with upraised arms as secondary figures; (ii) Siguas (early Early Intermediate Period) textiles representing bodiless frontal face heads showing tearlines, a headdress with a zigzag design and human hair hanging 'beard-like' from the chin region; and (iii) Siguas (late Early Intermediate Period) textiles which include single or multiple yellow coloured human figures with upraised arms, usually on a red background. None of these human figures have facial markings.

Looking further afield, we have noted that the undulating (or zigzag) motifs that appear as ' tear-lines' and as pervasive filler elements on some of the gold diadems find their counterparts in other Early and Middle Horizon southern Andean traditions.[32] These sinuous, serpentine motifs, appearing as they do in association with amphibians and continuous rows of circles used as filler elements, carry connotations of moisture and a general concern with water, rain, fertility and seasonal regeneration.[33]

If we are prepared to accept that the vertical facial markings around the mouths of the frontal faces on the far South Coast diadems represent beards, then we would suggest that the principal figure as well as the secondary faces are all male. The principal face and secondary faces appear in different combinations as follows: (i) a single frontal face (Fig. 1.1); (ii) two superimposed frontal faces (Fig. 1.8); (iii) a principal face flanked by two secondary faces (Fig. 1.7); (iv) two superimposed principal faces, the lower one of which is flanked by two secondary faces (Figs 1.3–5); and (v) a principal face with two superimposed secondary faces and flanked by two secondary faces (Fig. 1.6).[34]

These images, executed in gold and ultimately destined for burial, surely allude to core beliefs within the society that created them. Heroic ancestors figure prominently in surviving fragments of the once extensive oral histories of non-Inca cultures that were recorded at the time of contact. Andeans traced their descent from a supernatural creator through hero-ancestors to venerated ancestors. Ancestors lived as long as their mummies were preserved and they were the guardians of fertility. Entitlements to vital resources such as land and water were established through ayllus,[35] founded by ancestors[36] to whom they had constant recourse in myth and ritual. Such figures have always had an elemental connection with the forces of nature, combining celestial origins with responsibility for replenishing the springs, rivers and lakes that sustain life.[37] They embody a vitalizing and generating essence that continuously flows from supernatural realms into huacas (sacred animated matter), which comprise visible manifestations of this power in the natural world. Death would follow if this flow was interrupted.[38]

It would risk over-interpretation to insist that an identical set of elements is uniformly expressed in all the traditions of the Highlands, the South Coast and the far South Coast. Yet it is apparent that by the late Early Horizon comparable, parallel systems were developing among the different valley polities. They point to a core set of widely shared religious beliefs and the gradual emergence of a distinctively Andean iconic structure, key elements of which were ultimately incorporated into the ideology and art forged by later empires.

Notes

1 The dominant, recurring motif in the iconography is a frontal face but these objects do not appear to have served as masks in the strict sense of the term. The term diadem is preferred here instead of mask or pectoral for reasons that are discussed in the next section.

2 In the course of undertaking research for the exhibition *The Gilded Image: Precolumbian Gold from South and Central America*, Colin McEwan came upon three diadems that had been held in the British Museum's collections for many years. Comments made on one of these (Ethno +7819; see Fig. 1.5) by F. Galton Esq., F.R.S. (President of the Royal Anthropological Institute), were published in a note in the *Journal of the Anthropological Institute* of February 1889, titled 'Exhibition of Ancient Peruvian Breastplate'. This reads as follows: 'The President exhibited a gold breastplate, 9 1/4 by 13 inches in extreme measurement, rudely embossed, that had been found attached to the body of a Peruvian whose tomb was accidentally discovered in 1824, on removing some mounds of earth in the valley of Camaná, on the sea coast of Peru, latitude 16° 8' S. Alongside this body were found many others but not equally adorned, each under a different mound. This specimen, which belonged to him, was brought home by a relative of his, Captain, afterwards Admiral, Maling, then in command of the Pacific Station. The interest of the specimen lay in the fact that the use to which it had been applied had been observed and described. There were two similar plates of gold in the British Museum, but he had there been informed by Mr. Franks that their use was previously unknown, and that the information accompanying the present specimen was very acceptable. The buried Peruvian ornaments that were made of gold were at one time very easy to be procured, but now, owing to the long established practice of rifling the graves and of melting all the gold found in them, specimens of any kind were seldom met with, and one of the large size of that now exhibited was exceedingly rare.'

3 See, for example, Rocklin 1994. Some of the textiles have been around longer, at least since the 1930s.

4 See, for example, Barriaga 1952; Mujica *et al.* 1983; Rice, Stanish and Scarr 1989; Rodríguez 1990; Moseley *et al.* 1991; Stanish 1991; Goldstein 1993a and b. At the time of the Spanish conquest the people of the Sihuas, Majes and lower Colca formed a nation called Kunti, and the Sihuas Valley population owned camelid herds at the headwaters of the river.

5 Nasca 'masks' average 10–20 cm wide. By comparison the diadems from the far South Coast are 25–35 cm wide.

6 The examination of the three objects held in the British Museum's collections was undertaken by Susan La Niece and Nigel Meeks of the Museum's Department of Scientific Research (1998).

7 The thickness of Ethno +7820 (see Figs. 1.1–2) and Ethno n/n (Fig. 1.7) is fairly uniform at around 0.15 mm, whereas the thickness of Ethno +7819 (see Fig. 1.5) is less consistent, varying from 0.1–0.25 mm.

8 These measurements were carried out on the core metal, in polished section, of samples from each of the diadems, using energy dispersive X-ray analysis (EDX) in a scanning electron microscope (SEM). The precision of the measurements is ± 1% and the accuracy is similar. The gold sheet of all three diadems contains iron-rich inclusions. No other elements were detected by EDX or by air-path X-ray fluorescence analysis (XRF). All

three diadems show evidence of loss of copper by corrosion from their surfaces, but not of burnishing. The repoussé work was carried out before this corrosion attack (there is no compression of the matt, etched surface by working), but it is uncertain whether the corrosion occurred before, during or after burial. It is not possible to say therefore whether deliberate depletion gilding took place. The consistent evidence of surface corrosion on diadems showing differences in iconographic style and detail is one reason for arguing that these objects are authentic rather than modern forgeries. Furthermore, the find-date of one diadem is securely placed at 1824 (note 2) and at least one example in silver is known (note 34).

9 Very few analyses of southern Peruvian goldwork have been published. Some of these have been collated by Rovira (1994) and show a wide variation in composition not necessarily related to cultural group. Sheet metalwork generally has a copper content below 10%.

10 It is tempting to resort to describing this as a '*tumi*' shape, i.e. similar to the crescentic form of sacrificial knives used among North Coast cultures. However, applying this term is likely to cause confusion since the thin sheet gold objects from the far South Coast were clearly never intended to be used as knives. What is described as a 'tumi symbol' is found on feathered textiles which are alleged to be Nasca (see for example Gibson 1990: fig. 90, and Lavalle and Gonzalez 1991: 145–7, 163). This motif, which is centrally placed beneath a pair of rayed symbols, is clearly very similar to the form of the far South Coast diadems.

11 In 1965 Disselhoff excavated Early Intermediate Period Nasca-style remains at Cabezas Achatadas in the Camaná Valley. In 1972 Neira Avedaño found similar material at Pampa Tairona (north of Chala).

12 Ramirez 1977; Chávez and Hinojosa 1990; Márquez and Montero 1990; Valdivia and Zegarra 1990; Malpass *et al.* 1997; see also references cited in note 4 for the Mocquegua Valley.

13 'Siguas' is the spelling found in the older literature for this valley located in the Department of Arequipa and was the name used by its inhabitants at the time of the Spanish conquest. In more recent literature, including maps, it is spelt 'Sihuas'. The old spelling has been adopted to name the newly identified traditions in this and adjacent valleys and place them within the standard central Andean chronology. The finds of the Nasca-style textiles from the far South Coast differ in certain respects from those of the Nasca heartland, and the nature of the Nasca presence requires careful scrutiny. Haeberli has had the opportunity to make comparative studies of over 120 textiles from the area. Based on style, iconography, textile techniques and thirteen radiocarbon age ranges, he has proposed the following far South Coast 'Sihuas Valley' chronology in an unpublished paper (Haeberli 1988–9):

Siguas (late EH) tradition, approximately 200 BC–AD 100.
Siguas (EIP) traditions, approximately AD 150–750
Siguas-Nasca interaction, approximately AD 100–550.
Nasca (Cabezas Achetadas-La Chimba), approximately AD 200–400.

So far the pottery that probably accompanied these finds has not been described or illustrated, except in the case of Cabezas Achatadas. Excavation work has yet to be done to verify and refine this chronological framework. Issues to be resolved include, for example, the spread of innovations in textile techniques, such as discontinuous double interlocking

warp and weft, and cross-looping. Haeberli has only seen metal (copper or bronze) late EH Siguas pins. Two collectors in Peru have reported that late EH Siguas and EIP Siguas textiles have been found in the valleys of Oceña, Majes and Siguas, but they did not mention the Camaná. They also possessed Nasca 3 to Nasca 7 pottery allegedly from the Sihuas Valley.

14 Of over seventy Siguas (late EH) textiles forty have a frontal face with tearlines, radiating appendages around the head, and secondary figures. The calibrated radiocarbon results (first sigma) of five such textiles were in the range 200 BC to AD 100. The Paracas design of a bodiless front-face head with radiating appendages is termed the 'bodiless head motif' by Jane P. Dwyer to designate representations of the head of the Oculate Being. See, for example, Dwyer 1979: fig. 11; also Kajitani 1982, fig. 15, and note 28 below. This motif has also been called 'sun face' (King 1965).

15 This small textile fragment measures 25 × 56 cm and is said to have come from a valley in the Department of Arequipa. It is woven in interlocking tapestry with minor areas in slit tapestry (small squares of horizontal zigzag design), a weft-faced pattern (both bands with two stripes of concentric squares) and a border-band in cross-looping (not shown). The weft yarns are in camelid wool while the warp yarns are cotton. This textile has recently been dated as follows: radiocarbon age 2126+/– 56 BP; calibrated age: 95% confidence interval 395 to 1 BC; 68% confidence interval 345 to 322 BC plus 202 to 53 BC. The latter is the most likely age range of the two (Rafter Radiocarbon Laboratory, New Zealand; sample R:24578; date of measurement 4 March 1999).

16 The continued application of the adjective 'undulating' to describe this motif is intentional. The majority of Siguas (late EH) textiles with designs are executed in the discontinuous double interlocking warp and weft technique. This determined the rectangular, stepped, zigzag nature of designs. It is assumed that this rectangular tradition was retained for Siguas (late EH) interlocking tapestry designs.

17 Copper (or copper alloy) pins of a zigzag snake are allegedly found with Siguas (late EH) textiles.

18 This is particularly apparent in one gold diadem not illustrated here which has a 'minimalist' rectangular face with two small eyes, zigzag tearlines and a vertical noseline (see Sotheby's Sales Catalogue May 1998, Lot 23). The remainder of the decorative surface is filled with methodically arranged rows of undulating (or zigzag) motifs. The central face on this diadem bears a striking likeness to the frontal face motif found on many of the early Siguas textiles. The iconography of two other textiles is of particular interest in relation to that of the gold diadems. In addition to the principal highly stylized bodiless frontal face with stepped tearlines, they have similar secondary faces but without appendages. In one case (see illustration in Tribal Arts 1997 Vol.3, No.4.:45) these flank the principal face analogous to Fig. 1.3. In the other case (see illustration in HALI 73 (1994): 148) two faces are placed above and two below the principal face, nested between appendages. In this example, as is the case with most of the frontal face motifs, the undulating snakes appear between six of the eight stepped radial appendages.

19 Chávez and Chávez 1975.

20 Chávez and Chávez (1975: 47) suggest that the face markings on each might allude to a mask.

21 These are variously interpreted as llamas or alpacas (Chávez and Chávez 1975: 48).

22 As Chávez and Chávez (1975: 66) note, Rowe interprets the semi-subterranean temple at Tiahuanaco as a very early shrine, for which Stela 15, standing in its centre was the chief cult object. Kolata (1993: 78–81) notes that: 'The carved monuments of the Yaya-Mama group relate to a pan-Titicaca Basin ideology … a shared religious tradition … upon which Tiahuanaco drew for its subsequent expansion'.

23 There is one gold diadem which has representations of quadrupeds and amphibians (see Sotheby's Sales Catalogue May 1989, Lot 27). We have not had the opportunity of examining the object first hand to verify its authenticity.

24 Of course, as Chávez and Chávez indicate (1975: 65), the motif of a bodiless head with appendages is not confined to the southern Andes.

25 In Paracas 8–9 (Ocucaje) a bodiless frontal face is the principal motif. During Paracas 9 (Ocucaje) a full-bodied figure starts to replace the head. By Paracas 10 (Ocucaje) the full-bodied figure is associated with secondary figures, including smaller versions of the head. Many of the Paracas 10 (Ocucaje) figures have zigzag streamers or hair ending in snake or trophy heads. (See Dawson 1979.)

26 For similar representations of these lateral whiskers see e.g. Kajitani 1982: figs 13, 24; Rowe 1985: fig. 356). The whiskers or small mouth mask with whiskers does not appear in the Titicaca Basin but is found on the South Coast (Paracas, Topará and Nasca) and in the Cusco region. See for example Paracas 6 and Paracas Callango Basin phase 8 felines (Menzel, Rowe and Dawson 1964: figs 3b and 47c) and the Echenique gold plume from Cusco with a supernatural with feline characteristics (Rowe 1976: 6–20).

27 It is easy to be selective in the choice of images to illustrate this point. Clearly there is both temporal and spatial variation in the way that the principal attributes are combined. Here Dawson's observations on the Ocucaje mummy masks are pertinent: 'If … one seeks to distinguish a pantheon of distinct mythical identities instead of a single being, one finds no standardisation of these either. What seems to be the case is that the artists were drawing as much from the verbal imagery of myth as from design antecedents' (Dawson 1979: 102).

This comment notwithstanding, it is clear that there are discernible regularities in the structure and content of the iconography in each regional tradition paralleling those addressed here for the far South Coast.

28 The large eyes on some of the gold diadems are, in a general way, reminiscent of images of the Oculate Being. (Cf. Menzel, Rowe and Dawson 1964.)

29 We are grateful to Edward de Bock for drawing our attention to this material and in particular for sharing his observations on the iconographic details described here.

30 Like the Nasca and far South Coast objects, most, if not all, of these plaques also have perforations, presumably for suspension or sewing to a textile.

31 Another intriguing example of much later date is found in a painted textile from Chancay showing a figure with raised arms and a frontal mask on the abdomen replicating the face of the wearer above (see Lavalle and Gonzalez 1991: 295).

32 See e.g. the diadem mask with radiating tassels illustrated in Kolata 1992: fig. 12. In this example the tear 'drops' are picked out with turquoise inlay.

33 See e.g. Flores Ochoa 1977; Urton 1981: 174–80, and 1999.

34 This particular combination (a central principal face with two superimposed secondary faces and flanked by a pair of smaller secondary faces) is also found on a silver diadem in the collections of the Art Museum, Princeton University. This is the first time that we have come across the iconography described here on a silver diadem, and its discovery tends to reinforce our opinion that the gold diadems discussed here are authentic as opposed to being modern forgeries.

35 *Ayllu* is the Quechua term for a corporate land-holding collectivity self-defined as ancestor-focused kindred (Salomon and Urioste 1991: 21–3).

36 One such figure is Paria Caca, the creator deity featured in the Huarochiri manuscript. See Salomon and Urioste 1991, and Arce and Flores Ochoa 1994; see also Salomon 1995: 319–23 and Bastien 1995.

37 Ponce 1982; Gisbert 1994.

38 Salomon 1991:16; Flores Ochoa 1977: 211–37.

References

Arce, Elizabeth Kuon and Jorge A. Flores Ochoa
1994 Santiago en los Andes Peruanos. In *Historia y Cultura*, pp. 233–55. La Paz.

Avedaño, Máximo Neira
1990 Arequipa Prehispánica. In *Historia General de Arequipa*, 5-184. Arequipa.

Barriaga, P. Victor
1952 *Memorias para la Historia de Arequipa.* Tomo IV. Arequipa.

Bastien, Joseph W.
1995 The Mountain/Body Metaphor Expressed in Kaatan Funeral. In *Tombs for the Living: Andean Mortuary Practices*, ed. Tom Dillehay, pp. 355–78. Dumbarton Oaks, Washington DC.

Chávez, Sergio Jorge and Karen L. Mohr Chávez
1975 A Carved Stela from Taraco, Puno, Peru and the Definition of an Early Style of Stone Sculpture from the Altiplano of Peru and Bolivia. In *Ñawpa Pacha*, vol. 13. Institute of Andean Studies, Berkeley.

Chávez, José A. and Ruth R. Salas Hinojosa
1990 Castrato Arqueológico de la Cuenca del Río Ocoña. In *Gaceta Arqueológica Andina*, vol. V, no. 18–19: 15–20.

Dawson, Lawrence E.
1979 Painted Cloth Mummy Masks of Ica, Peru. In *The Junius B. Bird Pre-Columbian Textile Conference*, ed. Ann P. Rowe, Elizabeth P. Benson, Anne-Louise Schaffer. The Textile Museum & Dumbarton Oaks, Washington DC.

Flores Ochoa, Jorge A.
1977 Enqa, enqaychu, illa y khuya rumi. In *Pastores de Puna*, pp. 211–37. Instituto de Estudios Peruanos, Lima.

Disselhoff, H.D.
1969 Früh-Nazca im äussersten Süden Perus, Provincia de Camaná (Dep. Arequipa). In *Verhandlungen des XXXVIII Internationalen Amerikanisten Kongress*, vol. 1, pp. 385–91. Kommissionsverlag Klaus Renner, Munich.

Dwyer, Jane P.
1979 The Chronology and Iconography of Paracas-Style Textiles. In *The Junius B. Bird Pre-Columbian Textile Conference*, ed. Ann P. Rowe, Elizabeth P. Benson, Anne-Louise Schaffer. The Textile Museum & Dumbarton Oaks, Washington DC.

Gibson, Thomas
1990 *Feather Masterpieces of the Ancient Andean World*. Thomas Gibson Fine Art Ltd, London.

Gisbert, Teresa
1994 Santiago y el Mito de Illapa. In *Historia y Cultura*, pp. 299–310. La Paz.

Goldstein, Paul
1993a House, Community and State in the Earliest Tiwanaku Colony: Domestic Patterns and State Integration at Omo M12, Moquegua. In *Domestic Architecture, Ethnicity and Complementarity in the South-Central Andes,* ed. M. Aldenderfer, pp. 25–41. University of Iowa Press, Iowa City.
1993b Tiwanaku Temples and State Expansion: A

Tiwanaku Sunken Court Temple in Moquegua, Peru. *Latin American Antiquity* 4: 22–47.

Haeberli, Joerg
1988–9 Siguas Textile Traditions and Early Nasca-Style Textiles from the Department of Arequipa, Peru and the Multicultural Site of La Chimba, Sihuas Valley. Unpublished manuscript.

Kajitani, Nobuko
1982 The Textiles of the Andes. In *Senshoku no Bi (Textile Arts)*, no. 20, Fall. Kyoto Shoin.

King, Mary Elizabeth
1965 Textiles and Basketry of the Paracas Period, Ica Valley, Peru. Ph.D. dissertation. Tucson.

Kolata, Alan
1992 Tiwanaku: The City at the Center. In *The Ancient Americas: Art from Sacred Landscapes*, ed. Richard F. Townsend, pp. 316–33. The Art Institute of Chicago, Chicago.
1993 *Tiwanaku: Portrait of an Andean Civilization*. Blackwell, Oxford.

Lapiner, Allan
1976 *Pre-Columbian Art of South America*. Harry N. Abrams inc., New York.

Lavalle, José Antonio de, and José Alejandro Gonzalez García
1991 *The Textile Art of Peru* L.L. Editores, Lima.

Malpass, Michael A., P. de la Veracruz, M. Lopez, L. Linares, W. Yepez and C. Gonzales
1997 Archaeological Reconnaissance of the Upper Camaná River Valley, Peru. Unpublished report.

Márquez, Manuel García and Rosa Bustamente Montero
1990 Arqueología del Valle de Majes. In *Gaceta Arqueológica Andina*, vol. V, no. 18–19: 25–40.

Menzel, Dorothy, John H. Rowe and Lawrence E. Dawson
1964 *The Paracas Pottery of Ica: A Study in Style and Time*. University of California Press, Berkeley and Los Angeles.

Moseley, Michael E., R.A. Feldman, P. Goldstein and L. Watanabe M.
1991 Colonies and Conquest: Tiahuanaco and Huari in Mocquegua. In *Huari Administrative Structure: Prehistoric Monumental Architecture and State Government*, ed. W. Isbell and G. McEwan 121–40. Dumbarton Oaks, Washington DC.

Mujica, E., M. A. Rivera and T. F. Lynch
1983 Proyecto de Estudio sobre la complementaridad económica Tiawanaku en los valles occidentales del Centro-Sur Andino. In *Chungará* 11: 85–109.

Ponce Sanginés, Carlos
1982 *Tunupa y Ekako*, pp. 143–85. La Paz.

Ramirez, René Santos
1977 Presencia de Wari en el Valle de Siguas. In *Arqueología en Bolivia y Perú*, vol. 2: 393–403.

Rice, Don S., Charles Stanish and P. Scarr, eds
1989 *Ecology, Settlement and History in the Osmore Drainage*. British Archaeological Reports, International Series, 545 (i), Oxford.

Rocklin, Keith
1994 Water Symbolism in Nazca Textiles. In *HALI* 77: 108–15.

Rodríguez, Guillermo Galdos
1990 Naciones Ancestrales y la Conquista Incaica. In *Historia General de Arequipa*. Talleres de Cuzzi y Cia. S.A., Arequipa.

Rovira, S.
1994 Pre-hispanic goldwork from the Museo de América, Madrid: a new set of analyses. In *Archaeometry of Pre-Columbian Sites and Artifacts*, ed. D.A. Scott and P. Meyers, pp. 323–50. J. Paul Getty Trust, Getty Conservation Institute.

Rowe, John H.
1976 El Arte Religioso Del Cuzco En El Horizonte Temprano. In *Ñawpa Pacha* 14: 6–20. Institute of Andean Studies, Berkeley.
1985 Kunst in Peru und Bolivien. In *Das Alte Amerika*, ed. G.R. Willey. Propyläen Kunstgeschichte, Band 19. Propyläen Verlag, Berlin.

Salomon, Frank
1995 The Beautiful Grandparents. In *Tombs for the Living: Andean Mortuary Practices*, ed. Tom Dillehay, pp. 315–53. Dumbarton Oaks, Washington DC.

Salomon, Frank and George L. Urioste
1991 *The Huarochiri Manuscript*. University of Texas Press, Austin.

Stanish, Charles
1991 *A Late Pre-Hispanic Ceramic Chronology for the Upper Moquegua Valley, Peru*. In *Fieldana*, no. 16. Field Museum of Natural History, Chicago.

Urton, Gary
1981 *At the Crossroads of the Earth and the Sky*. University of Texas, Austin.
1999 *Inca Myths*. British Museum Press, London.

Valdivia, Julio M. and Manuel Cornejo Zegarra
1990 Visión sobre la Arqueología del Valle de Camaná. In *Gaceta Arqueológica Andina*, vol. V, no. 18–19: 21–4.

Acknowledgements

The task of piecing together the parts of this particular jigsaw puzzle has benefited from the help of a number of colleagues. In the first place we wish to thank Marilyn Hockey of the British Museum's Conservation Department for her skilled work of unfolding, cleaning and backing the three diadems in the Museum's collections, both preparing them for display and enabling them to be accurately drawn. Hans Rashbrook undertook the exacting task of rendering all the objects illustrated here as line drawings. These are an indispensable aid to comparison and interpretation and we thank him warmly for patiently executing the drawings to a consistently high standard. Susan La Niece and Nigel Meeks of the British Museum's Department of Scientific Research carried out the analytical work on the objects as part of their technical study of the whole range of the British Museum's collections of Precolumbian gold.

We must also thank Dr Helaine Silverman who kindly put us in touch with each other, Alan Sawyer and Mike Malpass for responding to our enquiries, and Gillett Griffin of Princeton University Art Museum who gave permission to inspect and photograph the silver diadem. We are also grateful to Karen and Sergio Chávez who took the trouble to reply under difficult circumstances, and to Edward de Bock who contributed many valued observations in the course of our discussions.

2

The Technology, Iconography and Social Significance of Metals

A Multi-Dimensional Analysis of Middle Sicán Objects

Izumi Shimada, Jo Ann Griffin and Adon Gordus

Introduction

Traditionally, interpretations regarding the cultural importance of different metals in the prehispanic Andes have usually been based on the conceptions and practices of the Incas and their subject populations as recorded by colonial Spanish writers. There is a consensus among these writers that precious metals were the prerogatives of the Inca and the ruling caste as well as of the Inca state cult of the sun, Inti. For example, Garcilaso de la Vega[1] relates how the Inca forbade anyone but royal members from wearing gold, silver, precious stones, coloured feathers, or vicuña[2] wool. Based on information provided by Garcilaso and other writers, Berthelot summarizes gold symbolism in the Inca empire:

> [G]old was the attribute of the sun god, Inti, and his supreme power was linked to it. In the mythological origins of the Inca, a golden stake had marked the valley of Cusco for the founding ancestor, Manco Capac, as the fertile site that the sun, his father, had chosen as the centre of [the Inca empire].[3]

In turn, Silverblatt suggests that gold and silver were a set of material symbols of gender parallelism that had fused with the political hierarchy and class structure imposed by the dominant Incas,[4] while Lechtman argues that tin-copper bronze was the utilitarian metal of the empire that was consciously disseminated and made accessible to the masses.[5]

In his comprehensive survey of Andean religion Augustinian Friar Antonio de la Calancha relates a widely spread coastal myth that describes how conflicts between the deity, Pachacamac, and his father, the Sun, and brother, Vichama, resulted in a series of creations and destructions.[6] In the last act of creation, to fill a world devoid of people, the Sun gave Vichama three eggs, one each made of gold, silver, and copper, from which kings and lords, royal and noble women, and common men and their wives and children were to come forth. Rowe feels that a similar 'origin myth' from Pacasmayo (Jequetepeque valley) legitimized and reinforced the 'great and immutable' differences between social classes in the Chimú Kingdom,[7] a powerful north coast rival that the Inca conquered around AD 1460–70. These myths underwrote the ruling elite's dogma regarding exclusive access to precious metals.

For the symbolic and social importance of metals in the pre-Chimú or pre-Inca era, it has been customary for scholars simply to project such 'schema' back in time, presupposing strong ideological continuity in time and space. This is an untested and, in many regards, questionable premise. In addition, the ethnohistorical observations and their modern interpretations cited above are rather rigid, inductive generalizations about official or elite dogma that do not inform us of earlier or non-elite views and situations.

Cobo himself speaks of the non-Incaic, local worship of mines, minerals, and metals, including gold nuggets, silver and cinnabar (mercuric sulfide), as their exceptional appearances were attributed to the presence of some divinity residing in them.[8] Similar practices of placing offerings and worshipping mines have been reported for the northern coast of Peru.[9] Excavations have demonstrated that the pre-Incaic tradition of arsenical copper production and use in the Lambayeque region on the north coast persisted even during Inca domination of the area. This persistence reveals the discrepancy between the aforementioned view of tin-copper bronze as the consciously disseminated, utilitarian metal of the Inca state and the reality in that province.[10] Further, antithetical to the heliocentric Incaic religion, Rowe notes that

> [I]n Pacasmayo at any rate the Moon (*Si*) was the greatest divinity. The weather and the growth of the crops were attributed to her and she was believed to be more powerful than the sun because she appeared by night and by day... The Sun was evidently considered to be a very inferior supernatural being...[11]

If the gender parallelism and the associated gold-silver symbolism noted earlier for the Inca culture is applicable here, could silver, rather than gold, have been the most valued metal and also related to females in Pacasmayo? At the same time, as shown later, this lunar-centric ideology cannot be generalized to the entire north coast.[12]

What is clear is that the retrogressive projection of the Inca vision and situation only encumbers the difficult task of illuminating the social and symbolic significance of diverse metals. This paper aims to elucidate their significance by examining a wide range of excavated Middle Sicán metal objects (*c.* AD 900–1100) from a multitude of complementary perspectives (technical, iconographic and compositional) and levels (individual artefacts, integral components of ceremonial regalia, and markers of social standing). In essence, this paper attempts an integrated analysis of metal objects and their contexts for patterns that may have social and/or symbolic significance. Because of the rarity of this kind of study, our paper emphasizes basic data presentation and explanation of the methodology. Many of our conclusions remain preliminary and untested. Various members of the Sicán Archaeological Project have addressed aspects of the main issues at hand directly or indirectly as part of our ongoing effort to achieve a 'holistic understanding' of Sicán metallurgy.[13] This 'holistic understanding' refers to the documentation and explication of the technology, organization and workers involved in this metallurgy at all stages of production and to the meanings and roles of its products.[14]

Cultural and environmental settings

The historical, social and environmental contexts of this study have been defined through our sustained program of regional study. Since 1978 our project has focused on defining the historical trajectory and material, organizational, and ideological characteristics of the Sicán culture.[15] The Sicán emerged in the Lambayeque region of the north coast of Peru around AD 700–800 (see chronology, p. 14) following the demise of the northern Mochica (or Moche).[16] The region boasts tremen-dous economic productivity with its extensive and fertile alluvial plains, perennial rivers with large annual discharge volumes, readily accessible fishing grounds along the Pacific coast, and mineral deposits in the surrounding Andean foothills.[17]

Of particular importance to this paper is the presence of numerous copper and arsenic-bearing ore deposits (arsenopyrite and its oxidized product, scorodite). Most of the some dozen prehispanic copper mines identified in the region were relatively small and exploited for superficial oxide and carbonate ores such as malachite.[18] The region also offered extensive growths of *algarrobo* (*Prosopis pallida*), a local hardwood well-suited for making high quality charcoal fuel.[19] These factors, together with a succession of complex societies, help account for prominent, persistent copper (and later copper-alloy) metallurgy in the Lambayeque region at least from the beginning of the first millennium BC.[20] As for precious metals, only one possible local source has been identified to date, an inferred 'bonanza-type' gold and silver deposit at Cerro Morro de Etén which may well have been mined out by the end of the second millennium BC.[21] Early colonial documents confirm the sparcity of prehispanic gold or silver mines on the north coast.[22] On the other hand, the adjacent north highlands and its eastern slope have long been known for gold and silver, including silver mining at Hualgayoc near Bambamarca and placer-gold mining in the Chinchipe river that merges with Marañon near Bagua.[23] Today, large-scale gold mining at Yanacocha in the north highlands north of Cajamarca and explorations in the upper reaches of the contiguous La Leche and Motupe valleys continue. Ramírez suspects that a major silver mine at Chilete in the upper Jequetepeque valley was mined before the onset of the Spanish exploitation in 1540.[24] Gold for late prehispanic precious metal production (Mochica and Sicán) is believed to have been largely imported from the north highlands or the Marañon drainage on the eastern side of the Andes.[25]

The Sicán chronology consists of the Early, Middle and Late periods. During the Middle Sicán or 'classic' period (AD 900–1100), its polity, centred at the site of Sicán in the mid-La Leche valley (see Fig. 2.3), established political and religious dominance over a 400-km stretch of the Peruvian coast, from at least the Chira valley in the north to the Chicama valley in the south. Middle Sicán religious art featured the highly distinct Sicán deity with its mask-like face and upturned ('winged') eyes,[26] and its earthly personification, the Sicán lord (Fig. 2.1).[27] The ubiquity and homogeneity of these two icons and the construction of monumen-

2.1 Modelled sheet-gold representation of the Sicán lord being carried on a litter. The lord holds a sceptre and a cup in his hands.

and accumulation of precious metals.[32] Precious metalworking must be seen as an integral part of broader ritual and status goods production and trade.[33] The range of functions and the extent of use of diverse metals, as well as the scale of their production documented for the Middle Sicán culture are all unprecedented in the prehispanic New World. In addition to ornamental and utilitarian usages, metals became the prestigious media of political, social and religious expression.

Overall, along with fishing and irrigation agriculture, metallurgical production formed a key element underpinning the Middle Sicán economy and culture as a whole. The economic wealth, political clout and religious prestige of the Middle Sicán culture were clearly unrivalled in Peru for its period.

Methodological considerations

The approach for this study is built on the belief that the cultural significance of a given metal can be elucidated through a detailed assessment of the mode, context and history of its use and production and its relationships with other metals and craft goods. Subsumed under the examination of this use and production is the analysis of material quality (including alloy composition),[34] manufacturing techniques and complexity (including the number of steps and required skill), and iconographic details and content (information). Results of this multi-dimensional analysis are interpreted against the background of regional sociopolitical context. In essence, what is attempted here is an internal analysis of the roles and meanings of metals in Middle Sicán culture by examining various intertwining lines of evidence. It is comparable to Menzel's study of ceramics from Late Ica (c.AD 1350–1570) tombs excavated by Max Uhle, in which she illustrated the potential of detailed stylistic and iconographic analysis for extracting social and symbolic meanings.[35] Her work emphasized tight chronological control, a long-term historical perspective, careful assessment of social relationships in the regional population (largely based on Spanish written accounts), and parallel pursuit of varied lines of evidence.[36] Though her work is rarely cited today, it presaged recent discussions on the 'interpretation of meanings' in archaeology, and approaches to style, funerary customs, and ethnic identity.[37]

The focus on metal objects necessitates a careful assessment of sampling problems. Different metals and objects are commonly ascribed different values or intended for different purposes, resulting in their uneven distribution across social

tal temples close to major waterways bespeak the central role that religion played in social and economic control and integration. The capital of Sicán was organized around its dozen monumental temples. Mould-made, black, single-spout bottles bearing the Sicán deity head spread rapidly and extensively over a much larger area, constituting the only coastal 'horizon style' known to date. The Late Sicán polity with its new capital at El Purgatorio (or Túcume Viejo) remained viable until c. AD 1375–1400 when it was conquered by the expanding Chimú Kingdom.[28]

During its first twelve years the Sicán Archaeological Project devoted much of its efforts to defining the chronology, environment and settlement pattern of the Lambayeque region, as well as the economy and technology of the Middle Sicán culture. It became apparent that metals permeated the Sicán culture unlike any preceding cultures, as our surveys and excavations documented the relative abundance of metallurgical debris, mines, and smelting sites in the region.[29] The first, large-scale Middle Sicán production of arsenical copper (also called arsenical bronze) was documented not only through their products but, more importantly, through excavation of workshops.[30] During the Middle Sicán, arsenical copper rapidly and permanently replaced copper in northern Peru.[31]

More recently, our excavations of Middle Sicán elite tombs showed an unprecedented diverse use boundaries. Both cultural and natural processes further complicate the picture. Copper, silver and their alloys (including arsenical copper, copper-silver alloys, and *tumbaga,* here referring to gold-silver-copper alloys that are ≤ 10-carat or 40% gold) are quite susceptible to corrosion and many of their products are found totally mineralized. In addition, in the prehispanic Andes most social segments had limited access to metal objects, resulting in curation (e.g. passing from one generation to the next), reworking (e.g. making a fish hook out of a broken needle), and/or recycling (e.g. defective and broken pieces, as well as scraps re-melted along with new metal to produce new objects). The extent of the last process is still largely unknown in prehispanic metallurgy,

logical relationships are not reliably defined. The theoretical 'representative sample' is nearly impossible to obtain largely due to destruction from pervasive grave looting and differential preservation of differently treated skeletons.

Realistically speaking, what is required is a burial sample of a regional population that is synchronic and includes an appreciable number of burials that vary in size, shape, location and content (i.e. representing as wide a range of the inferred social spectrum as possible). Only a sample such as this will allow us to discern significant patterning in burial treatment. We believe we have such a sample.

Prior to 1990, in the process of excavating various sites in and outside of Sicán, we encountered some 20 Middle Sicán burials. They ranged from those placed below the house floors of the craft production-residential site of Huaca del Pueblo Batán Grande to dedicatory sacrifices of young women inside columnar sockets atop the Huaca Rodillona and Las Ventanas temple mounds at Sicán. Most of the graves containing these burials were of relatively modest dimensions and similar construction, and consistent in the range, quantity and quality of associated goods. These graves were simple pits without any linings or structures and measuring less than 2 m in any one dimension. Typically, they contained a single skeleton in either extended or seated position. Sometimes we found the remains of simple cotton cloth that wrapped the body. Grave goods were usually limited to one to five pieces of one to four categories of objects, such as ceramic vessels, llama body parts, chalk lumps and arsenical copper objects.

Our cumulative burial sample did not include any of the 'elite personages' portrayed in ceramics and other media (Figs 2.1–2) and presumably interred in the sort of deep, richly endowed tombs looted earlier in this century.[38] In our efforts that began in 1990 to elucidate the social organization and demography of the Middle Sicán culture through interdisciplinary investigation of its mortuary practices,[39] we excavated inferred 'elite tombs' at Sicán (Fig. 2.3). These tombs were located largely on the basis of the knowledge of Sicán burial pattern gained from earlier, systematic examination of numerous looted tombs of diverse sizes at Sicán.[40] Looted tombs with traces of sumptuary or exotic goods, such as *Spondylus princeps,* traces of cinnabar paint and/or even tiny fragments of *tumbaga* objects, were invariably well over 2 m in depth. In some cases looters simply removed the fill, leaving much of the original tomb walls with ancient digging tool marks intact. Further, these tombs were under or close to

2.2 A close-up view of well-attired figurines in a miniature temple that decorated the back of a wooden litter seat. Each figure wears a diminutive Middle Sicán-style gold mask, tunic and headdress.

though it is likely to have been widely practised in respect to precious metals.

Metal objects in primary contexts are rare, except in graves and special ritual caches. It is quite difficult to obtain a 'representative sample' of metal objects, let alone a sample of any appreciable size, to establish their social and symbolic significance in the day-to-day world of the living. By default, we are left to focus heavily on funerary context metal objects as in this study.

Graves often provide favourable conditions for preservation and secure association for establishing the contemporaneity of diverse goods. At the same time, reliance on funerary context objects creates its own pitfalls and methodological challenges. For one, excavated burial samples often over- or under-represent or even entirely miss certain social segments. In some cases samples are too few to be statistically secure or their chrono-

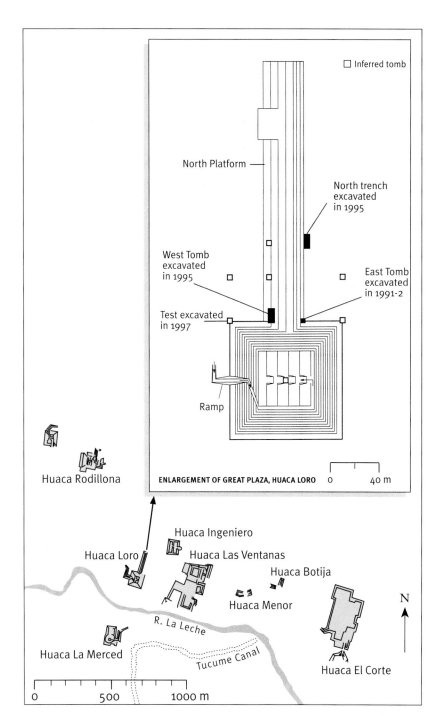

ENLARGEMENT OF GREAT PLAZA, HUACA LORO   0   40 m

□ Inferred tomb

North Platform

North trench
excavated
in 1995

West Tomb
excavated
in 1995

East Tomb
excavated
in 1991-2

Test excavated
in 1997

Ramp

Huaca Rodillona

Huaca Ingeniero

Huaca Loro

Huaca Las Ventanas

Huaca Botija

Huaca Menor

R. La Leche

Huaca La Merced

Tucume Canal

Huaca El Corte

N

0   500   1000 m

2.3 The site of Sicán, showing over a dozen major platform mounds and (inset) the reconstructed plan view of the Huaca Loro platform mound with the locations of the East and West Tombs.

the monumental temple mounds, an observation later supported by the results of radar survey in 1994, 1995 and 1997 at Huaca Loro.[41] A salvage excavation at Huaca La Merced Mound I in Sicán, following the 1983–4 flood that literally washed away much of the mound, documented what remained of an early Middle Sicán tomb (at least 2.3 m wide and 2.2 m deep) under the mound base.[42] Recovered items included a high-carat gold diadem and blackware double-spout bottle with *tumbaga* sheet-metal wrapping. Pedersen described a looted late Middle Sicán tomb that was

situated below an adobe platform called 'Huaca Menor' (part of the Huaca Las Ventanas complex at Sicán).[43] The tomb is said to have measured 14 × 14 m and 20 m in depth. Overall, a Middle Sicán 'elite' tomb at Sicán was tentatively defined as an excavated, rectangular pit greater than 2 m in at least two dimensions (width, length and/or depth) and proximate (<100 m) to the monumental platform mound(s) with a minimum height of 10 m.

Out of four inferred 'elite tombs' identified by 1991, three were excavated during the nine-month 1991–2 season and another during the seven-month 1995–6 season.[44] Radiocarbon dates and stylistic seriation of excavated ceramics indicate that these tombs were roughly contemporaneous, dating within the span of AD 960–1100 (at 95% confidence level).[45]

One tomb was situated under what had been Huaca Las Ventanas Mound III (destroyed by looters' bulldozer) and had an inverted pyramidal shape (15 × 15 m and 12 m deep). Its eastern half had been destroyed by looters. The intact western half contained remains of three complete and six partial bodies around the edges of a 3 × 3 m bottom. Also found at and near the bottom were a cluster of small tripod-painted bowls; blackware single-spout bottles; *tumbaga* sheet-wrapped, double-spout ceramic bottles; llama limbs and heads; two large shell bead clusters; a few strands of small amber beads; a cluster of *tumbaga* 'bells'; and cast (e.g. 'spear points') and sheet-metal arsenical copper objects (Fig. 2.4). Probably the most striking feature of the tomb is the way much of its interior surface was lined with layers of painted cotton cloth carefully pasted on *tumbaga* sheets.[46] Preserved paintings depicted mythological scenes of religious importance (see below). Gold objects were conspicuously absent.

Another shaft tomb, measuring 1.8 × 1.8 m and *c*.8 m in depth, was situated near the north-west corner of Huaca La Merced. Erosion by the La Leche river since the 1983–4 flood had exposed part of its vertical shaft. However, this, too, had already been looted. At the bottom we recovered shell beads, *tumbaga* bells, a partial skeleton and fragments of a *tumbaga* sheet-wrapped, double-spouted black bottle.

The other two deep shaft tombs, the Huaca Loro East and West Tombs (Fig. 2.3), had suffered minimal damage from looters and provided the great bulk of Middle Sicán metal objects to have been scientifically excavated thus far. Accordingly, this paper largely focuses on the objects from these two tombs.

The East Tomb, which was excavated in

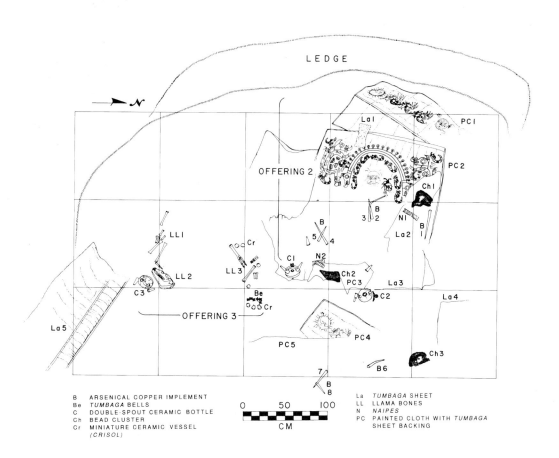

2.4 Grave offerings found near the bottom of the intact western half of the Huaca Las Ventanas tomb.

B   ARSENICAL COPPER IMPLEMENT
Be   *TUMBAGA* BELLS
C   DOUBLE-SPOUT CERAMIC BOTTLE
Ch   BEAD CLUSTER
Cr   MINIATURE CERAMIC VESSEL
        (*CRISOL*)

La   *TUMBAGA* SHEET
LL   LLAMA BONES
N   *NAIPES*
PC   PAINTED CLOTH WITH *TUMBAGA*
        SHEET BACKING

0   50   100
CM

1991–2, had been placed under the corner formed by the north basal terrace of the main body of the Huaca Loro truncated pyramid and the 150 m-long North Platform. The north–south longitudinal axis of the Huaca runs through the platform. Ground-penetrating radar survey of the Huaca Loro area in 1994 suggested that the East Tomb was just one of many deep shaft tombs placed in a lattice pattern along this axis on both sides of the platform and under the pyramid. The West Tomb, which was symmetrically situated from the East Tomb across the North Platform, was excavated in 1995–6 to test the hypothesis that it was in fact a part of a planned Middle Sicán elite cemetery under and around the Huaca Loro pyramid.[47] Corollary hypotheses were that the north–south axis served the symbolic role of separating deceased members of competing but complementary moieties and that physical distance between the Huaca centre and a given shaft tomb reflected generational or status differences. The East and West Tombs will be described in more detail later.

Though much of the solid adobe-and-mortar basal terrace that originally covered part of the mouths of the East and West Tombs had been removed by different groups of grave looters each using a bulldozer, there was enough architectural and stratigraphic evidence to indicate that inter-ment in these tombs occurred prior to construction of the Huaca Loro pyramid and North Platform. This reconstruction of the sequence of events was later reinforced by 1997 radar detection of a possible, intact shaft tomb at the north-west corner of the Huaca Loro pyramid base. A subsequent test excavation confirmed the tomb's location and sub-pyramidal stratigraphic position.[48] Tomb placement preceding pyramidal construction had earlier been noted in regard to Huaca Menor and La Merced Mound I.

Another aspect of our burial sample that requires clarification is the nature of the relationship between interred individual(s) and associated metal objects. Did the objects belong to and/or were they used by the deceased? Could they have represented tokens of respect or affection or even reflections of political motives of the living? The nature and degree of correspondence between the elaborateness of funerary rites and the material wealth interred, on the one hand, and the social standing of the accompanying deceased, on the other, can be quite varied and have been much debated since the 1960s.[49] Summarizing his survey of historic and prehistoric Andean and non-Andean mortuary practices, Brown found that complex societies with institutionalized social inequality (e.g. the Mochica) have positive correspondence.[50] It is evident that each case must be assessed on its own terms by considering the nature and size of its sample, as well as its context and internal patterning.

In our case, investigation since 1978 has established the critical environmental, historical and social contexts of the sample.[51] Various lines of evidence attest to the marked social differentiation and importance of its outward material expression. The iconography of the known corpus of Middle Sicán artefacts we have examined clearly illustrates this point.[52] An example is a mould-made blackware ceramic vessel that shows an elaborately attired personage being carried on a litter. Fig. 2.1 is a sheet-metal representation of the same. Though rare, fine blackline, pictorial representations on late Middle Sicán ceramic bottles show the persistence of the earlier Mochica convention of centrally placing key figures and depicting them larger than their peripherally placed attendants.[53]

Numerous monumental adobe temples at Sicán and other Middle Sicán sites constructed around AD 1000 further point to the centralization of power and social stratification.[54] All these structures were built by superimposing layers of a bonded lattice of adobe chambers, each filled with rubble, sand and/or other readily available materials. While this system allowed rapid attainment of a large volume with a minimum number of adobe bricks and human labour investment, it required continuous and centralized supervision of human and material resources.[55]

As noted earlier, at least in the case of the well-studied Huaca Loro temple, it was built atop a group of deep elite shaft tombs, thereby serving simultaneously as a protective seal, an impressive monument to the ancestors and an altar for their continuing worship; it was a highly visible and instructive material symbol of the power and permanence of a Middle Sicán elite group.[56] Presumably, its construction was commissioned and directed by living members of the elite group.

Overall, there are reasons to believe that in Middle Sicán society an individual's social importance could be gauged by tomb placement, content, and construction (e.g. size, depth and complexity), and that differential access to material goods and services reflected social standing.

Precious metal objects and their specific contexts

The Huaca Loro East Tomb
The description here emphasizes specific associations, manufacturing techniques and evidence that allows inferences regarding the usage of metal objects. Descriptions of other objects are presented elsewhere.[57]

At the bottom of a 3 × 3 m and 11 m-deep shaft was the intact burial chamber with seven niches on four walls. The chamber contained five individuals and c.1.2 tonnes of diverse grave goods (see Fig. 2.8), over two-thirds of which, by weight, were arsenical copper, tumbaga and high-carat gold-alloy objects. Grave goods were arranged concentrically and superimposed in layers on and around the inverted body of a robust male personage, some forty to fifty years of age, placed at the centre of the mat-lined, square-shaped burial chamber floor. The following description is organized by six arbitrary levels of grave contents, starting from the top (the last items to have been placed).

Levels 1 and 2 At the top of the grave content stratigraphy was a juvenile body (twelve to thirteen years of age, indeterminate sex) atop a detached litter seat. All preserved parts of the litter were made of cane and/or wood covered or wrapped with very thin tumbaga sheets (c.0.05 mm thick).

In the second level, placed against the northwest corner of the burial chamber was a 'chest', a tightly woven basket measuring 1.2 × 0.6 m and estimated to have been c.50 cm high. The interior and exterior surfaces were covered with very thin tumbaga sheet metal. The chest contained at least twenty-four superimposed layers of gold, gold-silver, and tumbaga ornaments and ritual paraphernalia laid one over the other – over sixty large objects overall.

The chest contents were carefully organized by size and category. At the bottom were the largest

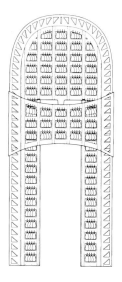
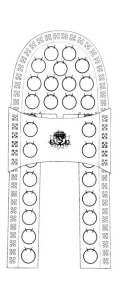
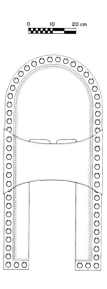

2.5 Reconstruction of the three parabolic headdresses found near the bottom of the chest, each with its matching double-convex ornament that was placed on the front of the crown.

2.6 Three kinds of crown ornaments from the chest: a set of gold feathers (left), ornament with rotating top (centre) and *tumi*-shaped ornament (right).

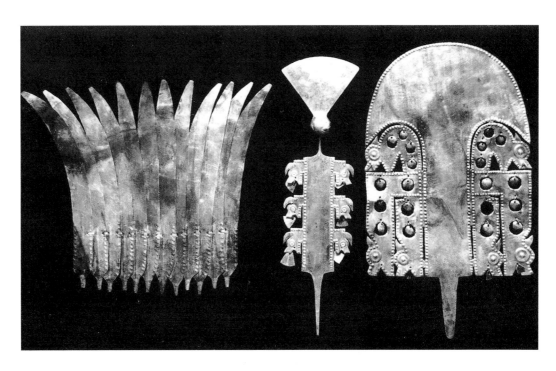

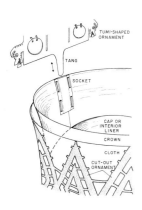

2.7 Diagram of the interior of a crown showing how the tang of a *tumi*-shaped ornament would have fitted into a socket. Also shown are an interior cloth liner that would have provided protection and a snug fit for the head, and an exterior wrap-around ornament.

objects, four gold and *tumbaga* parabolic head ornaments, three of which measured nearly one metre in length and some 40 cm in width (Fig. 2.5). These head ornaments were used in conjunction with crown and bi-concave forehead ornaments. Each had near its centre a long, pointed tang (arsenical copper or silver-copper alloys) that was apparently for insertion into a socket. Just such a socket was noted on the interior of a crown found in the chest (see below). Three of these headdresses had a nearly 2 m long sheet-metal strip with cut-out designs decorating its perimeter. All were additionally decorated with numerous gold bangles.

Overlaying them were fourteen gold discs (*c.*26–34 cm in diameter), each with a silver-alloy border, ridges in a 'spoked-wheel' pattern, and a circular centre covered with carefully pasted bird feathers. They may have been used as ornaments on the back of the head or crown as seen on various figurines mounted atop Middle Sicán *tumi*-knives.[58] The discs were, in turn, overlain by a dozen gold, gold-silver and *tumbaga tumi*-shaped head ornaments and six sets of eleven or twelve large gold feathers each, one set of ninety small gold feathers and three *tumbaga* 'fans' (Fig. 2.6). The above set of small feathers is believed to have trimmed the perimeter of an aforementioned parabolic headdress. The back side of these and larger gold feathers revealed imprints of what appear to have been the shafts of real bird feathers and string that tied them to the shafts of the gold feathers.[59]

Placed around the above sets of feathers were four gold rattles that were apparently mounted atop short wooden shafts long since perished; two wooden darts wrapped in *tumbaga* foil; numerous, small gold conical ornaments; and four gold head bands.

At the top of the chest were five crowns,[60] one at the centre and each corner of the chest. One crown had a pair of 'sockets' placed symmetrically opposed to each other on the interior top, so that a pair of *tumi*-shaped or other tanged ornaments could be inserted (Fig. 2.7). The interior surface of all crowns showed imprints of tightly woven liners that must have protected the head from sharp edges and, at the same time, provided a snug fit. Two of the five crowns were decorated with cut-out designs or perforations, while the remaining three were plain. The five intricately cut-out gold sheet-metal ornaments that were found near the five crowns had originally been sewn on to a cloth backing and placed on the crown exterior as interchangeable ornaments (Fig. 2.7). One of the plain crowns was found with such an ornament on its exterior. The colour and textural difference of the cloth backing would have served to highlight the cut-out designs.

Essentially, the chest contained precious sheet-metal head ornaments believed to have been used by the principal personage and the two accompanying women. Though these individuals wore various gold ornaments, none was buried with his or her head ornaments. In addition, the crowns and head bands had different circumferences, which approximated those of their skulls, and showed signs of use-related damage (e.g. disfigured holes for wires and lost bangles).

Table 2.1 Average gold, silver, and copper content of objects from the Huaca Loro East Tomb

Sample Type		Number		% Gold	% Silver	% Copper	Alloy
Group	Object	O	N	Av ± Sm	Av ± Sm	Av ± Sm	MP °C
Bangles	2-cm bangles	31	31	54.9 ± 0.2	32.2 ± 0.3	12.9 ± 0.1	890
	Tumi ornaments	12	12	42.4 ± 0.4	33.8 ± 0.6	23.8 ± 0.6	800
	Rattle rings	6	6	54.4 ± 1.6	34.9 ± 2.3	10.7 ± 0.8	900
	Headdress	28	28	51.3 ± 0.5	36.9 ± 0.4	11.8 ± 0.3	890
	Masks	7	7	46.5 ± 2.5	32.1 ± 2.0	21.4 ± 2.6	800
	Misc. bangles	12	12	55.6 ± 0.9	32.4 ± 1.5	12.0 ± 1.0	890
Feathers	Headdress	90	90	41.4 ± 0.2	37.7 ± 0.3	20.9 ± 0.4	800
	Set 1	11	11	43.8 ± 0.5	40.7 ± 0.6	15.5 ± 0.8	880
	Set 2	12	12	43.3 ± 0.7	40.1 ± 0.8	16.6 ± 1.3	850
	Set 3	12	12	43.1 ± 0.9	42.4 ± 0.9	14.5 ± 1.4	860
	Set 4	11	11	42.8 ± 0.5	40.6 ± 0.7	16.6 ± 0.8	870
	Set 5	6	6	60.0 ± 2.0	21.6 ± 0.7	18.4 ± 2.6	850
Ear-spools	Pair 1	2	6	66.4 ± 0.7	31.8 ± 0.7	1.9 ± 0.2	1020
	Pair 2	2	4	59.6 ± 1.3	38.1 ± 0.8	2.3 ± 0.6	1010
	Pair 3	2	6	68.6 ± 2.0	29.6 ± 2.1	1.8 ± 0.4	1030
	Pair 4	1	2	62.3 ± 1.3	34.6 ± 1.4	3.1 ± 0.1	1000
	Pair 5: mask	2	8	59.1 ± 1.0	34.7 ± 1.0	6.2 ± 0.4	950
Other groups	Crowns	5	5	54.5 ± 2.3	33.0 ± 2.3	12.5 ± 3.9	880
	Cones	12	12	42.0 ± 0.9	40.4 ± 0.6	17.6 ± 0.8	850
	Cup	1	1	54.9 ± 1.8	42.9 ± 4.1	2.2 ± 0.1	1000
	Dart throwers	2	6	50.9 ± 5.4	33.0 ± 7.0	16.1 ± 4.0	850
	30 cm discs	14	14	36.3 ± 1.2	40.0 ± 1.1	23.7 ± 2.0	790
	Staff gods	6	6	60.8 ± 3.7	28.5 ± 1.1	10.7 ± 3.4	900
	Masks	2	6	53.2 ± 7.6	35.1 ± 3.2	11.8 ± 7.6	850
	Mask tongue	1	1	12.0 ± 2.1	12.6 ± 6.5	75.4 ±21.0	1010
	Nails	5	5	47.2 ± 0.7	29.3 ± 1.9	23.5 ± 1.4	805
	Rattle rings	3	10	53.2 ± 1.8	31.7 ± 1.8	15.1 ± 2.4	860
	Square foils	4	4	40.6 ± 5.6	29.6 ± 0.7	29.8 ± 4.9	820
	Fan squares	4	4	50.9 ± 1.3	27.4 ± 2.0	21.7 ± 0.9	830
	Standards	4	4	54.6 ± 0.6	33.4 ± 0.5	12.0 ± 0.5	880
	Wires-staples	8	9	52.6 ± 2.3	31.4 ± 1.9	16.0 ± 1.3	860
	Tumis	11	13	50.8 ± 1.8	37.9 ± 1.4	11.3 ± 1.4	900
	All Samples*	328	363	48.2 ± 0.6	35.7 ± 0.1	16.1 ± 0.5	860

O is the number of separate objects sampled; N is the number of separate metal pieces sampled; Sm is the standard deviation of the mean (i.e. average) of N values; MP is the melting point temperature.
* Omits data for the (very high copper) tongue on animal mask. Assumes %Au + %Ag + %Cu = 100%.

2.8 A reconstruction drawing showing details of the contents and organization of the Huaca Loro East Tomb.

Level 2 had another but smaller cache of gold objects in Niche 5. The cache consisted mostly of the finished component parts of larger, more complex objects. A notable example is a set of six long gold feathers (*c.*60% gold, 21.6% silver, 18.4% copper; Table 2.1) and a complex, gold accessory ornament with some 350 small bangles that were to be mounted atop a staff. Another example is a rattle complete except for its handle.

Level 3 The next lower level of grave contents included fifteen bundles of arsenical bronze implements along or near the edges of the burial cham-

ber (Fig. 2.9). Each bundle consisted of some thirty implements tightly tied together by plant fibre cords (Fig. 2.10). There were 489 implements weighing some 200 kg overall. These implements were cast and hammered to shape but the great majority do not appear to have been finished or used.[61] At the proximal end they have an open socket (presumably for wooden hafts to be inserted) and taper to sharp points or blunt (rounded or squared) ends. They exhibit considerable variation in size, ranging from 30.4 to 43.7 cm in length, 2.0 to 4.1 cm in width, and 234.7 to 710.8 g in weight (including some corrosion products). Typically they are around 35 cm in length and 0.4 kg in weight. In addition, they vary in extent of corrosion, though most of them are relatively well preserved. In general appearance, they resemble 'digging stick' or spear points. However, given their incomplete or un-used character, a ready functional attribution is not possible. Further, as with many ceramic vessels found in Sicán tombs that were hardly fired (*c.*100-200°C),[62] these objects may have been strictly intended for funerary interment and not manufactured in the same ways or sizes as their counterparts made for use in the mundane world.

Also pertaining to the third level were two large piles (40–45 cm high) of *tumbaga* sheet-metal scraps, at the north-west and south-east corners (see below). The above chest of precious metal objects sat atop two bundles of arsenical copper implements and a *tumbaga* scrap pile. A surprise find at this level was two nearly identical sets of ornaments cut out of gold sheets and possibly intended for attachment to clothing. Each set consisted of a figurine representing the Sicán lord holding a staff in each hand and associated gold plaque with serrated borders. The staff had a diamond-shaped tip and large disc near the upper end of the shaft, much like the staff found lower in the burial chamber.

The third level (Fig. 2.10) also had two piles each of large (typically *c.*1 kg), whole *Spondylus princeps* and *Conus fergusoni* shells (totals of 179 and 141, respectively), all in the north-west sector of the burial chamber. At the time of interment, one of the *Spondylus* piles partially collapsed onto the top of a low *tumbaga* scrap pile and shells were found mixed with 'star-shaped' (four points) gold 'bells', two ceramic bottles and a wooden 'dart'. At the south-west corner was a cluster of varied objects atop a low pile (*c.*5–15 cm thick) of *tumbaga* sheet-metal scraps. The cluster included ceramic vessels, a set of wooden needles, small deposits of haematite and limonite paints, a small quartz crystal and a wire-framed ear ornament with

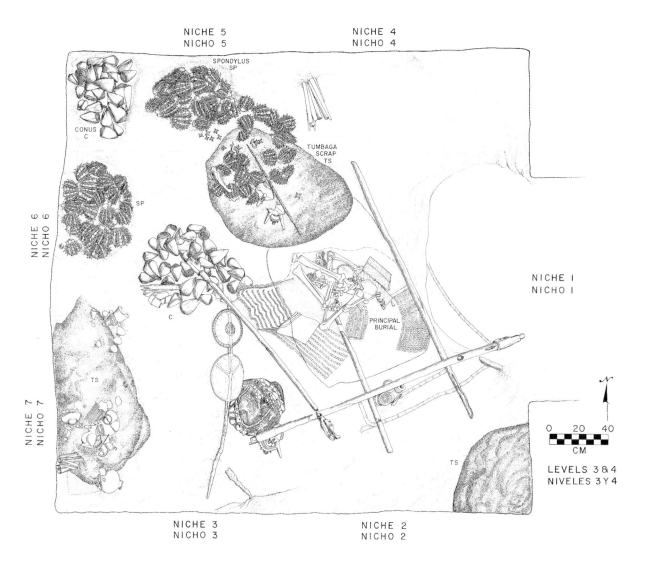

NICHE 5 / NICHO 5

NICHE 4 / NICHO 4

SPONDYLUS SP

CONUS C

NICHE 6 / NICHO 6

SP

TUMBAGA SCRAP TS

NICHE 1 / NICHO 1

PRINCIPAL BURIAL

C

NICHE 7 / NICHO 7

TS

N

0 20 40
CM

LEVELS 3 & 4
NIVELES 3 Y 4

TS

NICHE 3 / NICHO 3

NICHE 2 / NICHO 2

2.9 (above) Placing of Levels 3 and 4 grave goods around the principal personage at the centre of the chamber.

2.10 (below) Two bundles of cast arsenical copper implements, together with a pile each of *Spondylus* and *Conus* shells and a litter beam with its end carved into a mythical feline head (cf. Fig. 2.1 chief on a litter).

an amber disc set at the centre. Just east of the cluster was a *c*.2 m-long staff with a rhomboid wooden tip (*c*.30 cm long), wrapped in *tumbaga* sheet, and a metal shaft (totally mineralized), on which were mounted three *tumbaga* discs. The middle disc had gold ornaments with circular bangles.

The last major items of this level were four shafts belonging to the disassembled litter of Level 1. They were laid so as to define a roughly one-metre square area at the centre of the burial chamber, where the body of the principal personage was placed.

Level 4 The inverted body of the principal personage pertains to the fourth level (Fig. 2.9). He was buried wearing his personal ornaments: a gold *tumi*-knife was placed next to his left hand, a pair of gold shin-covers next to his crossed legs, a hinged gold backflap above his hips, and superimposed amber, shell and other bead pectorals on the chest. His head was detached and rotated so as to be right side up and placed in front of the body looking west (Fig.

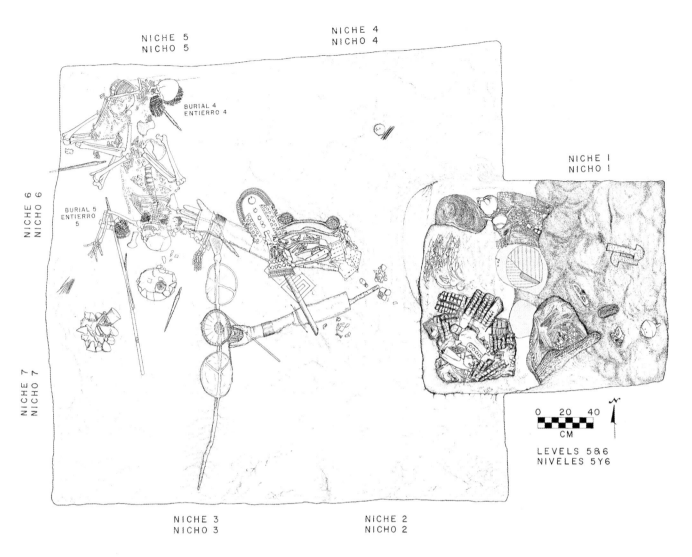

NICHE 5
NICHO 5

NICHE 4
NICHO 4

NICHE 1
NICHO 1

BURIAL 4
ENTIERRO 4

NICHE 6
NICHO 6

BURIAL 5
ENTIERRO 5

NICHE 7
NICHO 7

NICHE 3
NICHO 3

NICHE 2
NICHO 2

0   20   40
CM

LEVELS 5&6
NIVELES 5Y6

2.11 Placing of Levels 5 and 6 grave contents, including the opposing pair of women at the north-west corner (Burials 4 and 5).

2.5). The face was covered by a large gold mask. On his nose was an ingeniously designed nose clip kept in place by two parallel wire frames whose lower ends pressed against the base of the nose and lightly pinched the septum. The upper end held four bangles that hung slightly in front of the nose. A pair of large gold ear-spools (9.2 cm in diameter, 77.3 and 78.3 g in weight) covered his ears. Immediately below the ears were two sets of gold hanging ear ornaments. In essence, his head with the mask and nose and ear ornaments duplicated the Sicán deity head, the pervasive, hallmark icon of Middle Sicán art. All these items and the body of the principal personage were placed in the middle of a large, rectangular mantle (long since perished; roughly 155 × 130 cm) spread over the centre of the burial chamber. This mantle with nearly 2,000 gold foil squares (*c.*1.5 × 1.5 cm) sewn on in orderly rows separated the fourth and fifth levels.

Level 5 Grave contents of this level consisted of goods and bodies placed directly on the mat-lined

burial chamber floor (Fig. 2.11). The aforementioned mantle covered a wide array of sheet-metal objects. One notable item was a standard thought to have been displayed at the head of processions during the personnage's rule. It was composed of a 1.7 m-long wooden shaft wrapped in *tumbaga* sheets, and *tumi*-shaped and bi-concave ornaments mounted on the upper end of the shaft. The *tumi*-shaped ornament itself was multi-component; the badly mineralized body was probably made with silver-copper alloy sheet and had rows of small and large, hanging, gold discs. The crescent blade was decorated with a gold band with cut-out geometric designs, while a row of five 'mythical feline' heads cut out of gold sheet ornamented the opposing flanks. Imprints of small cut bird feathers were preserved on these outer gold sheet pieces. Attached to the corroded body (believed to have been made with a silver-copper alloy) of the biconcave ornament were four rows of circular bangles, a symmetrical pair of trapezoidal sheet-gold pieces with cut-out geometric

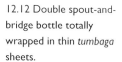

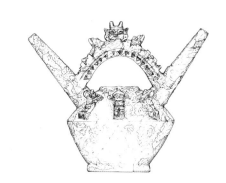

12.12 Double spout-and-bridge bottle totally wrapped in thin *tumbaga* sheets.

2.13 Four pairs of high-carat gold ear-spools that were found together just south of the body of the principal personage.

added up to 90 cm in length and were large and long enough to have inserted the entire arm. Though individual fingers, the rest of the hand, and the arm were separately sheet-wrapped, the glove as a whole was rigid. Joints were not articulated to allow independent movement of components. The rod is an enigma; it extended some 25 to 30 cm inward and outward beyond the end of the upper arm. If the gloves were worn at all by the principal personage during his life, the construction would have restricted him to simple lateral and up-and-down motions, such as offering a cup. It is quite possible that the thick rods were inserted at the time of his interment, so that the gloves could be anchored to the sides of his mummified body.

The left-hand glove held a gold beaker (*c.*13 cm high and 10 cm in diameter) with repoussé representations of the standing Sicán lord holding a staff in each hand. The base of this beaker, which was made of raised silver sheet ornamented with cut-out designs, showed evidence of a manufacturing mishap. Accidental overheating during the process of attaching the silver base to the bottom of the gold beaker melted a portion of the rim of the silver base and coated the beaker's base with a flash of the melted silver.[63]

South of the left glove beyond the edge of the mantle was a cluster of six pairs of gold earspools, a large group of beads (primarily of turquoise) and a double-spout ceramic bottle wrapped in sheet metal (totally mineralized; Fig. 2.12). There were two sizes among the ear-spools (Fig. 2.13); the larger measured *c.*10 cm in diameter and 73.5–77.9 g in weight, while the smaller had corresponding figures of 7.8–8.2 cm and 44.1–51.2 g. As a group, these ear-spools distinguished themselves by having been made of highly polished and workable, high-carat gold sheet (*c.*60–70% gold, 30–40% silver and 1–3% copper).[64] The larger ear-spools in particular displayed complex, innovative design and mastery of a number of difficult techniques, such as hand-forging of wires, granulation, mineral insets, x-shaped internal bracing that created the impression of a 'floating' design, and 'proto-braze' joining.[65] In addition to similar alloy composition, they displayed clear stylistic and technical unity with the gold ear-spools on the mask and head of the principal personage, suggesting they were made in the same workshop or even by same master goldsmith(s).

East of the gloves were additional gold objects, including a head band, a nose clip, a set of twenty 'bells', four square sheets with boot-shaped cut-out design (tunic or litter ornaments?), as well as a

designs and, at the centre, a cut-out sheet-gold figurine of the standing Sicán lord holding a staff in each hand.

The above standard straddled a pair of large gloves. They were assembled from four components: hands, bracelets of tiny turquoise and shell beads, a slightly tapering tubular section for forearms and upper arms, and heavy copper-alloy support rods (Fig. 2.11). The gloves were constructed with a substratum (perhaps of leather, badly deteriorated), which was covered with at least two layers of thin sheet gold. The first three parts

2.14 Forehead ornament with a sculptural rendering of a vampire bat head, which was formed with sheet gold.

set of four inferred tunic ornaments with numerous perforated circular bangles. Also found was a forehead ornament with a striking, sculptural 'bat' head (Fig. 2.14) mounted on a large rectangular plate with numerous bangles. This ornament is striking not only in appearance but also in regard to manufacturing techniques. The goldsmith literally 'tucked, gathered, clipped and stitched' gold sheets, in a manner somewhat analogous to handling textiles, to create a compelling and accurate high-relief rendering of a bat's facial details.[66] The head shows the short muzzle, folded nostrils, sharp fangs and long, narrow tongue characteristic of vampire bats (*Phyllostomidae* Family), which are relatively common today around the site of Sicán.[67] The eyes represented by the spherical amber beads (iris) capped with small, flat, circular turquoise beads (pupil) appear to have been tied down originally with a string (long perished) to allow rotation, while the *tumbaga* tongue moved sideways. The aforementioned tunic ornaments and bat headdress display the same manufacturing techniques, components and stylistic features, as well as similar alloy compositions, suggesting they may well have been made in the same workshop.

Underlying the shell clusters at the north-west corner were two gracile women, thirty to thirty-five years of age. A woman seated with her back against the north wall faced another woman in prone position on the floor (Fig. 2.11). Though superficially resembling each other in attire, there are at the same time important differences. Nearby on the floor, each had one silver-copper alloy (? – highly mineralized) *tumi*-knife, and two silver-rich alloy 'daggers' (*c*.1.5–1.6 cm wide, 34.5–35.6 cm long, including tang). Residue on the tang suggests these 'daggers' were originally inserted into a wooden hilt or shaft. Both wore tunics (long since perished) with gold foil squares (1.4 × 1.4 cm) sewn on the front in a regular lattice pattern.

However, the woman on the floor also had a shell bead pectoral and probably a shawl (perished) decorated with a row of large gold-foil squares (3.2 × 3.2 cm) sewn near the upper edge. In addition, there were a set of four cut-out gold figures in profile,[68] and four associated borders with cut-out geometric designs sewn around the margin of the right sleeve.

Below her left arm was a 'ceremonial dart thrower' (69 cm long, 2.7 cm in diameter) with plain gold sheet wrapped around a wooden rod and anchored by thirty (originally seventy-seven) hand-forged sharp, tiny gold nails (c.4.6–4.7 mm long, c.1 mm thick) dipped in tar. It had a silver-rich alloy lance-like point at its tip. Near the other end was a dart hook made of gold using lost-wax casting. Just south of her head lay another dart thrower assembled from five separate gold sheet parts. They were nailed onto a wooden core and ornamented with a repoussé representation of what appears to be a splayed 'Earth Monster' of the Manteño style of south coastal Ecuador.[69]

Level 6 The sixth and lowest level corresponds to the contents of Niche 1 dug into the east wall, the largest of the seven niches. The niche floor in reality was an eastward and downward extension of the burial chamber floor. The rectangular, flat-bottomed pit (c.1.8 × 1.5 m and 0.7–0.8 m deep) at the base of the niche was full of diverse, mostly metal, grave goods. First, c.300 kg of *tumbaga* sheet-metal scraps were packed into the back half of the pit. The scraps deposited in this niche and elsewhere in the burial chamber were essentially the small pieces that resulted from cutting and other steps of sheet-metal working. The shape of pieces that had been cut out can still be recognized in some scraps. Any successfully completed object would have generated a considerable quantity of scrap. Large objects such as *tumi*-shaped crown ornaments and masks that were missing some parts or folded were also found in scrap piles. Also included were partially used, oblong ingots (c.4.4% gold, 9.6% silver, 86% copper), what appeared to be bent and broken scribers, and rejects from mishaps in manufacturing, such as gold foil squares with poorly placed sewing holes. But, the great majority of the scrap comprised small pieces of thin depletion-gilded *tumbaga* sheets, commonly around 0.1 mm in thickness.[70]

The discovery of fine silt, spines and leaves of the local tree, *algarrobo*, and even some small, white bird feathers[71] and a few sherds in the scrap suggests that the scrap was gathered not only off workbenches, but also from the workshop floors. Though the designation 'scrap' may suggest something of little value, it was in reality a valuable, recyclable resource and carefully saved. Most scrap pieces had been tightly folded or crumpled, presumably to facilitate remelting. Three analysed samples of *tumbaga* sheet scraps had an average composition of c.13.4% gold, 29.4% silver and 57.2% copper,[72] implying that the 500 kg of scrap in the East Tomb may contain as much as 67 kg gold and 147 kg silver.

Near the top of the scrap heap at the back of the pit, two silver-alloy *tumi*-knives and one black ceramic bottle had been placed. Near the inner edge of the scrap pile at least six *tumbaga* masks (badly preserved) were found upside down at vertical or oblique angles as if they had been simply tossed on the heap. Near the masks lay an oblong concentration of depletion-gilded *tumbaga* foil squares (c.23.9% gold, 31.7% silver, 44.4% copper).[73] Given their regular lattice layout and superimposed nature (at least four layers), this concentration may represent a long-since-perished folded cloth that had had thousands of foil squares sewn on.

At the south-west corner of the pit next to the foil cluster were superimposed layers of orderly laid rows of an estimated 1,500 bundles of *naipes*, I-shaped objects cut out of arsenical copper sheets inferred to have been used as a standardized medium of exchange.[74] Though difficult to specify due to corrosion, each bundle seems to have consisted of some 12 to 13 *naipes* (all measuring c.5.0 × 3.0 cm) carefully tied together with a plant fibre cord. Altogether, this cache probably contains nearly 20,000 *naipes*, weighing some 25 kg in total. Two *tumi*-shaped head ornaments (one each of *tumbaga* and gold) and a wooden dart were placed atop the *naipe* heap.

Between two large clusters of mineral and shell beads towards the front of the niche was an impressive cache of what appear to be *tumbaga* sheet objects, predominantly masks (c.40 cm wide), *tumi*-shaped crown ornaments (same sizes as those in the chest in the second level), and large discs (estimated diameters of 30–35 cm). At least two dozen objects were packed tightly in a vertical but inverted position. Due to corrosion, they had become brittle and adhered to each other, and the exact alloy composition or number of objects in this cache remain undetermined.

Overall, the East Tomb contained some 750 kg of diverse objects representing the full range of metals produced by the Middle Sicán metalworkers, i.e. arsenical bronze, silver-copper, *tumbaga* and high-carat gold-alloys. Like their north coast Mochica predecessors,[75] Middle Sicán goldsmiths emphasized and excelled in sheet-metal making and working such as chasing and repoussé, raising, and mechanical and proto-braze joining. They also attained an impressive sophistication in alloying to meet their diverse needs. Their technical repertoire, preferences and associated technology were inherited by the later Chimú metalworkers, whose works are analysed by K. O'Day in a later paper.

Objects in the East Tomb were grouped

2.15 Isometric reconstruction view of the Huaca Loro West Tomb. Note its two-tier construction and placement below the north basal terrace of the Huaca Loro mound.

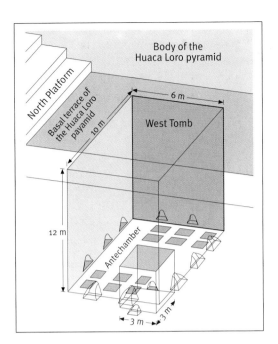

together by category and usually wrapped with or separated by organic mats and/or *tumbaga* sheets. Wrapping probably protected them and facilitated their placement as well as 'accounting' of the quantities of given categories. Though the presence of scraps, cast and partially forged objects, and finished component parts suggests strong concern with control of metalworking, we noted only one partially used ingot which was found in the scrap. The finished objects are clearly dominated by high-carat, sheet gold personal ornaments and ritual paraphernalia.

The West Tomb

In spite of physical proximity, the West Tomb presents a striking contrast to the East Tomb in regard to dimensions, internal organization, and skeletal and artefactual content. The West Tomb was physically imposing and had a complex, two-tier, nested construction – a tomb within a tomb

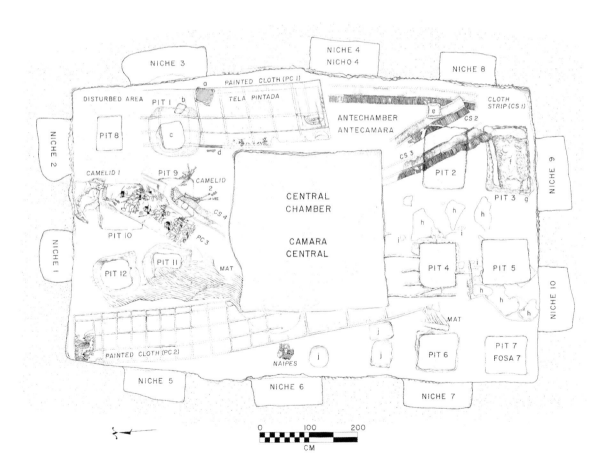

2.16 Organization and contents of the Antechamber, Huaca Loro West Tomb. Note how textiles, both painted (PC-1 to 3) and unpainted (CS-1 to 4), and a mat, as well as *tumbaga* sheets, cover the floor; a = red (haematite) pigment; b = red (haematite) and yellow (limonite) pigments; c = looters' hole; d = cinnabar paint; e = red (haematite) pigment; f = possible grey cloth remnant; g = grey cloth remnant; h = cloth remnant with *tumbaga* sheet backing; i = gilded *tumbaga* sheet; j = shallow depression.

(Fig. 2.15): (1) the 10 m (north–south) by 6 m (east–west) Antechamber at 12 m below surface with ten wall niches and twelve rectangular sub-floor pits (Fig. 2.16), and (2) the 3 × 3 m Central Chamber at the centre of the Antechamber, which descended another 3 m to a depth of 15 m and had a pair of symmetrically opposing niches on the north and south walls.

The Antechamber The twelve subfloor pits were organized into two symmetrically opposing groups of six pits each on the north and south sides of the Central Chamber. Each pit contained one or two young adult women making a total of nine for each group. Though most of the eighteen women were buried with ceramic vessels, textiles (perhaps vestiges of what were used to wrap the bodies), ceramic spindle whorls and lumps of chalk, only four individuals had metal objects. Two had a *tumi*-knife and the remaining two, one and two unidentifiable small objects. All objects appear to have been copper-based but had degraded into greenish corrosion products. The cache placed on the floor of Niche 8 included a *tumi*-knife, eight ceramic vessels, four wooden sticks and what appears to have been a reddish cloth.

The floor context objects were limited in range and quantity, except cloth. Much of the floor, including the sealed tops of some of the subfloor pits, had been covered with cloth strips (*c.*30–35 cm wide, over 5 m long) or painted textiles with or without gilded sheet-metal backing (*c.*1.15 m wide, over 4 m long; Fig. 2.16).[76] One deposit each of haematite and limonite had been placed on one painted cloth. Near the north-east corner two adult camelids were found close to a painted cloth.

The only notable metal objects were a *naipe* cluster placed directly in front of Niche 6. Like its counterpart in Niche 1 of the East Tomb, the cluster consisted of an estimated 240 orderly laid stacks of bundles, each of which, in turn, consisted of about a dozen *naipes* of the same size and shape (*c.*4.0 × 2.6 cm) tied together with organic fibre cords. Due to its corroded condition, a precise quantification of the *naipe* cluster is difficult. A roughly rectangular gold plate (*c.*2.2 × 4.6 cm; 17.6 g) found near the north-east corner of the Central Chamber mouth does not appear to have been associated with any feature or object. In fact, we encountered occasional small *tumbaga* sheet fragments on the floor and mixed in the earthen fill of the Antechamber. A set of a half dozen corroded 'bells' (copper-silver alloy?) was also found in the fill just above the Niche 1 mouth.[77]

The Central Chamber This space appears to have been reserved for placement of the principal personage and his grave goods. The personage, a relatively robust man of about thirty to thirty-five years of age with a serious puncture wound on his pelvis,[78] had been placed at the centre of the mat-lined floor in a cross-legged, seated position (Fig. 2.17). He wore full regalia, including a large *tumbaga* mask, *tumbaga* and gold headdress, a pair of gloves (*c.*55 cm long) and pectorals of mineral beads. The uppermost pectoral consisted largely of tabular, polished turquoise set in a *tumbaga* backplate. The other pectorals had lost their original forms as the threads that once held amber, sodalite, turquoise and *Spondylus* shell beads in place had deteriorated. Pressed against the chest below the pectorals were two gold cloth clips (in the form of a figure-8 and a bird in profile) that probably kept the two ends of a cloak (long since perished) together. Each glove consisted of a hand made of *tumbaga* sheets, an arm built of what appears to have been leather and some other organic substances (yet undefined), a bead bracelet and an arsenical copper rod which provided the structural support for the entire glove. The right glove held a totally mineralized (copper-silver alloy?) flaring cup with repoussé decoration (profile views of the Sicán lord?). Near his knee were a highly polished oblong stone (8 cm long, 2.6 cm wide), two polished, flat wooden implements,[79] a smooth lump of chalk and a small deposit of red haematite and orangish limonite paints.[80]

The principal personage was surrounded by a diverse range of grave goods including eight camelid heads, and the articulated feet of at least twenty-five camelids, both large and small forms;[81] earthen casts of nine rolls of strip cloth (*c.*13–14 cm wide) long since perished; two each of *tumbaga* sheet-covered double-spout ceramic bottles and short-neck jars; two *Spondylus princeps*; one *Conus fergusoni*; two wooden staffs (one with a carved *Spondylus princeps* [incomplete] and the other with a rhomboidal point at the proximal end [*c.*123 cm long]); at least half a dozen of what appear to be earthen casts of gourd vessels; and over a hundred crudely made miniature ceramic vessels known locally as *crisoles*, among other items (Table 2.2).

As if to flank the personage, a young adult woman was placed in each of the symmetrically opposing niches on the north and south walls of the Central Chamber. The south-side woman was cross-legged and seated, wore a shell bead pectoral and was accompanied by ceramic vessels. The north-side woman was tightly flexed and had

2.17 The main burial chamber (Central Chamber) and its contents. Diverse objects surround the centrally placed body of the principal personage.

**Table 2.2 Comparison of precious metal objects
found with the principal personages in the Huaca Loro East and West tombs**

Objects	West Tomb principal personage	East Tomb principal personage
Pair of ceremonial gloves	1	1
Beaker	1	1
Mask	1	1
Pairs of ear-spools	0	6
Pairs of ear ornaments	0	2
Nose ornament	1	2
Forehead ornament	0	1
Wide head band	0	1
Pair of shin covers	0	1
Tumi-knife	0	1
Cloth clip	2	0
Hip cover	0	1
Tunic	1	0
Tunic with gold foil	0	1
Set of tunic fringe ornaments	0	1
Staff	0	2

2.18 Reconstruction drawing of precious metal ornaments in the upper layers of the chest inside Niche 12 on the north wall of the Central Chamber.

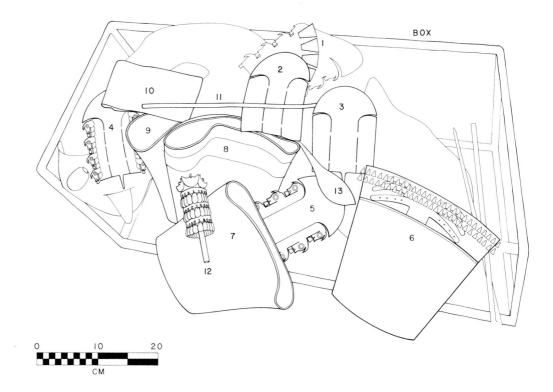

2.19 Reconstruction drawing of precious metal, beads and other ornaments in the lower layers of the chest.

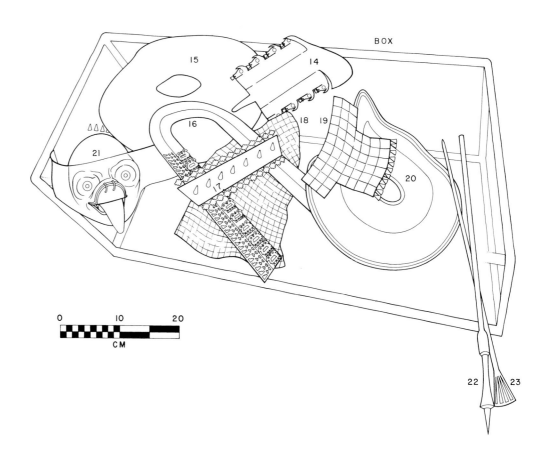

Table 2.3 Comparison of objects found in the chests in the Huaca Loro East and West tombs

Object category	West Tomb chest	East Tomb chest
Cylindrical crown	5	5
Crown wrap-around exterior ornament	0	4
Tumi-shaped crown-top ornament	5	12
Rotating crown-top ornament	0	1
Set of feather crown-top ornaments	0	6
Set of small feathers	0	1
Fans	0	3
Head band	0	4
Rattle	1	4
Forehead ornament	1	0*
Parabolic ornament with biconvex attachment	1	4
Large disc	2	14
Small disc with bangles	0	1
Dart thrower/dart	3	2
Cloth ornament	2	1**
Set of small cones	1	2
Indeterminate object	2	0
TOTAL	23	64

* Two forehead ornaments were found on the burial chamber floor.
** There were at least three inferred cloth ornaments on the burial chamber floor.

no accompanying grave goods. She was buried beneath a rectangular chest of tightly woven fibres (only its imprints remained; *c*.66 × 32 cm and over 18 cm high). This chest contained personal ornaments and ritual paraphernalia (Figs 2.18–19; Table 2.3). There were five *tumi*-shaped crown ornaments (nos 1–5 in Fig. 2.18), five cylindrical 'crowns' (nos 6–10), one wooden 'dart' (? no. 11), one rattle (no. 12), one forehead ornament with sculptural 'bat head' (no. 21 in Fig. 2.19), two large discs (nos 15, 20), a U-shaped headdress and accompanying forehead ornament (nos 16, 17), two tunic ornaments (? nos 18, 19), one wooden 'ceremonial dart thrower' (no. 22), a wooden sceptre (? no. 23) and two objects of unknown function.

Multi-dimensional analysis

Masks

Various categories of metal objects found in both the East and West Tombs of Huaca Loro allow us to compare material quality, manufacturing techniques and complexity, and iconographic content. The East Tomb mask (Fig. 2.20) demonstrates the impressive technical expertise of Middle Sicán goldsmiths.[82] It was fashioned out of a single gold-alloy sheet measuring 46 × 29 cm and 0.5 to 0.6 mm in thickness. To evenly anneal such a large sheet probably required a special large brazier and several workers to charge it with charcoal and

stoke it to maintain a high temperature. The sheet was hammered to a thickness that gave slight flexibility while maintaining overall structural rigidity. Though the mask as a whole was rather flat, the nose was realistically and masterfully raised and chased (*c*.4 cm high) without developing any visible stress cracks. The tool marks that remained visible from the raising and final shaping of the nose are quite small and even. They attest not only to the use and control of appropriately sized and shaped tools, and the care with which the work was conducted, but also a thorough understanding and exploitation of the workability of the sheet metal. The last quality was largely dependent on the high gold and silver content of the alloy employed (52% gold, 31% silver, 17% copper).[83]

Technical mastery is matched by iconographic detail. Hanging in front of the nose was a set of four high-carat, gold, teardrop-shaped bangles. They were supported by two wires coming out through holes at the base of the nostrils. In addition, a U-shaped ornament with small circular bangles surrounded the base of the nose. The eyes were made to resemble human eyes. On the 'whites' of the eyes (badly mineralized, but believed to have been made of a silver alloy) were large, highly polished, semispherical amber beads representing the irises and pierced, spherical emerald beads for the pupils.[84] The amber and emerald beads were threaded onto tapering gold wires anchored at the back of the eyes. The stylized ears retained fragile vestiges of rectangular pieces of cloth which had been stapled onto the sheet metal. The cloth in turn preserved faint traces of bird feathers which probably had been pasted or sewn onto it. The earlobes were decorated with a pair of full-sized, high-carat gold ear-spools. The unique and elaborate manner in which the ear-spools were assembled and stapled has been described elsewhere.[85] In essence, the back flanges of the ear-spools were placed on each earlobe of the mask (which closely matched the size and shape of the back flange). The three joining holes were then punched simultaneously through the flange and mask lobes. The flanges were then removed from the mask and the ear-spools were 'proto-brazed' together and finished. When completed, they were placed back on the mask and straps were put through each of the three holes and bent over on the back side.

In regard to style and overall shape, proportion and dimensions, the West Tomb mask (Fig. 2.21; measuring *c*.45 × 28 cm) is quite similar to the mask described above. However, important differences in technical and iconographic details abound (Table 2.4). The West Tomb mask was made by

2.20 (left) Middle Sicán elite ceremonial headdress composed of a large mask, biconvex forehead ornament with large bangles and small mask, cylindrical crown, parabolic ornament, and ninety feathers that were excavated from the Huaca Loro East Tomb. Our assembly of these components into this headdress is based on a good fit in their sizes and shapes (e.g. mask and forehead ornament), preserved vestiges (feathers and parabolic ornaments) and representations of various headdresses in ceramics and metal objects.

Table 2.4 Comparison between aspects of masks found in the Huaca Loro East and West tombs

Features	West Tomb principal personage	East Tomb principal personage	East Tomb Niche 1
Dimensions	45 × 28 cm	46 × 29 cm	c.35–40 × 22–5 cm
Composition	*Tumbaga*; relatively high in silver	52% gold, 31% silver 17% copper (neutron activation analysis)	*Tumbaga*
No. of components made (sheets per mask)	4 (nose and ears made of separate sheets)	1 single sheet	4 (nose and ears of separate sheets)
Eye construction	Repoussé outline Amber bead iris	Repoussé outline Silver alloy for the whites of the eye; amber beads as iris; emerald beads as pupil	Repoussé outline
Nose construction	Simplified form	Realistic, sculptural form	Simplified form
Nose ornaments	4 teardrop-shaped bangles with turquoise inlays hanging over the nose from wires	2 large teardrop-shaped bangles and 2 small discs hanging over the nose from wires and 9 small discs hanging from wires attached to a U-shaped frame stapled around the nose base	None
Ear ornaments	Ear-spool represented by a repoussé circle	Full-scale, complete high-carat ear-spool stapled on to the ear lobe of the mask; rectangular cloth (with metal backing?) stapled onto the ear above the ear-spool	None

2.21 (above) *Tumbaga* mask *in situ* covering the face of the principal personage of the Huaca Loro West Tomb. The top of the skull is visible behind the mask.

mechanically joining (laced with wire) four separate *tumbaga* sheets representing the nose, a pair of stylized ears, and the rest of the face. The nose was shaped much like a simple cone cut vertically in half rather than a realistic sculptural rendering. The nose ornaments were limited to four *tumbaga* bangles with turquoise inlay. Nostrils were indicated by a slight bulging. The eyes, though similar in size and shape to those of the East Tomb mask, and in having amber bead irises, lacked emerald bead pupils and piercing gold wires. There were no ear-spools, only circular repoussé outlines on earlobes that suggested them. At the same time, a

corroded staple at the centre of the earlobe indicates that originally there was some sort of perishable ornament there. Given the presence of amorphous corrosion product with some textile imprints adhered to much of the earlobes, we suspect that, much like the case of the East Tomb mask, feathers were stitched onto cloth that in turn was stapled onto the earlobes.

The composition of the constituent sheets of the West Tomb mask remains unknown. Their corroded, brittle state precluded taking rubbing samples for neutron activation analysis. However, the pale gold colour of the well-polished original surface and dark colour of corrosion products adhered to it suggest that the sheets were relatively high in silver and copper and low in gold but extensively depletion-gilded. No peeling of a thin gilt layer was observed.

The West Tomb mask is closer to the *tumbaga* masks in the East Tomb's Niche 1 in regard to manufacturing features, iconographic details, and inferred alloy composition. Those associated with the scrap pile have roughly the same size and shape and have the simple nose made out of a separate piece and circles of repoussé dots at the bottom of the rectangular, stylized earlobes symbolizing ear-spools. The upturned (or 'winged') eyes are indicated only by repoussé lines. Those masks found corroded together with *tumi*-shaped crown ornaments and other *tumbaga* objects in a cache cannot be described in detail. However, the apparent similarity in their size and shape and their multiplicity suggest that they may well have been used to decorate either a large cloth that temporarily enclosed an outdoor 'ritual space' or even, directly, wall faces.[86] The resultant effect would have been similar to or even more dramatic than the painting of similar masks on the adobe walls defining the central area of Huaca El Corte[87] or other key Sicán icons painted on cloth that covered *tumbaga* sheets lining the interior of the Huaca Loro West Tomb and Huaca Las Ventanas tomb.

The West Tomb mask can be better appreciated when we compare it to the one that covered the face of a seated adult male in a relatively shallow shaft tomb (*c.*1.5 × 0.8 m and *c.*3 m deep) between Huaca La Botija and Huaca El Corte at Sicán. The latter was a simple, totally mineralized 'copper' mask which was apparently fashioned out of a single hammered sheet.[88] The eyes and ear ornamentation were shown by means of repoussé lines. It had no nose ornaments or beads representing irises or pupils. The metallic composition of this mask has not been analysed and may well have been a copper-silver alloy. A 'copper' *tumi*-knife, ten small, folded 'gilded copper' (depletion gilded?) sheets that probably formed a necklace, a narrow 'copper' sheet of unknown function, shell and turquoise beads, and *crisoles* were found together with the mask.

The above comparisons show that, in spite of general stylistic and morphological similarities, these masks differ significantly at least in two, if not all three, dimensions being examined: (a) alloy composition and quality of other raw materials (e.g. beads) employed or their presence or absence, (b) the number of manufacturing steps, innovative character and skill required for the techniques employed, and (c) iconographic details and content. The total number of components and steps, as well as skill and practical knowledge needed in manufacture, must be considered when modelling the organization of craft production.[89] These measures also yield a notable difference among the masks compared. For example, preparation and mounting of a pair of complex ear-spools alone distance the East Tomb mask from the others.

The feat of sheet-metal working seen in the East Tomb mask may not be easy to fathom for those without personal experience in the making and shaping of a 0.6 mm thick sheet this large. A replicative sheet-metal making experiment was conducted in the spring of 1998 by J. A. Griffin[90] and I. Shimada using an ingot of the same alloy composition and magnetite hammers, both of which were expressly prepared for the experiment. It clearly brought home the impressive skill, prac-

tical knowledge, time and labour needed for the above work. Just to evenly anneal and hammer is a major challenge. The gold mask from the East Tomb can be described indeed as a technical and artistic masterpiece and occupies the high end of the wide variation in mask quality. The West Tomb mask occupies the mid-point of the range, while the remainder occupy the lower end.

Co-variation among the three dimensions: mask and headdress

A general pattern seems to be emerging: that is, masks made of higher-carat gold-alloy display greater technical mastery and iconographic details. At the same time our mask sample is small and represents only three excavated tombs. If we assume the authenticity and general contemporaneity of the Middle Sicán-style masks in museum collections we studied earlier (Fig. 2.22),[91] we find that masks with divergent manufacturing techniques and iconographic content appear to be made of high-carat gold alloys. Unfortunately, we have neither reliable data on their alloy composition and degree of gilding nor their original iconographic details (e.g. presence or absence of ear-spools and number and placement of bangles). A caution we issued earlier regarding the effects of the undocumented cleaning and restoration that many of these masks underwent still holds.[92]

Given our sample limitations, an effective approach to the question of co-variation would be to examine the Middle Sicán ceremonial headdresses in their totality. The Sicán gold mask has always been displayed by itself. Excavation of the East and West tombs and a complementary study of Sicán art, however, have revealed the mask as a component of an elaborate ceremonial headdress. As shown in Fig. 2.20, the East Tomb assembly consisted of a mask, a large forehead ornament (bi-concave in shape or a three-dimensional representation of a bat head), a cylindrical crown with slightly constricted mid-section, and a large parabolic head ornament with ninety gold feathers around its perimeter. Originally, large bird feathers were placed behind the gold feathers. The complete parabolic head ornament with its trimmings would have stood well over 40 cm above the top of the head. This ornament, in reality, had a narrow, stiff stem (tang) near the centre to be inserted into a 'socket' on the interior surface of the crown. In other words, the crown served as the support for large parabolic and bi-concave ornaments placed above and in front of it. In this case, the crown was an integral but largely hidden com-

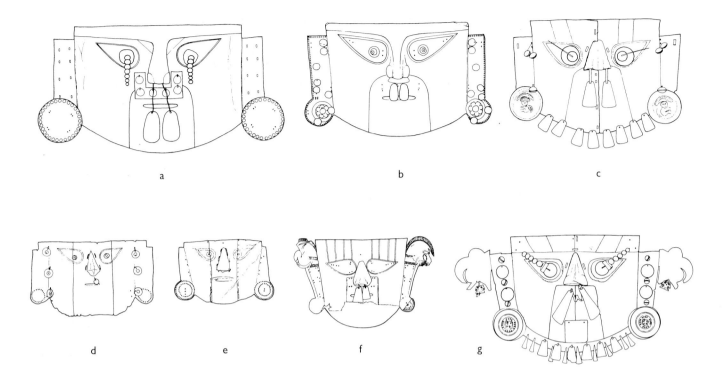

a b c

d e f g

2.22 Variation in size, shape, manufacturing and decorative details among Middle Sicán-style gold masks. Masks (a) and (b) were both made out of single sheets, while all the others were made of two to four separate sheets. (Dimensions are (a) 31.7 cm high, 63.5 cm wide; (b) 28.5 cm high, 48.3 cm wide; (c) 32.5 cm high, 44.6 cm wide; (d) 32.2 cm high, 61.9 cm wide; (e) 18.5 cm high, 31.7 cm wide; (f) 16.3 cm high, 25.4 cm wide; (g) 22.6 cm high, 36.2 cm wide.)

ponent of ostentatious display, differing from modern European crowns that are essentially static and used without other ornaments. It is probable that there were other supports such as strings to secure the above parabolic ornament. Conversely, a large disc placed on the back of the head as seen on the figurine mounted on the haft of the so-called 'Tumi de Illimo',[93] may have served as an ornament and a structural support. Overall, the formal ceremonial headdress would have measured well over 100 cm high and 60 cm wide, and weighed an estimated 2 kg.

The Sicán lord wearing this full headdress was probably carried on a litter to magnify the visual effect and to cope with the unwieldy size and weight. With each step of the litter bearers, the bangles, gold and bird feathers, and even the tongue of the bat head would have been set in motion to create a dazzling visual and auditory effect that would have captivated and impressed onlookers. Movement and articulation were an integral part of Andean sheet objects. In considering the original use of precious metal objects, we must see beyond their sheer quantity to the overall effect created by their movement, sound, colour and brilliance.

Middle Sicán polychrome friezes documented at Sicán (e.g. Huaca El Corte) and Ucupe[94] show the Sicán elite personage wearing impressive headdresses similar to those described above. Ceramic and gold objects, particularly modelled figures on blackware bottles and repoussé figures on gold beakers also show the diverse configurations of the multi-component headdress. Each of the eighteen Middle Sicán miniature figurines (set of three Sicán lords standing atop each of six temples) on the decorative panel placed on the back of a well-preserved wooden litter at the Museo de Oro del Perú (MOP-5720; Fig. 2.2) also wear detachable gold ornaments, including a mask, crown and some crown-top ornament.[95]

On a daily basis, however, the crown and earspools would have been sufficient to show one's high status. The circumferences of some crowns were decorated with cut-out designs. Impressions of cloth found on the backs of these cut-out ornaments, together with traces of threads on the small rectangular tabs (commonly 2–5 × 2–5 mm) found at regular intervals along the edges of the cut-out designs indicate that these ornaments were stitched on to a cloth backing. With the tabs hidden by threads (sewn over), the clean outlines of the objects would have emerged, giving an impression that they floated above the cloth. In other words, undecorated crowns were embellished with cut-out sheet-metal ornaments sewn on to cloth backing and wrapped around their circumference as seen in Fig. 2.8. In accordance with the individual's taste or context of use, the exterior appearance could have been readily changed. A pair of gold feather sets or tumi-shaped ornaments may have been used as additional ornamentation. The diversity of crowns and their ornaments found in both the East and West tomb chests does not surprise us, as

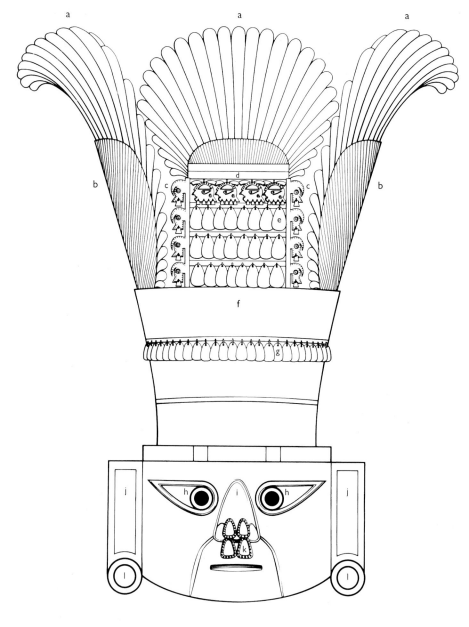

2.23 Reconstruction of the ceremonial headdress worn by the principal personage interred in the Huaca Loro West Tomb (most of the original components were found only as impressions or in a badly corroded state): (a) feather trim, inferred from faint impressions; (b) fan-shaped, painted support (inferred to have been split cane) for feather trim; (c) 'mythical feline heads' cut out of gold alloy sheet gold; (d) Sicán deity heads cut out of silvery-coloured gold alloy sheets; (e) gold bangles; (f) *tumbaga* crown with copper-alloy internal frame; (g) gold bangles; (h) polished, semi-spherical amber bead; (i) nose fashioned out of a separate *tumbaga* sheet; (j) ear fashioned out of a separate *tumbaga* sheet; (k) silvery-coloured gold-alloy bangles with turquoise inlay; (l) repoussé concentric lines representing ear-spools. The headdress including the crown is drawn somewhat larger than scale to show details.

high-status individuals may have played different roles in a variety of ceremonies, each requiring different ornaments. Similarly, different personages would be expected to wear different ornaments to reflect their gender, social position and role. Just such variation in head ornaments and ritual paraphernalia is seen among the aforementioned eighteen miniature figurines on the wooden litter.

As shown in Fig. 2.23, above the mask, the West Tomb principal personage wore a cylindrical crown with internal wire frame and row of bangles. All components of the crown were badly corroded or mineralized, suggesting that they were made of arsenical copper, copper-silver and/or *tumbaga* alloy(s). Protruding above the crown top were four evenly spaced, oval, thin, tightly woven supports, presumably for feather trimming above. Although only the imprints of the supports were found, they appear to have been made by binding thin split-cane pieces and decorated with yellowish, orangish and light bluish paint. The only well-preserved precious metal component of the headdress was a frontal ornament. It is possible that it was originally placed in front of the crown and post-depositional movement displaced it higher up as shown in Fig. 2.23. This ornament consists of a row of Sicán lord heads and three rows of bangles flanked on both sides by a strip with cut-out 'mythical feline' heads.

Clearly, the West Tomb headdress worn by the principal personage and those found in the chest pale in comparison with their counterparts in the East Tomb in regard to their overall number and size. It is noteworthy that, though objects in the chest largely duplicate in composition those found in a similar chest in the East Tomb, they are made predominantly of *tumbaga* (as opposed to high-carat gold) and are fewer in number. There were only two as opposed to fourteen large discs and one parabolic headdress as opposed to four. The forehead ornament with bat-head representation was found in the chest in the West Tomb, while the forehead ornament was placed on the burial chamber floor in the East Tomb. More importantly, the former appears to be made of *tumbaga* and lacks the facial details and bangles found on the gold version in the East Tomb.

To ascertain alloy composition of the West Tomb headdress, microgram rubbing samples were taken from individual pieces for neutron activation analysis by Gordus.[96] The average composition of the twenty-three sampled bangles is 38.0% gold, 32.7% silver and 29.3% copper (Table 2.5). The gold concentration among the samples is relatively consistent (44.07 to 32.73%), while those of silver

Table 2.5 Average gold, silver, and copper content of objects in the Huaca Loro West Tomb

Sample	Number		% Gold	% Silver	% Copper	Alloy
Type	O	R	Av ± Sm	Av ± Sm	Av ± Sm	MP °C
Mythical feline strip	2	10	36.2 ± 0.4	32.0 ± 0.7	31.8 ± 0.7	820
Bird-shaped clip	1	6	58.1 ± 0.5	33.0 ± 0.7	8.9 ± 0.5	930
Tumi-shaped clip	1	6	50.0 ± 0.5	36.8 ± 0.4	13.2 ± 0.4	900
Trapezoid strip	1	5	34.0 ± 0.4	46.1 ± 0.6	19.9 ± 0.4	810
Cones	6	18	35.1 ± 0.4	44.7 ± 0.6	20.2 ± 0.5	810
Cut strip	1	5	33.7 ± 0.6	44.6 ± 1.4	21.7 ± 1.1	790
Nose bangles*	4	15	41.2 ± 1.4	34.7 ± 1.0	24.1 ± 2.2	800
Crown pendants	23	67	37.8 ± 0.5	33.1 ± 1.0	29.1 ± 0.8	810
Total	39	132	38.9 ± 0.5	35.9 ± 0.7	25.2 ± 0.7	790

O is the number of separate gold objects sampled.
R is the number of separate metal rubbings used in average.
Sm is the standard deviation of the mean (i.e. average) of the R values.
MP is the melting point temperature.
* Omits data for (very high copper) samples taken from oxidized areas.
Assumes %Au + %Ag + %Cu = 100%.

and copper are quite varied (53.87 to 20.13% and 37.96 to 12.82%, respectively). This variability raises the possibility that the bangles were made from sheet scraps left over from the manufacture of other objects, rather than using one or two large sheets for all bangles. In addition, the average gold content of these bangles (38%) is lower than any group of bangles on East Tomb ornaments analysed in the same manner (see Table 2.1). For example, bangles on the parabolic head ornament mentioned above have a corresponding figure of 51.3%. Even the small gold cones (N = 6) found in the chest within Niche 12 (Central Chamber, West Tomb) yielded an average gold content of 35.4% as compared to 42.1% for the sampled East Tomb cones (N = 12). In fact, the overwhelming portion of nearly 1,000 rubbing samples from the East Tomb gold-alloy objects has a gold concentration above 40%.

Discussion and conclusion

An integrated analysis of the Middle Sicán ceremonial headdress revealed a patterned differentiation of gold and *tumbaga* objects in terms of the three dimensions examined. Material quality[97] appears to correlate positively with metalworking quality, particularly in the innovative character of design and accompanying technical solutions, and iconographic detail and content.

Some aspects of the above conclusion require an elaboration. The observed variation in material quality subsumes mineral beads used in complex metal objects, what may be called 'cross-craft' products.[98] The East Tomb gold mask was distinguished from the West Tomb *tumbaga* mask in having emerald beads as its pupils in addition to the amber irises that both masks have. The 'copper' mask from the aforementioned tomb near Huaca La Botija had no bead components to its eyes. The gold forehead ornament with sculptural bat head representation from the East Tomb had amber irises and turquoise pupils. The *tumbaga* version in the West Tomb had no beads.

At the same time, contrary to what one might expect, metalworking quality and skill (e.g. presence or absence of stress cracks, control over cutting, perforation, filing and/or polishing) do not relate consistently to alloy composition. The East Tomb gold mask and ear-spools can be justifiably described as a *tour de force* of prehispanic goldsmithing in terms of innovative designs, careful planning and flawless execution. At the same time, the fact that objects are made of gold does not guarantee that they are flawless or carefully manufactured.[99] For example, one of the five crowns found within the East Tomb chest shows well-executed chasing and perforations in the front but uneven hammer blows and perforations, as well as finely scribed guidelines on the back. We suspect that the front was begun by a skilled goldsmith who showed the apprentice how the remainder was to be done and went on to something else. Fine guidelines and/or unfiled edges were found on other gold objects from the same tomb. Gold foil squares with poorly placed sewing holes were apparently rejected and thrown into scrap piles found in the East Tomb.

Conversely, *tumbaga* objects such as three sets of 'fans' found in the East Tomb chest display even thickness, careful finish on edges and thorough polishing. In addition, in terms of the manufacture of sheet metal and its manipulation to make objects, *tumbaga* with relatively high copper content would have been generally harder and posed a greater technical challenge than high-carat gold.

The observed variation in workmanship in gold objects should be considered in regard to their usage, the organization of workshops involved in their manufacture, and the creativity of individual artisans. In the case of the above crown, the rough edges of perforations are found on the interior surface, which, at the same time, preserved imprints of some woven liner. It is likely that sharp edges did not come into a direct contact with the head and thus were left unmodified. On the other hand, the mask, ear-spools and nose ornaments worn directly on flesh are well finished.

The technical proficiency and expected performance of the craftsmen involved may well have been a more important factor in accounting for the above variation. Elsewhere, Griffin and Shimada[100] have argued that Sicán goldsmithing was conducted by a series of task-differentiated groups,[101] each of which was headed by one or a few master craftsmen assisted by numerous apprentices with different amounts of experience and training. In this scenario apprentices would have carried out repetitive and time-consuming tasks such as polishing, rough cutting, perforation and making bangles and small discs, as well as much of the early stages of certain tasks (e.g. re-melting of scraps, hammering, and annealing).

Master goldsmiths, at the same time, may well have vied with each other showcasing their talent and skill for personal gain. Helms presents various historical and ethnographic cases of highly skilled craftsmen achieving greater social prestige and status through their artistic and technical excellence and association with elite patrons, who are often influential public figures.[102] Such excellence is often seen to reflect personal qualities and skills 'derived from outside [supernatural] forces and beings'.[103] Often the excellence serves as metaphor for the capacity for leadership. Objects produced by these rare masters are said to be personalistic, finite, political and ideological in nature, instead of being impersonal, routine and materialistic as in the case of the products of ordinary craftsmen.[104] Metaphors of divine or mythical transformation and creation are often embodied in their products. Thus, highly skilled craftsmen have been recognized as political leaders in some societies. In other societies they and their elite patrons mutually reinforce their roles and importance. Among Sicán precious metal objects, the highly visible ear-spools and masks would most likely have displayed the talents and skills of master goldsmiths, as indeed we have documented.

As seen in the case of the East Tomb gold mask, there was also close horizontal articulation among the task-differentiated groups involved in the production of precious metal and other high-status items. In the case of the gold mask, the planned size and shape called for a ductile alloy high in gold and silver and low in copper (i.e. a material that could be deformed without breaking), while the sheet-metal workers had to produce a relatively thick sheet. Meanwhile, 'lapidarists' and 'featherworkers'[105] prepared beads for the eyes and ear ornaments, respectively. In other words, varied skill levels and compartmentalization of tasks were an inherent part of the Sicán goldsmithing.

This paper attests to the importance of iconography in differentiating gold from other metal objects. The most detailed representations of the Sicán deity and its earthly alter ego, the Sicán lord, in their respective regalia (including detail on the back) are found predominantly on gold objects such as *tumi*-knives and beakers.[106] The images of the Sicán lord are repeated on many gold objects in the East Tomb but are conspicuously missing from the metal objects of the West Tomb with the exception perhaps of the badly corroded cup held in the right-hand glove of the principal personage. In the East and West Tombs *tumbaga* objects are undecorated and bear only motifs of secondary religious significance[107] or partial and/or simplified versions of those expressed on gold objects. Although murals and textiles may display elaborate colouring and scenes, they are static and one-dimensional.

In essence, gold objects are the medium in which the highest technical and artistic[108] qualities among Sicán crafts are found. It is this very point that leads us to define the totality of high-carat gold objects as the 'aesthetic locus'[109] of Middle Sicán art. Cleland and Shimada define the Sicán aesthetic locus as 'those areas of material culture subjected to the highest standards of quality control, and requiring investment of the time and effort to finish goods made of highest quality materials to meet the standards of the society's most exacting consumers.'[110]

Gold objects constituted the artistic and technical standard bearers and pace setters of Sicán crafts and were emulated not only by *tumbaga* and arsenical copper objects, but also by ceramics.[111] Although, as Lechtman pointed out,[112] both gold and *tumbaga* served to convey elite religious, social and political dogma, *tumbaga* was evidently secondary to gold in its symbolic value in the Middle Sicán usage of precious metals.[113] In addition to the differences already enumerated above, in the East Tomb the personal ornaments placed on or near the body of the principal personage were all gold; *tumbaga* objects were essentially placed at the periphery of the burial chamber. In comparison with gold, *tumbaga* appears to have been produced on a much greater scale,[114] employed for a wider range of use,[115] and, we suspect, available to a wider range of social elite.[116] Overall, in the face of presumably limited supplies of gold and silver, depletion-gilded *tumbaga* would have been a most practical way of supplying gold- and silver-coloured sheet metals on demand.[117]

Arsenical copper was produced on an even greater scale[118] and was available to much of the

Middle Sicán populace. Simple Middle Sicán burials in shallow pits excavated at different locations in and outside of the site of Sicán were associated with either one to several relatively small arsenical copper objects or none at all. At the same time all shaft tombs examined thus far contained varied quantities and ranges of arsenical copper objects.

If *tumbaga* emulated the range of colour associated with high-carat gold and silver, was arsenical copper production partly motivated by its colour similarity to more prestigious precious metals? Many Sicán arsenical copper objects (e.g. prills, *naipes,* and cast 'digging stick tips') that have been analysed[119] contain greater than 2% arsenic (by weight). Lechtman reported that the hardness and malleability of copper is appreciably improved by as little as 0.5% arsenic and that the maximum useful arsenic concentration in regard to these two qualities is *c.*7–8%.[120] Effects of different arsenic concentrations in copper, however, are far from settled.[121] In this regard, it is worth considering the possibility that Sicán metalworkers took advantage of the silvery appearance that arsenical copper can acquire to make 'ritual or decorative' objects as Charles suggested.[122] This appearance results from inverse segregation at the time of solidification.[123]

Overall, in terms of associated metals, excavated Middle Sicán burials in the La Leche valley fall into four distinct groups: (1) those without metal objects; (2) those with arsenical copper artefacts; (3) those with arsenical copper and *tumbaga* objects (e.g. Huaca Las Ventanas and Huaca La Botija tombs); and (4) those with gold, *tumbaga* and arsenical copper objects (e.g. East and West Tombs at Huaca Loro). Thus, it has been hypothesized that access to different metal(s) served to define different social strata.[124] Within Groups 3 and 4, however, relative quantities of different metals may have reflected important status differences.

The differential distribution of certain images has already been documented in Middle Sicán ceramics. For example, representations of the Sicán deity with certain headdresses appear to be restricted to blackware double-spout bottles that occur only in elite shaft tombs. Similarly, jars decorated with the Sicán deity icon are found only at the site of Sicán,[125] while similar jars bearing secondary icons, mythical felines, are distributed widely in the Lambayeque region.

The frequent use of bird feathers stitched on cloth to cover a portion or even much of Sicán gold objects suggests that the concern with representations of sacred images surpassed that of displaying gold. The importance of avian symbolism in Sicán art is clear. The Sicán deity is often shown with both human and avian features (e.g. wings and talons) and the earthly ruler, the Sicán lord, is sometimes represented with false wings on his back.[126]

The preceding discussion on iconography brings us back to one of the questions raised at the beginning of this paper regarding the validity of the 'gold-silver' dichotomy for pre-Inca cultures. When all precious metal objects in our sample are examined as a whole, ranging from *tumbaga* scraps to gold ear-spools, they present an apparently seamless gradation of hues between pure gold and silver. In fact, given the documented expertise in surface depletion of copper and silver among Sicán goldsmiths,[127] they could have easily produced uniform gold and silver colours. What we have documented in this study, however, is wide tonal and compositional variation and a limited degree of surface depletion. At what point in tonal variation should a given colour be defined as gold or silver? Was there in fact a symbolic watershed? If the colours of gold and silver were of particular symbolic importance, why produce pale gold or reddish gold?

There are at least three possible explanations regarding the external colour of a given precious metal: (1) It was secondary to the knowledge that gold or silver was diffused throughout the metal even if only minimally present (art-historical concept of the 'essence of object');[128] (2) it was secondary to mechanical properties that were apparently suited to the manufacture and use of specific categories of objects; and (3) it was perceived as variable, relative to the associated icons and/or context of use. Evidence mustered here tends to support the second explanation.

Yet, the third view cannot be readily dismissed. The colour of the sun and the moon vary considerably depending on atmospheric conditions and time. If gold and silver symbolized the sun and moon in the Sicán mentality as some scholars have argued,[129] were their colours accordingly conceived as variable? A cosmographic scene painted on plastered cloth that lined the interior of the partially looted tomb at Huaca Las Ventanas (Fig. 2.24) is valuable in considering this question. The crescent moon with a seated mythical creature on the west end (proper left) of the scene was off-white in colour. The sun with anthropomorphic face and stylized flames around the circumference on the east end (proper right)[130] was painted in orangish red. The nose and cheeks were covered with bright red cinnabar paint. There is no colour approaching the conventional gold asso-

2.24 Reconstruction of a Middle Sicán 'cosmological vision' painted on a plastered cotton textile with *tumbaga*-sheet backing found in the Huaca Las Ventanas south sector tomb.

ciated with the sun icon in this scene. If the artisans so desired, the sun could easily have been painted yellow with a limonite-based paint (widely used by Sicán artisans) or covered with gold foil.

The general symbolic importance of the sun, the moon, gold, and silver in Sicán ideology is clear from our iconographic study. However, how they related to each other and the specific (or even general) meanings of associated colours remain undeciphered. Similarly, the symbolic meaning of the objects that combined gold and silver components (e.g. a *tumi*-shaped head ornament in the East Tomb)[131] still escapes us. It seems prudent at this stage of our understanding to entertain the idea that gold and silver held multiple meanings and were expressed by ranges of colours. This vision is akin to what has been documented for the Tukanoan cosmology of Colombia, in which the red sun symbolized oxygenated blood and infusion of new life.[132] It is also clear that the oft-heard gold-silver dichotomy is overly simplistic in dealing with Sicán goldsmithing and its symbolic dimension.

We end this paper with a caution. Given the limited sample size and range of contexts examined, conclusions reached and hypotheses offered in this study must be regarded as preliminary in character. Our samples of well-preserved, provenanced *tumbaga,* silver and arsenical copper objects for detailed contextual analysis are still too small. Too often they are lost due to the vagaries of natural elements or illicit looting. Just as the 'gold' in our study subsumed a good range of alloy composition (c.10 to 18 carats), the 'tumbaga' is similarly variable in composition (from only about 2 to nearly 10 carats). Elucidation of how technical, economic and/or ideological considerations account for this variation remains a major research task. Similarly, samples from funerary and non-funerary contexts outside of the Sicán heartland need to be examined to determine the applicability of the conclusions and hypotheses in this study. In this regard, a region-by-region assessment of relative availability of different metals as well as the sociopolitical and ideological contexts of their use need to be elucidated. For example, the paucity of precious metals and/or skilled artisans in provinces is likely to distort the picture defined for the elite at the Sicán. In such a circumstance, *tumbaga* or even arsenical copper objects may be accepted as the surrogate aesthetic locus, displaying detailed sacred images that would otherwise be restricted to the gold objects in the Sicán heartland. In the case of metal objects from the early Mochica 'royal tombs' from Sipán (c. AD 200–400), highly detailed religious icons are represented in gilded copper, highlighting the difficulty of making cross-cultural generalizations. By the same token, the extrapolation of the Inca conception and use of precious metals to earlier cultures is at best tenuous and misleading. This paper points to the need to undertake additional systematic, contextual and multi-dimensional study of metal in pre-Inca cultures.

Notes

1 Garcilaso 1966 (1609), Book Five, ch. XI: 263; Book Six, ch. XXXV, p. 394; see also Cobo 1979 (1653), Book II, ch. 36, p. 249.

2 The vicuña is a gracile, wild Andean camelid that has very fine hair.

3 Berthelot 1986: 80.

4 Silverblatt 1987.

5 Lechtman 1979: 25; 1993.

6 Calancha 1976 (1638), Book 2, ch. 19, pp. 930–35.

7 Rowe (1948: 47). The myth describes how Pachacamac sent to earth two pairs of stars; the first became the ancestors of kings and lords and the second those of the common people, servants and poor.

8 Cobo 1979 (1653), Book I, ch. 11, p. 45; see also Nash 1979.

9 Ramírez 1994: 95–6; Shimada 1994a: 53–4.

10 Epstein 1993; Epstein and Shimada 1984; Shimada et al. 1982.

11 Rowe 1948: 50; based on the writings of Antonio de la Calancha 1976 (1638).

12 Cf. Carrion 1940.

13 E.g. Carcedo 1989, 1992, 1997a,b; Carcedo and Shimada 1985; Cleland 1998; Cleland and Shimada 1992; Epstein 1993; Shimada 1998a; Shimada and Griffin 1994; Shimada et al. in press.

14 E.g. Shimada 1985, 1994a.

15 E.g. Shimada 1981a, 1990, 1995.

16 Shimada 1990, 1994b. The most current characterization of the Sicán culture is found in Shimada in press 1.

17 E.g. Craig 1985; Dillehay and Netherly 1983; Kosok 1959; Shimada 1982, 1985, 1994a, b.

18 Lechtman 1976; Merkel et al. 1994; Shimada 1994a.

19 Shimada 1982, 1985.

20 Shimada 1994a.

21 Bonanza-type gold and silver deposits refer to concentrations of these ores; Elera 1986; Shimada 1994a, 1994b.

22 Ramírez 1994: 96. Those rare, small mines said to have produced gold and/or silver may well have been rich prehispanic tombs. Sometime, large scale grave looting for precious metal objects in colonial era was described as 'mining'.

23 E.g. Bargalló 1955; Craig 1973.

24 Ramírez 1994: 96–7.

25 Craig 1973; Shimada 1982, 1994a, 1995.

26 It is difficult to distinguish these two icons in their simplified representations. In more detailed depictions, the Sicán deity is shown with wings and talons. More commonly, the deity is shown accompanied by mythical animals.

27 Shimada 1990, 1995.

28 Shimada 1990, 1995, in press 1; see also Heyerdahl et al. 1995, Trimborn 1979.

29 E.g. Shimada 1994a, 1995.

30 Merkel et al. 1994; Shimada 1985; Shimada and Merkel 1991.

31 Cleland and Shimada 1992.

32 E.g. Shimada 1995; Shimada and Griffin 1994; Shimada and Merkel 1993; Shimada and Montenegro 1993. See Pedersen 1976; Reichlen 1941, 1962; Tello 1937a, b, c; and Valcárcel 1937 for documentation of looted Middle Sicán precious metal objects.

33 Shimada 1994a, 1998b.

34 See Gordus and Shimada 1995; Gordus et al. 1996; Merkel et al. 1995.

35 Menzel 1976.

36 E.g. vessel forms and their technical-technological qualities, and grave-lot association.

37 E.g. Carr and Neitzel 1995; Conkey and Hastorf 1990; Dillehay 1995; Hodder 1982; Shennan 1989.

38 Pedersen 1976; Tello 1937a,b,c; Valcárcel 1937.

39 E.g. Baraybar and Shimada 1993; Shimada et al. 1998.

40 Shimada 1981a, b, 1995; Vreeland and Shimada 1981.

41 Shimada 1998b; Shimada and Watanabe 1995.

42 Elera 1984.

43 Pedersen 1976.

44 Shimada 1995; Shimada et al. 1998.

45 See Table 3 in Shimada 1995; Shimada et al. 1998.

46 Shimada 1995, 1998a.

47 Shimada 1998b; Shimada and Watanabe 1995.

48 Shimada 1998b.

49 E.g. Brown 1995; Buikstra 1995; Hodder 1982; Miller and Tilley 1984; Morris 1991; Shanks and Tilley 1982.

50 Brown 1995: 393–5.

51 E.g. Shimada 1981a, 1985, 1990, 1995.

52 E.g. American Museum of Natural History in New York, Bruning Museum in Lambayeque, Gold of Peru Museum and the National Museum of Anthropology, Archaeology and History, both in Lima.

53 E.g. see fig. 1 in Zevallos 1971.

54 E.g. Huaca Taco near Etén, Huaca Chornancap and Huaca Mayor at Chotuna, all in the lower Lambayeque valley.

55 Cavallaro and Shimada 1988; Shimada 1990, 1997a; Shimada and Cavallaro 1986.

56 Shimada 1998b; Shimada and Watanabe 1995.

57 E.g. Shimada 1995, 1997b.

58 See fig. 13 in Carcedo and Shimada 1985: 71.

59 See fig. 108 in Shimada 1995: 120.

60 They are basically cylindrical with outflaring tops and bottoms, and have internal wire frames.

61 Vetter 1993; see also Lechtman 1981.

62 Ursula Wagner, 1997, pers. comm.

63 Shimada and Griffin 1994.

64 Gordus and Shimada 1995.

65 Shimada and Griffin 1994.

66 Griffin 1998.

67 Ibid.

68 They represent identical Sicán lords each holding a staff.

69 Cordy-Collins 1982; Wilbert 1974; Shimada in press 2; Shimada et al. 1998.

70 McLoughlin 1996.

71 Sean McLoughlin, 1997, pers. comm.

72 Gordus and Shimada 1995.

73 Gordus and Shimada 1995; McLoughlin 1996.

74 E.g. Shimada 1985, in press 1; see also Holm 1966/67, 1975, 1978, 1980; cf. Hosler et al. 1990.

75 Jones 1979; Lechtman 1979, 1988.

76 Shimada 1998b.

77 The scarcity of metal objects seen above also characterizes the ten niches. Two niches each contained a young, adult female with accompanying goods much like the nearby pit burials. Another niche contained a 12- to 13-year-old individual with cinnabar paint on the face but no accompanying goods. The remaining seven niches had no human burials but traces of tumbaga sheets and/or textiles that had been carefully laid on the relatively flat niche base bottoms. In Niche 8 there were also eight ceramic vessels, four badly degraded (wooden ?) rods and a mineralized arsenical copper (?) tumi-knife.

78 Shimada et al. 1998.

79 One 14.5 cm long, 1 cm wide and 2.5–3.0 mm thick, and the other, 7.8 cm, 2.3 cm, and 4 mm.

80 These items may represent a potter's tool kit. The wooden implements, however, may have been used as spatulas for lime in chewing coca leaves.

81 Shimada and Shimada 1997.

82 Shimada and Griffin 1994.

83 Gordus and Shimada 1995.

84 Shimada and Griffin 1994; Shimada et al. 1997.

85 Shimada and Griffin 1994.

86 Shimada 1998a.

87 Shimada 1981a, b.

88 Alva 1986: 414, 416.

89 E.g. Carr and Neitzel 1995; Costin and Hagstrum 1995; Schiffer and Skibo 1987.

90 She is an expert goldsmith and metal conservator with some forty years of experience.

91 Carcedo 1989; Carcedo and Shimada 1985; see also Kauffmann-Doig 1989.

92 Carcedo and Shimada 1985: 67. See also Perkins 1997 for discussion of the effects of different cleaning agents and processes.

93 See the figure in Kauffmann-Doig 1989: 174.

94 Shimada 1981a,b; Alva and Meneses 1984.

95 Carcedo 1989, 1992; Carcedo and Shimada 1985.

96 Rubbing samples are well suited for gaining compositional information from the surface and near-surface of metal objects. For objects that were made of heterogeneous metals or had been heavily surface-treated, these samples are unlikely to yield compositional data representative of the whole artefacts. However, we were not permitted to carry out any sampling of the excavated precious metal objects that could be deemed 'destructive' (e.g. drilling or cutting). Permission from Dr Pedro Gjurinovic, then the Director of the National Institute of Culture of Peru, allowed us to conduct minimally destructive rubbing sampling for neutron activation analysis. Aware of the inherent limitations of rubbing samples, three successive rubbings were taken from each sampling locus (to an estimated depth of 30 microns) to obtain indications of both superficial and core composition. See Gordus et al. 1996 for results of an additional study comparing surface and core compositions using microprobe and neutron activation analysis.

97 Material quality in the sense of proportions of precious metals in the alloy used to manufacture a given object.

98 Shimada 1998a.

99 Shimada and Griffin 1994.

100 Griffin and Shimada 1997; Shimada and Griffin1994; Shimada 1998a.

101 E.g. alloying and remelting, sheetmetal production, shaping-joining, lapidary, and featherwork.

102 Helms 1993.

103 Ibid: 17.

104 Ibid: 16.

105 Though usually we consider them to be distinct groups of artisans working in separate locations, in the sort of horizontal integration of craft activities being discussed, the same artisans may have performed many of the tasks that we consider to be the domains of separate groups of crafts specialists; see Shimada 1998a.

106 Carcedo 1989; Carcedo and Shimada 1985.

107 Such as heads of the mythical felines that often accompany the Sicán deity in more complex representations.

108 In the sense of stylistic refinements and iconographic content.

109 Maquet 1979, 1985.

110 Cleland and Shimada 1994, 1998; Shimada 1995, 1998a.

111 See Cleland and Shimada 1998; Rondon 1965/66.

112 Lechtman 1984a: 63.

113 Shimada and Griffin 1994; Shimada *et al.* in press.

114 E.g. consider the quantity of scraps in the East Tomb.

115 E.g. wrapping ceramic vessels and backing painted cloth.

116 It was found in all shaft tombs considered in this study.

117 Shimada and Griffin 1994.

118 E.g. consider the presence of at least three smelting centres at Huaca del Pueblo Batán Grande, Cerro Huaringa and Tongorrape.

119 E.g. Epstein and Shimada 1984; Merkel *et al.* 1995.

120 Lechtman 1996: 481.

121 Cf. Budd 1991; Budd and Ottaway 1989; Charles 1967, 1973, 1974, 1980; McKerrell and Tylecote 1972.

122 Charles 1980: 171.

123 Charles 1974: 471.

124 Shimada 1994c, 1995; Shimada *et al.* in press; Shimada and Montenegro 1993.

125 Cleland and Shimada 1994, 1998.

126 See Shimada 1990: 321–5 and his figs 15, 16; see also Kauffmann-Doig 1986, 1992.

127 Lechtman 1984a,b; also McLoughlin 1996.

128 E.g. Lechtman 1984a, b.

129 E.g. Carcedo 1989, 1997a; Carrion 1940; Emmerich 1977; Kauffmann-Doig 1989, 1992.

130 Many metal objects associated with the early Mochica 'royal tombs' (Tombs 1–3) excavated at an adobe platform mound at Sipán were duplicated in 'gold' and 'silver' (in colour; Alva 1994; Alva and Donnan 1993). In the case of a necklace of gold and silver peanut beads from Tomb 1 ('Señor de Sipán'), gold and silver beads were placed in symmetrically opposing right and left halves, respectively. This differential placement of gold objects on the proper right and silver objects on the proper left is seen among various categories of objects in Tombs 1 and 2, but not in Tomb 3 ('Viejo Señor de Sipán'). Whether the right-left bipartition should be interpreted as marking the sun-moon or male-female or any other dichotomy or complementarity is not clear.

131 Among objects from Sipán, the bimetallic objects include one sceptre each from Tombs 1 and 2 and a backflap from Tomb 2.

132 Reichel-Dolmatoff 1981: 21.

References

Alva, Walter
1986 Una tumba con máscara funeraria de la costa norte del Perú. *Beiträge zur Allgemeinen und Vergleichenden Archäologie* 7 (1985): 411–21. KAVA, Deutschen Archäologischen Instituts, Bonn.
1994 *Sipán*. Colección Cultura y Artes del Perú, ed. José A. de Lavalle, Cervecería Backus & Johnston S.A., Lima.

Alva, Walter, and Christopher B. Donnan
1993 *Royal Tombs of Sipán*. Fowler Museum of Cultural History, Los Angeles.

Alva, Walter, and Susana Meneses de Alva
1984 Los murales de Ucupe en el valle de Zaña, norte del Perú. *Beiträge zur Allgemeinen und Vergleichenden Archäologie* 5 (1983): 335–60. KAVA, Deutschen Archäologischen Instituts, Bonn.

Baraybar, José Pablo, and Izumi Shimada
1993 A possible case of metastatic carcinoma in a Middle Sicán burial from Batán Grande, Peru. *International Journal of Osteoarchaeology* 3:129–35.

Bargalló, M.
1955 *La Minería y la Metalurgia en la América Española durante la Epoca Colonial*. Fondo de Cultura Económica, Mexico City.

Berthelot, Jean
1986 The extraction of precious metals at the time of the Inka. In *Anthropological History of Andean Polities,* ed. J. V. Murra, N. Wachtel and J. Revel, pp. 69–88. Cambridge University Press, Cambridge.

Brown, James A.
1995 Andean mortuary practices in perspective. In *Tombs for the Living: Andean Mortuary Practices,* ed. Tom D. Dillehay, pp. 391–405. Dumbarton Oaks, Washington, DC.

Budd, Paul
1991 A metallographic investigation of eneolithic arsenical copper artefacts from Mondsee, Austria. *Journal of the Historical Metallurgy Society* 25(2): 99–108.

Buikstra, Jane
1995 Tombs for the living … or … for the dead: the Osmore ancestors. In *Tombs for the Living: Andean Mortuary Practices,* ed. Tom D. Dillehay, pp. 229–80. Dumbarton Oaks, Washington, DC.

Calancha, Antonio de
1976 (1638) *Crónica Moralizada del Orden de San Agustín en el Perú*. Edición de Ignacio Prado Pastor, Lima.

Carcedo, Paloma
1989 Anda ceremonial lambayecana: iconografía y simbología. In *Lambayeque,* ed. José Antonio de Lavalle, pp. 249–270. Colección Arte y Tesoros del Perú. Banco de Crédito del Perú, Lima.
1992 Metalurgia precolombina: manufactura y técnicas de trabajo en la orfebrería Sicán. In *Oro del Antiguo Perú,* ed. José Antonio de Lavalle,

pp. 265–305. Colección Arte y Tesoros del Perú. Banco de Crédito del Perú, Lima.
1997a La plata y su transformación en el arte precolombino. In *Plata y Plateros del Perú*, ed. Juan Torres de la Pina y Victoria Mujica, pp. 19–117. Patronato Plata del Perú. Lima.
1997b Instrumentos utilizados en la manufactura de piezas metálicas que se encuentran en los museos: lítico y metal. Paper presented at the Simposio de Metalurgia Prehispánica de América. 49th International Congress of Americanists, Quito.

Carcedo, Paloma, and Izumi Shimada
1985 Behind the golden mask: Sicán gold artefacts from Batán Grande, Peru. In *The Art of Pre-Columbian Gold: The Jan Mitchell Collection*, ed. Julie Jones, pp. 60–75. Weidenfeld & Nicolson, London.

Carr, Christopher, and Jill E. Neitzel
1995 Integrating approaches to material style in theory and philosophy. In *Style, Society, and Person: Archaeological and Ethnological Perspectives*, ed. Christopher Carr and Jill E. Neitzel, pp. 3–20. Plenum Press, New York/London.

Carrion, Rebeca
1940 La luna y su personificación ornitomorfa en el arte Chimú. *Actas y Trabajos Científicos del 27 Congreso Internacional de Americanistas* 1: 571–87. Lima.

Cavallaro, Raffael, and Izumi Shimada
1988 Some thoughts on Sicán marked adobes and labor organization. *American Antiquity* 53: 75–101.

Charles, J. A.
1967 Early arsenical bronzes – a metallurgical view. *American Journal of Archaeology* 71(1): 21–6.
1973 Heterogeneity in metals. *Archaeometry* 15(1): 105–14.
1974 Arsenic and old bronze: excursions in the metallurgy of prehistory. *Chemistry and Industry* 12 (June 15): 470–74.
1980 The coming of copper and copper-base alloys and iron: a metallurgical sequence. In *The Coming of Age of Iron*, ed. T. A. Wertime and J. D. Muhly, pp. 151–81. Yale University Press, New Haven.

Cleland, Kate M.
1998 'Bronze transformation' – social and ideological impacts of Sicán metallurgical production. Paper presented at the 63rd Annual Meeting of the Society for American Archaeology, Seattle.

Cleland, Kate M., and Izumi Shimada
1992 Sicán bottles: marking time in the Peruvian bronze age. *Andean Past* 3: 193–235. Ithaca, New York.
1994 Cerámica paleteada: tecnología, modos de producción y aspectos sociales. In *La Tecnología y la Organización de Producción de las Cerámicas en los Andes Prehispánicos*, ed. Izumi Shimada, pp. 321–48. Fondo Editorial, Pontificia Universidad Católica del Perú, Lima.
1998 *Paleteada* pottery: technology, chronology

and sub-culture. In *Andean Ceramics: Technology, Organization and Approaches*, ed. Izumi Shimada, pp. 111–50. MASCA, The University Museum, University of Pennsylvania, Philadelphia.

Cobo, Bernabé
1979 (1653) *History of the Inca Empire*. Translated and ed. Roland Hamilton. University of Texas, Austin.

Conkey, Margaret and Christine A. Hastorf (eds)
1990 *The Uses of Style in Archaeology*. Cambridge University Press, Cambridge.

Cordy-Collins, Alana
1982 Earth mother/earth monster symbolism in Ecuadorian Manteño art. In *Pre-Columbian Art History*, ed. Alana Cordy-Collins, pp. 205–30. Peek Publications, Palo Alto.

Costin, Cathy L., and Melissa Hagstrum
1995 Standardization, labor investment, skill, and the organization of ceramic production in late prehispanic highland Peru. *American Antiquity* 60(4): 619–41.

Craig, Alan K.
1973 Placer gold in eastern Peru: the great strike of 1942. *Revista Geográfica* 79: 117–28.
1985 Cis-Andean environmental transects: late Quaternary ecology of northern and southern Peru. In *Andean Ecology and Civilization*, ed. Shozo Masuda, Izumi Shimada and Craig Morris, pp. 23–44. University of Tokyo Press, Tokyo.

Dillehay, Tom D. (ed.)
1995 *Tombs for the Living: Andean Mortuary Practices*. Dumbarton Oaks, Washington, DC.

Dillehay, Tom D., and Patricia J. Netherly
1983 Exploring the upper Zaña valley in Peru. *Archaeology* 36(4): 22–30.

Elera, Carlos G.
1984 Características e implicaciones culturales en dos tumbas disturbadas de Huaca La Merced, complejo arqueológico de Batán Grande, Lambayeque, costa norte del Perú. Report submitted to the Instituto Nacional de Cultura, Lima.
1986 Investigaciones sobre Patrones Funerarios en el Sitio Formativo del Morro de Eten, Valle de Lambayeque. Bachelor thesis, Especialidad de Arqueología, Pontificia Universidad Católica del Perú, Lima.

Emmerich, André
1977 *Sweat of the Sun and Tears of the Moon: Gold and Silver in Pre-Columbian Art*. Hacker Art Books, New York.

Epstein, Stephen M.
1993 Cultural Choice and Technological Consequences: Constraints of Innovation in the Late Prehistoric Copper Smelting Industry of Cerro Huaringa, Peru. Doctoral thesis, Department of Anthropology, University of Pennsylvania, Philadelphia.

Epstein, Stephen M., and Izumi Shimada
1984 Metalurgia de Sicán: una reconstrucción de la producción de la aleación de cobre en el Cerro de los Cementerios, Perú. *Beiträge zur Allgemeinen und Vergleichenden Archäologie* 5

(1983): 379–430. KAVA, Deutschen Archäologischen Instituts, Bonn.

Garcilaso de la Vega, El Inca
1966 (1609) *Royal Commentaries of the Incas and General History of Peru, Part I*. Translated by Harold V. Livermore. University of Texas, Austin.

Gordus, Adon A., and Izumi Shimada
1995 Neutron activation analysis of microgram samples from 364 gold objects from a Sicán burial site in Peru. In *Materials Issues in Art and Archaeology IV*, ed. P. B. Vandiver, J. R. Druzik, and J. L. Galvan , pp. 127–42. Materials Research Society Proceedings, vol. 352. Pittsburgh.

Gordus, Adon A., Carl E. Henderson and Izumi Shimada
1996 Electron microprobe and neutron activation analysis of gold artefacts from a 1000 AD Peruvian grave site. In *Archaeological Chemistry: Organic, Inorganic, and Biochemical Analysis*, ed. Mary V. Orna, pp. 83–93. American Chemical Society Symposium Series 625. Washington, DC.

Griffin, Jo Ann
1998 The construction of a Sicán gold ornament: a sculptural bat head. *Boletín Museo del Oro* 41 (1996): 83–97

Griffin, Jo Ann, and Izumi Shimada
1997 Die Goldbearbeitung im vorspanischen Amerika. In *Sicán – ein Fürstengrab in Alt-Peru: Eine Ausstellung in Zusammenarbeit mit dem peruanischen Kulturministerium*, ed. Judith Rickenbach, pp. 91–101. Museum Rietberg, Zürich.

Helms, Mary W.
1993 *Craft and the Kingly Ideal: Art, Trade, and Power*. University of Texas, Austin.

Heyerdahl, Thor, Daniel H. Sandweiss and Alfredo Narváez
1995 *Pyramids of Túcume: The Quest for Peru's Forgotten City*. Thames and Hudson, London.

Hodder, Ian
1982 *Symbols in Action*. Cambridge University Press, Cambridge.

Hodder, Ian (ed.)
1982 *Symbolic and Structural Archaeology*. Cambridge University Press, Cambridge.

Holm, Olaf
1966/67 Money axes from Ecuador. *Folk* 8–9: 135–143. Copenhagen.
1975 Monedas primitivas del Ecuador prehistórico. *La Pieza* 3. Casa de la Cultura Ecuatoriana, Guayaquil.
1978 Hachas monedas del Ecuador. In *Actas y Trabajo del 3º Congreso Peruano, El Hombre y La Cultura Andina I*, ed. Ramiro Matos, pp. 347–61. Lima.
1980 Monedas primitivas del Ecuador prehistórico. *Cuadernos Prehispánicos* 8(8): 53–67. Guayaquil.

Hosler, Dorothy, Heather N. Lechtman and Olaf Holm
1990 *Axe-Monies and Their Relatives*. Studies in Pre-Columbian Art and Archaeology 30. Dumbarton Oaks, Washington, DC.

Jones, Julie
1979 Mochica works of art in metal: a review. In *Pre-Columbian Metallurgy of South America,* ed. E. P. Benson, pp. 53–104. Dumbarton Oaks, Washington, DC.

Kauffmann-Doig, Federico
1986 Los dioses andinos: hacia una caracterización de la religiosidad andina fundamentadas en testimonios arqueológicos y en mitos. *Vida y Espiritualidad* 3: 1–16. Lima.
1989 Oro de Lambayeque. In *Lambayeque,* ed. José Antonio de Lavalle, pp. 163–214. Colección Arte y Tesoros del Perú. Banco de Crédito del Perú, Lima.
1992 Mensaje iconográfico de la orfebrería lambayecana. In *Oro del Antiguo Perú,* ed. José Antonio de Lavalle, pp. 237–63. Colección Arte y Tesoros del Perú. Banco de Crédito del Perú, Lima.

Kosok, Paul
1959 El valle de Lambayeque. *Actas y Trabajos del II Congreso Nacional de Historia del Perú: Epoca Pre-Hispánica 1*: 69–76. Lima.
1965 *Life, Land and Water in Ancient Peru.* Long Island University Press, New York.

Lechtman, Heather N.
1979 Issues in Andean metallurgy. In *Pre-Columbian Metallurgy of South America,* ed. E. P. Benson, pp. 1–40. Dumbarton Oaks, Washington, DC.
1981 Copper-arsenic bronzes from the north coast of Peru. *Annals of the New York Academy of Sciences* 376: 77–122.
1984a Andean value systems and the development of prehistoric metallurgy. *Technology and Culture* 25(1): 1–36.
1984b Pre-Columbian surface metallurgy. *Scientific American* 250(6): 56–63.
1988 Traditions and styles in Central Andean metalworking. In *The Beginning of the Use of Metals and Alloys,* ed. Robert Maddin, pp. 344–78. MIT Press, Cambridge, MA.
1993 Technologies of power: the Andean case. In *Configurations of Power,* ed. J. S. Henderson and P. Netherly, pp. 244–80. Cornell University Press, Ithaca.
1996 Arsenic bronze: dirty copper or chosen alloy? A view from the Americas. *Journal of Field Archaeology* 23: 477–514.

McKerrell, H., and R. F. Tylecote
1972 The working of copper-arsenic alloys in the early Bronze Age and the effect on the determination of provenience. *Proceedings of the Prehistoric Society* 38: 209–219.

McLoughlin, Sean D.
1996 A Metallurgical Characterisation of Precious Metal Alloys from Batán Grande, Peru. M.Sc. thesis in Archaeometallurgy, Institute of Archaeology, University College London, London.

Maquet, Jacques
1979 *Aesthetic Anthropology.* Undena, Malibu, California.
1985 *The Aesthetic Experience: An Anthropologist Looks at the Visual Arts.* Yale University Press, New Haven.

Menzel, Dorothy
1976 *Pottery Style and Society in Ancient Peru: Art as a Mirror of History in the Ica Valley, 1350–1570.* University of California Press, Berkeley.

Merkel, John F., A.I. Seruya, Dafydd Griffiths and Izumi Shimada
1995 Metallographic and microanalysis of precious metal objects from the Sicán period at Batán Grande, Peru. In *Materials Issues in Art and Archaeology IV,* ed. P. B. Vandiver, J. R. Druzik, and J. L. Galvan , pp. 105–126. Materials Research Society Proceedings, vol. 352. Pittsburgh.

Merkel, John F., Izumi Shimada, C.P. Swann and R. Doonan
1994 Investigation of prehistoric copper production at Batán Grande, Peru: interpretation of the analytical data for ore samples. In *Archaeometry of Pre-Columbian Sites and Artefacts,* ed. D. A. Scott and P. Meyers, pp. 199–227. The Getty Conservation Institute, Marina del Rey, CA.

Miller, Daniel, and Christopher Tilley (eds)
1984 *Ideology, Power and History.* Cambridge University Press, Cambridge.

Morris, Ian
1991 The archaeology of ancestors: the Saxe/Goldstein hypothesis revisited. *Cambridge Archaeological Journal* 1: 147–69.

Nash, June
1979 *We Eat the Mines and the Mines Eat Us.* Columbia University Press, New York.

Pedersen, Asbjorn
1976 El ajuar funerario de la tumba de la Huaca Menor de Batán Grande, Lambayeque, Perú. *Actas del 41 Congreso Internacional de Americanistas* 2: 60–73. Mexico City.

Perkins, Rachael N.
1997 The Technology, Deterioration and Benzotriazole Treatment of Electrochemically Gilded Copper Alloy Artefacts from Peru. B.Sc. thesis in Archaeological Conservation, Institute of Archaeology, University College London, London.

Ramírez, Susan H.
1994 Ethnohistorical dimensions of mining and metallurgy in sixteenth-century northern Peru. In *In Quest of Mineral Wealth: Aboriginal and Colonial Mining and Metallurgy in Spanish America,* ed. Alan K. Craig and Robert West, pp. 93–108. *Geoscience and Man* 53. Louisiana State University, Baton Rouge.

Reichel-Dolmatoff, Gerardo
1981 Things of Beauty Replete with Meaning – Metals and Crystals in Colombian Indian Cosmology. In *Sweat of the Sun, Tears of the Moon: Gold and Emerald Treasures of Colombia,* ed. D. Seligman, pp. 17–33, exh. cat., Natural History Museum of Los Angeles County. Terra Magazine Publications, Los Angeles.

Reichlen, Henry
1941 Etude technologique de quelques objets d'or de Lambayeque, Pérou. *Journal de la Société des Américanistes* 33: 119–54.
1962 Un bijou d'or de Lambayeque, Pérou. *Objets et Mondes* 2(2): 77–84.

Rondón, Jorge
1965/66 Morfología de la cerámica en relación a las normas prestadas del metal. *Revista del Museo Nacional* 34: 82–4. Lima.

Rowe, John H.
1948 The kingdom of Chimor. *Acta Americana* 6: 26–59.

Schiffer, Michael B., and James M. Skibo
1987 Theory and experiment in the study of technological change. *Current Anthropology* 28: 595–622.

Shanks, Michael, and Christopher Tilley
1982 Ideology, symbolic power and ritual communication: a reinterpretation of Neolithic mortuary practices. In *Symbolic and Structural Archaeology,* ed. Ian Hodder, pp. 129–54. Cambridge University Press, Cambridge.

Shennan, Stephen J. (ed.)
1994 *Archaeological Approaches to Cultural Identity.* Routledge, London/New York.

Shimada, Izumi
1981a Temple of time: the ancient burial and religious center of Batán Grande, Peru. *Archaeology* 34(5): 37–44.
1981b The Batán Grande-La Leche archaeological project: the first two seasons. *Journal of Field Archaeology* 8: 405–46.
1982 Horizontal archipelago and coast-highland interaction in north Peru: archaeological models. In *El Hombre y su Ambiente en los Andes Centrales,* ed. Luis Millones and Hiroyasu Tomoeda, pp. 185–257. National Museum of Ethnology, Suita, Japan.
1985 Perception, procurement and management of resources: archaeological perspective. In *Andean Ecology and Civilization,* ed. Shozo Masuda, I. Shimada and Craig Morris, pp. 357–99. University of Tokyo Press, Tokyo.
1990 Cultural continuities and discontinuities on the northern north coast, Middle-Late Horizons. In *The Northern Dynasties: Kingship and Statecraft In Chimor,* ed. Michael E. Moseley and A. Cordy-Collins, pp. 297–392. Dumbarton Oaks, Washington, DC.
1994a Prehispanic metallurgy and mining in the Andes: recent advances and future tasks. In *In Quest of Mineral Wealth: Aboriginal and Colonial Mining and Metallurgy in Spanish America,* ed. Alan K. Craig and Robert West, pp. 37–73. *Geoscience and Man* 53. Louisiana State University, Baton Rouge.
1994b *Pampa Grande and the Mochica Culture.* University of Texas Press, Austin.
1994c The role of metals in Middle Sicán society. In *The Illustrated Encyclopedia of Humankind, Vol. 4: New World and Pacific Civilizations,* ed. Goran Burenhult, pp. 94–5. Weldon Owen Pty Limited, Sydney.
1995 *Cultura Sicán: Dios, Riqueza y Poder en la Costa Norte del Perú.* Banco Continental, Lima.
1997a Organizational significance of marked adobe bricks and associated construction features

on the north Peruvian coast. In *Architecture and Civilization in the Prehispanic Andes,* ed. Elisabeth Bonnier and Henning Bischof, pp. 62–89. Archaeológica Peruana II. Völkerkundliche Sammlungen der Stadt Mannheim im Reiss-Museum, Mannheim.

1997b Das Grab von Huaca Loro und die Sicán-Kultur. In *Sicán – ein Fürstengrab in Alt-Peru: eine Ausstellung in Zusammenarbeit mit dem peruanischen Kulturministerium,* ed. Judith Rickenbach, pp. 33–79. Museum Rietberg Zürich.

1998a Sicán metallurgy and its cross-craft relationships. *Boletín Museo del Oro* 41 (1996): 27–61.

1998b Sicán monumental architecture: symbols of ancestor worship and social hierarchy. Paper presented at the *Kay Pacha* Conference, University of Wales, Lampeter.

In press 1 Late prehispanic coastal states. In *Pre-Inka States and the Inka World,* ed. Laura Laurencich Minelli, University of Oklahoma Press, Norman.

In press 2 Exotic goods and archaeological methodology: how viable are our data on interregional interaction? In *Commerce and Exchange in the Andes: Highland-Lowland Interaction from an Archaeological and Ethnohistorical Perspective,* ed. J. F. Cárdenas-Arroyo and Tamara L. Bray. Universidad de los Andes, Quito.

Shimada, Izumi, and Raffael Cavallaro
1986 Monumental adobe architecture of the late pre-hispanic northern north coast of Peru. *Journal de Société des Américanistes* LXXI: 41–78.

Shimada, Izumi, and Jo Ann Griffin
1994 Precious metal objects of the Middle Sicán. *Scientific American* 270(4): 60–67.

Shimada, Izumi, and John F. Merkel
1991 Copper alloy metallurgy in ancient Peru. *Scientific American* 265: 80–86.
1993 A Sicán tomb in Peru. *Minerva* 4(1): 18–25.

Shimada, Izumi, and Jorge Montenegro
1993 El poder y la naturaleza de la elite Sicán: una mirada a la tumba de Huaca Loro, Batán Grande. *Boletín de Lima* 15(90): 67–96.

Shimada, Izumi, and Hirokatsu Watanabe
1995 Ground penetrating radar: large scale application on coastal Peru. Paper presented at the 60th Annual Meeting of the Society for American Archaeology, Minneapolis.

Shimada, I., Stephen M. Epstein and Alan K. Craig
1982 Batán Grande: a prehistoric metallurgical center in Peru. *Science* 216: 952–9.

Shimada, I., K.B. Anderson, H. Haas and J.H. Langenheim
1997 Amber from 1000-year old prehispanic tombs in northern Peru. In *Materials Issues in Art and Archaeology V,* ed. P.B. Vandiver, J.R. Druzik, and J.F. Merkel, pp. 3–18. Materials Research Society Proceedings, vol.462. Pittsburgh.

Shimada, Izumi, Adon Gordus, Jo Ann Griffin and John Merkel
In press Sicán alloying, working and use of precious metals: an interdisciplinary perspective. In *Metal in Antiquity,* ed. Paul Budd and Suzanne Young.

Shimada, Izumi, Robert Corruccini, Julie Farnum, Kazuharu Mine, Rafael Vega-Centeno and Victor Curay
1998 Sicán population and mortuary practice: a multi-dimensional perspective. Paper presented at the 63rd Annual Meeting of the Society for American Archaeology, Seattle.

Shimada, Melody J., and Izumi Shimada
1997 Camelid and human offerings: a view from the north coast of Peru. Paper presented at the 62nd Annual Meeting of the Society for American Archaeology, Nashville.

Silverblatt, Irene
1987 *Moon, Sun, and Witches: Gender Ideologies and Class in Inca and Colonial Peru.* Princeton University Press, Princeton.

Tello, Julio C.
1937a Los trabajos arqueológicos en el Departamento de Lambayeque. *El Comercio,* 29, 30 y 31 de Enero, Lima.
1937b La búsqueda de tesoros ocultos en las huacas de Lambayeque. *El Comercio,* 11 de Marzo, Lima.
1937c El oro de Batán Grande. *El Comercio,* 18 de Abril. Lima.

Trimborn, Hermann
1979 *El Reino de Lambayeque en el Antiguo Perú.* Haus Völker und Kulturen Anthropos-Institut, St. Augustin.

Valcárcel, Luis E.
1937 Un valioso hallazgo arqueológico en el Perú. *Revista del Museo Nacional* VI: 164–8. Lima.

Vetter, Luisa María
1993 *Análisis de las Puntas de Aleación de Cobre de la Tumba de Un Señor de la Élite Sicán, Batán Grande, Lambayeque, Perú.* Memoria de Bachiller, Especialidad de Arqueología, Pontificia Universidad de Católica del Perú. Lima.

Vreeland, James M., and Izumi Shimada
1981 Burial and looting traditions at Batán Grande, Peru. Paper presented at the Annual Meeting of the Institute of Andean Studies, Berkeley.

Wilbert, Johannes
1974 *The Thread of Life: Symbolism of Miniature Art from Ecuador.* Studies in Pre-Columbian Art and Archaeology, no. 12. Dumbarton Oaks, Washington, DC

Zevallos, Jorge
1971 *Cerámica de la Cultura 'Lambayeque' (Lambayeque I).* Universidad Nacional de Trujillo, Trujillo.

Acknowledgements

We are grateful to the Shibusawa Ethnological Foundation of Tokyo for three research grants issued to Izumi Shimada to support field and laboratory work (1990–98) that provided the data for this paper. The Museo de la Nación in Lima kindly provided space for our documentation, conservation, and analysis of excavated artefacts during 1992–4. Many people helped to make our work in Lima productive and pleasant. In particular, we thank Paloma Carcedo de Mufarech, Leticia Dargent de Bocangegra, Pedro Gjurinovic, Laurence Le Ber, John Merkel, Jorge Montenegro and Yutaka Yoshii. We also thank the Bruning National Archaeology Museum in Lambayeque for its assistance during excavation of the Huaca Loro East and West tombs. An earlier version of this paper was presented by I. Shimada at a conference held on 18 May 1996 at the Museum of Mankind (British Museum). I. Shimada is grateful for the assistance of the Peruvian embassies in London and Washington, DC, in making the trip to London for the conference possible and hospitality of J. F. Merkel and his family during his stay there. Lastly, we are indebted to Melody Shimada and Colin McEwan for their editorial assistance.

3

The Goldwork of Chimor

The Technology and Iconography of Wealth Accumulation

Karen O'Day

Introduction

The Chimor empire controlled the largest territory of all Late Intermediate Period (AD 1000–1470) polities, spanning approximately 1,000 km of Peru's coast (see map p. 15). From its capital Chan Chan on the North Coast of Peru the empire gradually expanded its coastal

3.1 Gold ear-spools showing richly attired Chimú nobles brandishing pairs of beakers in outstretched hands.

domain to encompass Tumbes in the north and the Chillon Valley in the south. In the late fifteenth century the Incas conquered and forcibly incorporated Chimor into their own growing empire.

The nobles at the apex of Chimor's social order adorned themselves with brilliant goldwork; different lines of evidence suggest that the privilege of wearing gold ornaments was largely restricted to the highest social echelons (Figs 3.1–2).[1] There was a direct connection between gold and the nobility, for the technology and iconography of metalworking served to display their unique position and status, and to assert their divine authority

to rule. Chimú metalsmiths fashioned gold ornaments that combine skilful manipulation of many pieces of sheet metal with a profuse and highly structured iconography. This distinctive technological and iconographic combination is the subject of this paper.

Research

In recent decades archaeological and ethnohistorical research has revealed much about the composition and organization of Chimor. The Chan Chan-Moche Valley Project (1969–74) mapped the capital's royal compounds, addressed subsistence strategies and uncovered evidence of a large artisanal class that devoted its skills to full-time metalworking, weaving, and wood sculpting.[2] Early colonial administrative and judicial documents, as well as indigenous oral histories recorded by Spaniards, also provide insights into coastal leadership and artistic production.[3]

Nevertheless, the technology, iconography and design of Chimú goldworking, like much of the imperial artistic corpus, has not been addressed fully.[4] One obstacle has been the misidentification of Middle Sicán art as Chimú,[5] only recently clarified by archaeological research at the Sicán capital Batán Grande (see Shimada, this volume). The accomplishments of Chimú metallurgists have also been underestimated: 'The men of Chimor were not great artists, but they were superlative engineers and craftsmen, and they produced in great quantities.'[6] Here I will reassess the quality and quantity of Chimú goldwork based on the archaeological and ethnohistorical evidence. First, the Inca response to Chimú metalworkers testifies to their artistic skill, for the conquest of Chimor by the Incas around 1470 entailed the resettlement of many of Chan Chan's metalworkers at Cusco

3.2 Gold ear-spools,
shoulder straps and pectoral
(ear-spools: diam. 15.5 cm;
pectoral: height 20 cm,
length 49 cm).

and other Inca centres.[7] These transplanted artists contributed their North Coast skills to Inca metalwork, testifying to Inca appreciation of the conquered metalsmiths' arts.[8] The Incas were no less impressed by the sheer abundance of Chimor's gold and silver, as too were the Spaniards on their arrival some fifty years later.[9]

The great quantity of high-quality metalwork represents one important aspect of Chimú metallurgy. Anthropologists such as Heather Lechtman note that most ancient central Andean polities employed gold and silver in social and political display.[10] All aspects of Andean metallurgical production expressed cultural values and priorities: mining, processing, alloying, joining, surface treatment and iconography.[11] The technology of production and iconography are inextricably

bound together in the complex process of creating objects intended for ostentatious display.

The overwhelming majority of Chimú goldwork lacks provenance due to the persistent looting of Chan Chan and other Chimú centres begun by the Incas and continuing to this day.[12] As John Topic states, 'no hoards of ingots or storerooms filled with textiles' are known to have survived at Chimú centres.[13] Notwithstanding this critical lack of context, it may still be possible to extract information from the goldwork about the messages it delivered while adorning noble bodies. Here I attempt to draw together the strands of archaeological, ethnohistorical, and art historical research, as well as evidence from the goldwork itself, to show how Chimú sheet-metal technology and iconography was deployed to accumulate and display wealth.

Gathering gold

Among Andean cultures metals were especially valued for their colours, and gold in particular was associated with the sun and its generative powers.[14] The first evidence of metalworking, recovered at Waywaka, involved small gold sheets, indicating that this metal acquired symbolic significance as early as *c.*1900–1450 BC.[15] Subsequently, attempts to achieve the desired golden colour may have played a role in stimulating the development of procedures for gilding objects with a low gold content, a technology practised for nearly two millennia by North Coast metalsmiths.[16] Gold is above all immutable, a quality that served to mark noble status and social position.[17] An indigenous North Coast oral record documented by Fray Antonio de la Calancha in 1638 conveys just such a link between gold and nobles.[18] In this account the Sun sent gold, silver and copper eggs to create humanity. The gold egg produced the lords, and their women came from the silver, but commoners emerged from the copper egg.

While the symbolic value of gold can be assessed, the sources of the gold exploited by Chimú metallurgists are not known with certainty.[19] Unlike copper which is plentiful, naturally occurring gold is not abundant on the Peruvian coast.[20] On the other hand, placer gold is commonly found in river beds of the eastern Andean slopes, well beyond the imperial boundaries. Chimú traders apparently secured access to this via trade routes across the highlands and beyond.[21] For example, coastal names and consonants in patronyms of the Cajamarca region are perhaps due to the presence of coastal groups monitoring

3.3 Aerial view of Chan Chan looking north-west and showing the rectangular outlines of the large royal compounds (*ciudadelas*).

water flow to their irrigation systems.[22] Arsenic-bearing ores for the production of arsenical copper objects were possibly acquired from the Quiruvilca region.[23] Chimú pottery found in north-eastern Peru suggests outlying colonies, probably founded to cultivate coca and acquire bird feathers, wood, plants and gold nuggets.[24] Studies of Chimú feather crowns, ear-spools, neckpieces and garments reveal a preference for the feathers of tropical birds like the Blue-and-Yellow Macaw, and such birds may even have been kept captive.[25] Gold ornaments, like colourful feathers of rain forest birds, display the wearer's connection to the rich realm on the other side of the Andes:

> Those who create and/or acquire goods and benefits from some dimension of the cosmological outside are not only providing goods and benefits per se but also are presenting tangible evidence that they themselves possess or command the unique qualities and ideals generally expected of

persons who have ties with distant places of supernatural origins and, therefore, are themselves 'second creators.' Evidence of inalienable connections with places of cosmological origins thus conveys a certain sacrality which readily translates into political-ideological legitimacy and facilitates successful exercise of power.[26]

The distant origin of gold, together with its alluring attributes, contributed an 'other worldly' dimension to the display of wealth accumulation.

Defining the empire

Chimú social hierarchy may be broadly divided into noble and commoner constituents with the former perhaps being divided into royal and non-royal lineages.[27] The Anonymous History of 1604 lists successive kings from the dynastic founder named Taycanamo to regional lords of the early colonial period.[28] Spanish administration and judicial documentation, chroniclers' observations, and archaeological investigation of Chan Chan itself, however, suggest dual organization of political authority.[29] Therefore, gold was probably the privilege of a large and well-structured noble class.

The internal organization of the enormous compounds, or *ciudadelas*, at Chan Chan point to their function as elite residences or palaces (Fig. 3.3).[30] Their architectural configuration unmistakably conveys a sense of inaccessibility and exclusion with access to the inner precinct restricted to one

ENLARGEMENT OF RIVERO

3.4 Plan of central Chan Chan, with an enlargement of Ciudadela Rivero showing its division into three major sectors including administrative quarters, storage facilities and the funerary platform Huaca La Misa.

entrance and walls 9 m high and 2 m thick (Fig. 3.4).[31] Their architectural attributes underscore the separation of the world within from that without, and evoke another North Coast creation myth also recorded by Fray Antonio de la Calancha, which recounts how the nobility arose from different stars to the commoners.[32] This fundamental distinction between the nobility and commoners is embodied in the material form of the *ciudadelas*.

Personal adornment seems to have given material expression to an 'ideology of separation' just as boldly as the *ciudadelas*.[33] Chimor's nobles

sheathed themselves in the most prized materials, an act of transformation according to Mary Helms:

Indeed, some persons of authority, even while yet living, seemingly surpass the basely human condition altogether by becoming political-ideological icons. As such they are transformed not only by attributes of sacrality, distinctive behaviour, and exemplary personal qualities but also by richly textured and elaborately designed costumes, gems, and other regalia often derived and/or crafted from materials obtained from geographically distant, mystically charged domains by long-distance acquisition or equivalent acts, such as hunting. Such costumes and regalia elevate and transform the very person of the chief into an aesthetically (and thus morally) potent, supra-human 'crafted object' indicative and expressive of the lofty qualities that constitute the sheer ideal.[34]

The nobility sought to acquire materials from afar to enhance their own special status. The objects constituting their sets of gold adornment vary, but ear ornaments and pectorals are typical (Fig. 3.2).[35] Another set of pectoral and ear ornaments was reportedly discovered in a grave in the Huarmey Valley, part of the southern portion of the empire, along with 1,200 sequins, a pair of bracelets, band of beads, nose ornament, stopper, spear thrower, digging stick tip and slab for metalworking or spacing nets (Figs 3.5–6).[36] The varied components may indicate that the owners commissioned their own 'custom-made' sets or, alternatively, acquired them over a period of time. Some of the objects of the Huarmey set, particularly the spear thrower and digging stick, suggest a male owner, as do the garment sets of turban, tunic and loincloth.[37]

The nobility probably also comprised lesser-ranked nobles by privilege, including a retinue of bureaucrats and administrators. They resided in and around thirty-five elite compounds at Chan Chan with enclosing walls and restricted access, as well as in smaller compounds located near commoner residences rather than in the *ciudadelas* themselves.[38] A silver ornament found in one elite compound links this group of nobles with precious metals.[39]

The highest-ranking nobility, especially the *ciudadela* residents, evidently sought to separate themselves from the commoners who formed the majority of the city's population. Metalworkers, weavers and wood sculptors composed a large portion of this group. An estimated 7,000 full-time artists practised their specialities between 1350 and 1400 and this number increased just prior to the Inca conquest.[40] Inside four neighbourhoods, or *barrios*, one group of artists dwelt

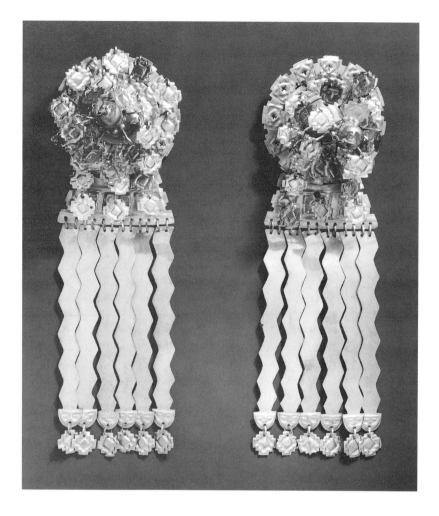

in irregularly arranged structures with workshops.[41] A second group of artists lived in retainers' quarters set atop platforms adjacent to *ciudadelas*.[42] Both groups were charged with artistic production primarily devoted to noble adornment. Some artists wore wooden ear-spools to signal their importance and status within the social order.[43]

Although the Chan Chan elite represented the apogee of the imperial hierarchy, those who lived outside Chan Chan had to be woven into the social fabric. Imperial administrative centres throughout Chimor's domain, such as Manchan in the Casma Valley and Farfán in the Jequetepeque Valley, collected tribute from the surrounding areas, monitored natural resources and human labour, and produced metalwork and textiles.[44] The successful operation of these centres depended upon provincial administrators, perhaps nobles transferred from Chan Chan as well as local leaders incorporated into the imperial system.[45] Unusual architectural features at some centres indicate that certain administrators possessed considerable status. For instance, one compound at Farfán contained a burial platform similar to those found only in the *ciudadelas* at Chan Chan (Fig. 3.4).[46] The important role of administrators possibly conferred the right to wear and use gold objects, some perhaps borrowed by their superiors at Chan Chan.[47] In this way the 'ideology of separation' may have been extended beyond the capital via portable goldwork and textiles, simultaneously linking nobles throughout the empire and distinguishing them from commoners. Finally, a population of ruralists tended the agricultural fields and irrigation canals.[48] At Cerro la Virgen near Chan Chan archaeologists have discovered textiles and copper fishhooks, the metal ranked below gold and silver. These commoners apparently did not merit the privilege of wearing ear ornaments.[49]

Building wealth

Chan Chan was the centre of imperial artistic production, which included lavish sculpting of friezes on the walls of *ciudadelas* and some elite compounds, metalworking, weaving and wood

3.5 (above left) Gold
ear-spools (diam. 8.1 cm).

3.6 (left) Gold pectoral
(height 31.5 cm,
width 38.4 cm, diam. 10 cm).

sculpting.[50] Large-scale metalworking seems to have gathered momentum between 1300 and 1375. After the conquest of the Lambayeque region around 1350 artistic activity increased, possibly due to the forcible relocation of artists from conquered outlying areas to the capital.[51] During this peak period of production, the two groups of artists at Chan Chan performed different work; *barrio* residents hammered ingots into sheets and the retainer residents worked these sheets into finished works of art.[52] Thus, the unusual architectural connection of *ciudadelas* and retainers suggests that the nobility lived in close proximity to these artists who transformed sheet metal into salient works of art. Retainer artists and their skills may therefore have been regarded as 'items' to acquire, much like gold or feathers.[53]

Although the skills of the *barrio* and retainer artists distinguished one from the other, metalworkers, weavers, and wood carvers often practised their specialities in the same workshops, an arrangement termed 'horizontal integration' because it allowed substantial and efficient interaction of specialists in different media.[54] Chimú textiles, especially garments and bags covered with metal plaques, testify to the importance of combining fibre and metal.[55] Thus, the nobility organized the large-scale production of metalworking and weaving, which complemented the more visible monumental projects such as the great irrigation canals and *ciudadelas*.[56]

Sheet-metal construction dominates the corpus of Chimú goldwork. Sheets were hammered and annealed to achieve the desired forms, and then joined by ingenious metallurgical and mechanical techniques, including soldering and stapling. This preference for sheet work, which characterizes ancient central Andean metallurgy, has provoked speculation. On the one hand, the paucity of cast objects has been attributed to the absence in the highlands and coast of the stingless bee, provider of the wax necessary for casting.[57] However, Heather Lechtman contends that cultural values influence the choice of technologies, a view that places less emphasis on technological or ecological determinants; beeswax could have been obtained from the eastern Andean forests, like the gold itself.[58]

Inca sheet metalwork has been described as 'architectural',[59] and this characterization may also be applied in the Chimú case if the construction of the objects themselves is considered. A finished object of sheet construction comprises an assemblage of individual pieces fashioned by many artists. In Chimú goldwork the numerous sheets often maintain their visual independence or integrity within the total construction. For example, the ear ornaments of the Dumbarton Oaks set display a profuse accumulation of small gold sheets (Fig. 3.5).[60] Each ornament consists of four main elements: disc, rod, trapezoidal plaque and six serpents. The dynamic stepped or zigzag contours, distinguish each component from its neighbours. Fourteen gold loops join the disc and plaque and identical loops connect the serpents and six stepped squares. Strap hangers projecting from the disc, rod and plaque support thirty stepped squares from each ornament. The stepped contour of each square is mimicked by steps embossed at the edges helping to distinguish it from the many neighbouring elements. Finally, the bird at the apex of each rod is an assembly of tiny gold pieces. Approximately one hundred gold sheets and pieces make up the more complex ornaments! The components swayed and shimmered as the wearer moved, each contributing to the total effect of the whole. The profusion of dangling and projecting elements tends to visually dominate the avian and serpentine iconography; the layered dangles overshadow the birds even though these birds actually project further than the layers. Thus, iconography becomes subordinate to the repetitive display technique emphasized by Chimú's metalsmiths: the exploitation of the 'brilliance of gold and silver by a variety of reflecting planes, often achieved with hinged bangles and filaments'.[61]

Comparable accumulation of precious materials may be found in Chimú textiles. In one case thirty medallions of red camelid fibre have been applied to the front of a tunic (perhaps originally part of a garment set), and red and yellow tassels dangle from these medallions (Fig. 3.7).[62] More dangling tassels attached directly to the tunic partly obscure the eight yellow units with images of frontal figures.[63] The faces of these figures are themselves woven with red fibre, thus blending into the dropping red tassels. Eighteen red tabs hanging from the bottom of the tunic in turn split into thirty-six yellow tabs.

These abundant dangling and projecting elements can express the wearer's 'acquisitive power' and 'conspicuous consumption' of gold or dyed camelid fibre.[64] Moreover, the importance of displaying accumulated precious materials generates imitation of such activities; garments present rows of embroidered or tapestry bird feathers, evoking the application of real feathers.[65] Both the tunic and gold ear ornaments testify to the acquisition of artistic and technological skill. Each individual sheet, much like the medallions and tassels of the tunic, proclaim the wearer's ownership of

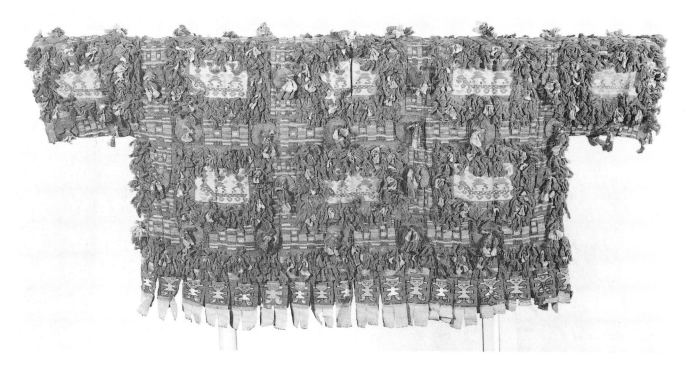

3.7 Tunic of the Bird Lot style (51.5 cm x 108 cm) made from gauze and tapestry with camelid fibre medallions and tassels.

the cherished materials and the artistic resources needed to transform them. This visual strategy parallels the gathering of skilled artists in retainers attached to *ciudadelas*. The acquisition and ownership of skilled labour become a primary message, relegating the zoomorphic and anthropomorphic motifs themselves to a secondary role. If the skills required for art production are a direct means of adding value to precious raw materials,[66] then gold ornaments and textiles are themselves potent displays of the expertise and energy invested in their manufacture.

Chimú sheet work is preceded by earlier North Coast sheetworking traditions and drew directly upon its Moche and Middle Sicán predecessors (see Shimada, this volume). All three traditions include objects that juxtapose gold and silver (see Fig. 3.9).[67] They also experimented with other novel combinations of high-status metals.[68]

The construction techniques of these successive North Coast traditions are clearly related, as demonstrated by the pair of Chimú ear ornaments discussed above, a pair of Moche wood, gold, and turquoise ear-spools recovered from the Tomb of the Warrior Priest at Sipán, and the enormous Middle Sicán gold-alloy funerary masks. In the Moche case several of the individual pieces, such as the warrior's club, shield and necklace, comprise independent elements that can be removed from the composition. Sicán metalworkers often built gold-alloy masks by joining several sheets. These antecedents, however, tend not to empha-

size the individual elements over the iconography; the Moche warrior is not visually overwhelmed by his many components and attributes, unlike the birds projecting from the Chimú ear ornaments. The sheets of the Sicán masks were originally adorned with paint and feathers which unified the multiple sheets,[69] again unlike the abundant and dynamic squares that become a primary visual message of the Chimú ear ornaments. Although it represented the outcome of a long tradition of three-dimensional sheet work, the Chimú application of that technology produced its own distinctive variants, exemplified by dazzling multi-component masterpieces.

Depicting wealth

Sheet-metal technology conveys half of the message of Chimú goldwork; iconography and composition contribute in equal measure. The iconography frequently portrays nobles, their privileges, and pursuits. In this way the goldwork differs from the *ciudadela* friezes in which humans are rather scarce.[70] The addition of high-status human beings and some of their activities in gold iconography creates a revealing distinction between the two media. The intimate relationship between ornament and wearer may account for this trend; nobles signalled their status by the gold ornaments they wore, reinforced by the use of golden 'doubles' on their ears or other body parts (cf. the Moche warrior

3.8. Pair of gold ear-spools portraying a noble travelling on a litter (diam. 13.5 cm).

ear-spools buried with the Warrior Priest). Indeed, gold ornaments, as well as textiles, typically depict human beings in possession of various high-status indicators, such as headdress and ear-spools (Figs 3.1–2, 3.8–9).[71]

Goldwork also illustrates noble privileges, such as being borne on a litter, a mode of transportation documented on the North Coast by the famous Middle Sicán litter of wood, silver, and gold and a litter of wood and fibre discovered in a burial at Manchan.[72] Gold ear-spools portraying high-status individuals on litters accord with these extant examples (Fig. 3.8). The noble with elaborate crescent-shaped headdress, tunic, ear-spools, drinking vessel and fan rests on a litter carried by two individuals and gazes towards the beholder.[73]

In addition to representations of nobles and their privileges, acquisitional activities are depicted. The best-known case involves scenes of diving for *Spondylus* shell, a red- or purple-rimmed bivalve nurtured by the warm waters off the Ecuadorian coast. A recently excavated adobe relief in Ciudadela Uhle at Chan Chan portrays *Spondylus* diving, proclaiming the 'Chimu lords' connections with divine powers and their central role in the supply of this highly valued material.'[74] A pair of gold-copper alloy ear-spools reinforces this link between Chimor's nobles and *Spondylus* shell (Fig. 3.9). Each ear-spool presents a rectangular raft supporting two figures who collect the trilobed shell from divers. Other

divers, beneath the boat in the scene, harvest more shells underwater. Chimú lords, like their Middle Sicán counterparts, wore images of acquisition of this bivalve, highly valued as a ritual offering for rain and river water to irrigate the crops planted in the coastal desert.[75] The ear-spools mark the role of the ruling elite in securing and regulating the relationship between three precious materials: gold, *Spondylus* shell and water. All three originate outside the immediate confines of the empire, including the water from the mountains, and thus convey the wearer's connection with distant, resource-rich locales. The ear-spools portray the divers, who reached hidden depths of 25 m or more beneath the ocean surface to gather the shells.[76] They performed a service for the nobility analogous to the role of the *barrio* and retainer artists.

Ostentatious and repetitive accumulation is also expressed in the goldwork. George Kubler observed: 'The predilection for a few ornamental figures in stereotyped repetition is a fundamental trait of Chimu art.'[77] Indeed, this compositional preference appears in *ciudadela* architecture, friezes, textiles and goldwork.[78] I suggest that the emphasis on repetition can itself be viewed as another acquisitive visual strategy, analogous to the profusion of individualized gold sheets. The pectoral, two shoulder straps and ear-spools of one adornment set display one such composition (Fig. 3.2). The pectoral contains approximately ninety profile figures in six registers and each

3.9. Pair of gold-copper alloy ear-spools with silver alloy shafts, showing diving for *Spondylus* shells (diam. 11.1 cm).

shoulder strap presents one stack or column of three frontal figures. Thirty undecorated tabs frame the bottom of the straps and pectoral, resembling the tabs hanging from the tunic discussed above (Fig. 3.7). Each ear-spool presents ten frontal human heads wearing headdress, earspools and pectoral. The repetition of the iconographic units in orderly registers, columns or circles promotes quick visual comprehension of the numerical regularities.

The orderly presentation of iconographic units seems to be an important visual strategy in Chimú art. The same tunic features eight blocks each containing two frontal figures and tabs forming a row of eighteen figures that in turn multiply into thirty-six yellow tabs. The composition of a loincloth panel (Fig. 3.10), with six registers containing fifty-one frontal figures with headdresses and staffs, recalls the gold pectoral (Fig. 3.2). This mode of expression resembles the profuse marine imagery of the *ciudadela* friezes that 'extends beyond direct subsistence concerns to a more generalized concept of abundance.'[80] Goldwork and textiles, like the friezes, employ repetition and standardization, which in itself constitutes an important visual message underlining the pervasive power of the state.[81]

Accumulating the wealth

The technology, iconography and composition of Chimú goldwork combine to convey the unequivocal message that to accumulate was noble. A few surviving Chimú scales, fibre nets with metal or bone balance beams, are also preserved, suggesting that accountants or other specialists played a role comparable to Inca *quipucamayocs*.[82] Little else is known about such potentially informative aspects of the empire.[83] On the other hand, the value placed on accumulation may be conveyed by the punishment for stealing: death.[84]

The artistic messages underline the preoccupation with the accumulation of exotic materials. A procedure for succession, termed 'split inheritance', has been posited for the empire. In this system the successor receives title and status without material wealth such as residences or territory.[85] Deceased rulers retain their property while the new potentate must strive to acquire new wealth. If split inheritance was in fact practised, it would have effectively codified a cycle of noble wealth accumulation.

The *ciudadelas* provide the most conspicuous evidence for elite accumulation. Every *ciudadela*, as well as some elite compounds, contain innumer-

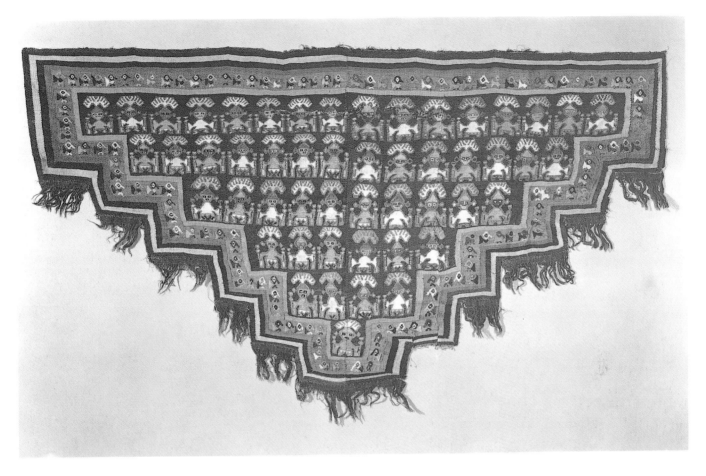

3.10. Tapestry panel from a loincloth, cotton and wool, Toothed Crescent Headdress Style, North Coast Peru, Chimú (61.7 cm x 107.5 cm).

able rooms two to four metres square with walls one metre thick and a single high-threshold entrance (Fig. 3.4),[86] which have been identified as storage facilities.[87] Partial excavation of some compartments has revealed little in the way of material remains, since during the Inca conquest they had been meticulously emptied of the stored goods: textiles, gold and silver objects, and *Spondylus* shell.[88] Nevertheless, the friezes of marine imagery that adorn some storage areas offer a link between visual and physical accumulation of goods in the surroundings.[89]

Ciudadelas also contain burial platforms interpreted as the resting places of Chimor's nobles.[90] They typically include many cells: twenty-five in the Laberinto platform, forty-five in Tschudi (Fig. 3.4),[91] and between fifteen and one hundred cells estimated for the other platforms.[92] These platforms are among the most looted parts of Chan Chan, but *Spondylus* shell, pottery, textiles, featherwork, carved wood, weaving tools and metal objects, such as pairs of gold and silver drinking vessels, have been recovered, possibly deposited during funerary rituals.[93] Since *ciudadela* design emphasizes inaccessibility, exclusion and containment, it has been suggested that in their accumulative functions they resemble museums.[94]

Conclusions

According to one commentator, 'the act of acquisition in itself becomes a mark of exceptionality, exclusivity, and ability to control.'[95] Chimú goldwork conveys amassed wealth through the symbolic value of the metal, iconographic themes and repetitive compositions. The artistic message of Chimor has been characterized as follows: 'The point of the designers seems to have been to subvert specific readings in order to convey a generalized impression of abundance, luxury, and perhaps sanctity; through iconography to a certain extent, but through formal composition as well.'[96] Goldwork contributed to these state-regulated proclamations and directly linked them to their noble wearers.

Mastery of the technology conferred authority on those who managed and controlled it.[97] The technology of sheet work empowered and also enriched those who wore it. If wealth accumulation distinguished Chimor's nobles, as ethnohistoric, archaeological and art historical evidence suggests, then gold ornaments were not merely objects to possess and display but also a vital means of portraying the distinctions that set the ruling elite apart.

Notes

1 Moseley 1990: 27–8; Cordy-Collins 1996: 224; Pillsbury 1993: 77, 277.

2 J. Topic 1990.

3 Netherly 1977, 1984, 1988, 1990; Rostworowski de Diez Canseco 1977, 1989, 1990.

4 Joanne Pillsbury (1993, 1996) has noted the scarcity of research on the empire's means and messages of visual expression. Her work concentrates on interpreting the imagery on the adobe friezes throughout the empire.

5 Anton 1972 is one example of the confusion of Middle Sicán and Chimú art in past decades.

6 J. Rowe 1948: 47. For two similar assessments see Bennett and Bird 1960: 208 and Sawyer 1968: 75.

7 J. Topic 1990.

8 María Rostworowski de Diez Canseco has been the most vocal advocate of Inca recognition of the talent of North Coast metalworkers, counselling researchers not to overlook the influence of these artists on Inca art (Rostworowski de Diez Canseco 1988: 112; 1990: 456 and n.13). Inca appreciation of Chimor's weavers may be inferred from Chimú-style textiles found in Inca archaeological contexts outside of the North Coast. Such textiles apparently were incorporated into Inca redistribution and their production at imperial weaving workshops may have been tailored to Inca specifications (A. Rowe 1984: 121–4; Young-Sánchez 1994: 45).

9 Cabello Valboa in Netherly 1988: 108; Vázquez de Espinosa 1969 (1620): 273–4.

10 Lechtman 1984a.

11 Shimada 1994a.

12 Bray 1985: 76; Ramírez 1996: 121–51.

13 J. Topic 1982: 161.

14 Lechtman 1993: 253; 1996: 38–42.

15 Grossman 1972; Burger 1992: 127.

16 Lechtman 1973, 1984a, 1984b, 1993; Lechtman, Erlij, and Barry 1982.

17 Patterson 1971: 297; Lechtman 1984a: 14–15. The immutability of gold, versus silver, is demonstrated by a pair of Moche backflaps in the tomb of the Warrior Priest at Sipán, Alva and Donnan 1993: fig. 120.

18 Moore 1996: 175–6.

19 This remains an unanswered question about most North Coast metallurgy. Shimada 1994b: 267, n. 52; Lechtman, Erlij and Barry 1982: 29.

20 Patterson 1971; Lechtman 1976: 9–15, 40; Shimada, Epstein and Craig 1983; Shimada 1994b: 200. Izumi Shimada (1994b: 44) cautions against this generalization, noting that rivers on the Peruvian coast carry some gold nuggets and citing Cerro Morro de Etén in the Lambayeque Valley as a possible gold source. Moseley (1979: 69) cites the Tumbes River as a potential source for coastal polities.

21 Root 1949: 205; Patterson 1971; Moseley 1979: 69; Topic and Topic 1983: 250; Mackey 1987: 123; Netherly 1988; Parsons and Hastings 1988: 197–8; Rostworowski de Diez Canseco 1990: 450–5, 457; T. Topic 1990: 192.

22 Rostworowski de Diez Canseco 1985, 1990: 454.

23 Lechtman 1976; J. Topic 1990: 161–5; Lechtman 1991.

24 Shimada 1994b: 37.

25 O'Neill 1984: 146–50.

26 Helms 1993: 49.

27 Day 1982a: 63; Topic and Moseley 1986: 155.

28 J. Rowe 1948: 39–40.

29 Netherly 1984, 1990; Rostworowski de Diez Canseco 1990: 448–9; Zuidema 1990: 489; 500–503.

30 Day 1982a: 63–4.

31 Day 1982a: 55–6; Kolata 1983: 362–3; Conrad 1990; Kolata 1990: 140–42.

32 J. Rowe 1948: 47.

33 Moore 1996: 173–9.

34 Helms 1993: 170.

35 Unfortunately, only a small number of complete gold sets are known; this discussion is limited to two sets. Many other original sets were probably split up when found by looters.

36 Boone, ed. 1996: 225–59.

37 A. Rowe 1980: 106–7; 1984: 28–9.

38 Klymyshyn 1982.

39 Ibid: 141.

40 J. Topic 1990: 152.

41 Ibid: 155.

42 J. Topic 1982: 148–9, 156–8; 1990: 161.

43 J. Topic 1982: 164; Topic and Moseley, 1986: 156; Moseley 1990: 28.

44 Mackey 1987: 125–8; Mackey and Klymyshyn 1990: 198.

45 Mackey 1987: 129.

46 Perhaps the deceased was the military commander Pacatnamú or a member of Chimor's royalty. Mackey 1987: 127.

47 Moseley 1990: 27–8.

48 Keatinge 1982; Topic and Moseley 1986: 155–6; J. Topic 1982: 170.

49 S. Pozorski 1982: 187–9; J. Topic 1982: 171.

50 J. Topic 1990: 166–70; Mackey and Klymyshyn 1990: 211; Pillsbury 1993

51 J. Topic 1990: 149–50.

52 J. Topic 1990: 170; Moseley 1992: 47.

53 Helms 1993, ch. 5.

54 J. Topic 1990: 164–5.

55 A. Rowe 1984: figs 148, 150, 152, 167, 168, 169, and pl. 23.

56 Lechtman 1993: 246; Day 1982a: 55–6; Pozorski and Pozorski 1982; Topic 1990: 170.

57 Root 1949: 223; Bird 1979; Lechtman 1979: 30–31; Moseley 1979: 71; Helms 1981: 216–17; Lechtman 1984a: 34; Bruhns 1994: 178.

58 Bird 1979: 51.

59 Helms 1981: 219–20.

60 A similar pair of ear-spools, albeit of less profusion, is in the collection of El Museo Arqueológico Rafael Larco Herrera, Lima (Berrin 1997: cat. no. 183).

61 Kubler 1990: 407.

62 For such a garment set see Musées royaux d'Art et d'Histoire, Brussels, 1990: cat. no. 275.

63 The labour required to create these medallions and tassels rivals that of the gold sheets. See Stone-Miller 1994: 17 for the daunting process, from herding camelids to extracting the materials for the red dye from the cochineal beetle.

64 Chimú garments, bags and miniatures with silver plaques sewn onto their surfaces also participated in this expression (A. Rowe 1984: figs 152, 167, pl. 23; Stone-Miller 1994: pl. 42).

65 A. Rowe 1984: figs 54, 55, and pl. 11.

66 J. Topic 1990: 165.

67 Root 1949: 219; Alva and Donnan 1993: 221–2; Berrin, ed., 1997: 207.

68 Berrin, ed., 1997: fig. 159.

69 Muro and Shimada 1985: 65.

70 Pillsbury 1993: 82, 89, 267–75.

71 For example, in the pair of ear-spools illustrated in Fig. 3.1 accurate representation of the noble gives way to accumulation; six danglers added to the bottom of his tunic replace his legs. Jones, ed., 1985: cat. no. 77.

72 Mackey 1987: 127; Shimada 1995: fig. 22; Netherly 1977.

73 A pair of gold ear-spools in the collection of the Minneapolis Institute of Arts illustrates a similar scene (Los Angeles County Museum of Art, 1964 : fig. 183) as does another pair in the Museo Nacional, Lima (Kubler 1990: fig. 350).

74 Pillsbury 1993: 151–64; 1996: 334.

75 Cordy-Collins 1990; Pillsbury 1993: 159–64. The trilobed shells are also portrayed in art. The silver plaques sewn onto a textile (A. Rowe 1984: pl. 23) bear one embossed shell, depicting at once the acquisition of precious metal and accumulation of many shells.

76 Cordy-Collins 1990: 396.

77 Kubler 1990: 407.

78 Moore 1996: 77; Pillsbury 1993: 81–5, 268.

79 Personal adornment that conveys acquisition through repetition is created with silver as well (A. Rowe 1984: fig. 184; Berrin, ed., 1997: cat. nos 157 and 158).

80 Pillsbury 1993: 281.

81 Repetition appears in other Late Intermediate period art such as Middle Sicán textiles and metalwork and Chancay textiles. Earlier art styles also utilize repetition, suggesting that it may have been a key visual strategy with widespread currency in the central Andes rather than a neutral compositional device.

82 Boone 1996: pl. 73. I am indebted to Rebecca Stone-Miller for pointing out these scales, a topic that merits research.

83 Moseley 1990: 29; Ramírez 1990: 509–19.

84 J. Rowe 1948: 49.

85 Conrad 1982: 106–8.

86 Day 1982a: 60; Klymyshyn 1982: Table 2; 139; 1987: 103; Moore 1996: 79.

87 J. Topic 1982: 172–3; Keatinge 1982: 202; Klymyshyn 1982; Kolata 1990: 130–32; Earle 1992: 336; Moore 1996: 71, 86.

88 Day 1982a: 60, 64; 1982b: 333; D'Altroy & Earle 1992: 33, 51–9; Earle: 1992: 336–7.

89 Pillsbury 1993: 292–3.

90 Day 1982a: 64; Conrad 1982: 88; Kolata 1990: 133.

91 Conrad 1982: 94.

92 Ibid: fig. 5.1.

93 Ravines 1980: 216; A. Rowe 1980; T. Pozorski

1980: 241; Conrad 1982: 99, 103; Rios and Retamozo 1982.
94 Conklin 1990: 64–5.
95 Helms 1993: 165.
96 Pillsbury 1993: 298.
97 Lechtman 1993: 254.

References

Alva, Walter, and Christopher Donnan
1993 *Royal Tombs of Sipán*. Fowler Museum of Cultural History, Los Angeles.

Anton, Ferdinand
1972 *The Art of Ancient Peru*. Thames and Hudson, London.

Bennett, Wendell, and Junius Bird
1960 *Andean Culture History*, 2nd edn. American Museum of Natural History, New York.

Berrin, Kathleen, ed.
1997 *The Spirit of Ancient Peru: Treasures from the Museo Arqueológico Rafael Larco Herrera*. Thames and Hudson, London.

Bird, Junius
1979 Legacy of the stingless bee. *Natural History* 88 (9): 49–51.

Boone, Elizabeth Hill, ed.
1996 *Andean Art at Dumbarton Oaks*, vol. 1. Dumbarton Oaks Research Library and Collection, Washington, DC.

Bray, Warwick
1985 Ancient American metallurgy. In *The Art of Precolumbian Gold: The Jan Mitchell Collection*, ed. Julie Jones, pp. 76–84. Little, Brown and Company, Boston.

Bruhns, Karen Olsen
1994 *Ancient South America*. Cambridge University Press, Cambridge.

Burger, Richard L.
1992 *Chavin and the Origins of Andean Civilization*. Thames and Hudson, London.

Clark, Grahame
1986 *Symbols of Excellence: Precious Materials as Expressions of Status*. Cambridge University Press, Cambridge.

Conklin, William J.
1990 Architecture of the Chimu: memory, function, and image. In *The Northern Dynasties: Kingship and Statecraft in Chimor*, ed. Michael E. Moseley and Alana Cordy-Collins, pp. 43–74. Dumbarton Oaks Research Library and Collection, Washington, DC.

Conrad, Geoffrey W.
1982 The burial platforms of Chan Chan: some social and political implications.
In *Chan Chan: Andean Desert City*, ed. Michael E. Moseley and Kent C. Day, pp. 87–117. University of New Mexico Press, Albuquerque.
1990 Farfan, General Pacatnamu, and the Dynastic History of Chimor. In *The Northern Dynasties: Kingship and Statecraft in Chimor*, ed. Michael E. Moseley and Alana Cordy-Collins, pp. 227–42. Dumbarton Oaks Research Library and Collection, Washington, DC.

Cordy-Collins, Alana
1990 Fonga Sidge: shell purveyor to the Chimu kings. In *The Northern Dynasties: Kingship and Statecraft in Chimor*, ed. Michael E. Moseley and Alana Cordy-Collins, pp. 393–418. Dumbarton Oaks Research Library and Collection, Washington, DC.

1996 Chimu. In *Andean Art at Dumbarton Oaks*, vol. 1, ed. Elizabeth Hill Boone, pp. 223–76. Dumbarton Oaks Research Library and Collection, Washington, DC.

D'Altroy, Terence, and Timothy K. Earle
1992 Staple finance, wealth finance, and storage in the Inka political economy. In *Inka Storage Systems*, ed. Terry Y. LeVine, pp. 31–61. University of Oklahoma Press, Norman.

Day, Kent C.
1982a Ciudadelas: their form and function. In *Chan Chan: Andean Desert City*, ed. Michael E. Moseley and Kent C. Day, pp. 55–66. University of New Mexico Press, Albuquerque.
1982b Storage and labor service: a production and management design for the Andean area. In *Chan Chan: Andean Desert City*, ed. Michael E. Moseley and Kent C. Day, pp. 333–49. University of New Mexico Press, Albuquerque.

Earle, Timothy
1992 Storage and the Inka imperial economy: archaeological research. In *Inka Storage Systems* (Terry Y. LeVine, ed.): 327–42. Oklahoma University Press, Norman.

Grossman, Joel
1972 An ancient goldworker's tool kit. *Archaeology* 25 (4): 270–75.

Helms, Mary W.
1981 Precious metals and politics: style and ideology in the Intermediate Area and Peru. *Journal of Latin American Lore* 7 (2): 215–38.
1993 *Craft and the Kingly Ideal*. University of Texas Press, Austin.

Jones, Julie, ed.
1985 *The Art of Precolumbian Gold: The Jan Mitchell Collection*. Little, Brown and Company, Boston.

Keatinge, Richard
1982 The Chimu empire in a regional perspective: cultural antecedents and continuities. In *Chan Chan: Andean Desert City*, ed. Michael E. Moseley and Kent C. Day, pp. 197–224. University of New Mexico Press, Albuquerque.

Klymyshyn, Alexandra M. Ulana
1982 Elite compounds in Chan Chan. In *Chan Chan: Andean Desert City*, ed. Michael E. Moseley and Kent C. Day, pp. 119–43. University of New Mexico Press, Albuquerque.
1987 The development of Chimu administration in Chan Chan. In *The Origins and Development of the Andean State*, ed. Jonathan Haas, Sheila Pozorski and Thomas Pozorski, pp. 97–110. Cambridge University Press, Cambridge.

Kolata, Alan. L.
1983 Chan Chan and Cuzco: on the nature of the ancient Andean city. In *Civilization in the Ancient Americas: Essays in Honor of Gordon R. Willey*, ed. Richard M. Leventhal and Alan L. Kolata pp. 345–71. University of New Mexico Press, Albuquerque.
1990 The urban concept at Chan Chan.
In *The Northern Dynasties: Kingship and Statecraft in Chimor*, ed. Michael E. Moseley and Alana Cordy-Collins, pp. 107–44.

Dumbarton Oaks Research Library and Collection, Washington, DC.

Kubler, George
1990 *The Art and Architecture of Ancient America*. The Penguin Group, London.

Lechtman, Heather
1973 The gilding of metals in Precolumbian Peru. *Application of Science in Examination of Works of Art* (William Young, ed.): 38–52. Museum of Fine Arts, Boston.
1976 A metallurgical site survey in the Peruvian Andes. *Journal of Field Archaeology* 3: 1–42.
1979 Issues in Andean Metallurgy. In *Pre-columbian Metallurgy of South America*, ed. Elizabeth P. Benson, pp. 1–40. Dumbarton Oaks Research Library and Collection, Washington, DC.
1984a Andean value systems and the development of prehistoric metallurgy. *Technology and Culture* 25 (1): 1–36.
1984b Precolumbian surface metallurgy. *Scientific American* 250(6): 56–63.
1991 The production of copper-arsenic alloys in the Central Andes: highland ores and coastal smelters? *Journal of Field Archaeology* 18: 43–76.
1993 Technologies of power: the Andean case. In *Configurations of Power: Holistic Anthropology in Theory and Practice*, ed. J.S. Henderson and P.J. Netherly, pp. 244–79. Cornell University Press, Ithaca.
1996 Cloth and metal: the culture of technology. In *Andean Art at Dumbarton Oaks*, vol.1, ed. Elizabeth Hill Boone, pp. 33–43. Dumbarton Oaks Research Library and Collection, Washington, DC.

Lechtman, Heather, Antonieta Erlij and Edward J. Barry, Jr.
1982 New perspectives on Moche metallurgy: techniques of gilding copper at Loma Negra, northern Peru. *American Antiquity* 47 (1): 3–30.

Los Angeles County Museum of Art
1964 *Gold Before Columbus*. Los Angeles County Museum of Art, Los Angeles.

Mackey, Carol J.
1987 Chimu administration in the provinces. In *The Origins and Development of the Andean States* (Jonathan Haas, Sheila Pozorski, and Thomas Pozorski, eds.): 121–29. Cambridge University Press, Cambridge.

Mackey, Carol J., and A.M. Ulana Klymyshyn
1990 The southern frontier of the Chimu empire. In *The Northern Dynasties: Kingship and Statecraft in Chimor*, ed. Michael E. Moseley and Alana Cordy-Collins, pp. 195–226. Dumbarton Oaks Research Library and Collection, Washington, DC.

Moore, Jerry D.
1996 *Architecture and Power in the Ancient Andes: The Archaeology of Public Buildings*. Cambridge University Press, Cambridge.

Moseley, Michael
1979 *Peru's Golden Treasures*. Field Museum of Natural History, Chicago.
1990 Structure and history in the dynastic lore of Chimor. In *The Northern Dynasties: Kingship and Statecraft in Chimor*, ed. Michael E. Moseley and Alana Cordy-Collins, pp. 1–42. Dumbarton Oaks Research Library and Collection, Washington, DC.
1992 *The Incas and Their Ancestors*. Thames and Hudson, London.

Muro, Paloma, and Izumi Shimada
1985 Behind the golden mask: Sicán gold artifacts from Batan Grande, Peru. In *The Art of Precolumbian Gold: The Jan Mitchell Collection*, ed. Julie Jones, pp. 61–75. Little, Brown and Company, Boston.

Musées royaux d'Art et d'Histoire
1990 *Inca-Perú: 3000 ans d'histoire*. Imschoot, uitgevers, Ghent.

Netherly, Patricia J.
1977 Local Level Lords on the North Coast of Peru. Ph.D. dissertation, Cornell University.
1984 The management of late Andean irrigation systems on the North Coast of Peru. *American Antiquity* 49 (2): 227–54.
1988 El Reino de Chimor y el Tawantinsuyu. In *La frontera del estado Inca* (Tom D. Dillehay and Patricia Netherly, eds.): 105–29. BAR International Series 442, Oxford.
1990 Out of many, one: the organization of rule in the North Coast polities. In *The Northern Dynasties: Kingship and Statecraft in Chimor*, ed. Michael E. Moseley and Alana Cordy-Collins, pp. 461–87. Dumbarton Oaks Research Library and Collection, Washington, DC.

O'Neill, John P.
1984 Introduction: feather identification. In Anne Rowe, *Costumes and Featherwork of the Lords of Chimor: Textiles from Peru's North Coast*, pp. 145–50. The Textile Museum, Washington, DC.

Parsons, Jeffrey R., and Charles M. Hastings
1988 The Late Intermediate Period. In *Peruvian Prehistory*, ed. Richard W. Keatinge, pp. 190–229. Cambridge University Press, Cambridge.

Patterson, Clair C.
1971 Native copper, silver, and gold accessible to early metallurgists. *American Antiquity* 36 (3): 286–321.

Pillsbury, Joanne
1993 Sculpted Friezes of the Empire of Chimor. Ph.D. dissertation, Columbia University.
1996 The thorny oyster and the origins of empire: implications of recently uncovered *Spondylus* imagery from Chan Chan, Peru. *Latin American Antiquity* 7 (4): 313–40.

Pozorski, Sheila G.
1982 Subsistence systems in the Chimú state. In *Chan Chan: Andean Desert City*, ed. Michael E. Moseley and Kent C. Day, pp. 177–96. University of New Mexico Press, Albuquerque.

Pozorski, Thomas G.
1980 Las Avispas: plataforma funeraria. In *Chanchan: metrópoli chimú*, ed. Rogger Ravines, pp. 231–42. Instituto de Estudios Peruanos, Lima.

Pozorski, Thomas, and Sheila Pozorski
1982 Reassessing the Chicama-Moche intervalley canal: comments on the 'Hydraulic engineering aspects of the Chimu Chicama-Moche intervalley canal.' *American Antiquity* 47 (4): 851–68.

Ramírez, Susan E.
1990 The Inca conquest of the North Coast: a historian's view. In *The Northern Dynasties: Kingship and Statecraft in Chimor*, ed. Michael E. Moseley and Alana Cordy-Collins, pp. 507–37. Dumbarton Oaks Research Library and Collection, Washington, DC.
1996 *The World Upside Down: Cross-Cultural Contact and Conflict in Sixteenth-Century Peru*. Stanford University Press, Stanford.

Ravines, Rogger
1980 Religión y culto de los muertos. In *Chanchan: metrópoli chimú*, ed. Rogger Ravines, pp. 212–16. Instituto de Estudios Peruanos, Lima.

Rios, Marcela, and Enrique Retamozo
1982 *Vasos ceremoniales de Chan Chan*. Instituto Cultural Peruano Norteamericano, Lima.

Root, William C.
1949 Metallurgy. In *Handbook of South American Indians*, ed. Julian Steward, 5: 205–25. Government Printing Office, Washington, DC.

Rostworowski de Diez Canseco, María
1977 Coastal fishermen, merchants, and artisans in Pre-Hispanic Peru. In *The Sea in the Precolumbian World*, ed. Elizabeth P. Benson, pp. 167–86. Dumbarton Oaks Research Library and Collection, Washington, DC.
1985 Patronyms with the consonant F in the Guarangas of Cajamarca. In *Andean Ecology and Civilization*, ed. Shozo Masuda, Izumi Shimada and Craig Morris, pp. 401–21. University of Tokyo Press, Tokyo.
1988 *Historia del Tahuantinsuyu*. Instituto de Estudios Peruanos, Lima.
1989 *Costa peruana prehispánica*. Instituto de Estudios Peruanos, Lima.
1990 Ethnohistorical considerations about the Chimor. In *The Northern Dynasties: Kingship and Statecraft in Chimor*, ed. Michael E. Moseley and Alana Cordy-Collins, pp. 447–60. Dumbarton Oaks Research Library and Collection, Washington, DC.

Rowe, Ann Pollard
1980 Textiles from the burial platform of Las Avispas at Chan Chan. *Ñawpa Pacha* 18: 81–148.
1984 *Costumes and Featherwork of the Lords of Chimor: Textiles from Peru's North Coast*. The Textile Museum, Washington, DC.

Rowe, John Howland
1948 The Kingdom of Chimor. *Acta Americana* 4 (1–2): 26–59.

Sawyer, Alan R.
1968 *Mastercraftsmen of ancient Peru*. The Solomon R. Guggenheim Foundation, New York.

Shimada, Izumi
1994a Pre-hispanic metallurgy and mining in the Andes: Recent Advances and Future Tasks. In *In Quest of Mineral Wealth: Aboriginal and Colonial Mining and Metallurgy in Spanish America*, ed. Alan K. Craig and Robert C. West,

pp. 37–74. Department of Geography and
Anthropology, Louisiana State University, Baton
Rouge.
1994b *Pampa Grande and the Mochica Culture*.
University of Texas Press, Austin.
1995 *Cultura Sicán: dios, riqueza y poder en la
costa norte del Perú*. EDUBANCO, Lima.

Shimada, Izumi, Stephen Epstein
and Alan K. Craig
1983 The metallurgical process in ancient North
Peru. *Archaeology* 36(5): 38–45.

Stone-Miller, Rebecca
1994 *To Weave for the Sun: Ancient Andean
Textiles in the Museum of Fine Arts, Boston*.
Thames and Hudson, New York.

Topic, John R.
1982 Lower-class social and economic
organization at Chan Chan. In *Chan Chan:
Andean Desert City*, ed. Michael E. Moseley and
Kent C. Day, pp. 145–75. University of New
Mexico Press, Albuquerque.
1990 Craft production in the Kingdom of Chimor.
In *The Northern Dynasties: Kingship and State in
Chimor*, ed. Michael E. Moseley and Alana
Cordy-Collins, pp. 145–76. Dumbarton Oaks
Research Library and Collection, Washington,
DC.

Topic, John R., and Michael E. Moseley
1986 Chan Chan: a case study of urban change in
Peru. *Ñawpa Pacha* 24: 153–82.

Topic, John R., and Theresa Lange Topic
1983 Coastal-highland relations in northern Peru:
some observations on routes, networks, and scale
of interaction. In *Civilization in the Ancient
Americas: Essays in Honor of Gordon R. Willey*,
ed. Richard M. Levanthal and Alan L. Kolata, pp.
237–59. University of New Mexico Press,
Albuquerque.

Topic, Theresa Lange
1990 Territorial expansion and the Kingdom of
Chimor. In *The Northern Dynasties: Kingship
and State in Chimor*, ed. Michael E. Moseley and
Alana Cordy-Collins, pp. 177–94. Dumbarton
Oaks Research Library and Collection,
Washington, DC.

Vázquez de Espinosa, Antonio
1969 (1620) *Compendio y Descripción de las
Indias Occidentales*. Ediciones Atlas, Madrid.

Young-Sánchez, Margaret
1994 Textile traditions of the Late Intermediate
Period. In *To Weave for the Sun: Ancient Andean
Textiles in the Museum of Fine Arts, Boston*, ed.
Rebecca Stone-Miller, pp. 43–9. Thames and
Hudson, New York.

Zuidema, R. Tom
1990 Dynastic structures in Andean cultures. In
*The Northern Dynasties: Kingship and State in
Chimor*, ed. Michael E. Moseley and Alana
Cordy-Collins, pp. 489–505. Dumbarton Oaks
Research Library and Collection, Washington,
DC.

Acknowledgements

The present essay is profoundly different from the
first version that was submitted due to the assistance of several individuals. I am greatly indebted
to Rebecca Stone-Miller for her boundless support
and suggestions for improvement. Many thanks
also go to Joanne Pillsbury and Michael Moseley
for reading a draft and offering important comments. I owe a tremendous amount of gratitude to
Colin McEwan for his editorial advice and
patience.

4

Clothed Metal and the Iconography of Human Form among the Incas

Penny Dransart

The Inca human figurines that survived the European invasion and conquest of the Andes are very reduced simulacra of human beings. Anatomically detailed, these miniature figurines wear scaled-down versions of full-sized garments. Despite this anatomical completeness, the Incas evidently did not intend them to be viewed unclothed, unlike Western art, in which the nude has been such an important artistic tradition since classical times and earlier. In this paper I consider in what sense clothed figurines may be regarded as iconographic. I argue that concepts of meaning and form are interrelated in the iconography of Inca figurines and that a fuller appreciation of the underlying principles expressed visually by the figurines is possible with an examination of the archaeological contexts in which they have been found. These principles have to do with the expression of gender and the wrapping of metal and shell in cloth.

Is there such a thing as an iconography of Inca art?

Inca art is often considered to be geometric in character and therefore not amenable to iconographic analysis.[1] In Erwin Panofsky's classic definition iconography is concerned with subject matter or the meaning of works of art, rather than their form.[2] One of the aims of iconographic analysis is to identify what Panofsky calls 'conventional subject matter', presented visually in the motifs, that is images, or combinations of motifs, which are stories and allegories.[3] Given the apparently non-figurative appearance of much Inca art, and the absence of an interpretative key, there are enormous barriers for understanding the meaning of that art. Patricia Lyon admits that although a few examples of Inca sculpture have

survived (and these are recognizably figurative), Inca art is characterized by its geometric tendencies, which began to predominate in the Andes as the influence of the Wari Empire collapsed.[4] In contrast, earlier Andean art styles, such as that of Moche, are more fully figurative, and they also may be narrative-like in character. It would seem that such art (unlike Inca art) presents a body of material which invites the viewer to seek images, stories (or narrative) and allegories. With the figurines studied here, we have stylized but recognizable human forms in clothing that is decorated in an abstract manner. The clothed figurines present a nexus of figurative and apparently non-figurative imagery.

We should recognize the probability that Inca art was not intended to convey narratives, just as Panofsky points out that not all European art can be seen to serve such a function. He cites landscape painting, still life and genre, as well as 'non-objective' art, as European art forms in which one can identify the motifs that constitute the primary or natural subject matter, but 'the whole sphere of secondary or conventional subject matter is eliminated and a direct transition from motifs to content is effected'.[5] Thus even if much of Inca art was not intended to convey 'stories', its forms would have transmitted meanings ('content') and visual values that were understandable to people conversant with the conventions employed by Inca artists. This content is referred to by Panofsky as 'intrinsic meaning';[6] it is a sphere in which the character of meaning and form is less easily dichotomized.

It is useful to explore the historical process whereby meaning and form came to be regarded as possessing a relative independence. Writing in the 1930s, the art historian Henri Focillon observed that if form can be said to have its own content, then 'the fundamental content of form is a *formal* one' (emphasis in original).[7] He argued that the content of the subject matter is harder to grasp. This notion of separability between meaning and form had earlier been advocated by the Bloomsbury art critics Roger Fry and Clive Bell, whose writings were informed by the sculptures of Epstein, Brancusi and Gaudier Brzeska.[8] In *Art* (1914) Clive Bell proposed that aesthetic experience might be expressed in a 'significant form' that transcends specific cultural contexts. Roger Fry (1920) also sought the appeal of aesthetic form in non-Western art, an appeal that was unaccompanied by any concern to understand the meanings attributed to that form by the people who produced the art in question. His book *Vision and Design* consisted of essays in aesthetics, and it included a chapter on Ancient American art. Barbara Braun has shown that the sculptor Henry Moore was deeply influenced by such thinking, and she has discussed Moore's admiration for the 'truth to material' he perceived in Precolumbian sculpture.[9] In his sketchbooks Moore drew an Inca 'silver' figurine of a camelid, among other examples of Precolumbian works.[10] Thus the art-critical appreciation of Inca and other Precolumbian art has contributed to twentieth-century theoretical approaches to iconography in which a distinction between meaning and form has been advocated. George Kubler's 1962 view of art as a system of formal relationships, in which the forms have their own autonomy, is perhaps the most consistent formulation of such an approach.

In her examination of illustrations by Gonzalo Fernández de Oviedo (1478–1557) of American subjects, Kathleen A. Myers argues that there is an evident awareness 'of the interrelatedness of form and content' in Oviedo's work, which she sees as characteristic of Renaissance thought.[11] Myers discusses the underlying principles of Oviedo's illustrations by relying on Panofsky's third level of iconographic analysis, that of intrinsic meaning. Her paper provides a useful reminder that the conceptual separation of meaning and form in art has not always prevailed in the past.

Reference to Myers's consideration of a set of illustrations contained within a written text underscores the fact that Panofsky intended his method to be applied in a literary context. He stressed that knowledge of the relevant literary sources is a prerequisite for interpreting correctly the images or narrative of secondary or conventional subject matter.[12] While my concern here is with his third level, the realm of intrinsic meanings, he also suggests that knowledge of literary sources provides a helpful corrective in order to understand the contemporary concepts that informed the underlying principles of the art.[13] However, there are no contemporary literary sources of a kind employed by students of medieval and Renaissance art that we may consult in the case of prehispanic art. In an application of Panofsky's methodology to Moche art, Anne Marie Hocquenghem confronts the problem by looking to ethnohistorical and ethnographic records as independent bodies of material that may be used in order to interpret Moche iconography.[14] This has an unfortunate end result; her final analysis is of Andean art rather than of Moche iconography. It is significant in this respect that Hocquenghem speaks of *the* Andean ceremonial calendar,[15] as though such a thing could remain substantially unmodified both cross-culturally and through time. In contrast, my concerns are restricted to art of the Inca period. The lack of contemporary literary sources for Inca art means that Panofsky's reference to 'other documents of civilization historically related to that group of works' must be interpreted in a manner that Panofsky did not originally intend.[16]

Panofsky himself may not have approved such a procedure. W.J.T. Mitchell reminds us that the author of iconology was reluctant to make direct comparisons between Renaissance and non-Western art of the same period, although he considers that Panofsky's use of the term iconology implies a broader field of study that was not limited to Western visual images alone. There is, however, a fundamental problem if we wish to revive Panofsky's iconology in a postmodern framework. Mitchell locates this problem in the dominance of the word over the image. He comments that in iconology, a 'discursive science of images' is promised, 'a mastering of the icon by the logos'.[17]

The method used here is to examine archaeological sites in various parts of the Andes for information that can be used to situate the clothed figurines in a culturally specific setting.[18] Contextual information is available to expand our understanding of such figures in miniature human form; it will constitute the historically related record rather than conventional 'documents'. The patterning of material culture may also be compared with, and perhaps more importantly contrasted with, some relevant written accounts dating from the colonial period following the invasion of the Inca empire by the Spanish in 1532. However, the use of colonial documents highlights the problem addressed by Mitchell in the need for a critical iconology to be sensitive to 'the resistance of the icon to the logos'.[19] While it is relatively easy to name the underlying principles that sixteenth-century Europeans deployed in their cultural productions (for example, a tetralogy of the elements[20]), the underlying principles that were given visual expression in Inca art escape a facile naming process in the present. Paradoxically, the resistance of Inca images to words make them vulnerable to being dominated by verbal processes in an intercultural exchange that prioritizes the logos.[21] At the time of European contact European observers had their own perceptual frameworks through which to interpret Andean visual forms. Superficial formal similarities in the visualization of cosmologies may have suggested a certain parallelism in the semiotic codes deployed by two very different cultures. However, as Cecilia Klein has observed in a study of Aztec art, the apparent similarities should not lead us to conflate the different social and moral messages that those visual forms conveyed.[22]

Heather Lechtman has approached what Panofsky calls intrinsic meaning from a different angle, from a technological perspective.[23] In her study of metallurgical traditions in the prehispanic Andes (1979), she has explored concepts of what 'metalness' may have meant to the peoples who produced items wrought from different metals,[24] and the value systems that such objects conveyed to the makers and users.[25] The 'idea systems' Lechtman observes in Andean traditions of metalworking help provide a means for studying both meaning and form in metal objects in a non-narrative context. However, it should be recognized that the meanings expressed in terms of the relative worth of the inorganic elements employed to make art objects, and as expressed in terms such as colour values, are largely abstractions.

Humanity portrayed in miniature

The Inca human figurines considered here appear as miniature women and men who present themselves in static poses. They are made of metal alloys (gold, silver, copper), shell and stone. Where they have been found in conditions that favour the preservation of organic remains, they are dressed in miniature versions of full-sized Inca-style garments. This clothing has the effect of masking their gestures, which in any case are restricted to a few variants of the same standing pose. Any narrative message that they may have conveyed appears to have been de-emphasized.

The full complement of materials used to create the figurines includes the inorganic elements or shell from which their bodies are made, as well as camelid and plant fibres, and feathers in their garments. The combinations of organic and inorganic

elements in the presentation of these figurines seem to have followed standardized norms.

Few systematic studies analysing the composition of Inca figurines of metal have been published. Two female figurines from the high-altitude shrine of Pichu Pichu in southern Peru are identified as being made from a silver-copper alloy and a gold-silver alloy respectively.[26] A silver figurine from Cerro El Plomo was identified as comprising 94.4% silver, 5.1% copper, less than 0.4% gold and traces of tin.[27]

Because the figurines have not been subjected to the same level of scrutiny as pre-Incaic metalwork, it is not known whether the alloys were given surface enrichment and depletion gilding or silvering treatments. Lechtman has demonstrated that such surface techniques were characteristic of Chimú and earlier metalwork. She argues that the gold or silver constituted an essential quality that characterized the outward appearance of the object, although it was only minimally present in the interior.[28] This she regards as 'a metallurgical concept based upon an attitude about the requisite external appearance of certain kinds of object, where the external appearance of the object depended upon its internal condition'.[29] The surfaces of the objects were coated with overlays of other metals or precious stones and paint.[30] The significance of this argument to the Inca figurines is that the golden or silver surface representing the human skin was scarcely seen. It is notable that specially made clothing hid it. Only the face is just about visible under the splendid garments (Fig. 4.1).[31] This clothed aspect means that although the figurines are ethnically marked as Inca, they display an underlying cultural principle, which was widespread in the Andes, of covering or dressing metal in non-metallic substances.

Many of the surviving Inca metal figurines vary between about 50 mm and 150 mm in height and weigh between 7.8 g and 56.8 g. There are some taller ones, notably a solid silver male figurine from Pachacamac, 243 mm tall and weighing 1397 g,[32] and a female figurine from near Lauramarca in the region of Cusco (now in the Museo Arqueológico, Cusco), which is 245 mm in height and weighs 524 g.[33] Another male figure in the Royal Museum of Scotland, Edinburgh, is 228 mm tall.[34]

Most of the figures are hollow and were assembled from metal sheets soldered at the sides.[35] Typically, the figures stand with the feet apart, and with the arms bent towards the midriff or chest. The fingers are sometimes held tip to tip, a gesture that is reminiscent of the deceased

4.1 (above) Miniature Inca clothed figurine found on Cerro El Plomo, Chile.

4.2 (above right) Drawing by Guaman Poma of the deceased Inca emperor Guayna Capac, who died in Ecuador, being carried back on a litter to Cusco.

4.3 (right) Miniature Inca gold male figurine of unknown provenance (height 58 mm).

emperor Guayna Capac as depicted by Guaman Poma (Fig. 4.2).[36]

Female figurines often have the face and hair outlined in relief; the hair is divided into two braids, and hair fastenings are sometimes indicated. The hands of both male and female examples are usually empty, but a hollow gold female figurine illustrated by Benson holds a full spindle in the right hand.[37] Male figurines are represented with stretched earlobes, although the ear-spools, which indicated the status of the noble Inca men who wore them, are not usually present (Fig. 4.3). Other features associated with males are a protuberance in one cheek (often the left), as though the figurine were masticating a quid of coca.[38] They also wear a conical, Inca style hat which is flat on top.

Metalwork made by hammering and cutting out sheets of metal in order to produce three-dimen-

4.4 Inca male figurine with horizontal inlays, reputedly from Pachacamac.

sional objects was preferred over methods favouring the castability of metal in the geographical area comprised by Ecuador, Peru, Bolivia, Chile and north-western Argentina.[39] However, cast Inca figurines are also known, such as the large solid silver male figure in Baessler's fig. 541, as cited above. These figurines adopt similar postures to their hollow counterparts.

There are also examples of cast figurines inset with inlays of substances that have not always survived. The inlays form horizontal bands at the level of the cheekbones, shoulders, midriff and elbows or waist, hips, thighs or knees, and lower calf or ankles. This use of inlaid material is considered to be an Inca innovation.[40] Both female and male figurines have been published with inlaid transversal bands.[41] Another type of figure has the upper part of the body cast in one metal or alloy, and the lower part in another.[42] To date, such figurines have not been reported from high-altitude shrines. However, it seems that they were dressed, since Baessler reported one 'from Pachacamac' dressed in a brown tunic with an embroidered hem, and wrapped in a brown shawl.[43] It was accompanied by two further tunics, and had a plaited band serving as a turban round the head.[44] An illustration of the figurine without its clothing is presented in pl. 37 of Baessler's book (Fig. 4.4). It is not clear where these figurines were found – whether they were taken from the site of Pachacamac itself or from some other site in the vicinity. In the 1903 report on Max Uhle's work at Pachacamac no reference is made to human figurines of the type discussed here.[45]

Carved shell figurines are less often described in the published literature. Perhaps this relative lack of interest betrays Western preoccupations with precious metals. Usually, the material is identified as *Spondylus princeps,* the spiny bivalve that lives in the warm waters along the coast of Ecuador and southern Colombia. Shell figurines adopt a similar standing posture as their metal counterparts, but they are much smaller in size. The male shell figurines from Cerro Taapaca and Cerro Las Tórtolas measure only 35 mm and 40 mm in height, respectively.

The small size of the shell figurines means that there is often far less anatomical detail than is the case with their metal counterparts. This may be the reason why one of the shell figurines from Túcume has been misidentified as female in a recent publication.[46] There are two shell male figurines from the site: the smaller male figurine is very similar to the male from Cerro Gallán in that both lack the details of the characteristic Inca hat. However, the top of the head in both cases is hat-

shaped. A careful description of a similar shell figurine from Cerro Aconcagua by Schobinger, Ampuero and Guercio shows that although the genitals are not depicted, the figurine can be sexed as male by the absence of long hair and by the presence of four horizontal incised lines across the top of the head representing the conical, flat-topped hat.[47]

Shell, metal and stone, the raw materials used to fashion the bodies of Inca miniature figurines, are products of water and earth. To the Incas *Spondylus* was a high-status material, and it was presumably as 'noble' as gold and silver are in Western value systems. Trade routes controlling the supply of *Spondylus* were jealously guarded.[48] In a sixteenth-century Spanish account Cabello Valboa explained that the Inca emperor Topa Ynga (also known as Tupac Yupanqui) made 'profound adoration' on seeing the Pacific Ocean when he arrived in Ecuador, and he acclaimed the ocean as *Mamacocha*, or 'mother of the lakes'.[49] An equivalent concept concerned the domain from which the ores were mined for the bodies of the metal figurines. *Mama* is the Quechua term for a vein of metal, but it also a term of respect for a mother or a woman.[50] Mamacocha and Pachamama, mothers of the sea and earth, were two domains that provided the raw materials for making the bodies of the figurines discussed here.

The clothed aspect

Figurines with a full complement of clothing, in addition to the examples reported from Pachacamac[51] and those excavated at Túcume,[52] have also been found at high-altitude shrines. At these sites the clothing has been preserved in the permafrost at altitudes in excess of 5,000 or 6,000 m above sea level. Sites with such finds are known from the following mountain-top shrines: Nevado Pichu Pichu and Ampato in Peru; Cerro Taapaca, Volcán Pili, Volcán Copiapó and Cerro El Plomo in Chile; and Cerro Gallán, Cerro Las Tórtolas, Nevado Mercedario and Cerro Aconcagua in Argentina (Fig. 4.5).[53]

When the clothing is intact, the dress follows standardized conventions. Female figurines are clad in a rectangular cloth, wrapped round the body and fastened with pins of 'silver'. These pins, known as *tupu,* have a long shaft and a flattened, semi-circular top. Typically, the top is pierced, and two pins are attached to an elaborately embroidered cord, from which two rectangular pieces of *Spondylus* shell are suspended by two short lengths of braid, plaited from deep red camelid fibre yarns (Fig. 4.6). An unattached third

pin secures a second cloth, a shawl, which is either folded in half and wrapped round the shoulders with the fold uppermost, or, if it is more rectangular in shape, it is wrapped round the figurine in a single layer. A broad belt, furnished with a tubular cord and a tassel at each end, is wrapped round the waist, above the first cloth and below the shawl. On the head is placed a cap, provided with a fringed flap which hangs down over the back. Both cap and flap are covered with feathers, either orange-red or white. Orange feathers are known on caps from Cerro Gallán, Volcán Pili and Cerro Las Tórtolas. White feathers are associated with a second figurine from Las Tórtolas, with the figurines from Cerro Copiapó and with another from an imprecise findspot in the Diaguita area of Chile.[54] A full-sized cap with back flap and covered with white feathers was recovered from Cerro Esmeralda, Chile; it was associated with an adult woman who was accompanied by a more soberly dressed girl.[55]

Apart from the feather headdress, which only seems to occur in the highly specialized contexts of high-altitude shrines and other ritual sites such as Cerro Esmeralda and Túcume, the clothes of female figurines are miniature versions of garments worn by Inca women that are known in museum collections and from other archaeological contexts (Fig. 4.7).[56] Notable examples of women's clothing were displayed by a group of forty-six Inca women, who were found in a cemetery on a terrace forming part of the so-called sun temple at Pachacamac by Max Uhle.[57] Uhle termed this 'the cemetery of the sacrificed women', as some of the bodies show signs of strangulation; all the women were identified as

4.5 Map of the southern Andes mountain shrines where human offerings have been found often accompanied by miniature clothed figurines (see Fig. 4.8).

4.6 Miniature Inca cord with two silver pins attached. The pins were used to hold together the shoulders of the Inca women's dress, with the pins pointing upwards and the semi-circular head downwards (length of cord approximately 230 mm).

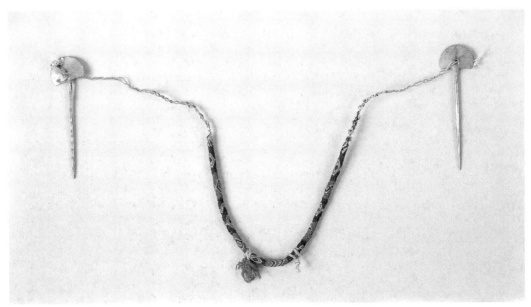

4.7 Miniature Inca woman's shawl (height 81 mm, width 146 mm).

adult. A further example of a woman in Inca dress was found on Nevado Cajón in Salta, Argentina; her clothed remains should be identified with the so-called *momia de los Quilmes,* according to Beorchia Nigris.[58] Both full-sized and miniature dresses and shawls are decorated with bands of zigzag designs or very stylized angular double-headed motifs (Figs 4.7 and 4.8). Although various colours appear in the plain weave stripes flanking these pattern bands, the colours used to execute these motifs are generally (but not always) red and yellow.

Male figurines wear a tunic, above which there is a rectangular shawl. This tends to be of a more oblong shape than the almost square cloths worn by many of the female figurines. It is knotted by the corners under the chin. In addition, male figurines may be equipped with a long, narrow plait of black camelid fibre, which is sometimes wrapped round the hat, and a small feather plume. Sometimes they have a bag with a shoulder strap. All these accessories are present in the costume of the male shell figurine from Volcán Pili.[59] It should be noted that the yellow tunic and the vicuña-coloured shawl worn by this figure are monochrome, apart from the characteristic Inca colours used to edge the borders and a row of zigzag embroidery round the lower edge of the tunic. The shell male figurine from Cerro Gallán,

Argentina, is similarly dressed in a black tunic and a white shawl,[60] while a silver male from Cerro Aconcagua, Argentina, has a light brown shawl and a dark green tunic.[61] In contrast, the gold and shell figurines from Aconcagua have monochrome shawls and patterned tunics. The tunic design of the gold male is the 'Inca key chequerboard' as designated by Rowe (1979); this design is related to the double-headed zigzag motifs of the women's clothing (Fig. 4.9). The shell figurine from Aconcagua, like another shell figurine from Cerro Las Tórtolas (Argentina), wears a chequerboard tunic of black and white squares with a plain red triangular area round the neck opening.[62] Both these pattern types occur in full-sized men's tunics, as discussed in detail by Rowe (1979). It is tempting to regard the patterned textiles as more significant in iconographic terms, but it should be remembered that the plain garments worn by the male figurines from Pili, Gallán and Aconcagua also form constituent parts of the iconography as discussed here.

Although the miniature garments worn by the figurines appear to be closely modelled on Inca adult clothing, the absence of a breechcloth on the males is puzzling, given the prominence this garment is accorded in accounts of Inca initiation rites.[63]

Both female and male figurines display similar imagery on their clothing, but there is a clear dichotomy expressed in the form of their main garments. The women wear a large cloth wrapped round the body, held in place by pins, while men wear a tunic with four openings for arms, legs and neck.[64]

4.8 Mummified body of a young woman found on Cerro Esmeralda. A white-feathered headdress worn by the young woman was found in a deteriorated condition and is not on display.

4.9 Inca mummy of a high-ranking man with a copper mask and a tunic displaying the so-called 'Inca key chequerboard' pattern.

Archaeological contexts

In this section the archaeological evidence is examined for evidence that may reveal some of the underlying principles in the iconology of Inca miniature human figures. In 1935 Valcárcel reported a pair of female silver figurines from Sacsahuaman, the 'fortress' site on the outskirts of Cusco.[65] However, their findspot did not favour the preservation of organic material and they lack the clothing and other contextual information that is available from sites elsewhere.

Most of the figurines considered in the preceding section were found at high-altitude shrines in the southernmost parts of the Inca empire. On Nevado Mercedario several archaeological features were encountered on the northern face. A silver female figurine was found with a textile bag covered with white feathers in a tumulus measuring 2 m in diameter.[66] Nearer the summit there was a group of three dry stone structures, circular in plan, built against the incline of the mountain; one of these contained a shell female figurine.[67] On Cerro Gallán, three separate drystone structures with a rectangular plan, measuring 1.30 m by 1.60 m, each contained a figurine.[68] Two of the figurines are silver and female; the third is shell and male. The smallest, the shell figurine, was in the largest structure. During excavations on Volcán Copiapó figurines were found in a platform.[69] A silver female figurine with a white headdress was found at a depth of 1.30 m to 1.35 m below the surface, which was marked by a rectangle of stones. A shell male figurine was found with a black feather plume at 1.60 m to 1.65 m beneath the surface, marked by a circle of stones.

Figurines have been recovered from mountain or hill-top sites where human remains have also been encountered. These sites include Ampato, Cerro Aconcagua, Cerro El Plomo and Nevado de Pichu Pichu. Cerro Esmeralda should perhaps also be listed, as the remains of shell figurines and the traces of metal on clothing of the two women raise the possibility of the presence of metal figurines, which were not recovered.[70] Of these sites, Ampato and Aconcagua have reliable data collected under archaeological control. The skeletal remains from Pichu Pichu have been identified as probably those of a young woman;[71] a female figurine was also found at the presumed tomb, but the finds were not recovered by archaeologists.[72] A similar situation applies in the case of El Plomo, the findspot of a young boy dressed in clothing associated with the Titicaca area, rather than in imperial Inca style.[73] The figurines found on the mountain included clothed females in silver[74] and shell[75]; their clothing is of an imperial Inca style that closely corresponds with that of the other figurines. A hollow gold male and a cast silver figurine, said to have weighed 3 kg, have also been reported from Cerro El Plomo.[76] Evidently these figurines were not buried with the young boy.[77]

More is known about the findspots of items from Aconcagua and Ampato. Three dressed male figurines were reported as being in the same fill as a boy aged seven or eight years of age on Aconcagua.[78] Dressed female figurines have also been found on Ampato, where one of shell accompanied a young girl on the ridge of the summit, and lower down, a silver male figurine was with the remains of a boy.[79] The same-sex groupings are significant with respect to the underlying principles with which the iconography of the Inca figurines is concerned, as discussed further below.

Clothed figurines are not only found on high-altitude shrines. At Túcume the figurines were excavated from a structure known as the Temple of the Sacred Stone, from phase ST-5, which dates from the Inca period.[80] In the courtyard in front of the temple there was a pit that contained a silver female figurine clad in a plainweave cloth; she was on her own. Further pits were found east and west of the doorway into the Temple. The western pit contained two female figurines. One was of *Spondylus* shell and was clothed in a dress, shawl and white feather headdress. It was sewn to a small log. Higher in the pit was another female figurine, a hollow silver one, dressed in a red and white dress and shawl with silver *tupu* pins, and an orange-red feather headdress.[81] To the east of the doorway another pit contained two male shell figurines wearing tunics: the taller one (64 mm) was higher up the pit and had better preserved clothing, while the smaller one (54 mm) was lower down the pit with less well preserved clothing.

It is perhaps significant that neither of the Túcume males had a feathered plume as part of their dress. There seems to be a strongly defined hierarchy of figurines, with the female ones in the western pit displaying the highest status. They are dressed in a similar manner to figurines from high-altitude shrines. The more soberly dressed female figurine in the courtyard pit provides a useful reminder that not all figurines represented the uppermost levels of Inca society.

At least five miniature human figurines were recovered by George A. Dorsey, who dug up an Inca site overlooking the Bahía de Drake in 1892, on the Isla de La Plata, Ecuador.[82] He found one silver, one copper and one shell figurine, and at least two gold figurines.[83] These items were found with other cultural material in the fill above two human skeletons, which were not recovered due to their poor state of conservation. It has been suggested that the individuals were both female because Dorsey found six full-sized *tupu* pins with the remains, which would correspond with the requisite set of three pins for each woman or girl.[84]

Inca figurines have also been found underwater in Lake Titicaca. Carved stone boxes were located at a site 130 km north-east of Khoa, a small island in the lake. A cuboid box with a lid contained two gold male and two silver male figurines, and a cylindrical box held a gold male figurine and a silver camelid figurine.[85] In yet another box there were three miniature gold *tupu* pins, but the figurine was missing.[86] A gold female figurine, 60 mm tall, was found south of the archaeological site; Reinhard suggests that it was dropped by a looter.[87] As with the Isla de La Plata figurines, the clothing has not survived. However, the three *tupu* pins imply a full set of clothing for the female figurine, and a gold plaque along with the male figurine in the cylindrical stone box suggests that it may have been attached to clothing that has not survived.

The pattern that emerges from a consideration of the contextual information revealed by archaeological research demonstrates that human figurines either occur alone or that they form same-sex groupings. A tabulation based on gender and material of figurines from known findspots is displayed in Table 4.1.

Information in sixteenth- and seventeenth-century chronicles

The chronicler Cristóbal de Molina commented that 'persons of gold and silver' accompanied children dedicated to Inca deities; the children were sent back to their communities of origin where they were sacrificed for the benefit of the

Table 4.1 Occurrence of female and male figurines according to material at Inca ritual sites.[88]

Female figurines					Male figurines		
Gold	Silver	Copper	Shell	Stone	Gold	Silver	Shell
High-altitude shrines							
3	12		5	1	3	2	7
Túcume, Sacsahuaman and Isla de La Plata							
2	5	1	2				2
Lake Titicaca							
1					2	2	
TOTALS							
6	17	1	7	1	5	4	9

community.[89] Records kept during the campaign of extirpation of idolatry led by Hernández Príncipe at Aixa, near Ocros, central Peru, in 1621, contain details of how the priest exhumed the remains of a sacrificed girl on the top of a high mountain. She had been buried alive, as a sacrifice to the sun, in order to have her father's governorship of the region formally confirmed and ratified by the Inca emperor. The priest listed among her grave goods small vessels, silver *tupu* pins and charms.[90] If these 'charms' were human figurines, then the items that accompanied her were similar to those found by Dorsey in the burial at Isla de La Plata, Ecuador. This complex of goods is also similar to that occurring with the burial of the young woman and the girl on Cerro Esmeralda, Chile.

However, the archaeological record gives a somewhat different picture than the scant details contained in the chronicles. Whereas the written accounts refer to single burials, we have seen that the archaeological details show interments of either single persons or same-sex groupings at ritual sites. In addition, the age range represented by these persons is wider than the boys and girls referred to in the chronicles (Molina specifically mentions children ten years old[91]). Young men and women as well as girls and boys have been found at high-altitude shrines and on Cerro Esmeralda.

Father Pablo José de Arriaga, another seventeenth-century extirpator of idolatry, refers in a report to a *saramama*, or 'maize mother', made from a maize stalk clothed as a woman in dress, shawl and *tupu* pins.[92] It is recorded in central Peru that people danced to and with the maize as part of the observances to Lliviac, the divinity of thunder and lightning. Irene Silverblatt says this was done to ensure a good harvest, and she suggests that *saramamas* were believed to engender maize in abundance.[93] It is possible that the anthropomorphized maize presented a local, more popular version of the metal and shell figurines that were used in the state-sponsored cults of the Inca empire. The reference to Lliviac is suggestive because a female figurine from Volcán Pili and two children found placed 6 m apart near the summit of Ampato show signs of having been struck by lightning.[94] It is possible that the double-headed serpents woven into the dresses and shawls of the female figurines, and into some of the male tunics, were associated with lightning.[95] The zigzag imagery in red and yellow was repeated on the face of the young boy sacrificed on Cerro El Plomo. His face was covered with a layer of red ochre, and four yellow diagonal lines of highly poisonous orpiment or arsenic sulphide were painted running from his cheekbones to the nose and corner of his mouth.[96]

The high-altitude shrines in Chile and Argentina and the burial at Isla de La Plata, Ecuador, were probably established as part of the project of imperial expansion that took place under the emperors Tupac Yupanqui and Guayna Capac between about 1470 and 1530. However, the underlying principles that gave form to rituals that involved both real humans and smaller simulacra of humans on the mountain tops had been generated in central Peru.

The hollow silver female figure weighing 3 kg, mentioned above as one of the finds reported from Cerro El Plomo,[97] would presumably not be categorized as a miniature. There are references to life-sized figures in the seventeenth-century accounts at the imperial capital of Cusco. An author of mixed Inca-Spanish descent, Garcilaso de la Vega, El Inga, gave an account of Cusco in a book intended for a European readership. In a series of chapters he examined a complex of buildings in Cusco, named by him 'the house and temple of the Sun';[98] he recalled the garden of gold and silver as it had existed in Inca times:

> It contained many herbs and flowers of various kinds, small plants, large trees, animals great and small, tame and wild, and creeping things such as snakes, lizards, and snails, butterflies and birds, each placed in an imitation of its natural surroundings. There was also a great maize field, a patch of the grain they call *quinua,* and other vegetables and fruit trees with their fruit all made of gold and silver in imitation of nature… Finally there were figures of men, women, and children cast in gold and silver, and granaries and barns, which they call *pirua,* to the great majesty and ornamentation of the house of their god, the Sun.[99]

Elsewhere, Garcilaso refers to the writings of Spanish authors who had seen the life-sized hollow statues of humans and animals with bodies of gold and silver.[100] In his account he conformed to the usual Spanish practice of referring to the Sun as the principal Inca divinity. Yet it is known that the Inca rulers, empress and emperor, considered themselves to be children of the Sun and Moon. Gold was considered to be the 'sweat of the sun' and silver 'the tears of the moon'.[101] It would seem that both these raw materials were embodied in human form by the empress and emperor. It is also known from the work of Guaman Poma that, while the emperor was considered to be the embodiment of the Sun and Moon, in death he was called *yllapa* (thunder-lightning).[102] If the miniature Inca figurines represented children of these elemental Inca divinities,[103] then no easy one-to-one identifications can be observed in the metals used to form the bodies of the figurines; silver and gold alloys were used alike for both female and male miniatures (Table 4.1). There is no gender dichotomy expressed in terms of the raw materials selected for the figurines. The most obvious outward expression of sexual difference occurs in the dress, which formed the outward marker of gender identity. This was reinforced by the arrangements noted above in which same-sex pairings or groupings of figurines occur at ritual sites.

An eighteenth-century painting in the Convent of St Teresa, Cusco, of a vision of the Virgin and Child to St Rose of Lima with native Andean donors retains this characteristic gender grouping.[104] The Andean wife and her daughter appear at the right of the canvas, while her husband and son are on the left. Teresa Gisbert points out that this arrangement is characteristic of medieval Flemish paintings where the kneeling donors are inserted into a religious scene.[105] However, the European formula of portraying mother and daughters on one side of the picture and father and sons on the other, as had been the customary arrangement for worship in church, was superseded in the late sixteenth century when family groups were portrayed as a mixed group.[106] The eighteenth-century Cusco painting would be curiously anachronistic unless the division of the family according to gender corresponded with a deeply rooted Andean tradition.[107] Gisbert characterizes Andean Baroque art as a fusion based on European mannerist styles that incorporated prehispanic religious elements into hispano-Christian forms. Although it has its own distinctiveness, Andean colonial art developed in step with changes that were occurring in Europe.[108]

Not only were art styles fused in the colonial period, the Spanish chroniclers, writing in the sixteenth and seventeenth centuries, viewed Inca art and institutions through their own perceptual frameworks. They were, at times, amazed by the coincidences with European practices that they saw in such an utterly different culture from their own. With wonderment they questioned whether the parallelism they observed in religious practices was the deception of the devil or the effect of what Fernando Cervantes has called 'Satan's incorrigible mimetic desire'.[109] One of

the notable cases of apparent parallelism the Spanish observed was the institution known as the *acllahuasi*, the houses of women chosen to dedicate their lives to the royal Inca cults of the Sun, Moon, Stars and holy shrines. Spanish observers tended to refer to these houses as 'convents', which, as Sabine MacCormack demonstrates in the case of the conquistador Juan Ruiz de Arce, led him to confuse the functions of the different houses in the imperial city of Cusco according to a Spanish model.[110] However, the institution of the *acllahuasi* demonstrates that single-sex corporate groups characterized at least some aspects of Inca society and provides a living counterpart to the same-sex groupings represented on ritual sites. The social organization of the Incas was given cultural expression in the distinctive garments worn by its members, which emphasized the gender, rank and ethnic identity of the wearer.[111] It was given further expression in the spatial organization of single- or same-sex groupings of figurines at certain sites, such as Túcume, Aconcagua, Isla de La Plata and Lake Titicaca.

The process of viewing another society through a foreign perceptual framework is evident in a work on Inca religion written by Father Bernabé Cobo in the seventeenth century, who relied heavily on sixteenth-century manuscripts among his sources.[112] We should recognize that the work conformed to the scholarly standards which prevailed at the time. In fact, the work is organized according to the Aristotelian or scholastic divisions employed in natural philosophy. Cobo himself mentioned that his account of Inca deities followed these divisions:

> Descending in the order that we are following here to the things that are in the closest and most familiar to us, such as those that are made up of the elements that we call perfectly mixed, both animate and inanimate, the fact that these Indians had specific gods for every kind of creature or thing within this whole category or list of perfectly mixed things – from the noblest of these creatures, which is man, to the lowest of them all...[113]

The translator and editor of the edition of Cobo's work used here has appended a footnote to explain that the Aristotelian or scholastic divisions to which Cobo alluded were divided into two basic categories: 'simple bodies' or elements and 'perfectly mixed elements'. The paradigm is presented in Table 4.2.

Although the chroniclers do not specifically discuss the occurrence of Inca figurines at high-altitude shrines and as votive deposits in Lake

Table 4.2 Paradigm of elements according to scholastic divisions[114]

I. Simple: air, water, earth and fire

II. Perfectly mixed
      A.   Inanimate: stones, metal, etc.
      B.   1. Plants
              2. Animals
                    a) Rational: humans
                    b) Irrational: all others

Titicaca, the thematic treatment of the iconography (including the contexts in which the figurines are found) might, from a Spanish perspective, have corresponded conveniently with existing European categories. In such a scheme, using the contemporary European classification, the imagery would refer to the 'simple elements': air, water, earth and fire (including lightning). The figurines themselves are made from 'perfectly mixed' elements in the scholastic divisions of natural philosophy. However, we should note that the study of the substances employed in the iconography of the Inca figurines demonstrates that Inca classifications would have cross-cut European categories.[115] Shell and metal were both used in making the bodies of the figurines, respectively products of water and earth. The clothing with which these bodies were wrapped are products of the animate world (camelid fleece, bird feathers and, to a lesser extent, plant fibres). This shows that the underlying principles of Inca iconography were ordered on a significantly different classificatory basis than the European model employed by Cobo. Although some apparent parallels between the classification of substances used in Inca and European art may have been perceived by Europeans, this study shows that the intrinsic meanings of Inca miniature figurines responded to underlying principles that emphasize the otherness of Inca culture with respect to European cultures of the sixteenth and seventeenth centuries. The dressed model humans constituted embodied forms in 'noble' materials that included gold, silver and shell taken from the domains of earth and sea. Such substances were probably used to express relationships with Inca divinities, the character of which was utterly different from European notions of divinity.

Conclusion

Clothed Inca figurines have been found in votive contexts (at high-altitude shrines, temple sites, on islands and in Lake Titicaca). As configurations of substance, form and imagery, the figurines would have conveyed intrinsic meanings to the Incas who made and used them. These meanings were expressed in the gender-specific garments with which the figurines were dressed, and in the groupings in which they have been found at particular sites. The fashioning of inorganic and organic substances into human shapes responded to underlying cultural principles that differed greatly from those of the Spanish observers of the Incas in the early colonial period.

The principles that were expressed visually in the clothed miniatures were derived from a nexus of culturally specific meanings. Elsewhere, I have suggested that Inca clothing served as an outer skin for the wearer, and that it stood in a metonymic relationship to the self.[116] Ethnographically, the language of weaving is employed by Qaqachaka women in Bolivia, who conceive of their houses as nests of concentric wrapped cloths, imbued with generative powers that animate the inhabitants. Qaqachaka women also refer to the cloths with which they wrap their babies as 'the mother nest'.[117]

Lechtman (1996) regards both cloth and metal as products of specific technological behaviour. She argues that the internal structure of many alloys in the Andes is the product of a manipulation of the microstructure that generates and releases the colour of the object, and that the inner essence of the object is part and parcel of its structure.[118] A complex nexus of ideas is given visual form in the clothed figurines.

Both female and male figurines display a 'kinship' with the elemental divinities of earth, moon, sun and lightning in the substances from which their bodies were formed and in the imagery woven into their clothing. However, their clothing also marks a strong gender difference that is reinforced by the same-sex groupings or solitary figures that have been found at ritual sites. It is this contextual information that helps elucidate the underlying principles that conditioned the iconography of the figurines. However, this 'iconography' is not amenable for study according to standard definitions of iconography as developed for a study of Western art. In particular, the drawing of distinctions between 'meaning' and 'form' cloud rather than clarify our understandings of the importance of the visual arts of the Incas.

Notes

1 Julie Jones, for example, described it as 'intellectual and ordered ….[c]ompact, integrated and simple' (1964: 5).

2 Panofsky 1974: 26.

3 This is the second of the three levels he says are involved in iconographic analysis. His first level consists of primary or natural subject matter (Panofsky 1974: 28-9). For the third level, which has to do with intrinsic meaning, see note 6 below.

4 Lyon 1983: 161.

5 Panofsky 1974: 32.

6 Ibid: 30. Panofsky used the term iconology for the study of intrinsic meaning, this being his third level of iconographic analysis.

7 Focillon 1966: 4.

8 Braun 1989: 159.

9 Ibid: 158.

10 Ibid: 163, n. 14. A detailed study of the relationships between Inca human and animal figurines would constitute a separate study, and for reasons of space cannot be explored here. Illustrations of camelid figurines made from metal alloys have been published by, among other authors, Morris and Thompson (1985, pl. 2 and col. pl. XIV) and McEwan, La Niece and Meeks (1996, figs 6 and 7). These miniature camelids often occur with, or appear in similar contexts to, human figurines. It should be noted that most of the camelid figurines are not wrapped in garments as are the human ones.

11 Myers 1993: 190.

12 Panofsky 1957: 35.

13 Ibid: 38.

14 Hocquenghem 1989: 22–3.

15 Ibid: 26.

16 Panofsky 1957: 39.

17 Mitchell 1995: 293.

18 The figurines discussed here are ones which have either been found with their clothing preserved or, in the case of unclad figurines, where there are indicators such as dress pins that suggest that they were once clothed.

19 Mitchell 1995: 296.

20 In ancient European thought the tetralogy of the elements concerned the four substances that were thought to be the foundation of everything: fire, air, water and earth.

21 Dransart 1995.

22 Klein 1995: 263.

23 Another approach to understanding the interrelatedness of form and meaning in the Andes is evident in the work of Mirko Lauer. Writing about Andean retables produced by Peruvian rural communities, Lauer discussed the relationship between images and the substance from which they are made. He observed that 'the object *is* its representation' under precapitalist conditions of production (1982: 149, emphasis in original). In this view modelled matter and meaning can present a unity of representation and material support.

24 Lechtman 1979.

25 Lechtman 1984.

26 Linares Málaga 1969: 281.

27 Oberhauser and Fuhrmann in Mostny 1957: 81.

28 Lechtman 1979: 32.

29 Ibid: 33.

30 Ibid: 32.

31 Most of the dressed figurines included in museum displays have had the clothing rearranged so as to make the face visible. It is interesting that a well-preserved female figurine excavated from a pit west of a structure identified as a temple at Túcume is illustrated as having the face all but hidden from view (Narváez 1995: fig. 81).

32 Baessler 1904: pl. 37, fig. 541.

33 Doering 1952.

34 Idiens 1971.

35 Schuler-Schomig 1972: 28–9; Lechtman in Rowe 1996: 308–9.

36 Guaman Poma 1980: 379.

37 Benson 1981:153.

38 It is interesting to note that the female figurines are not portrayed with a quid of coca in the mouth, nor do they have a little coca bag as part of their dress. In contrast, Guaman Poma (1980) drew noble Inca women with coca bags that resemble the miniature versions that accompany the dressed male figurines.

39 Lechtman 1979: 31.

40 Bray 1990: 310.

41 Rivero and Tschudi 1851: pl. XLIV; Kelemen 1956: pl. 204.

42 Rivero and Tschudi 1851: pl. XLIV.

43 Baessler 1904: pl. 37, fig. 543. I wish to thank R. Nigel Smith for providing a translation from the German.

44 Ibid: 135. This band may or may not represent a *llaut'u*, glossed as *ci[n]gulo que traen por sombrero*, or 'band which they wear for a hat', by Gonçalez Holguín (1989 [1608]: 212). Guaman Poma illustrated noble Inca men wearing *either* a band wrapped round the head, which he describes as being of different colours such as green or red (1980: 87, 97), *or* helmets. His drawing of a 'captain', or lord, from the Lake Titicaca area shows a man wearing a flat-topped, conical hat wrapped with a band or braid (1980: 71), but the dress of this personage is marked as ethnically non-Inca (the tunic and shoes are different and his headdress has ornaments attached typical of his region). For a further discussion of the *llaut'u* as an ethnic marker see Adorno 1987: 109–12). The dressed male figurine illustrated by Bray (1990: 314) has the band tied round the body of the figurine to hold the wrapped mantle in place.

45 Uhle 1991.

46 Narváez 1995: 109.

47 Schobinger, Ampuero and Guercio 1984–5: 183. This type of headgear is known in the literature as *gorro tipo fez* ('a fez-type hat'; Iriarte and Renard 1998: 86).

48 Paulsen 1974.

49 Cabello Valboa 1951: 322.

50 Gonçalez Holguín 1989: 225.

51 Baessler 1904: 135, fig. 543; Bray 1990: 314, fig. 242.

52 Narváez 1995.

53 For further details consult McEwan and Van de Guchte (1992), Dransart (1995) and Reinhard (1996). Other dressed or partially clad figurines without known findspots are known in museum and private

collections. See Damian (1995: 85, fig. 50); Dransart (1995: Appendix D); Sotheby (1994: cat. no. 35).

54 Beorchia Nigris 1987; Museo Chileno de Arte Precolombino 1986; Reinhard 1992b: 88.

55 Checura Jeria 1977: 136.

56 Further details of the miniature shawl and accompanying cord in the Museum of Mankind are given in Dransart (1995: 55, no. 22). Following criteria established by Anne Pollard Rowe (1977), I identified the shawl as a warp-faced weave with camelid fibre warp and a cotton weft that was used paired. Rowe has published revised criteria for examining weaves that have closely comparable warp-faced and weft-faced counterparts (A. Rowe 1995–6). She has amended her analysis of Inca women's garments and now considers the miniature shawls to be executed in weft-faced weaves. The shawl in Fig. 4.7 should probably be considered to have a cotton warp (used paired) and camelid fibre weft. I wish to thank Alexandra Morgan for showing me Rowe's 1995–6 article.

57 Uhle 1991: 84.

58 Beorchia Nigris 1987: 41.

59 Dransart 1995: Appendix B, nos 17 and 18.

60 Ibid: nos 10 and 11.

61 Schobinger *et al.* 1985: 182.

62 Naville 1958: 5; Schobinger 1986: 317.

63 Dransart 1995: 9–10.

64 Dransart 1992: 146.

65 Valcárcel 1935: 180.

66 Beorchia Nigris 1987: 127.

67 Ibid: 126.

68 Rebitsch 1967: 54–5.

69 Reinhard 1992a: 157–63.

70 Checura Jeria 1977: 133.

71 Dr Luis Fernán Zegarra, cited by Linares Málaga 1969: 290.

72 Linares Málaga 1969: 275.

73 Mostny 1957.

74 Ibid.

75 Medina Rojas 1958: 54.

76 Ibid: 54.

77 Mostny 1957: 46.

78 Schobinger 1986: 298.

79 Reinhard 1996: 68 and 74.

80 Narváez 1995: 107.

81 Ibid: 109.

82 Dorsey 1901.

83 McEwan and Silva 1988: 169.

84 Dransart 1995: 10.

85 Reinhard 1992c: 431.

86 Siñanis 1992: 448.

87 Reinhard 1992c: 433.

88 Based on Beorchia Nigris 1987; Dransart 1995; McEwan and Silva 1988; Narváez 1995; Reinhard 1996 and 1997; and Valcárcel 1935.

89 Molina 1947 (1577): 133.

90 Hernández Príncipe 1923: 61–2.

91 Molina 1947: 133.

92 Arriaga 1968: 204.The Spanish administrator Polo de Ondegardo also mentioned 'maize mothers' of

maize stalks dressed in fine shawls (cited in Silverblatt 1987: 25).

93 Silverblatt 1987: 25–7.

94 Luis Ramírez Aban, pers. comm. 1987; Reinhard 1996: 74.

95 In the Quechua myths recounting inter-ethnic struggles, collected at Huarochirí (central Peru), a battle between the divinities Pariacaca and Huallallo Carhuincho took place. The latter caused an enormous double-headed serpent to rise against the thunderbolts of Pariacaca. Infuriated, Pariacaca transfixed the serpent with a gold rod, and it was transmuted into rock (Taylor 1987: 259–61).

96 Mostny 1957: 31.

97 Medina Rojas 1958: 54.

98 Garcilaso 1989 (1609): 179.

99 Ibid: 188.

100 Ibid: 316, 318. Unfortunately, Garcilaso did not say whether or not these statues were dressed with woven garments.

101 Coutts 1990.

102 Guaman Poma 1980: 290. See also fig. 4.2.

103 Thomas Patterson (1983: 166) has proposed a model based on kin and affinal relationships for understanding relationships between the Inca oracle of Pachacamac and other branch oracles, which were considered to be the wife and children of the Temple of Pachacamac.

104 Gisbert 1980: fig. 91; Mujica Pinilla 1995: 178, pl. 80.

105 Gisbert 1980: 90.

106 Musées Royaux de Beaux Arts 1973: 67.

107 Note also that Guaman Poma (1980) separates the Inca royal lineage according to gender.

108 Gisbert 1980: 11.

109 Cervantes 1991: 22.

110 MacCormack 1991: 65, N12.

111 Adorno has argued that clothing can serve as a vestimentary code (1987: 103).

112 Cobo 1990.

113 Ibid: 35.

114 Cobo 1990: 254.

115 Dransart 1995: 2.

116 Dransart 1992: 146.

117 Arnold 1992: 55–6.

118 Lechtman 1996: 42.

References

Adorno, R.
1987 Sobre el lenguaje pictórico y la tipología cultural en una crónica andina. *Revista Chungará* 18 (August): 101–43.

Arnold, D.Y.
1992 La casa de adobes y piedras del Inka: género, memoria y cosmos en Qaqachaka. In D.Y. Arnold, D. Jiménez A. and J. de D. Yapita, *Hacia un Orden Andino de las Cosas*. Hisbol/ILCA, La Paz.

Arriaga, P.J. de
1968 (1621) La extirpación de la idolatría en el Perú. *Biblioteca de Autores Españoles*, vol. 209, pp. 191–277.

Baessler, Arthur
1904 *Altperuanische Metallgeräte*. Berlin.

Bell, C.
1914 *Art*. Chatto and Windus, London.

Benson, E.
1981 Commentary texts. In *Museums of the Andes*. Newsweek, Inc. and Kodansha Ltd, Tokyo.

Beorchia Nigris
1987 *El Enigma de los Santuarios Indígenas de Alta Montaña*. San Juan, Argentina: CIADAM.

Braun, B.
1989 Henry Moore and Pre-Columbian Art. *Res: Journal of Anthropology and Aesthetics* 17/18: 158–97.

Bray, W.
1990 Le travail du metal dans le Pérou prehispanique. In *Inca Perú: 3000 ans d'histoire*, ed. S. Purin, pp. 292–315. Musées Royaux d'Art et d'Histoire, Brussels.

Cabello Valboa, M.
1951 (1586) *Miscelanea Antártica*. Universidad Nacional Mayor de San Marcos, Lima.

Cervantes, F.
1991 *The Idea of the Devil and the Problem of the Indian: the case of Mexico in the sixteenth century*. Institute of Latin American Studies Research Papers no. 24, University of London.

Checura Jeria, J.
1977 Funebria incaica en el Cerro Esmeralda (Iquique, I Región), *Estudios Atacameños* 5: 125–141.

Cobo, B.
1956 (1653) *Obras*, ed. P. Francisco Mateos. Biblioteca de Autores Españoles, Tomo 92. Madrid.
1990 *Inca Religion and Customs*, trans. and ed. R. Hamilton. University of Texas Press, Austin.

Coutts, H. (ed.)
1990 *Sweat of the Sun: Gold of Peru*. City of Edinburgh Museums and Art Galleries, Edinburgh.

Damian, C.
1995 *The Virgin of the Andes: Art and Ritual in Colonial Cuzco*. Grassfield Press, Miami Beach.

Doering, H.U.
1952 *The Art of Ancient Peru*. A. Zwemmer Ltd, London.

Dorsey, G.A.
1901 *Archaeological Investigations on the Island of La Plata, Ecuador*. Field Columbian Museum Publication 56, Anthropological Series II(5).

Dransart, P.
1992 Pachamama: the Inka Earth Mother. In *Dress and Gender: Making and Meaning in Cultural Contexts*, ed. R. Barnes and J.B. Eicher, pp. 145–63. Berg, New York and Oxford.
1995 *Elemental Meanings: Symbolic Expression in Inka Miniature Figurines*. Institute of Latin American Studies Research Papers, University of London.

Farago, C. (ed.)
1995 *Reframing the Renaissance: Visual Culture in Europe and Latin America 1450–1650*. Yale University Press, New Haven and London.

Focillon, H.
1966 (1948) *The Life of Forms in Art*. George Wittenborn Inc., New York.

Fry, R.E.
1920 *Vision and Design*. Chatto and Windus, London.

Garcilaso de la Vega, El Inca
1989 *Royal Commentaries of the Incas and General History of Peru*, Part One, trans. Harold V. Livermore. University of Texas Press, Austin, Texas.

Gisbert, T.
1980 *Iconografía y Mitos en el Arte*. Gisbert y Cia. S.A., La Paz.

Gonçález Holguín, D.
1989 (1608) *Vocabulario de la Lengua General de Todo el Peru Llamada Lengua Qquichua o del Inca*. Lima: Universidad Nacional Mayor de San Marcos.

Guaman Poma de Ayala, F.
1980 *El Primer Nueva Crónica y Buen Gobierno*, ed. J.V. Murra and R. Adorno. Siglo Veintiuno and Instituto de Estudios Peruanos, Mexico.

Hernández Príncipe, R.
1923 (1621) Mitología Andina, *Inca* I: 25–68.

Hocquenghem, A.M.
1989 *Iconografía mochica*. Pontificia Universidad Católica del Perú Fondo Editorial, Lima.

Idiens, D.
1971 *Ancient American Art*. Royal Scottish Museum, Edinburgh.

Iriarte, I. and S.F. Renard
1998 Textiles del norte de Chile en la colección Echeverría y Reyes del Museo Etnográfico de la Universidad de Buenos Aires. *Boletín del Comité Nacional de Conservación Textil* 3: 81–101.

Jones, J.
1964 *Art of Empire: The Inca of Peru*. The Museum of Primitive Art, New York.

Kelemen, P.
1956 *Medieval American Art: Masterpieces of the New World before Columbus*. Macmillan, New York.

Klein, C.
1995 Wild woman in Colonial Mexico: an encounter of European and Aztec concepts of the other. In C. Farago (ed.) 1995, pp. 244–63.

Kubler, G.
1962 *The Shape of Time: Remarks on the History of Things*. Yale University Press, New Haven and London.

Lauer, M.
1982 La estructura del objeto plástico. In *Crítica de la Artesanía: Plástica y Sociedad en los Andes Peruano*, ch. VIII. Desco, Lima.

Lechtman, H.
1979 Issues in Andean metallurgy. In *Pre-Columbian Metallurgy of South America*, ed. E.P. Benson, pp. 1–40. Dumbarton Oaks Research Library and Collections, Washington DC.
1984 Andean value systems and the development of prehistoric metallurgy, *Technology and Culture* 25(1): 1–36.
1996 Cloth and metal: the culture of technology. In *Andean Art at Dumbarton Oaks*, ed. Elizabeth Hill Boone, pp. 33–43. Dumbarton Oaks Research Library and Collection, Washington, DC.

Linares Málaga, E.
1969 Restos arqueológicos en el nevado Pichu-Pichu. In *Mesa Redonda de Ciencias Prehistóricas y Antropológicas* II, pp. 273–94. Pontificia Universidad Católica del Perú, Instituto Riva-Agüero, Seminario de Antropología, Lima.

Lyon, P. J.
1983 Hacia una interpretación rigurosa del arte antiguo peruano. *Historia y Cultura* 16: 161–73.

MacCormack, S.
1991 *Religion in the Andes: Vision and Imagination in Early Colonial Peru*. Princeton University Press, Princeton, New Jersey.

McEwan, C. and M.I. Silva Itturalde
1988 ¿Qué fueron a hacer los incas en la costa central del Ecuador? In *Relaciones Interculturales en el Area Ecuatorial del Pacífico durante la Epoca Precolombina*, ed. J.F. Bouchard and M. Guinea. BAR International Series 503: 163–85.

McEwan, C. and Maarten Van de Guchte
1992 Ancestral Time and Sacred Space in Inca State Ritual. In *Ancient Americas – Art from Sacred Landscapes*, ed. Richard F. Townsend. The Art Institute of Chicago.

McEwan, C., S. La Niece and N. Meeks
1996 The Gilded Image: Precolumbian Gold from South and Central America. *Minerva* 7(3), May/June: 10–16.

Medina Rojas, A.
1958 Hallazgos arqueológicos en el Cerro El Plomo. *Arqueología Chilena* 4.

Mitchell, W.J. T.
1995 Iconology, ideology, and cultural encounter: Panofsky, Althusser, and the scene of recognition. In C. Farago (ed.) 1995, pp. 292–300.

Molina, C. de
1947 (1577) *Ritos y Fábulas de los Incas*. Editorial Futuro, Buenos Aires.

Morris, C. and D. E. Thompson
1985 *Huánuco Pampa: An Inca City and Its Hinterland*. Thames and Hudson, London.

Mostny, G. (ed.)
1957 La momia del Cerro el Plomo. *Boletín del Museo Nacional de Historia Natural* XXVII(1).

Mujica Pinilla, R.
1995 El ancla de Santa Rosa de Lima: mística y política en torno a la Patrona de América. In J. Flores Araoz, R. Mujica Pinilla, L.E. Wuffarden and P. Guibovich Pérez, *Santa Rosa de Lima y su Tiempo*, pp. 54–211. Banco de Crédito del Perú, Colección Arte y Tesoros del Perú, Lima.

Musées Royaux des Beaux Arts
1973 *Art Ancien*, 8th edn. Musées Royaux des Beaux Arts, Bruxelles.

Museo Chileno de Arte Precolombino
1986 *Diaguitas, Pueblos del Norte Verde*. Museo Chileno de Arte Precolombino. Santiago.

Myers, K.A.
1993 The representation of New World phenomena: visual epistemology and Gonzalo Fernández de Oviedo's illustrations. In *Early Images of the Americas: Transfer and Invention*, ed. J.M. Williams and R.E. Lewis, pp. 183–213. University of Arizona Press, Tucson.

Narváez, A.
1995 The pyramids of Túcume: the monumental sector. In T. Heyerdahl, D.H. Sandwiess and A. Narváez *The Pyramids of Túcume: The Quest for Peru's Forgotten City*, pp 79–130. Thames and Hudson, London.

Naville, R.
1958 Sanctuaires incas dans la cordillère des Andes. *Bulletin de la Société Suisse des Américanistes* 16 (September): 1–5.

Panofsky, E.
1974 (1955) Iconography and iconology: an introduction to the study of Renaissance art. In *Meaning in the Visual Arts: Papers in and on Art History*, pp. 26–54. The Overlook Press, Woodstock, New York.

Patterson, T.C.
1983 Pachacamac – an Andean oracle under Inca rule. In *Recent Studies in Andean Prehistory and Protohistory*, ed. D.P. Kvietok and D.H. Sandweis, pp. 159–74. Cornell University, Papers from the Second Annual Northeast Conference on Andean Archaeology and Protohistory, Latin American Program.

Paulsen, A.C.
1974 The thorny oyster and the voice of god: *Spondylus* and *Strombus* in Andean prehistory, *American Antiquity* 39(4): 597–607.

Rebitsch, M.
1967 Santuarios indígenas en altas cumbres de la Puna de Atacama. Informe sobre las cuatro expediciones argentino-austríacas 1956–1965. *Anales de Arqueología y Etnología* 21: 51–125.

Reinhard, J.
1992a An archaeological investigation of Inca ceremonial platforms on the Volcano Copiapo, Central Chile. In *Ancient America: contributions to New World archaeology*, ed. N.J. Saunders, pp. 145–72. Oxbow Monograph 24, Oxford.
1992b Sacred peaks of the Andes. *National Geographic* (March): 84–111.
1992c Investigaciones arqueológicas subacuáticas en el lago Titikaka. In Carlos Ponce Sanguinés, Johan Reinhard, Max Portugal, Eduardo Pareja, Leocadio Ticlla, *Arqueología Subacuática en el Lago Titikaka: Informe científico*, pp. 419–30. La Palabra Producciones, La Paz.
1996 Peru's ice maidens: unwrapping the secrets. *National Geographic* 189(6) (June): 62–81.
1997 Sharp eyes of science probe the mummies of Peru. *National Geographic* 191(1) (January): 36–43.

Rivero y Ustariz, M.E. de, and J.D. de Tschudi
1851 *Antigüedades Peruanas*. Litografía de Leopoldo Müller (Atlas), Vienna.

Rowe, A.P.
1977 *Warp-Patterned Weaves of the Andes*. The Textile Museum, Washington DC.
1995–6 Inca weaving and costume. *The Textile Museum Journal* 34–5: 4–53.

Rowe, J.H.
1979 Standardization in Inca tapestry tunics. In *The Junius B. Bird Pre-Columbian Textile Conference*, ed. A.P. Rowe, E.P. Benson, A.-L. Schaffer, pp. 239–64. The Textile Museum and Dumbarton Oaks, Washington DC.
1996 Inca. In *Andean Art at Dumbarton Oaks*, ed. Elizabeth Hill Boone, pp. 301–20. Dumbarton Oaks Research Library and Collection, Washington, DC.

Schobinger, J.
1986 La red de santuarios de alta montaña en el Contisuyo y el Collasuyo: evaluación general, problemas interpretativos. *Comechingonia Número Especial El Imperio Inka*, pp. 295–317, Volumen Homenaje al 45° Congreso Internacional de Americanistas.

Schobinger, J., M. Ampuero and E. Guercio
1984–5 Descripción de las estatuillas que conforman el ajuar acompañante del fardo funerario halloado en el cerro Aconcagua (Provincia de Mendoza). *Relaciones de la Sociedad Argentina de Antropología* XVI: 175–90.

Schuler-Schomig, I. von
1972 *Werke indianischer Goldschmiedekunst. Im Museum für Volkerkunde, Berlin*. Gebr. Mann, Berlin.

Silverblatt, I.
1987 *Moon, Sun, and Witches: Gender Ideologies and Class in Inca and Colonial Peru*. Princeton University Press, Princeton, New Jersey.

Sotheby
1994 Catalogue No. 35, 15 November 1994. New York.

Taylor, G.
1987 *Ritos y Tradiciones de Huarochirí del Siglo XVII*. Instituto de Estudios Peruanos and Instituto Francés de Estudios Andinos, Lima.

Uhle, M.
1991 (1903) *Pachacamac: A Reprint of the 1903*

Edition (introduced by I. Shimada). University
Museum Monograph 62, Philadelphia.

Valcárcel, L.E.
1935 Los trabajos arqueológicos en el
Departamento del Cusco. Sajsawaman
redescubierto (IV). *Revista del Museo Nacional*
IV(2): 161–205.

Acknowledgements

I wish to thank Colin McEwan for inviting me to
contribute to the conference held at the Museum of
Mankind. In addition, I wish to thank Warwick
Bray, Alexandra Morgan and Bill Sillar for showing me some of the items listed in the bibliography.

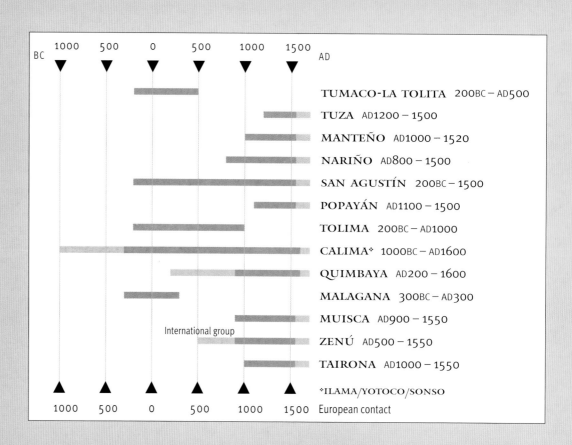

BC 1000 500 0 500 1000 1500 AD

TUMACO-LA TOLITA 200BC – AD500

TUZA AD1200 – 1500

MANTEÑO AD1000 – 1520

NARIÑO AD800 – 1500

SAN AGUSTÍN 200BC – 1500

POPAYÁN AD1100 – 1500

TOLIMA 200BC – AD1000

CALIMA✤ 1000BC – AD1600

QUIMBAYA AD200 – 1600

MALAGANA 300BC – AD300

International group

MUISCA AD900 – 1550

ZENÚ AD500 – 1550

TAIRONA AD1000 – 1550

✤ILAMA/YOTOCO/SONSO

1000 500 0 500 1000 1500 European contact

ECUADOR AND COLOMBIA

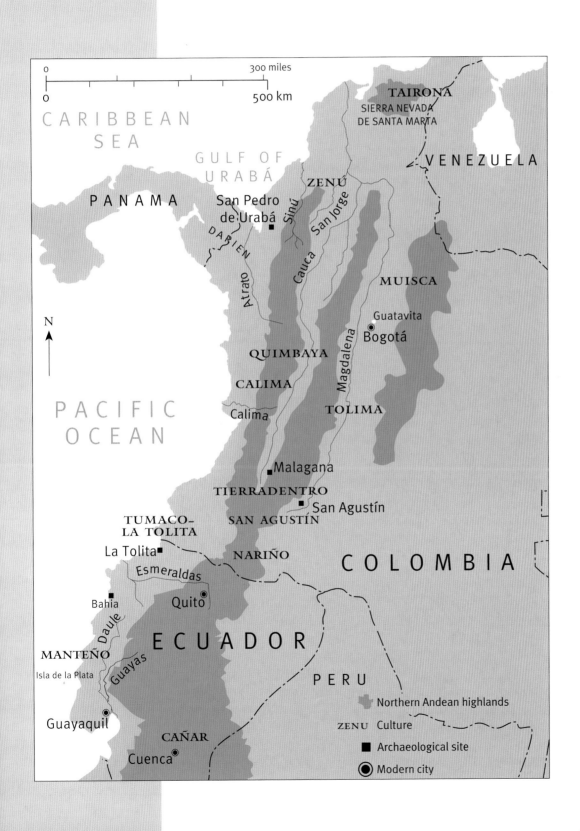

CARIBBEAN SEA

GULF OF URABÁ

PANAMA

TAIRONA

SIERRA NEVADA
DE SANTA MARTA

VENEZUELA

ZENÚ

San Pedro
de Urabá

Sinú

DARIEN

San Jorge

Cauca

Atrato

MUISCA

Guatavita

Bogotá

QUIMBAYA

Magdalena

N

PACIFIC
OCEAN

CALIMA

Calima

TOLIMA

Malagana

TIERRADENTRO

San Agustín

SAN AGUSTÍN

TUMACO–
LA TOLITA

La Tolita

NARIÑO

COLOMBIA

Esmeraldas

Bahia

Daule

Quito

ECUADOR

MANTEÑO

Guayas

PERU

Isla de la Plata

Northern Andean highlands

ZENÚ   Culture

Guayaquil

CAÑAR

Cuenca

■ Archaeological site

◉ Modern city

0 ——————— 300 miles
0 ——————— 500 km

5

Malagana and the Goldworking Tradition of Southwest Colombia

Warwick Bray

Towards the end of 1992 the Museo del Oro in Bogotá was offered a group of spectacular gold objects in a previously unknown style. Investigations showed that these items had come from a newly discovered site at the Hacienda Malagana, near the town of Palmira in the floodplain of the Cauca valley at 1,000 m above sea level (see map on previous page).

The story of the 'Malagana Treasure' began with an agricultural accident when a tractor, working in an apparently featureless sugar cane field, fell into a collapsed tomb, and the driver saw the glint of gold. According to local rumour, he removed the gold, abandoned both his tractor and his job, and discreetly sold the artefacts. The secret could not be kept for long, and the initial find stimulated what can only be called a gold rush.

Between October and December 1992 Malagana was invaded by treasure hunters from all the surrounding areas.[1] Newspaper reporters who visited the scene estimated that 5,000 people had converged on the cemetery and, despite the presence of both the police and the army, the situation escalated out of control, with at least one murder.[2] In a few months of frenzied digging, huge quantities of gold, pottery and other artefacts were looted, and the scientific context of a unique archaeological discovery was largely destroyed.

In a rescue operation the Museo del Oro managed, over a period of time, to amass a large and representative collection of Malagana goldwork. The catalogue of this collection lists more than 150 accessions,[3] many of them multiple sets of beads and pendants, and an even greater quantity of material is in private hands. Some observers estimate that the total weight of gold removed from the cemetery was between 140 and 180 kg.[4] Other informal estimates are even higher.

Excavations at the Hacienda Malagana

The first scientific excavations at Malagana were carried out in March 1993, when the treasure hunt was still at its height.[5] During the few days before the archaeologists were forced to retreat, they were able to excavate three graves and to demonstrate that the site had a complex history of occupation. One of the tombs, already partially looted, still contained two pots and two gold beads like those in Fig. 5.7:19, 24. These two little beads are the only gold objects professionally excavated from the main cemetery area. The excavation also gave the first radiocarbon date for Malagana: AD 70 ± 60 (uncalibrated) from a buried soil containing fragments of pottery.

At the end of 1994, when the site was once again a peaceful cane field, excavation resumed under the direction of Marianne Cardale de Schrimpff, Leonor Herrera and Carlos Armando Rodríguez with a team of Colombian archaeologists. By that time the destruction of the cemetery area was complete, so the excavators concentrated on an undamaged zone of domestic occupation some 500 m away. Here they uncovered the remains of household activities (though any wooden structures had long decayed), excavated seventeen burials (two of which contained small items of gold jewellery) and established the basic history and chronology of the Malagana settlement.[6]

The site proved to have a long and complicated stratigraphy. Four periods of occupation were distinguished and are named, from the earliest to the most recent, 'Proto-Ilama' (the provisional name for a phase still poorly understood), then 'Ilama', 'Malagana' and 'Sonsoid' (see chronology, p. 92). Only the first three of these are relevant to the present study.

In the habitation area the initial Proto-Ilama occupation floor gave radiocarbon dates of 300 BC ± 50 years and 250 BC ± 100. The pottery trodden into this floor seems related to (and possibly ancestral to) the mature Ilama style known from the neighbouring Calima region in the western cordillera, with dates in the first millennium BC (see chronology, p. 92).[7]

After a break marked by the accumulation of clays and other alluvial deposits, people using pottery identical to the Ilama wares of Calima were present in the excavated area. A single radiocarbon date of 290 BC ± 60 comes from this occupation.

From the end of the Ilama period the histories of Calima and Malagana began to diverge. In the cordillera the Ilama style developed into what is called the Yotoco style;[8] in the Palmira region of the Cauca valley Ilama was followed by the style we now call Malagana. Reciprocal trade in ceramics and gold artefacts between these two regions demonstrates that the old contacts were maintained, but the people of Malagana now had a distinct regional culture with an easily recognizable style of its own.[9]

For this period at the Hacienda Malagana there are four radiocarbon determinations: 180 BC ± 150, 140 BC ± 60, 90 BC ± 60 and AD 30 ± 85 (information from Marianne Cardale and Leonor Herrera). On present evidence there seems to be no significant occupation after the second century AD. These radiocarbon dates confirm what the ceramic cross-links had already suggested, that the main occupation at the Malagana site falls roughly between the fourth century BC and the second century AD, and is contemporary with late Ilama and early Yotoco in the cordillera. The significance of these connections between Calima and Malagana is discussed below.

There are, however, two chronological problems: (a) we cannot yet be sure that the entire history of settlement at Malagana is represented within the excavated area, and (b) because of the way in which the main cemetery was looted, we cannot directly associate the gold artefacts with any particular subperiod(s) or assume that all the radiocarbon dates from the habitation area can be applied to the tombs. On the positive side, even though the precise duration of occupation at the Hacienda Malagana is still uncertain, we now have a good approximation for the age of the goldwork.

The context of the Malagana gold

The excavations in the domestic area of the site unearthed a few tiny beads and scraps of gold wire, lost or discarded by the inhabitants, but any study of Malagana goldwork must be based on the finds from the main cemetery. Because these tombs were looted without any record, background information on the artefacts is minimal. It is clear that hundreds of tombs were destroyed but (apart from the objects themselves) our only sources of information are the recollections of people who took part in these events. Their accounts are unverifiable, sometimes inconsistent, and may not be accurate in every detail, but from conversations with eyewitnesses the archaeologists have obtained a general idea of the funerary rituals and have been able to reconstruct twenty-nine grave groups (see the Appendix, p. 110).[10] To this can be added the seventeen graves from the domestic area.

The tombs at Malagana consisted of rectangular pits, some of them shallow, others 3 m or more in depth. Usually there was only a single corpse, laid on its back on the tomb floor and oriented north–south or east–west, though a few skeletons were in flexed positions, others were incomplete, and a small number had been burned. Two burials were of heads only. Informants agree that most of the graves contained either no gold whatsoever or just one or two simple trinkets, sometimes with a few pots, stone beads or shells. The poorest graves contained no offerings at all.

By contrast, a few tombs, clearly the burials of the Malagana elite, contained most of the goldwork and all the largest and finest artefacts. The contents of nine such tombs are listed in the Appendix, but we must bear in mind that fragile organic materials (wood, feathers, basketry, textiles, foodstuffs) are not preserved in the tropical conditions at Malagana. All the tombs except one are said to have held a single body. The exception, Tomb 6, was a pit 3 m deep and contained three skeletons, though the gold items were associated exclusively with the principal corpse, which was laid out on a row of stone *metates* (maize-grinding slabs). The accompanying bodies may have been those of wives or retainers, as described in the first Spanish accounts from South America more than a thousand years later.

The information in the Appendix also shows that even the richest burials had very little pottery, and sometimes none at all. Instead the emphasis was on jewellery and regalia. If we can rely on reports that each tomb contained the property of a single individual, it appears that some members of the governing group (in death, and presumably in life as well) were richer than others. Assuming that this pattern is not simply a statistical accident, it may indicate that various degrees of rank and status existed within the Malagana elite.

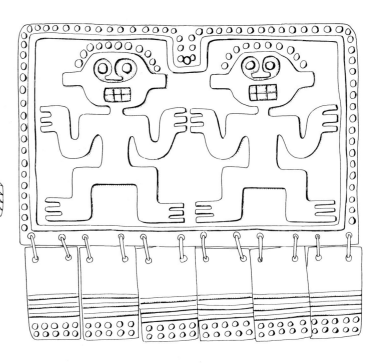

5.1 Hanging plaques (probably ear ornaments) in Malagana style. Each is one of a pair. The figures on the right-hand plaque may be wearing masks similar to the one in Fig. 5.2.

Very occasionally we have detailed eyewitness accounts of the layout of the offerings within the tomb. The following description, taken from the archives of the Museo del Oro, refers to what must have been one of the richest graves at the site (see also Appendix, Tomb 1). The tomb consisted of a rectangular shaft about 3 m deep, filled with gravel and river sand containing specks of alluvial gold.

The floor was paved with rectangular slabs of a white granitic stone foreign to the Cauca floodplain, and a single course of more rounded stones had been placed around the base of the walls to define the funerary area. A conical object of carved stone lay somewhere in the burial zone.

The body was stretched out on its back on the floor of the tomb, and the face was covered by

5.2 Malagana-style mask (width 57.2 cm).

three large sheet-gold masks, one on top of the other. In the neck area were tubular gold beads and little gold birds, together with necklaces of coloured stone beads, carved emeralds and red *Spondylus* shell, and enough tiny stone beads to form a string about 50 m long. Gold beads were found in the neck area and in a single row on the chest (for comparable examples see Fig. 5.7:17). A sheet-gold mask concealed the feet of the corpse. The published accounts also list two pendant-plaques and two plaques for sewing onto textiles. A set of bone tubes (or cylindrical beads) found just below the waist may have been attached to a loincloth or kilt like those represented on miniature gold figurines,[11] and the legs of the skeleton were separated by a line of rock crystal beads. In a niche in the wall above the head of the corpse were two Ilama-style pots: one a bowl with four feet and the other an *alcarraza* (a vessel with two spouts joined by a bridge handle) in the form of a recumbent woman. A layer of between fifty and one hundred stone slabs of various sizes covered and protected the entire funerary deposit.

Reports by other finders confirm that items of jewellery were usually found in their correct places on the skeletons, with other belongings (such as lime-flasks) placed conveniently to hand. Extra items were piled in the corners of the tombs, an observation confirmed by marks in the surface patina of gold artefacts showing where one object had rested on another.

By combining these first-hand accounts with the study of the objects themselves, we can re-create the ceremonial costume of an elite personage. Around the head was a golden crown or a diadem hung with bird effigies and stylized human figures cut out of sheet metal, or plaques with repoussé designs like those in Fig. 5.1. Similar plaques also served as ear-danglers, though the more common type of ear decoration was a bobbin-like spool (Fig. 5.18e). The septum of the nose was perforated to take a nose-ring or a crescent-shaped ornament of sheet gold (Fig. 5.18c). Some of the masks have decoration on their cheeks, and this may represent face paint, tattoos or scarification. It is not clear whether the gold masks were used in life or were made exclusively for the tomb. Some masks seem too large to wear (Fig. 5.2) and others have no eye holes, but experiment shows that many of them could have been worn and that, in spite of the eye discs, the wearer can see quite well. Other masks are much smaller and probably served as costume accessories (Fig. 5.3).

The upper body must have been almost invisible under a mass of necklaces. Spacer beads,

which keep the strands separate, have up to twelve holes, and the beads must have been arranged to form wide collars. Imprints of these can still be seen in the patina on sheet-metal breast ornaments (Fig. 5.12). Men and women wore decorative bands around their arms and legs, but we also have sets of gold bracelets or broad cuffs made from hammered sheet metal. The miniature gold figurines depict many different kinds of kilts, loincloths or waist-belts, and some of the embossed and perforated plaques may have been sewn to garments of one kind or another.

This is an idealized re-creation. The funerary offerings indicate that not every member of the elite owned a full set of regalia, nor can we be sure that all these items were worn at the same time. Since we have no information about the age or sex of the corpses in individual tombs, the

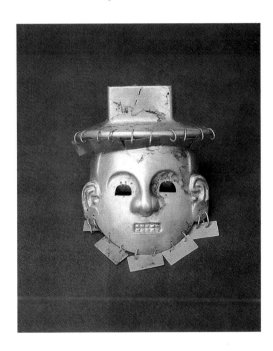

reconstruction artificially combines men's and women's items into a single composite outfit. It is evident, too, that this was a costume for ceremonial or ritual occasions, not for everyday wear, and representations in both gold and pottery suggest that for most of the time the people of Malagana wore very little clothing.

Form and decoration in Malagana goldwork

The gold objects from Malagana fall into three groups: imported items (discussed in later sections of this paper), categories unique to Malagana, and Malagana versions of artefacts common to all the cultures of southwest Colombia. A good

5.3 Miniature sheet-gold mask from Malagana (one of a set) with holes at the sides for attachment to some kind of backing (height 9.3 cm).

5.4 Large sheet-metal cut-out human figure (height 42 cm).

deal of the goldwork may have been produced locally. Although no workshops have yet been discovered, one of the tombs in the cemetery yielded a metalworking tool in the form of a carved bone with bead designs in high relief (see Appendix, Tomb 7), and other tombs contained bits of wire, sheet-metal offcuts and broken artefacts that seem to be scrap metal.

Very few formal categories are, in fact, unique to Malagana. Most of these are beads and pendants (see below), but the list also includes large cut-out human figures (Fig. 5.4), and the composite creature, combining human, bird and crocodilian features, illustrated in Fig. 5.5.

Most of the gold pieces from Malagana have their functional counterparts elsewhere (see Tables 5.1–2). Full-sized masks, lime-flasks and lime-dippers, trumpets and rattles, chisels, axes, ceremonial staffs, diadems, breastplates and pectorals, are all pan-Colombian forms, though each

5.5 (above) Sheet-metal creature combining human, bird and crocodilian elements, from Malagana (height 11.9 cm).

5.6 (above right) Malagana-style 'tweezer ornament' (height 23 cm).

local culture made its own regional variants. There is, however, one artefact that is restricted to the Southwest and has been found at Malagana, San Agustín and in Calima. In general appearance it looks like a set of tweezers (Fig. 5.6), but is too large to be functional and is always elaborately decorated, frequently with designs based on the human face. It is also depicted on Malagana pottery. The function of these tweezer-ornaments remains unknown but their size, and the quality of

At the naturalistic end of the range (Fig. 5.7:1–10) is a small group of beads copying items from everyday life: humans, birds, armadillos, monkeys, crabs, lizards, mosquitos, flowers, shells and shell artefacts, and even ceramic *alcarrazas*. A second group of beads (Fig. 5.7:23, 25, 30) is composed of creatures, usually birds or

5.7 (above) Beads and pendants from Malagana.

5.8 (above right) Pottery vessel in the form of two human figures, from the cemetery at Malagana (height 18 cm). The same personage, with a protruding stomach and a headdress with side pieces, is also represented in gold (cf. Fig. 5.7:9).

the workmanship, link them with the finest of the breastplates and pectorals, and suggest that they were worn somewhere on the body. Museum reconstructions often show them dangling from arm bands, but the 'tweezers' do not normally occur in matching pairs and this arrangement is pure speculation.

What sets Malagana apart from other archaeological sites in the Colombian Southwest is the proliferation of beads made from rock crystal, coloured stones, gold and the gold-copper alloy, *tumbaga*. Transparent crystal beads seem to have been charged with symbolic power and were an important element in burial rituals,[12] while the gold beads lead us into a world of images whose meaning and significance are lost to us. Fig. 5.7 illustrates a small selection of these gold beads. More than 120 different forms have been recorded but, leaving aside simple tubes, spheres and geometrical shapes, they can be broken down into a few general categories.

insects, reduced to semi-abstract forms, and often terminating in little spheres; their natural origins can still be recognized, but they do not belong to identifiable species. Others (Fig. 5.7:18) are clearly works of imagination. By a process of further reduction we come eventually to a series of almost completely abstract forms (Fig. 5.7:19–21, 27–8) whose human or animal inspiration is all but lost.

Another type of ornament, abundant at Malagana but hardly known elsewhere, consists of dropper-shaped 'Christmas tree decorations' with two or three circular openings in the lower part and a suspension hole at the top. These items are made from two sheet-gold components joined, without solder, at the 'equator', and are covered with complex incised designs (Fig. 5.9b–c). They are very light in weight, were evidently suspended or attached to something else, and may have been incorporated into beaded collars or sewn onto clothing.

The line between 'beads' and 'pendants' is an arbitrary one. As a general rule, small items found in large numbers and in matching sets are best called 'beads', while larger ones, fewer in number and made as individual pieces, can be designated 'pendants'. There is some overlap between the two categories, but if we adopt this distinction we see that most of the pendants at Malagana are three-dimensional castings in the form of human figures, some of them naturalistic, others apparently masked (Fig. 5.7:16).

A second group of objects that raises problems

they have simple stems and the decorative tops are hammered and chiselled into 'palm tree' shapes[14] or complex representational designs (Fig. 5.10) that are very different from the cast, three-dimensional figures on Calima dippers. The same process of 'Malaganization' can be seen in the *poporos* (lime-flasks) from the site. The finest of them are in the shape of naked human figures, both men and women, but they are clearly 'Malagana people'. Identical figures, with the same faces and the same distinctive hair styles, occur right across the board, from miniature gold beads and pendants to modelled pottery vessels (compare Figs 5.7:9 and 5.8).

The goldsmiths of Malagana also had a liking for boldly embossed, curvilinear designs, often symmetrical about a vertical axis and depicting representational themes such as animals (real or supernatural), human beings and stylized faces (Figs 5.6 and 5.11). These designs are so far known only on metalwork. Another set of motifs, incised rather than embossed, consists of straight-

5.9 Hollow sheet-gold items from the Malagana cemetery: (a) quadruped of unknown function (length 8 cm) and (b–c) two 'dropper-pendants', a little under natural size. The head and body of (a) were made separately and then joined; its crisscross decoration can be matched on llama pottery from Calima and the Malagana site. Item (c) has been drawn upside down in order to emphasize the human figure motif.

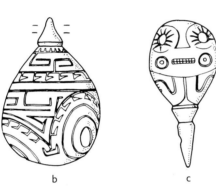

a

b

c

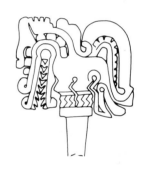

5.10 (right, top) Decorated top of a lime-dipper from the Malagana cemetery. The item is made from gold-rich *tumbaga* with a depletion-gilded surface. Tool marks show that the design was cut out with a chisel and then engraved.

5.11 (right) Bracelets from (a) Rio Chiquito (Tierradentro) and (b) Malagana. On each bracelet the figurative panel is repeated four times. The orientation alternates, and the bracelets can be worn either way up.

of nomenclature, though of a different kind, is a series of beads and pendants in the form of flat, cut-out human figures with the limbs bent at the elbows and knees (Fig. 5.7:13–14). These were first discovered in the Tolima archaeological zone and became the defining artefacts of a 'Tolima style' of goldwork,[13] but they have since been found over a much wider area that now includes Malagana, San Agustín and Tierradentro. Although no longer appropriate, the term 'Tolima figure' is retained as a descriptive shorthand, but without any assumptions about the place (or places) of manufacture.

What gives Malagana goldwork its distinctive appearance is a combination of shape and decoration. The large, flexible masks, for example, are unique in having protuberances on top of the heads, flanges at the sides, and hanging discs covering the eye sockets (Fig. 5.2). Malagana lime-dippers lack the thickened stems characteristic of their Calima and Quimbaya counterparts; instead

a

b

5.12 Breast ornament of sheet gold. Around the lower face are marks in the surface patina left by multi-strand necklaces of tubular beads.

style, one that is internally coherent and is distinct from those of neighbouring areas. Once we have learned to recognize this Malagana style, we can identify Malagana products exported to other regions and can distinguish foreign trade pieces at Malagana itself. This in turn allows us to extend our enquiry and to examine the role of Malagana in southwestern Colombia as a whole.

The Southwest Colombian Metallurgical Tradition

From about 500 BC to AD 500 the cultures of the Colombian Southwest participated in a regional goldworking tradition distinct from those of the rest of the country. In the 1980s Colombian archaeologists formally named this the 'Southwest Colombian Metallurgical Tradition', defined by a shared technology, by a cultural preference for certain categories of gold artefacts (Tables 5.1–2), and by similarities in art styles and iconography.[15] In the Amerindian world the subject matter of what we would call 'art' is never merely decorative; instead, the imagery is charged with symbolic, and often religious, meaning, reflecting a system of beliefs about the nature of the universe, mankind's place within it, and the proper structure of society. It is likely, therefore, that the Southwest Metallurgical Tradition is as much an ideological phenomenon as a technological one.[16]

The Southwest Tradition links the archaeological zones of Tumaco, Calima, Tierradentro, San Agustín, Tolima and – more peripherally – Nariño and Quimbaya. Malagana can now be added to this list and, within the group as a whole, has particularly strong connections with Calima, Tierradentro and San Agustín.

Throughout the Southwest gold is more readily available than copper. In consequence, metal-smiths generally worked in good quality gold, though there are always a few objects of gold-copper alloy (*tumbaga*) and some of these have been depletion-gilded to give a more golden surface. The Southwestern jewellers were masters of lost-wax casting, producing huge quantities of miniature human and animal figures, beads and pendants, but what characterizes the tradition above all is the manufacture of large and showy items in hammered and embossed gold sheet (Fig. 5.12). This is a logical decision: gold is easier to beat out than copper or *tumbaga*, and the use of gold sheet gives maximum surface glitter for minimal weight. Three-dimensional objects (lime-flasks, large human and animal effigies, or the ornaments illustrated in Fig. 5.9) were made by joining preformed components, and gold foil was

line geometric patterns, bands of criss-cross incision, net-and-cross designs (Fig. 5.11b), meanders and squared spirals. These geometric motifs are arranged in panels and are employed to fill up empty spaces within the overall design (see, for example, the body of the creature in Fig. 5.5). Similar 'fillers' occur on both the incised Ilama pottery and the resist-painted Malagana wares.

These are just a few of the formal and decorative attributes that link Malagana metal artefacts to each other, and the metalwork to the pottery. Together, they allow us to define a Malagana

Table 5.1 Distribution of artefacts of the Southwest Colombian Metallurgical Tradition
(* = Malagana form, + = local equivalent)

	Malagana	Calima	Tierradentro	S. Agustin	Tumaco	Tolima	Quimbaya
Gold trumpets (Archila 1996, cf. pl. 76)	*	+		+			
Gold-covered sea shells	*	+		+			
Lime flasks	*	+			*		
Lime-dippers with ornamental tops	*	+	+			+	+
Masks	*	+	+	+	+		+
Nose-piece (Fig. 5.18c)	*			*			
Nose-pieces (Fig. 5.15)	*	*+					
Breast ornaments (cf. Fig. 5.14)	*	*					
Breastplates with recurved tops (embossed)	*	+	+				
Breastplates with recurved tops (plain) (cf. Archila 1996, fig. 32a)	*	+		+			
Bobbin-shaped ear-spools (Fig. 5.18e)	*	+	+	+			+
Spacer bead (cf. Archila 1996, fig. 7b)	*				*		+
Tweezer ornament (cf. Figs 5.6, 5.18a)	*	+		+			
Diadem (cf. Archila 1996, pl. 84)	*	*					
H-shaped diadems (Archila 1996, fig. 1d)	*	+	+				
Diadems with hanging elements (cf. Archila 1996, Cuadro 3, 2)	*	+					
Bird-beak crowns (cf. Bray 1992, fig. 138)	*	+	+				
Dropper ornaments (cf. Fig. 5.9)	*		*				
Depilatory tweezers	*	*+	+			*+	*+
Masked figure pendant (Fig. 5.7:16)	*	*					
Figure pendant (cf. Labbe 1998: 89)	*	+					+

Table 5.2 Distribution of Malagana-style beads in the archaeological regions of Southwest Colombia
(* = identical, + = closely similar to Malagana form)

	Malagana	Calima	Tierradentro	S. Agustin	Tumaco	Tolima	Quimbaya
Tolima figures (cf. Fig. 5.7:13–14)	*		*	+		*+	*+
Beads: insectiforms	*	+	+			+	
Beads: zoomorphs (various)	*					+	+
Falcon beads (cf. Fig. 5.7:3)	*			*		+	+
Beads (cf. Fig. 5.7:30)	*	+					
Beads (cf. Fig. 5.7:15)	*					*	*
Beads (cf. Fig. 5.7:25)	*	*				*	
Beads (cf. Fig. 5.7:29)	*			+			
Beads (cf. Fig. 5.7:20)	*	+					
Beads (cf. Fig. 5.7:27–8)	*	+					
Beads (cf. Fig. 5.7:19)	*	*					
Beads (cf. Archila 1996, fig. 16b)	*	+				+	+
Beads (cf. Fig. 5.7:21)	*			+			
Beads: miniature decorated globular (Archila 1996, fig. 18a)	*	*					
Beads: conjoined miniature spheres (Archila 1996, fig. 17b)	*	*					
Perforated emerald beads	*	+			*		

5.13 Marine shell covered with gold foil, from the Malagana cemetery.

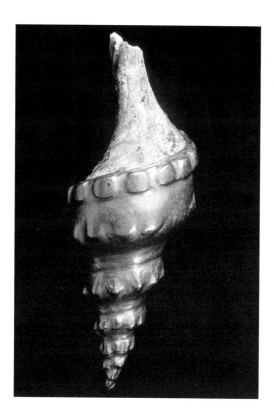

used to cover sea shells (Fig. 5.13), wooden staffs, bone trumpets, etc. Where necessary, the sheathing was attached to the backing with small gold pins, or components were joined by folding together (crimping) the edges of the metal sheets.

Malagana is strategically located at the centre of the Colombian Southwest, and archaeology shows that it maintained trade contacts with all its neighbours. The Rio Cauca provides a natural route to the south, into the Colombian Massif where the three ranges of the Andes converge. These mountains have deposits of obsidian (a natural volcanic glass used to make mirrors as well as tools), are the source of both the Cauca and Magdalena rivers, and also encompass the headwaters of other major rivers draining west to the Pacific and east to the Amazon lowlands. In this crossroads region are two of Colombia's best-known archaeological sites, Tierradentro and San Agustín. The Cauca and Magdalena valleys also give easy access northwards to the Tolima and Quimbaya zones. Another set of trade routes, marked in some areas by a network of unpaved roads,[17] led westwards over the cordillera and through the Calima region, to link up with the rivers that meander through the rain forests to the Pacific coast. By examining the metallurgical relationships between the Malagana chiefdom and its neighbours we can gain insight into the political and economic conditions that prevailed throughout the whole of Southwest Colombia.

Links with the west: Calima and Tumaco

Earlier sections of this paper have emphasized the relationship between Malagana and the Calima region, especially during the Ilama period, when the pottery of the two areas was almost identical. In Calima, as at Malagana, goldworking was well developed before the end of the Ilama phase[18] and reached its climax during the Yotoco period. But, despite close and continuous contact, the products of Malagana and Calima goldsmiths remained distinct and easily recognizable. This can be demonstrated by comparing sets of elite regalia from Malagana (discussed above) and Calima;[19] item for item, the categories of jewellery are virtually the same, but the two styles are different and the ideas are interpreted in different ways.

Looking at the problem quantitatively, there are surprisingly few unambiguous Calima gold artefacts at Malagana, and few Malagana pieces (apart from the ubiquitous beads) in the cordillera of Calima. Nevertheless, there are some significant parallels between Malagana and Calima goldwork. The large heart-shaped pectorals (Fig. 5.14) are identical in the two regions; the elaborate nose-piece, which is one of the greatest treasures of Malagana (Fig. 5.15), has its counterpart in Calima;[20] cast gold pendants in the form of masked human figures (Fig. 5.7:16) are common to both areas; so, too, are diadems with embossed human figures.[21] For many categories of artefact where the total sample is very small, we can no longer be certain of the place of manufacture, and some items traditionally labelled 'Calima' may one day have to be reassigned.

The people of Calima may well have been the middlemen who transmitted materials from Tumaco and the Pacific coast to the landlocked communities of the Cauca valley. A number of tombs at Malagana contained beads made from *Spondylus* (thorny oyster) shell, and the cemetery also yielded marine snails of various kinds, including entire spindle shells (*Fusinus* genus), some of them covered in gold foil. At least one of these *Fusinus* shells still contained powdered lime and must have served as a *poporo*. Some of the little gold beads and pendants from Malagana are also in the form of Pacific molluscs, including tiny models of *Oliva* shells with their spires cut off (Fig. 5.7:8). The original shells probably served as beads or were worn in bunches as dance rattles.

Emeralds are another Pacific item to reach Malagana. Sixteenth-century Spanish authors mention a source (or sources) of emeralds on the Pacific slope of the Ecuadorean Andes, and

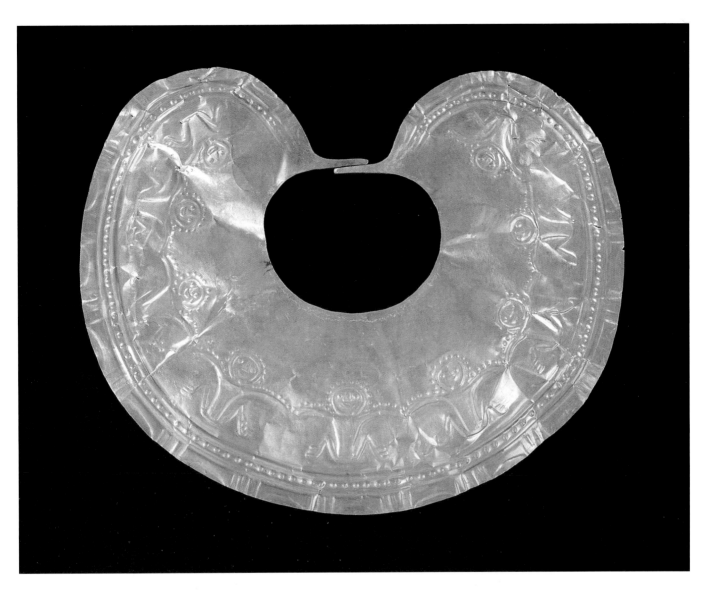

5.14 (above) Sheet gold breastplate with embossed human figures, from the Malagana cemetery (width 47.7 cm). Similar items have been found in Yotoco-period tombs in Calima.

5.15 (right) Nose ornament from the cemetery at Malagana (width 25.5 cm).

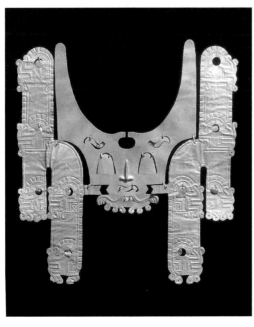

emeralds have been found sporadically, usually by looters, in the Pacific lowlands of Ecuador and the Tumaco region of Colombia. A few emeralds are recorded from tombs of the Yotoco period in Calima, and from there the trail continues to the Cauca valley, where the Malagana cemetery has yielded perforated emerald beads (some of them copying the shape of the gold ones in Fig. 5.7:20), a gold lizard-like creature (a larger version of Fig. 5.7:4) with an emerald crystal in place of the head, and a little bird carved from emerald matrix with a gold overlay. In general terms the range of minerals used for beads at Malagana is almost exactly matched in the Tumaco region, and many of those materials are foreign to both areas.

Some gold items from Malagana are also imports from the Pacific, including a pair of little cast figures with Tumaco-style head deformation (Fig. 5.16),[22] a lime-flask in the shape of a mythical creature (Fig. 5.17), and perhaps also a pair of

5.16 Pair of miniature cast gold figures from Malagana (height 3.4 cm). The general form and in particular the head deformation are similar to those of clay figurines from the Tumaco region.

gold discs with repoussé feline heads.[23] These seem to be oversized versions of the ear discs from highland Nariño on the Ecuador-Colombia frontier, but identical discs are also represented on Jama-Coaque figure-jars from coastal Ecuador.[24] If the two large discs were really found at Malagana – and there must always be room for doubt – they would be the earliest on record for Colombia.

Links with the south: San Agustín and Tierradentro

One unexpected consequence of the Malagana discovery is the new light it sheds on the archaeology of these two areas of the Colombian Massif.

5.17 Lime-flask in Tumaco style from the Malagana cemetery (height 17.2 cm; see Appendix, p. 110, Tomb 28). It consists of two repoussé elements joined around the centre, where pin holes are visible, and originally had a stopper made of gold. The lower part is in the shape of a crocodile head, and the upper element is some kind of anthropomorphized animal.

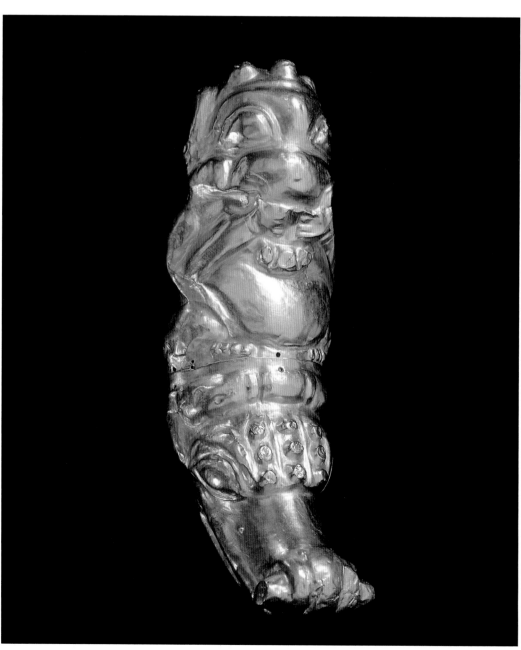

5.18 Gold items
from Vereda Ciénega
Grande, San José
de Isnos, San Agustín
(not to scale).
The incised decoration
on (d) is not indicated.

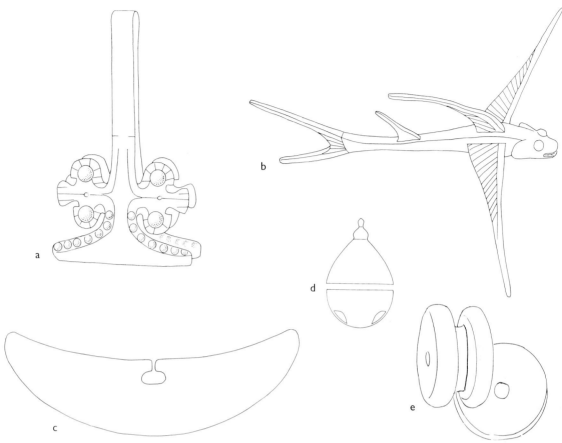

The core area of San Agustín is not a single archaeological site, but a cluster of smaller ones scattered over more than 500 sq. km of rolling foothills near the headwaters of the Río Magdalena. The entire landscape is man-made, with house-platforms, trackways, ancient fields and drainage ditches, cemeteries of shaft graves, and several large burial mounds covering stone-built funerary chambers. Associated with these megalithic structures are more than 300 stone statues in the shapes of humans, animals and supernatural beings.[25] Some of these statues have their faces covered by masks with empty eyes and mouths; others wear ornaments (diadems, ear-spools, nose-rings, necklaces) that seem to be representations of gold jewellery.

Since the age of the San Agustín statues roughly corresponds with the time of the Malagana tombs we might expect to find comparable rich burials, but the archaeological evidence from San Agustín was initially disappointing. Duque and Cubillos found a few simple ornaments of sheet gold dating to the first century BC,[26] and there is evidence for a metallurgical workshop at the site, with both hammering and casting, from about the time of Christ,[27] but these early excavations unearthed nothing dramatic.

There is, however, one old discovery at San Agustín (on the site of the Tourist Hotel) that foreshadows Malagana. In 1948, in a tomb at this locality, Luis Duque Gómez excavated five pottery vessels, a quantity of stone beads and thirty-six gold items, most of which can now be matched at Malagana.[28] The metal finds consisted of two H-shaped diadems, a crescentic nose-piece (cf. Fig. 5.18c), twenty-nine beads similar to those in Fig. 5.7:29, and three pendants in the shape of stylized 'Tolima' figures with forked tails.

Our impression of San Agustín goldwork changed dramatically in the 1980s when the Museo del Oro acquired several groups of gold objects unearthed by non-archaeologists. Two of these groups included objects in pure Malagana style. From a single tomb at Vereda Ciénega Grande, in the municipio of San José de Isnos, came a fragmentary stone statue and eight pieces of jewellery, all in fine gold (Fig. 5.18): a pair of ear-spools; two nose-pieces identical to those from the Tourist Hotel; a small tweezer ornament; a flat disc; a dropper-shaped ornament exactly like the Malagana specimens in Fig. 5.9; and a pendant in the form of a flying fish. The second group of material, also from San José de Isnos, consisted of repoussé ear-spools, a nose-ring of clay covered with gold foil, and a necklace of Malagana-style beads with a pendant in the form of a headless human figure.[29] Other miscellaneous finds, in the Museo del Oro and in private collections, also link San Agustín with Malagana. Falcon-beads (Fig. 5.7:3), bearing an obvious resemblance to the flying fish, occur at both localities, as do elongated breastplates with recurved tops,[30] shells covered with gold foil, and crowns composed of several miniature bird heads made from gold, stone or shell.[31]

Seventy-five km north of San Agustín is the Tierradentro region, noted for its deep subterranean burial chambers with painted walls and for statues carved in a simplified version of the San Agustín style. Ilama pottery has recently been discovered in Tierradentro,[32] and there have been occasional finds of both Malagana and Yotoco-related vessels. There are also historical reports of burials as rich as those of Malagana. In 1756 the Spanish priest Fray Juan de Santa Gertrudis visited Tierradentro and described his experiences in a book called *Maravillas de la Naturaleza* (Wonders of Nature). In the village of El Pedregal he noted, 'they found a tomb so rich that when the gold ornaments they had dug up (tigers, monkeys, toads, snakes, etc.) were put on a tray, a negro using all his strength could not lift them'.[33] Nothing found by the archaeologists has lived up to this eighteenth century account, but the subsequent finds from Tierradentro are clearly within the Southwestern Metallurgical Tradition and demonstrate close links with Malagana.

One of the first discoveries from the area was a gold mask in the form of a fanged creature with a protruding snout and a decorated band or flange forming a headdress.[34] The animal face can be matched on San Agustín statuary, as can the headdress.[35] This same form of head band, with its curvilinear, broad-line repoussé decoration, is also characteristic of certain Malagana masks in gold and in clay.[36]

These hints of Malagana connections were confirmed in the 1970s when gold objects were discovered in simple pit-graves. The Museo del Oro has two of these funerary offerings. One grave-lot, from the municipio of Páez, consists of a double-spouted pot of a form also recorded at Malagana, a complete gold mask and part of another, an ear-spool, an H-shaped diadem similar to those of Calima and San Agustín, a tongue-shaped breast ornament with an embossed lizard,[37] a bird-pendant and a necklace of *tumbaga* figure-plaques.[38] From the same general area, though not from the same tomb, came a 'Tolima figure' similar to Fig. 5.7:14.[39] The second tomb group, from Río Chiq-

uito, also has Malagana connections. Among the gold offerings were a Malagana-style bracelet (Fig. 5.11a),[40] and the pottery included a two-chambered whistling jar, in the shape of a human figure, of a type that subsequently turned up in some numbers at the Malagana cemetery.[41]

To summarize, reanalysis of the goldwork from San Agustín and Tierradentro clarifies some problems but creates new ones. On present evidence, the similarities with the material from Malagana are so many, and so specific, that only two interpretations seem possible; either the people of the Massif were importing most of their goldwork from Malagana (or from some unknown site of the same culture) or they were manufacturing 'Malagana-style' artefacts themselves.

Links with the east and north: Tolima and Quimbaya

By comparison with the southern connections, Malagana's links with the north and east are less evident, though this impression may be due more to lack of data than to lack of contact. This is particularly true of Tolima, in the Magdalena valley, where there has been little archaeological activity and the basic cultural sequence has still to be worked out. Besides the 'Tolima figures' already discussed, the goldwork of this region includes beads similar to those of Malagana (cf. Fig. 5.7:13–15, 26), and the basin of the Río Saldaña (in the southernmost part of Tolima) has produced several gold pieces in the Yotoco style of Calima.[42] The Saldaña area is rich in alluvial gold, and southern Tolima also has sources of copper (near Natagaima) that may have entered into the *tumbaga* alloys all over the Southwest.[43] Nevertheless, the total sample of gold artefacts is not large and consists mainly of isolated finds without context or date. For the moment all we can say is that the goldsmiths of Tolima were participating in the Southwest Colombian Metallurgical Tradition and that the Río Magdalena seems to have been a trade artery that linked areas as far apart as Tolima and San Agustín.

Although the Cauca valley, like the Magdalena, was one of Colombia's most important trade routes, the Quimbaya archaeological zone was marginal to the Malagana world and (with its strong metallurgical connections to the Caribbean lowlands) was at best a frontier member of the Southwestern Metallurgical Tradition. 'Tolima' pendants and lime-dippers related to those of Calima have been found there; one or two Malagana pots reached the southern part of the region, and there are Malagana-like beads in the famous

'Treasure of the Quimbayas',[44] but direct contacts between the two areas seem to have been limited.

Conclusion: gold and politics in Southwest Colombia

One way of testing a hypothesis is to see whether it can accommodate new data. By this criterion, the Malagana discovery has validated the belief in a Southwest Colombian Metallurgical Tradition and has given us new information about the workings of a regional trading network that stretched from the Quimbaya zone to San Agustín and from the Magdalena valley to the Pacific. This 'interaction zone', an area of approximately 400,000 sq. km, is the political and economic world within which Malagana played a role.

The area directly governed by the Malagana chiefs is very much smaller than this. Since we have no documentary information about the politics of Colombia at the start of the Christian era, the Malagana 'homeland' can only be defined in archaeological terms – as the territory in which Malagana-style artefacts predominate in the archaeological record. It must be emphasized that this is a purely archaeological construct; it does not assume that this territory was politically unified (still less that the Malagana site was its 'capital'), nor that the area was occupied by a single ethnic or tribal group. Because we do not have, and never will have, any idea what the Malagana people called themselves or what language(s) they spoke, these kinds of question remain unanswerable.

Identifying the boundaries of the Malagana 'homeland' is not easy. We know very little about the archaeology of this part of the Cauca valley, and the problem can only be tackled indirectly, by eliminating areas known to have been occupied by non-Malagana groups. This disposes of the western cordillera, the central cordillera (though with much less certainty) and the Cauca valley north of the town of Guacarí. This process of elimination leaves the Malagana people in possession of the floodplain of the Cauca valley from about 25 km north of the Malagana site to a still undetermined frontier in the south. This southern boundary probably falls somewhere between the city of Cali, where one piece of Malagana gold has been found, and the point where the mountains close in and the floodplain terminates. If these guesses are correct, the 'Malagana archaeological zone' may have extended for no more than 40 to 80 km along the Rio Cauca. Within this area farmers and treasure-hunters have made sporadic finds of Malagana-style artefacts at several localities,[45] and a second Malagana site, at Coronado in the suburbs of Palmira, has recently been excavated by Colombian archaeologists.

We do not know the precise status of the ruler of Malagana or how far from the site his jurisdiction extended, but by local standards Malagana is a large settlement, rich and cosmopolitan in its material culture. The emerging picture suggests that it was the nucleus of an early chiefdom, a prototype for those that the first Spanish travellers observed in the Cauca valley[46] and northwards to Panama and beyond.[47] These sixteenth-century chiefdoms were territorially small, either at war with their neighbours or trading with them along established routes with recognized market centres. The word 'chiefdom' masks a wide range of variability,[48] but in general terms these societies were hierarchical and non-egalitarian, with power (political and spiritual) concentrated in the hands of a ranked elite headed by a chief. In part, the power of the chiefs derived from their access to foreign trade goods and to the esoteric knowledge that came with these. Certain materials, including gold, were charged with supernatural qualities (see Oliver, this volume), and the use of gold regalia – in death as well as in life – both asserted and legitimized the power of the chief. Gold objects were symbols of prestige and authority, functioning as insignia of rank and as charms or amulets, defining tribal or lineage identity, and linking the earthly world with the supernatural.

Projecting sixteenth-century information back into the prehistoric past is a dangerous exercise, and analogies in themselves 'prove' nothing. Nevertheless, the material evidence from Malagana, and from Southwest Colombia in general, fits easily into the kind of world described by the conquistadors, and helps us to imagine the real people who made and used the Malagana goldwork.

Appendix: Malagana tomb groups

This Appendix summarizes the contents of nine rich Malagana tombs (information abstracted from Herrera *et al.* 1994, Cuadro II). The numeration follows the system used in their chart, not the schemes used by the relevant museums and archives.

Tomb 1: Two pots; three [should be four] large gold masks; necklaces of tubular and zoomorphic beads; hanging plaques, sheet-gold plaques for sewing onto textiles; bone tubes; beads of *Spondylus*, rock crystal and coloured stone. See also Archila 1996: 55, 58–9 and Bray *et al.* 1998: 142. There are minor differences between the three published accounts.

Tomb 2: A pot in the form of a woman; a gold mask; necklaces; a miniature human figure in gold; beads of rock crystal and green stone.

Tomb 3: A gold pectoral in the form of an animal mask with danglers (Archila 1996: pl. 42); ear pendants; anthropomorphic beads; a nose-ring; a necklace of shell beads.

Tomb 4: Ear pendants; a necklace of hammered gold beads; a necklace of crystal beads.

Tomb 5: Three pots; a necklace of gold beads in the forms of humans and animals.

Tomb 6: Three gold masks; two diadems; beads and nose-rings; twisted wire; a gold bead in the form of a miniature *Passiflora* flower (Archila 1996, pls 28–30); a sheet-gold item in the shape of a maize cob; beads of green stone, rock crystal and *Spondylus* shell.

Tomb 7: A double-spouted *alcarraza* and miniature *alcarrazas*; pottery jars and bowls; a necklace of gold beads; a gold miniature in the shape of a masked figure; a gold lime-dipper topped by a bird; a gold-sheathed sea shell; tweezers for removing facial hair; nose-rings; green stone beads; a bone flute; shells; a bone carved with human and animal figures for working metal beads.

Tomb 28: A plain heart-shaped pectoral and the repoussé example shown in Fig. 5.14 (Archila 1996, pl. 2i); a gold mask; a Tumaco-style lime-flask in sheet gold (Fig. 5.17); a diadem with a repoussé human figure (Archila 1996, pl. 84); eight cast plaques, square with projecting human heads (Archila 1996, pl. 88); gold pendants and beads (cf. Fig. 5.7:17, 27–8); a piece of chipped obsidian. A single pot is also reported.

Tomb 29 (from 'near Malagana'): A gold mask; depilatory tweezers; a heavy gold nose-ring; a small cast figure; a sheet-gold animal head; beads of gold, crystal and *Spondylus* shell.

Notes

1 Botiva *et al.* 1994; Botiva and Forero 1994.

2 *El Caleño*, 23 January 1993; *El Tiempo*, 9 March 1993.

3 Archila 1996.

4 Herrera *et al.* 1994: 156.

5 Botiva and Forero 1994.

6 Rodríguez *et al.* 1993; Herrera *et al.* 1994; Bray *et al.* 1998.

7 Cardale de Schrimpff 1992.

8 Bray 1992.

9 For illustrations of Malagana pottery see Archila 1996 and Labbé 1998.

10 Herrera *et al.* 1994.

11 E.g. Labbé 1998: no. 61.

12 Bray *et al* 1998: 140–44.

13 Pérez de Barradas 1958.

14 Archila 1996: pl. 27.

15 Plazas and Falchetti 1983, 1985, 1986.

16 See, for example, Legast 1995 on the animal symbolism.

17 Cardale and Herrera 1995; Cardale de Schrimpff 1996.

18 Cardale de Schrimpff *et al.* 1989.

19 Bray 1992: 105.

20 Cf. Reichel-Dolmatoff 1988: 20; Plazas and Falchetti 1983: 4.

21 Compare Archila 1996: pl. 84, or Bray *et al.* 1998: fig. 14, with Plazas and Falchetti 1985: fig. 8.

22 Ortiz 1996: no. 267 bis.

23 Archila 1996: fig. 32a.

24 Valdez 1992: fig. 16.

25 Reichel-Dolmatoff 1972.

26 Duque and Cubillos 1979: 26–33.

27 Duque 1966: 408.

28 Duque 1966: 203–5; Bray 1978: nos 253–4.

29 *Boletín Museo del Oro* 22: 117–18.

30 Cf. Archila 1996: fig. 32a.

31 Bray 1992: fig. 138.

32 Gnecco and Martínez 1995.

33 Rojas de Perdomo 1995: 111, my translation.

34 Pérez de Barradas 1937, 1954: 32; Reichel-Dolmatoff 1972: 128 and pl. 12; Plazas and Falchetti 1983: 16.

35 Reichel-Dolmatoff 1972: pl. 67.

36 Archila 1996: pl. 42; Bray *et al.* 1998: fig. 2.

37 Falchetti de Sáenz 1978; Reichel-Dolmatoff 1988: fig. 187.

38 Bray 1978, nos 458–63.

39 Ibid: no. 464.

40 Duque 1979.

41 Cf. Bray *et al.* 1998: fig. 3; Archila 1996: pl. 25.

42 Pérez de Barradas 1954.

43 Pérez de Barradas 1958, Texto: 53–8.

44 Pérez de Barradas 1966, Texto: figs 27–8; Plazas and Falchetti 1985: 49.

45 Bray *et al.* 1998.

46 Trimborn 1949.

47 Drennan and Uribe 1987; Helms 1979.

48 Drennan and Uribe 1987.

References

Archila, Sonia
1996 *Los Tesoros de los Señores de Malagana.* Museo del Oro, Banco de la República, Bogotá.

Botiva Contreras, Alvaro, and Eduardo Forero Lloreda
1994 Malagana: guaquería vs arqueología. *Boletín Museo del Oro* 31 (1991): 124–9.

Bray, Warwick
1978 *The Gold of El Dorado.* Times Books, London.
1992 El período Yotoco. In Marianne Cardale de Schrimpff, Warwick Bray, Theres Gähwiler-Walder and Leonor Herrera, *Calima: Diez Mil Años de Historia en el Suroccidente de Colombia*, pp. 75–124. Fundación Pro Calima, Bogotá.

Bray, Warwick, Leonor Herrera and Marianne Cardale de Schrimpff
1998 The Malagana chiefdom, a new discovery in the Cauca Valley of southwestern Colombia. In *Shamans, Gods and Mythic Beasts: Colombian Gold and Ceramics in Antiquity*, ed. Armand J. Labbé, pp. 121–54. American Federation of Arts (New York) and University of Washington Press.

Cardale de Schrimpff, Marianne
1992 La gente del período Ilama. In Marianne Cardale de Schrimpff, Warwick Bray, Theres Gähwiler-Walder and Leonor Herrera, *Calima: Diez Mil Años de Historia en el Suroccidente de Colombia*, pp. 25–71. Fundación Pro Calima, Bogotá.
1996 *Caminos Prehispánicos de Colombia. El Estudio de Caminos Precolombinos en la Cuenca del Alto Río Calima, Cordillera Occidental, Valle del Cauca.* Fundación de Investigaciones Arqueológicas Nacionales, Banco de la República, Bogotá.

Cardale de Schrimpff, Marianne,
and Leonor Herrera
1995 Caminos y comerciantes en el suroccidente de Colombia entre 2500 y 1500 AP. In *Perspectivas Regionales en la Arqueología del Suroccidente de Colombia y Norte del Ecuador*, ed. Cristóbal Gnecco, pp. 195–222. Universidad del Cauca, Popayán.

Cardale de Schrimpff, Marianne,
Warwick Bray and Leonor Herrera
1989 Ornamentos y máscaras de oro de la cultura Ilama. Metalurgia del período formativo tardío en la cordillera occidental colombiana. *Boletín Museo del Oro* 24: 55–71.

Drennan, Robert D., and Carlos A. Uribe (eds)
1987 *Chiefdoms in the Americas*. University Press of America, Lanham.

Duque Gómez, Luis
1966 *Exploraciones Arqueológicas en San Agustín*. Bogotá: Instituto Colombiano de Antropología, Revista Colombiana de Antropología Supplemento no. 1 (1964).
1979 La pieza del Museo. *Boletín Museo del Oro* 2, centrefold.

Duque Gómez, Luis, and Julio César Cubillos
1979 *Arqueología de San Agustín: Alto de los Idolos, Montículos y Tumbas*. Fundación de Investigaciones Arqueológicas Nacionales, Banco de la República, Bogotá.

Falchetti de Sáenz, Ana María
1978 Pieza del Museo. *Boletín Museo del Oro* 1, centrefold.

Gnecco, Cristóbal, and José Ricardo Martínez
1995 Dos alcarrazas Ilama en Tierradentro. *Boletín Museo del Oro* 32–3: 178–81.

Helms, Mary W.
1979 *Ancient Panama: Chiefs in Search of Power*. University of Texas, Austin and London.

Herrera Angel, Leonor, Marianne Cardale de Schrimpff and Warwick Bray
1994 Los sucesos de Malagana vistos desde Calima. Atando cabos en la arqueología del suroccidente colombiano. *Revista Colombiana de Antropología* 31: 145–71.

Labbé, Armand J.
1998 *Shamans, Gods and Mythic Beasts: Colombian Gold and Ceramics in Antiquity*. American Federation of Arts (New York) and University of Washington Press.

Legast, Anne
1995 Iconografía animal prehispánica en el suroccidente de Colombia. In Cristóbal Gnecco (ed.), *Perspectivas Regionales en la Arqueología del Suroccidente de Colombia y Norte del Ecuador*: 263–97. Universidad del Cauca, Popayán.

Ortiz, George
1996 *In Pursuit of the Absolute: Art of the Ancient World. The George Ortiz Collection* (revised hard cover edition). Bern.

Pérez de Barradas, José
1937 Máscara de oro de Inzá. *Revista de las Indias* 1: 3–7.

1954 *Orfebrería Prehispánica de Colombia, Estilo Calima*. Banco de la República (Bogotá), Madrid.
1958 *Orfebrería Prehispánica de Colombia, Estilos Tolima y Muisca*. Banco de la República (Bogotá), Madrid.
1966 *Orfebrería Prehispánica de Colombia, Estilos Quimbaya y Otros*. Banco de la República (Bogotá), Madrid.

Plazas, Clemencia, and Ana María Falchetti
1983 Tradición metalúrgica del suroccidente colombiano. *Boletín Museo del Oro* 14: 1–32.
1985 Cultural patterns in prehispanic goldwork from Colombia. In *The Art of Precolumbian Gold: The Jan Mitchell Collection*, ed. Julie Jones, pp. 47–59. Weidenfeld & Nicolson, London.
1986 Patrones culturales en la orfebrería prehispánica de Colombia. In *Metalurgia en América Precolombina*, ed. C. Plazas, pp. 210–46. Banco de la República, Bogotá.

Reichel-Dolmatoff, Gerardo
1972 *San Agustín, A Culture of Colombia*. Praeger, New York.
1988 *Orfebrería y Chamanismo. Un estudio iconográfico del Museo del Oro*. Colina, Medellín.

Rodríguez, Carlos Armando, Leonor Herrera Angel and Marianne Cardale de Schrimpff
1993 El proyecto arqueológico de Malagana (1994). *Boletín de Arqueología* 8(3): 59–70.

Rojas de Perdomo, Lucía
1995 *Arqueología Colombiana: Visión Panorámica*. Intermedio Editores/Círculo de Lectores, Bogotá.

Trimborn, Hermann
1949 *Señorío y Barbarie en el Valle del Cauca*. Madrid: Consejo Superior de Investigaciones Científicas, Instituto Gonzalo Fernández de Oviedo.

Valdez, Francisco
1992 Symbols, ideology, and the expression of power in La Tolita, Ecuador. In *The Ancient Americas: Art from Sacred Landscapes*, ed. Richard E. Townsend, pp. 229–43. Art Institute of Chicago.

Acknowledgements

I have benefited from conversations with many colleagues involved in the Malagana project, and especially thank Marianne Cardale, Leonor Herrera, Carlos Armando Rodríguez, David Stemper, Sonia Archila, Ana María Falchetti, and Clemencia Plazas (Director of the Museo del Oro at the time of the discovery). After so many years of collaboration it is often impossible to remember where any particular idea originated. I must also thank Alan Myers and Caroline Cartwright for their advice about shells. Illustrations of items from the Gold Museum (identified in the Illustration Credits, p. 240) were provided by the present Director, Clara Isabel Botero, and Roberto Lleras. Figs 5.5 and 5.16 are reproduced, with the author's kind permission, from Ortiz 1996, and the drawings are the work of Tessa Rickards.

6

The Iconography and Symbolism of Metallic Votive Offerings in the Eastern Cordillera, Colombia[1]

Roberto Lleras-Pérez

Geographic and archaeological setting

The region known as the Eastern Cordillera (Cordillera Oriental) comprises the easternmost branch of the northern Andean range which begins at the Colombian Massif in the heart of Colombia and extends northwards approximately 1,300 km to near the Caribbean Sea. The Eastern Cordillera divides the mountainous part of the country from the eastern plains of the Amazon and Orinoco basins. A branch of the Eastern Cordillera originates at the Santurban Massif and follows a north to north-eastern direction into Venezuelan territory where it is known as the Serranía de Mérida.

Nowadays there is a general chronological framework for the human occupation of the southernmost part of the central region which includes a cultural periodization covering nearly 20,000 years and provides an explanation for cultural developments in this area. The Muisca, Lache, Guane and Chitarero cultures represent the later prehispanic period; it is generally accepted that these groups might have started to assume distinct identities by around AD 300. The most striking feature of this period is the close linguistic relationship of the groups inhabiting the Eastern Cordillera at the time of the Spanish conquest.

There is only a very fragmented knowledge of the neighbours and relatives of the Muiscas (Guane, Lache and Chitareros) living in other areas of the central Eastern Cordillera. For some time attention has been called to the close similarities between the archaeological materials of the Eastern Cordillera and the Serranía de Mérida in Venezuela, particularly the Tachira, Quibor and coastal Falcon areas.[2] The snow peaks of Mérida are regarded as a sacred site by the Eastern Cordillera Uwas[3] and there seems to

have been an active circulation of certain kinds of gold ornaments in the Venezuelan Andes before the arrival of the Spaniards.[4] The reported findings of gold ornaments to the east of the present border of Colombia are, nevertheless, extremely scarce.

Linguists and archaeologists[5] believe that during the first centuries of the Christian Era there was a massive migration of Chibcha speakers from their ancestral territory in Central America (Costa Rica) to northern South America. This common origin may help explain why the groups inhabiting the Eastern Cordillera share many features of their material culture.

It has been proposed that there were two different phases in the development of the Chibcha groups.[6] The best-documented period is the later one and particularly the years immediately preceding and following the Spanish conquest. The most detailed information on language, religion, sociopolitical organization, economic production and interchange, as well as many details of daily and ritual life, comes from this period.

Among the Chibcha groups the Muisca were the largest. Different models have been proposed to explain their chiefdom structure.[7] There was a basic or, perhaps, two basic types of social and kinship units, the Utas and the Sybins, which had separate territories and obeyed the authority of their respective leaders (*capitanes*). Utas and Sybins might have been organized in pairs as part of dualistic structures or in triads forming double oppositions.[8] They formed larger units, known to the Spaniards as villages, which obeyed chiefs (*caciques*) and had control over larger territories. Villages were not always politically independent; groups of villages were, in turn, under the authority of powerful chiefs (*uzaques*). Finally, the *uzaques* obeyed the great regional lords.

Sacrifice and offerings among the Chibcha

Muisca religion was extremely complex and is not yet fully understood. There were at least four principal deities: Chibchacum and his wife, creators of the world; and Bachue and his son, creators of humanity. A culture hero, Bochica, saved the Muisca people from flooding and taught them cultivation and weaving. Finally, a multitude of minor spiritual entities, such as lakes and mountain tops, were considered sacred, and the Sun and the Moon were worshipped and had special temples dedicated to them. Religious services were provided by specialized shamans (*jeques*).

Sacrifice and votive offerings played an important role in religious practices, and a large part of metallurgical production was devoted to the latter. It is clear, in fact, from the colonial accounts that offering was a very special and deeply rooted custom among the Muisca people. There are some descriptions revealing how the shamans prepared and performed the offerings and what the temples looked like. Apart from these special places, called Cucas, offerings were deposited in other locales which were held to possess a special significance or occupy a special liminal region between the aquatic, terrestrial and celestial worlds. Lakes were one such preferred site for offerings, but the list also includes mountains, hilltops, crossroads, springs, rivers and creeks, open fields, house and temple foundations, caves and gorges.

As for sacrifice, its meaning and purpose remain obscure. Sacrifice was practised during special ceremonies, perhaps related to certain calendrical dates. The best-known form was the one called by the Spanish the 'Sacrifice of the Gavia' (Gull): victims were tied to the upper part of a high pole erected in a special site of the village, probably next to the temple or the chief's dwellings, and warriors would kill them by throwing darts. The blood running down the pole was collected in bowls and offered to the Sun. Some votive figures represent the sacrificial post and the victim tied to it. The victims were small children, seven to eight years old, chosen from birth for this purpose and brought up with utmost care. Sacrifices of children were also common at the consecration of important buildings; their skeletons are usually found beneath the most important posts.

Metallurgy in the Eastern Cordillera

The Prehispanic metallurgy of the Eastern Cordillera in Colombia has the peculiarity, not shared with other archaeological areas in South America, of having an overwhelming proportion of its production (nearly 56%) exclusively devoted to votive objects. Furthermore, several adornments were also finally intended as votive offerings, thus increasing to 62.5% the proportion of objects used as offerings.

On the basis of the available information it is not yet possible to propose a proper chronological framework for metallurgy. Dating has been carried out whenever appropriate samples are spotted, but without a proper selection guided by research objectives. There are, though, fourteen radiocarbon dates directly associated with metal artefacts, which agree fairly well, both among themselves and with other chronological data for Eastern Cordillera archaeological materials.[9] According to them, metallurgy was present in this region from around AD 300 and remained in production for some 1,200 years until the early colonial period (c.1600).

The earliest date corresponds to what most archaeologists agree as the beginning of the occupation of the cordillera by Chibcha-speaking groups. The ceramic chronology has enabled us to propose the existence of Early and Late periods both for the Muisca[10] and Guane cultures.[11] Ten of the dates associated with metal objects fall in the Early Period (AD 300 to 1100), thus indicating that metallurgy was a cultural feature that these groups brought with them into their newly occupied territory or was developed shortly after their arrival. Two dates corresponding to imported items (seventh and tenth centuries AD) reveal that exchange with neighbouring areas also occurred in early times.

Metallic votive offerings

While most of the votive offerings from the Eastern Cordillera are undoubtedly miniatures, not much has been said about this topic for this particular region; a fact which contrasts with the interpretations that relate miniaturization, landscape and control mechanisms in the central Andes and elsewhere (see also Dransart, this volume).[12] The production of votive figures as miniatures in the Eastern Cordillera was not an accidental one. In a certain sense the figures reproduce, to scale, part of the real world of the Indian communities. They evince an intention to represent and obtain control over nature and society, and this in turn determines both what is represented and how the patterns of representation are established. On the other hand miniatures become a very convenient and manageable way of producing symbols with their own complete meaning. These may be deposited in large groups and express more complex ideas.

6.1 (right) Gold votive figure
of a woman with staff
(female figures category).

6.2 (below) Woman
heavily adorned
(female figures category).

Muisca votive figures have attracted the atten-tion of archaeologists, historians and scholars from early in the history of the study of metalwork in Colombia. The first works on this topic, which included the interpretation of the most attractive figures, followed concepts derived from chroni-clers or from mythology and were far from sys-tematic. The basic principle of the classificatory system that I have developed is the definition of types or typical depictions which, independently of minor variations, seem to convey a specific meaning of their own. Care has been taken not to overemphasize details, as this would produce an excessively complex typology making classifica-tion unnecessarily difficult. It is considered that, ethnographically, the representation of any given figure follows the same general patterns in differ-ent places, providing cultural traits and beliefs were shared, although the details may vary. Sev-enty-six typical depictions distributed in eight major groups have been identified.

The classification of anthropomorphic figures starts from the most conspicuous characteristic: gender. Feminine, masculine and unsexed figures are identified. Next, all the other attributes of the figures are considered; figures appear wearing dif-ferent types of ornaments and carrying staffs, weapons, miscellaneous objects and birds. In most cases attributes appear combined; this makes it necessary to establish the types of combinations that occur. Another major group consists of scenes with one or more people in a specific setting.

Animal representations are organized from sky to earth and water, that is to say, first flying ani-mals, next walking animals and reptiles, and last amphibians and fishes. In the case of jaguars and snakes there are different types of the same animal, since meaningful variations are found. Objects are placed last; they are organized so that objects of personal use, such as clothing and weapons, come first and household objects, such as furniture, are last. Finally geometric and unde-fined objects are described.

Female figures

One hundred and sixty female figures (9.6% of votive figures) are divided into seven subgroups, according to their additional elements or to special body positions (Figs 6.1–2). Usually figures are standing up, with legs straight or slightly bent and arms straight or crossed, facing front.

Subtype	Description	Frequency	% of group
Women, heavily adorned	Wearing no dress and adorned with elaborate headdress, danglers, ear ornaments and necklaces.	9	5.6
Women with bowl, lime container and tray	Holding a bowl with one or both hands, a lime container held in a hand or hanging at the waist. The three elements appear by themselves or in couples.	7	4.4
Women with staff and birds	With staff and birds or one of the two elements.	60	37.5
Women with weapons	With spearthrowers and occasionally darts.	11	6.9
Women seated holding knees	Seated with legs bent and arms crossed over the knees, thus forming a kind of container.	2	1.3
Women with child	Carrying a small child, sometimes in a cradle.	21	13.1
Women without additional elements	With no special additional elements and no special body position.	50	31.3

Male figures

Male figures total 495 (29.6% of votive offerings); they are divided into eleven subgroups according to their additional elements or to special body positions. Usually figures are standing, with legs straight or slightly bent and arms straight or crossed.

Subtype	Description	Frequency	% of group
Men, heavily adorned	Adorned with elaborate headdresses, diadems or crowns, rectangular nose ornaments, various necklaces, ear ornaments and danglers.	20	4.0
Men with bowl, lime container and tray	With a bowl held in one or both hands, a lime container in a hand or hanging at the waist or a hallucinogen tray held in one hand. The three elements appear either by themselves or in couples.	22	4.4
Men with staff and birds	With one or two staffs and/or one or two birds. Staffs are held in one hand and birds are depicted seated on the shoulder or the head.	125	25.3
Men with weapons	Carrying one or two spearthrowers, with or without darts, an axe and/or club.	112	22.6
Men seated holding knees	Seated with legs bent and arms crossed on top of knees, thus forming a kind of receptacle.	42	8.5
Men with tools	With objects different from staffs or weapons, presumably tools, in their hands.	9	1.8
Men without additional elements	Without special ornaments.	97	19.6
Priests with weapons, staff and birds	Always combining three elements: spearthrower, staff and birds. They have been named 'priests' as a way of identification.	41	8.3
Warriors with trophy head	Heavily armed with spearthrowers, darts and clubs. One or occasionally two trophy heads hanging from the wrists or held at the end of sticks. The term 'warrior' is used for identification.	14	2.8
Men seated on benches	Heavily ornamented man seated on a four-legged bench.	7	1.4
Masked men	Wearing a mask, sometimes held with one or both hands. Face can clearly be seen behind the mask.	6	1.2

Unsexed figures

Unsexed figures total 181 (10.8% of votive figures); they are divided into seven subgroups according to their additional elements or to special body positions. Usually figures are standing up, with legs straight or slightly bent and arms straight or crossed, facing front.

Subtype	Description	Frequency	% of group
Unsexed figures, heavily adorned	With elaborate headdress, rectangular nose ornament, ear pendants, danglers and necklaces.	4	2.2
Unsexed figures with staff and birds	Carrying a staff and/or bird seated on the shoulder.	44	24.2
Unsexed figures with weapons	Carrying a spearthrower and, in some cases, darts.	7	3.8
Unsexed figures, seated	Seated with legs bent and arms crossed over knees, thus forming a receptacle.	14	7.7
Unsexed figures without additional elements	Without additional elements.	105	58.2
Unsexed warriors with trophy head	With spearthrower and darts or club, and carrying a trophy head hanging from the waist or held in a stick.	3	1.6
Mummies	With body fully wrapped in bandages.	4	2.2

Scenes

Sixty-seven scenes have been found (4.0% of votive figures). They are divided into eight subgroups according to their characteristics. Their only common feature is that they portray one or more persons.

Subtype	Description	Frequency	% of group
Double-headed human figures	Person with one pair of legs, two trunks, one pair of arms and two heads.	2	3.0
Couples embracing	Couple making love.	2	3.0
Chiefs on litters	Important person, heavily adorned, seated on a litter. The word 'chief' is used as a means of identification.	6	8.9
Enclosures with one human figure	Heavily adorned important person standing in the middle of an enclosure.	12	17.9
Enclosures with main and secondary figures	Heavily adorned important person in the middle of an enclosure surrounded by secondary figures.	4	6.0
Rafts with human figures	Raft made of bent logs in the middle of which there is a main figure, heavily adorned and very large surrounded by secondary figures.	2	3.0
Alligator with human inside	Small alligator with short tail. The belly is open and a human face is seen inside.	1	1.5
Sacrificial posts	Sacrificial post with a human figure on its upper part.	38	56.7

Animals

Animals total 214 (12.8% of votive figures). They are divided into fourteen groups according to the species, when it proved to be identifiable, or, if not, to broader biological families or orders.

Subtype	Description	Frequency	% of group
Birds – eagles, hawks, condors	With a hook-shaped beak like that of condors, hawks, eagles and similar birds of prey.	16	7.5
Birds – pheasants, doves, parrots	With a plain beak, generally represented with its wings closed.	14	6.5
Jaguars	Feline, most probably a jaguar, even though in some cases pumas or other felines might be represented.	35	16.4
Jaguars on litters/trays	Jaguar or similar feline standing on a litter or on one of the ends of a hallucinogen tray.	3	1.4
Jaguars, serpentiform	Feline with fangs, whiskers and ears, usually with short legs. The most prominent feature is the extremely long and undulating tail.	7	3.3

Deer	Deer seated with its head pointing frontward.	3	1.4
Lizards	Lizard or small iguana.	2	0.9
Turtles	Turtle with incised carapace.	4	1.9
Snails	Shell of a snail, sometimes with danglers.	34	15.9
Snakes	Snake with rounded head, usually having human or jaguar face with whiskers and fangs	86	40.2
Snakes, coiled	Snake coiled and having a human face; sometimes whiskers are also represented.	3	1.4
Snakes, double	Couple of snakes side by side.	2	0.9
Insect	Insect of undefined species.	1	0.5
Unidentified animals	Not identifiable to any species or genus.	4	1.9

Objects of personal use

Objects of this type total 405 (24.2% of votive figures). Miniature objects of personal use are divided into seventeen types according to the function of the real objects they represent and their additional elements.

Subtype	Description	Frequency	% of group
Staffs	Type used by chiefs, priests and important persons as a symbol of status and authority.	109	26.9
Staffs with birds	Complex or very complex staff adorned with one or two birds.	105	25.9
Staffs/spearthrowers, double or multiple	Staff or a spearthrower bifurcated or with multiple endings.	7	1.7
Spearthrowers	Type used for hunting and battle.	85	21.0
Spearthrowers with birds	Miniature spearthrower adorned with one or occasionally two birds.	17	4.2
Axes/weapons	Trapezoidal axes and clubs are the most frequent.	4	1.0
Quiver with spears	Cylindrical quiver ending in a rounded base and with darts or spears inside.	1	0.2
Blowguns	Blowgun of the type used for hunting.	4	1.0
Bows	Miniature bow with its cord.	3	0.7
Shields	With frame, adorned with birds and danglers.	20	4.9
Hallucinogen trays	Tray of the type used for the inhalation of hallucinogens.	23	5.7
Lime containers	Miniature lime container, together with its dipper pin.	6	1.5
Bag	Cotton bag of the type used to carry coca leaves and lime containers.	1	0.2
Masks	Miniature mask with human features.	6	1.5
Robes	Robe or textile. Designs are visible on the surface.	2	0.5
Belts	Textile belt or band woven in a twisted fashion.	4	1.0
Drums	Cylindrical drum.	8	2.0

Household objects

Objects of this type total ninety (5.4% of votive figures). Miniature household objects are divided into eleven types according to the function of the real objects they represent and their additional elements.

Subtype	Description	Frequency	% of group
Cradles, empty	Cradle made with wooden sticks tied together; there is no human figure in it.	11	12.2
Cradles with babies	Cradle made with wooden sticks with a child (male or female) lying inside.	30	33.3
Benches	Four-legged bench used by chiefs and priests.	3	3.3
Hammock	Miniature hammock with suspension rings.	1	1.1
Weaving looms	Miniature weaving loom with an irregular wooden frame and textile bands held inside.	2	2.2
Baskets	Miniature basket with handles.	25	27.8

Ceramic vessels	Miniature ceramic vessel; forms include bowls and jars.	2	13.3
Bell	Miniature bell or rattle; no sound function.	1	1.1
Fence	Row of crossed wooden sticks forming a fence.	1	1.1
Jaguar pelts	Pelt of a jaguar or similar feline, including its skull and tail, stretched on a rectangular wooden frame.	2	2.2
Deer pelts	Pelt of a deer stretched on a rectangular wooden frame.	2	2.2

Undefined and unknown objects

In this group I have included two types with a total of sixty-three objects (3.8% of votive figures).

Subtype	Description	Frequency	% of group
Undefined/ geometrical objects	Variety of objects of unknown function, or highly schematized representations, including complex geometrical objects.	8	12.7
Unknown objects	No precise description available.	55	87.3

Main iconographic traits

Many people, animals and objects drawn from both the everyday and the ritual life of the Indian communities of the Eastern Cordillera are represented in metal figures. Seventy-six different categories of representations convey an idea of what was considered important in religious terms. If the intention was, indeed, to represent what made up the universe of the community, then it is worth looking also at the range of people and things which existed in the region but were not modelled in metal. The subjects that do not appear include: anthropomorphic figures representing diseased or malformed persons; anthropozoomorphic figures; various kinds of animals; most types of scenes, such as fighting and hunting; all types of buildings (except enclosures); and all forms of vegetation (with the possible exception of a cactus tree).

Representations of malformations and disease are common in north-western South America, especially in the Pacific Coast, from the Tumaco area in southern Colombia to northern Peru.[13] They also appear in the metal and terracotta votive figures of other cultures such as, for example, southern Italy[14] and Jaina Island, Mexico.[15] Diseases causing conspicuous malformations and genetically determined anatomical defects have been reported for Muisca and other Chibcha populations of the Eastern Cordillera.[16] They are completely absent in the votive offerings of the region.

There are many differences between the iconography of the votive and non-votive sets of objects, and one concerns the representation of sexual characteristics. In the non-votive group there are no representations of sexual organs or sexual intercourse whatsoever; yet in the votive group sex is a most prominent feature of anthropomorphic figures. While only two examples of sexual intercourse are found, sexual organs are clearly depicted in nearly three-quarters of the figures. Taking all the above into account, there seems to be a pattern determining what is acceptable within the iconographic universe of votive items that is rigidly adhered to and differs radically from the patterns governing the decoration of adornments.

Anthropozoomorphic motifs are clearly not as common in the Eastern Cordillera as in other goldworking areas of Colombia. There is one, however, which is extremely important and constitutes the core of adornment iconography: birdmen. One would expect this shamanistic motif to be occasionally, if not frequently, present in votive figures. I was unable to record a single figure depicting the combination of bird and human characteristics found in pendants and breastplates. Birds appear by themselves, decorating staffs, spearthrowers, benches and trays, or on the head or shoulders of anthropomorphic figures – never combined with men in one single figure (Fig. 6.3).

The range of animals represented in votive figures is quite different from those appearing on adornments. Even though birds are present in the votive group, they have less pre-eminence. At the same time other animals, very scarce or completely absent in adornments, acquire an important role, as is the case with jaguars and snakes. Both are frequent and enormously varied in their representations. Another animal absent in the votive context is the frog, otherwise common in necklaces and pendants.

The range of scenes is rather limited. While

6.3 Man with staff and birds
(male figures category).

most of them seem to convey very special ritual activities (i.e. a sacrifice, an offering or an important person standing in the middle of an enclosure), others refer to domestic or, at least, not distinctly ritual activities; this is the case with couples embracing and the alligator that has eaten a man. The existence of other types of scenes could, therefore, be expected. Hunting, and especially deer hunting, was a very important activity with ritual connotations.[17] War was an ever-present part of life in certain areas of Muisca territory since it was the only way of keeping the Magdalena valley tribes at bay.[18] On the other hand, weapons, people carrying them and warriors with trophies are frequently depicted. There are, however, no figures depicting actual combat or hunting scenes.

Enclosures, with or without people in them, occur quite frequently (Fig. 6.4). Some even have a rough representation of the avenues that opened in front of them and served for ritual competitions.[19] Not one shows the buildings (such as houses and temples) which stood inside.[20] Nor are houses and temples found as separate images.

There are, finally, no representations of trees or plants of any kind. One object, which I have not been able to examine personally, looks very much like a cactus tree. If it is indeed a cactus, then it would be the only such case. Plants and vegetable products are represented in metal objects elsewhere in prehispanic Colombia (e.g. in Calima, Quimbaya and Palmira objects). Moreover, they played an important role in the life of Chibcha communities of the Eastern Cordillera; their range of uses included, naturally, some ritual ones such as the building of temples with special logs of *Guayacan* brought from the eastern Orinoco Basin plains.[21] Coca plants were highly valued for their leaves, as were tobacco and some other lesser-known varieties, but none were represented in votive contexts.

Despite this, it is worth looking again at the iconographic universe of votive items. Human figures form a very important part of the group (Fig. 6.5), both in quantitative and qualitative terms; they number 932 (including scenes and objects with human figures), which is 55.6% of all the votive figures. There are three times more male than female figures and, as a whole, men tend to be more elaborate than women; the simplest type of figure for both sexes (women/men without additional elements) forms a much larger proportion of the female group (31.3%) than of the male one (19.6%). On the other hand, complex, elaborate and large figures tend to be more frequent in the male than in the female group.

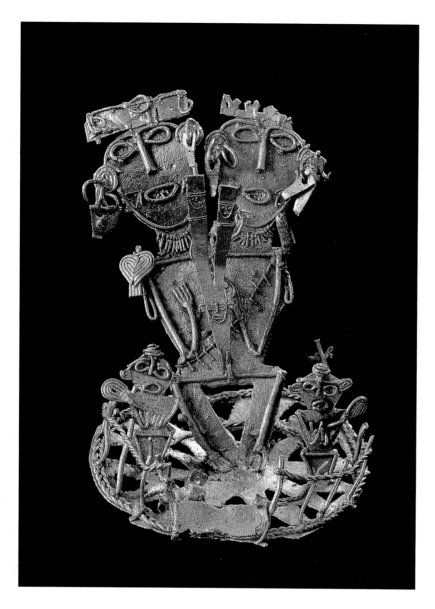

6.4 (above) Enclosure with main and secondary figures (scenes category).

6.5 (above right) Man sitting on a bench (male figures category).

The existence of a large group of unsexed figures (181 or 10.8% of the votive items) is extremely interesting. As I have already pointed out, the absence of sex organs is not due, at least in an overwhelming majority of the cases, to the representation of garments which might have covered them. Most of the categories and attributes present in the male and female groups are also present in the unsexed figures, even though they are even less elaborate and complex than the female figures. The simplest type (without additional elements) constitutes the majority (58%) of the group.

The categories that I established for the classification reflect the most conspicuous characteristics, but they do not account for the wide range of variation present in anthropomorphic figures. Apart from sexual features and attributes such as staffs, birds, weapons, lime containers, trays,

bags, benches, adornments and body postures, there are many different types of headdresses[22] and forms and positions of parts of the head and body.[23] The range of different figures is such that, to a certain point, it can be said that there are no two figures alike in every detail. Whether these differences are due to regional variation in the manufacture of types or whether they are just the expression of particular stages of production in different workshops will have to be investigated. It is evident, nonetheless, that the final form of votive figures was not determined by very strict models; this may also explain the limited use of matrices to cast votive figures. As long as basic attributes were present, details could vary widely.

The scenes constitute another interesting group. Even though limited in number (67 or 4% of votive items), they are, by far, the most elaborate objects. Some scenes are readily identifiable as

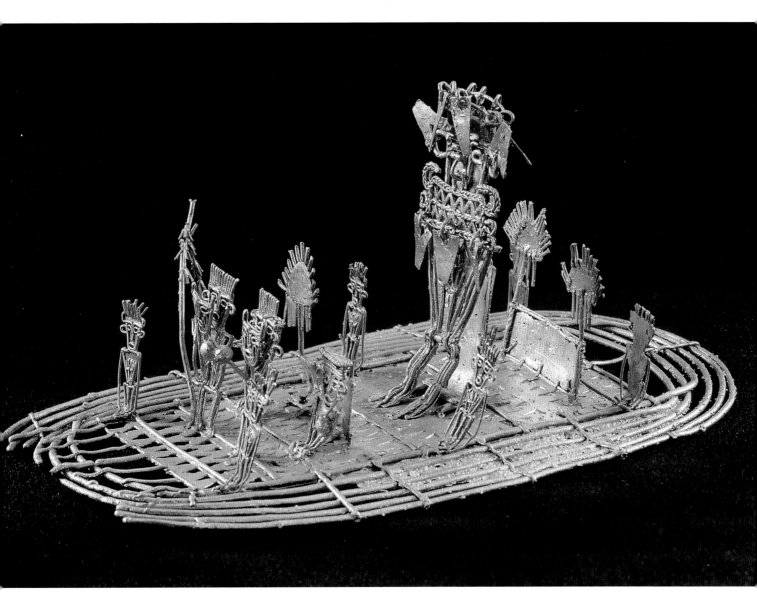

6.6 Raft (scenes category).

depictions of significant events or acts of ritual life which are well known from the ethnohistoric documentation;[24] that is the case with chiefs on litters, enclosures, rafts (Fig. 6.6) and sacrificial posts. There are some other, somewhat problematic, scenes: double heads springing from single unsexed bodies; couples making love; and an alligator with a human head inside its open belly. These later types are extremely rare.

I have already mentioned that jaguars and snakes are especially important in the group of animal votive figures (Figs 6.7–8). Both are known to have had special significance in Muisca and Guane mythology. Jaguars were hunted and their skins used by shamans for ritual occasions,[25] sometimes they were kept captive in cages belonging to the Chiefs.[26] In Guane and northern Muisca pottery jaguars and their skin pattern are often depicted. Snakes were regarded as ancestors

of humanity in the myth of Bachue, one of the main accounts of the origin of humanity.[27] This goddess emerged from Iguaque lake as a snake and then became a woman; after her life on Earth she and her son became snakes again and returned to the depths of the same lake.

The importance of birds representing the drug-induced imaginary flights of shamans has already been mentioned. Birds, however, are divided into two distinct groups, one of which clearly represents species which are not characterized by their ability to fly, or at least to reach great heights, such as pheasants and parrots. Another significant animal is the deer; both species existing in the Eastern Cordillera (*Odocoileus virginianus* and *Mazama sp.*) were regarded as special prey reserved for important people.[28] There is an association in Muisca language between deer (*boychica*), weaving and the cultural hero (*Bochica*),

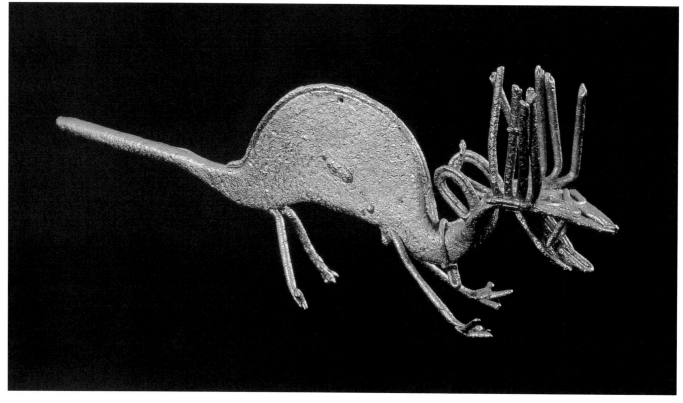

6.7 (top) Serpentiform
jaguar (animals category).

6.8 (bottom) Jaguar
(animals category).

who taught the art of weaving.[29] The significance
of the other animals represented (lizards, turtles,
snails, insects and unidentified mammals) is not
referred to in documents directly linked with
Indian communities of the Eastern Cordillera.

Objects, both for personal use and belonging to
the household, form another big group (495 or
29.6% of votive items). A large proportion (214)
is represented by staffs (with or without birds).

Even though Spanish chroniclers do mention
staffs,[30] they have never been regarded as very
important items. They are probably a symbol of
status and authority, a type of authority which was
in many cases linked with religion and shamans,
as is suggested by the frequent association with
birds.

Spearthrowers were the preferred type of
weapon among Chibcha speakers in the region

6.9 Man with weapons (male figures category).

With the exception of the Guanes, most of the groups inhabiting the Eastern Cordillera have traditionally been regarded as peaceful.[32] Recent studies have shown, nevertheless, that internal conflicts were rife in the years preceding the arrival of the Europeans.[33] It is very likely that war, and the need to fight in order to defend the territories of the communities, has been overlooked as a strong force shaping the life of these societies (Fig. 6.10).

Another group of objects is directly related to the use of drugs: hallucinogen trays (Fig. 6.11), lime containers and bags (Fig. 6.12). They come as no surprise in view of what is known about the use of substances such as coca and *yopo* in the region. There are, finally, several other categories of objects, which are difficult to interpret. An interesting type are cradles, with or without babies (Fig. 6.13). This miscellany includes ritual objects of shamanic use (masks, benches, drums) and ordinary objects (robes, belts, weaving looms, baskets, vessels, etc.), which may have had, in spite of their modest appearance, certain symbolic importance.

Additional characteristics of votive depictions

It is very unlikely that each category of votive offering had a significance of its own, independent from the whole group. The analysis of the sample has shown the recurrence of types, which, apart from minor details, clearly depict the same icon and must, therefore, share much the same meaning. On the other hand, Muisca votive offerings were subject to rigid norms; Spanish chroniclers agree in saying that *jeques* (shamans) determined the type of figure to be offered.[34] In this case it is also quite improbable that the characteristics of the offering were determined by individual needs. This notion is a Judaeo-Christian concept,[35] first applied to American Indians by the sixteenth-century European historians, and has persisted unchallenged in spite of its inability to explain the basic facts of prehispanic offerings. Furthermore, detailed studies of votive offerings in the Old World have shown that their character was, in many cases, very different from the Judaeo-Christian model.[36]

Surface colour is a conspicuous property of metal objects, which is usually achieved intentionally by alloying basic metals or by special surface treatments.[37] This property was accurately determined for 43.9% of the sample; the findings confirm a preference for two groups of colours, whitish yellows (36.6%) and pinkish yellows (31.0%), which were obtained by alloying

(Fig. 6.9); as votive figures, they are very frequent (102) and share with staffs, though to a lesser degree, the association with birds. Shields, blowguns, axes, quivers and bows constitute categories that, due to their use, it is possible to associate with spearthrowers. The iconography of weapons and people carrying them is usually associated with societies frequently involved in war; offerings of real weapons are common in these cases.[31]

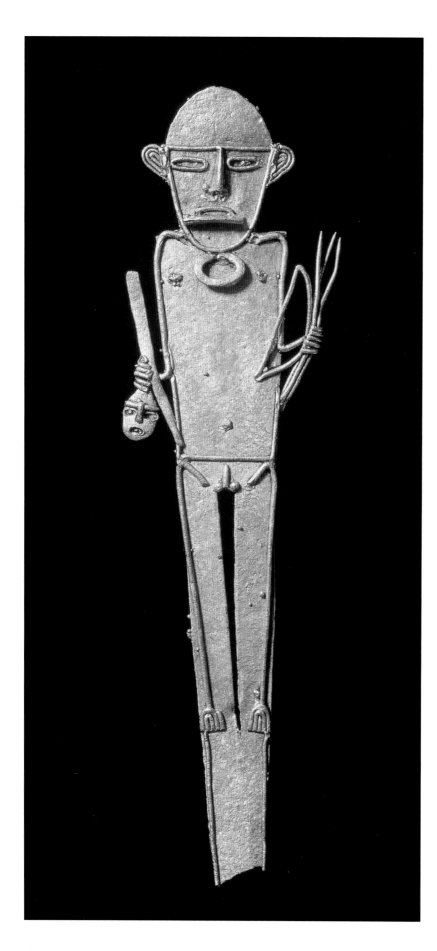

between 70 and 90% gold with 20 to 10% silver (the rest being copper) for the first group, and 60 to 90% gold with 40 to 10% copper for the second group. The remaining 32.4% ranges across several shades of reddish yellows without any definite concentration.

There is no way of knowing the particular significance of the two principal groups of colours but, nevertheless, this bipolar trend agrees with the 'strong tendency towards binary oppositions' found by Osborn[38] among the modern Uwas of the Eastern Cordillera, as well as their colour classification patterns.[39] This prominent feature also seems to have prevailed in prehispanic times.[40] The available data does not show any clear pattern of surface colour emerging for particular types of objects or for specific sites.

Manufacturing technique is predominantly lost-wax casting (82.5%) but, nonetheless, hammering intervenes, either as the sole technique or in conjunction with casting, in 19.9% of the objects. Hammering was an important technique in the Eastern Cordillera and it was extensively used. The importance and use of hammering are better understood when votive items are separated from adornments. In the votive group only 1.4% of the objects are hammered while in the adornments group this figure rises to 37.9%; taking into account the secondary use of hammering for finishing purposes, it must be concluded that this technique was applied to nearly 40% of Eastern Cordillera adornments.

Lost-wax casting with stone matrices is not as frequent as is commonly believed; just 9.3% of the sample was manufactured in this way. The technique is restricted mainly to necklaces and to model human and bird figures in pendants and breastplates. There is no extensive use of it to manufacture votive figures. Lost-wax casting with core was not very frequent either; only 142 objects (4.73% of sample) have cores. There are reasons to believe that goldsmiths in the Eastern Cordillera did not master this technique. Most of the objects cast with cores reveal manufacturing defects, such as voids and porosity. This, however, did not greatly affect the production of tri-dimensional complex objects which were cast in solid blocks.

Finishing is rather coarse for most objects (72.5%), but again there is a marked difference between the votive items and the adornments. Polished and well-polished votive figures amount to just 1.9% of the group; with respect to adornments this figure rises to 59%. It is not possible,

6.10 Warrior with trophy head
(male figures category).

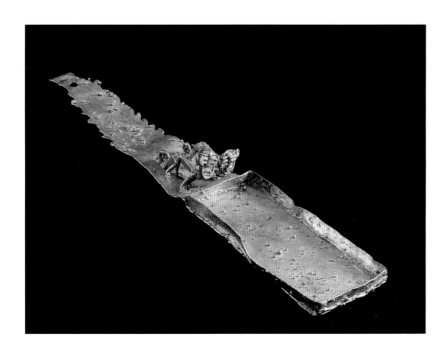

then, to continue to assert that Eastern Cordillera adornments as a whole are characterized by a coarse and careless finish. Surface depletion gilding is present in 2% of the sample; it was possibly used also to obtain certain surface colours not present in the alloy used.

Metallurgical composition is available for just 9.9% of the objects, mainly votive figures. The data show a marked concentration in the range of high to medium gold-content *tumbagas* (40 to 80% gold). Copper is used to a much greater extent than in other prehispanic cultures, with the exception of Nariño in southern Colombia; pure copper and copper-rich (up to 80% Cu) objects amount to nearly 10% of the sample. This proportion is only a fraction of the original one; many copper objects were lost in their burial sites, due to severe corrosion, and many others were not collected by treasure hunters, because they were regarded as valueless.

6.11 (above) Jaguars on a tray (objects of personal use category).

6.12 (right) Lime container (objects of personal use category).

6.13 (far right) Cradle with baby (household objects category).

Another striking fact of metallurgical composition is the consistent presence of silver in relatively high quantities. While most of these results can be explained by the presence of native silver in alluvial gold, one set of very high values (up to 31%) suggests that in some cases it was intentionally added to the alloy, possibly as a means of obtaining very whitish colours. It must be noted that silver is scarce in the Eastern Cordillera and its neighbourhood; apart from the mines which possibly existed near Sogamoso, the nearest sources would have been in the Central Cordillera (Mariquita and La Plata), but it is not certain that they were exploited in prehispanic times.

Votive assemblages and votive grammar

To understand the Muisca votive system, it is important to take into account that many objects were not found on their own but as part of assemblages. The concept of votive assemblage as used in this study requires a precise definition in order to avoid confusion. This is most important, since this work is being carried out in museum collections which lack much contextual information. Votive assemblages in the Eastern Cordillera resemble what López Luján[41] has termed 'caches'. The most important link between the objects making up the assemblage is their contemporaneity; to constitute a cache they must have all been interred at roughly the same time or within a short period, no longer than the life span of a single person. This is usually established by spatial association – the concept of proximity is most important – which is often determined by a container or by any other archaeological structure in which the objects are placed.

Apart from contemporaneity and spatial proximity, the other important condition is that a significant number of expressly votive objects be present. The precise number or proportion is not easily established, since it depends on various factors. Those factors include the total number of objects in the group; the number and relative importance of non-votive objects; the type of site; the presence or absence of votive containers; and the quality and quantity of non-metallic objects. If the group has a clearly votive setting (i.e. a vessel in a hilltop), then the presence of only a few votive figures suffices to classify it as a votive assemblage. If the group comes from a non-votive setting, then a larger proportion of votive figures would be required to distinguish it from other types of groups, such as funerary offerings. Provided that the setting is characteristically votive, a group might be considered as a votive assemblage

even if it contains no proper votive figures; as pointed out, votive offerings were by no means limited to votive figures. Seventy votive assemblages were identified.

The seventy votive assemblages recorded are composed of a minimum of two and a maximum of fifty-seven metallic objects. The size of assemblages, as a general rule, tends to be small. Half of the assemblages recorded have between two and seven elements, while those having more than twenty elements amount to just 15.6%. With respect to the distribution of objects in size categories the larger number of small assemblages counterbalances the smaller number of large assemblages so that overall there is an even distribution.

The number of objects in votive assemblages, 807, accounts for 26.9% of the total number of objects recorded (3,001). Of this total, 196 are non-votive objects and 611 are votive figures; globally speaking, votive assemblages are composed of 24.3% of non-votive objects and 75.7% of votive figures. A proportion of 14.8% of non-votive objects (total 1,326) was found as part of votive assemblages, while 36.5% of votive figures (total 1,675) form part of assemblages. With respect to the relative heterogeneity of votive assemblages, it was found that they are composed of between one and twenty-two different types of objects.

Forty-nine assemblages (70%) have between two and seven different types of objects, while fifty-six (80%) have between two and nine. Thirteen (18.6%) have ten or more types, and five (7.1%) have fifteen or more types. These figures show that variation is limited and that the range of different objects is nearly always low; extremely varied assemblages are unusual.

Another aspect is that of figure predominance, which occurs if any type is present in two out of two, three, four or five objects; three out of six, seven or eight objects; and 25% or more from a total of nine or more objects. If there are two similar and closely related types in the assemblage (i.e. staffs and staffs with birds), then there is combined predominance. If there are two very different types in equal or very close proportions, there is shared predominance.

Out of seventy assemblages, thirty-seven (52.9%) have some type of figure predominance. Predominances are divided in the following manner: twenty-two (59.5%) are simple; nine (24.3%) are combined; five (13.5%) are shared; and one (2.7%) is both combined and shared. The most frequent predominant types are: men with staffs and birds (8); men with weapons (5); staffs with birds (5); staffs (4); spearthrowers (4); unsexed figures without additional elements (4); men without additional elements (3) and necklaces (non-votive) (3). Non-votive objects are predominant in nine cases, of which six correspond to simple predominances, one is a shared predominance between two non-votive types and another a shared predominance between a votive and a non-votive type.

Dualism and dualistic equilibrium

Native American cultures have a special character, which differs greatly from Western culture. The study of the religious systems of several prehispanic and present-day societies has enabled us to gain some insights into what is a very complex vision of the cosmos.[42] Dualism, that is the concept of the whole cosmos and each of its parts as entities composed of opposed complementary principles,[43] seems to be prevalent amongst these societies. Elsewhere, I have proposed that dualistic modes of thought played a significant role in shaping conceptions and patterns of life among Eastern Cordillera groups through different applications of the same underlying principle.[44] An exploration of dualism as it applies to the iconography of votive figures raises interesting questions.

Gender represents the most obvious expression of a dualistic opposition,[45] and tends to reflect the deepest cultural patterns of dualistic thought. I have already called attention to the importance of the representation of gender in anthropomorphic figures, where there are three clearly distinguished groups: female, male and unsexed figures. These groups encapsulate the basic principles involved in dualistic oppositions. In this case it is a complex form of dualistic opposition, which has been recognized elsewhere in South America,[46] involving a triad (three elements) linked by a double opposition. Male figures represent a pole of one of the oppositions, whose other pole is constituted by the unsexed figures; they in turn form another opposition with female figures as shown in the following diagram:

This dualistic pattern can be recognized in

other cultural expressions of the Eastern Cordillera groups.[47] It represents an elaborate form of the simple binary opposition, in which a third element is introduced as a buffer between the extremes (male and female) and in itself incorporates the properties of both. In this way the third element can interact with both the others. The range of possible oppositions includes male–female, male–unsexed, female–unsexed. Anthropomorphic figures probably not only represented but also contained in themselves the essence of basic dualistic principles; to make an offering of them would, therefore, have definite effects upon the equilibrium of these principles in the cosmos.

Reichel-Dolmatoff has drawn attention to the widespread belief among Chibcha-speaking communities that humans are responsible for the preservation of the harmony and equilibrium of the cosmos.[48] In spite of our limited understanding of the full range and depth of religious beliefs among Eastern Cordillera groups, it seems likely that they all shared the notion that man can effectively alter, by means of his actions, the equilibrium of heaven and earth. There are several ways in which this equilibrium can be upset, and mythology is full of descriptions of catastrophic events which are marked by a disruption in the harmony between opposing principles.[49] Restoring the equilibrium and maintaining a watchful eye on any disturbance is the work of religious specialists, shamans or *jeques*, and is achieved mainly through two fundamental actions: sacrifice and offering.

Equilibrium could be upset by an excess of either one of two opposing principles, and restoring the balance demanded the offering of an opposing essence, according to the nature of the disturbance. This underlying rationale probably explains the existence of male and female votive figures. But the equilibrium of the cosmos was certainly not such a simple matter. It must have involved other more subtle oppositions and complementary poles than just a straightforward male–female pair. Complex dualistic visions of the cosmos include oppositions related to existence (life–death); direction and movement (up–down, left–right, still–moving, etc.); colour and brightness (black–white, white–red, dark–bright, etc.); temperature (cold–hot); form and shape (square–round, flat–volume, etc.); smell; taste; texture; sound; and many others which are applied to the understanding of physical phenomena, social events, settlement patterns, kinship and descent, and are often reflected in language.[50]

The very complex nature of the votive offerings

First Opposition   Second Opposition

| MEN | ◄──► | UNSEXED
'Female'   'Male' | ◄──► | WOMEN |

of the Eastern Cordillera suggests that they are the representation of an equally complex system of dualistic oppositions. I have identified the basic principle as a sexual one consisting of a double opposition of three linked principles. The particular attributes of those figures that have enabled me to propose a more refined classification must, therefore, represent secondary dualistic oppositions operating alongside the main one. When our understanding of the full range of religious beliefs is so limited, the identification of the pairs of principles involved in those oppositions becomes speculative and even entirely hypothetical. Nevertheless, it is worth looking at the most conspicuous secondary oppositions and attempting an interpretation of their significance.

Both aggressive and passive attributes seem to be present in various groups, including anthropomorphic figures and those intended for personal use. Warfare was a pervasive concern for the communities of the Eastern Cordillera and is represented as a principle of aggression in a wide array of figures. People armed with weapons and the weapons themselves possibly represent the aggression pole of this dualistic opposition, counterbalanced by the passive principle most probably depicted through figures such as those seated holding knees, people with staffs and household objects. An event, such as the raid by a neighbouring group on a defenceless village, for example, would have altered the equilibrium between aggression and passiveness and may have demanded corrective action such as the offering of large quantities of figures containing the aggression principle.

Another opposition is that between barren and fertile. Fertility seems to be depicted by women with children and children in cradles. The principle of barrenness is expressed through empty cradles. Fertility, of the land as well as the people, is a matter of continuing concern. Natural phenomena, such as droughts, plagues and diseases, upset the equilibrium of fertility, thus demanding corrective actions which often include offerings.[51] The opposite situation, excess fertility, is likely to have been less problematical. It is not surprising, therefore, that figures representing the fertility principle would be much more abundant than those representing the barren principle.

Yet another opposition, which appears in the votive iconography, is that of domination–submission. I believe it is clearly depicted in social terms, with the figures of heavily adorned people, chiefs on litters, and enclosures with one human figure representing the domination principle, and people without additional elements representing the submission principle. Even so, the way in which this opposition was conceived and, therefore, the meaning of its iconographic expression are not limited to the social sphere. As a universal dualistic pair, they extend to all levels of the cosmos. Whenever the equilibrium between what rules and what is meant to be ruled was disturbed, the appropriate remedial measures were required, including perhaps offering elements of some of those principles.

In the context of Amerindian mythology jaguars can be seen to embody the colour, power and strength of the sun.[52] Snakes, on the other hand, are linked with darkness, humidity and the underworld. These two types of animals, which are prevalent in the votive iconography seem to express, therefore, the opposition between brightness and darkness or, from another angle, the world above and the world below. Contrary to what one might suppose, snakes appear more frequently than jaguars. The dominance of the principle of darkness, the underworld, may reflect the overwhelming importance of the earth as the place where life originates.

There is, however, a special characteristic in this opposition. As described above, a variety of jaguars acquire a definite serpentiform shape while, on the other hand, some snakes have very short limbs and feline whiskers and fangs. There is, in fact, a continuum between jaguars and snakes corresponding to another type of dualistic opposition, whereby opposite principles generate an unstable synthesis in danger of reverting to the original principles.[53] The following diagram explains the opposition:

Original opposition

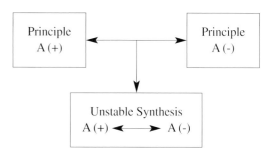

One series of figures that deserves special attention comprises those that incorporate the representation of both principles of the opposition. I have identified this type of dualism underlying the Muisca myth of origin:[54] A single original principle unfolds into its opposite and itself, eventually generating two opposed independent principles which remain linked by their complementarity.

The outcome of this process is illustrated by the diagram:

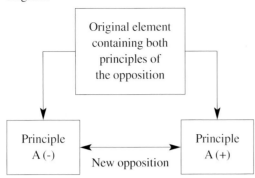

I believe that a particular type of scene, enclosures with main and secondary figures, may well express a domination–submission opposition. The raft scenes, which share with enclosures the depiction of main and secondary figures, might also express such an opposition, even though other important iconographic elements are certainly present in them. A similar variation, this time related to the fertility–barrenness opposition could be depicted in the figures of couples embracing.

The identification of the oppositions that have been analysed does not exhaust the significance of votive iconography. There is, however, a risk of indulging in over-interpretation and conjecture without solid supporting evidence. One final point must be noted: as a general rule, in all the oppositions I have examined, including the main one (male–unsexed–female), there is a dominant principle, one that is more frequent and noticeable. The other principle, less frequent and conspicuous, can be considered as secondary. In the main opposition the dominant principle is male; in the aggression–passiveness opposition it is, undoubtedly, aggression; in the fertility opposition the dominant principle is fertility; in the domination opposition it is, definitively, domination; and in the brightness–darkness opposition the underworld seems to be dominant.

These observations may also help account for the range of 'absent' representations that have been mentioned earlier. Certain anthropomorphic and anthropozoomorphic figures, various kinds of animals, certain types of scenes, all types of buildings and all forms of vegetation are excluded from the votive repertoire because they do not convey any symbolic meaning within the system of oppositions. The primary aim was to express basic principles, not to produce portraits of people, animals and objects. The overall pattern of presence and absence of figures and themes will only make complete sense when it is read as an expression of meaning within a system that may be understood as a visual, symbolic language.

Notes

1 This paper is a revised excerpt of the Ph.D. thesis 'Prehispanic Metallurgy and Votive Offerings in the Eastern Cordillera, Colombia', written under the supervision of Drs Warwick Bray and José Oliver and submitted to University College London in April 1997. The research was based on a sample of 3,001 objects from museums and collections in Colombia and various countries in Europe. The second part of this investigation dealt with the classification and analysis of 1,675 votive objects from that region. Only those votive figures will be described and discussed in this paper.

2 Lleras and Langebaek 1987; Oliver 1989.

3 Osborn 1985.

4 Langebaek 1990; Oliver 1989.

5 Constenla 1992; Lleras 1990.

6 Broadbent 1986; Lleras 1990; Langebaek 1995.

7 Hernández Rodríguez 1975; Reichel-Dolmatoff 1985a; Langebaek 1987; Londoño 1984a, b.

8 Lleras 1992.

9 Lleras and Vargas 1990; Langebaek 1995.

10 Langebaek 1995.

11 Lleras and Vargas 1990.

12 McEwan and Van de Guchte 1992; Van de Guchte 1990.

13 Reichel-Dolmatoff 1965.

14 Girardon 1994.

15 Corson 1976.

16 Boada 1987; Cardenas 1990.

17 Simon 1981 (1625).

18 Ibid.

19 Castellanos 1955 (1601).

20 Ibid.

21 Silva Celis 1945.

22 Peréz de Barradas 1958.

23 Plazas 1975.

24 Aguado 1956; Castellanos 1955 (1601); Simon 1981 (1625).

25 De la Cruz 1984.

26 Londoño 1990.

27 Zerda 1883.

28 Simon 1981 (1625).

29 Londoño, pers. comm.

30 Cetros in Castellanos 1955 (1601).

31 Bradley 1990.

32 Uricoechea 1971 (1854).

33 Londoño 1983, 1984a, b.

34 Aguado 1956; Castellanos 1955 (1601); Simon 1981 (1625).

35 Mauss 1966; Evans-Pritchard 1956.

36 Pinch 1993; Bergman 1985; Englund 1985.

37 Lechtman 1973.

38 Osborn 1995

39 Faust 1990.

40 Lleras 1992.

41 López Luján 1995.

42 Rostworowski 1986; Reichel-Dolmatoff 1981, 1985b, 1988; Osborn 1990, 1995; Faust 1990.

43 Lévi-Strauss 1966.

44 Lleras 1992, following Lévi-Strauss 1966.

45 Ibid.

46 Rostworowski 1986.

47 Lleras 1992.

48 Reichel-Dolmatoff 1985b.

49 Kroeber 1946.

50 Constenla 1992; Correa 1992.

51 López Luján 1995.

52 Reichel-Dolmatoff 1988.

53 Lleras 1992.

54 Ibid.

References

Aguado, Fray Pedro de
1956 *Recopilacion Historial*, Biblioteca de la Presidencia de la República, Bogotá.

Bergman, Jan
1985 Religio-Phenomenological Reflections on the Multi-Level Process of Giving to the Gods. In *Gifts to the Gods*, ed. Linders and Gullog. *Acta Universitatis Uppsaliensis*, no.15. Uppsala.

Boada, Ana María
1987 *Excavación de un asentamiento indígena en el Valle de Samaca (Marin Boyaca)*. FIAN, Banco de la República. Bogotá.

Bradley, Richard
1990 *The Passage of Arms – An Archaeological Analysis of Prehistoric Hoards and Votive Deposits*. University Press, Cambridge.

Bray, Warwick
1978 *The Gold of El Dorado*, exh. cat., the Royal Academy of Arts. Times Books, London.
1984 Across the Darien Gap: A Colombian View of Isthmian Archaeology. In *The Archaeology of Lower Central America*, ed. F.W. Lange and D.Z. Stone. School of American Research Advanced Seminar Series, University of New Mexico, Albuquerque.

Broadbent, Sylvia
1986 Tipólogía Cerámica en el Territorio Muisca, Colombia. In *Revista de Antropología*, Universidad de los Andes, Bogotá.

Cardenas, Felipe
1990 Reconstrucción química de la paleodieta en restos arqueológicos humanos del territorio muisca. Unpublished. WAC II, Barquisimeto.

Castellanos, Juan de
1955 (1601) *Elegias de Varones Ilustres de Indias*. Biblioteca de la Presidencia de la República, Bogotá.

Constenla, Adolfo
1992 Sobre el estudio diacrónico de las lenguas chibcha y su contribución al conocimiento del pasado de sus hablantes. Unpublished. VI Congreso de Antropología en Colombia, Bogotá.

Corson, Christopher
1976 *Maya anthropomorphic figurines from Jaina Island, Campeche*. Studies in Mesoamerican Art, Archaeology and Ethnohistory, no. 1. Ballena Press, Ramona, California.

Correa, François
1992 Analisis formal del vocabulario de parentesco muisca. In *Boletín Museo del Oro* 32–3.

De la Cruz, Martha Lucia
1984 Represión religiosa en el altiplano cundiboyacense durante la Colonia, estudio preliminar. Unpublished. Universidad de los Andes, Bogotá.

Englund, Gertie
1985 Gifts to the Gods – a necessity for the preservation of cosmos and life. Theory and Praxis. In *Gifts to the Gods*, ed. Linders and Gullog. *Acta Universitatis Uppsaliensis*, no.15. Uppsala.

Evans-Pritchard, E.E.
1956 *Nuer Religion*. Oxford University Press, Oxford.

Faust, Franz X.
1990 Apuntes al sistema Médico de los Campesinos de la Sierra Nevada del Cocuy. In *Boletín Museo del Oro* 26.

Girardon, Sheila Patricia
1994 Italic Votive Terracotta Heads from the British Museum: a stylistic appraisal in their religious and historical settings. Ph.D. Thesis, University College, London.

Hernández Rodríguez, Guillermo
1975 *De los Chibchas a la Colonia y la República, del clan a la encomienda y al latifundio en Colombia*. 1949, Biblioteca Basica Colombiana, Colcultura, Bogotá.

Kroeber, Alfred Louis
1946 The Chibcha. In *Handbook of South American Indians*, vol. 2, ed. Julian Steward. Smithsonian Institution, New York.

Langebaek, Carl
1987 *Mercados, poblamiento e integración étnica entre los muiscas, siglo XVI*. Colección Bibliográfica, Banco de la República, Bogotá.
1990 Aguilas y caricuries. Venezuela y su coparticipación en el area orfebre de Colombia. In *Revista Colombiana de Antropología*, vol. XXVII, Bogotá.
1995 Heterogeneidad versus homogeneidad en la arqueologia colombiana : una nota critica y el ejemplo de la orfebreria muisca. In *Revista de Antropología y Arqueología*, no. 7, Universidad de los Andes, Bogotá.

Lechtman, Heather.
1973 A Tumbaga Object from the High Andes of Venezuela. In *American Antiquity*, vol. 38, no. 4, New York.

Lévi-Strauss, Claude
1966 *The Savage Mind*. Weidenfeld and Nicolson, London.

Lleras, Roberto
1990 *Diferentes oleadas de poblamiento en la prehistoria tardia de los Andes Orientales*. Unpublished. WAC II, Barquisimeto.
1992 Las estructuras de pensamiento dual en el ambito de las sociedades indígenas de los Andes Orientales. Unpublished. VI Congreso de Antropología en Colombia, Bogotá.

1997 Prehispanic Metallurgy and Votive Offerings in the Eastern Cordillera, Colombia. Ph.D. Thesis, University College London.

Lleras, Roberto and Carl Langebaek
1987 Producción agrícola y desarrollo sociopolítico entre los chibchas de la cordillera Oriental y serranía de Mérida. In *Chiefdoms in the Americas,* ed. Drennan and Uribe. University Press of America, Lanham.

Lleras, Roberto and Arturo Vargas
1990 Palogordo; La Prehistoria de Santander en los Andes Orientales. In *Boletín Museo del Oro* 26.

Londoño, Eduardo
1983 La conquista de la laguna de Cucaita para el Zaque. Un hecho militar prehispanico muisca conocido por documentos de archivo. Unpublished. Departamento de Antropología Universidad de los Andes, Bogotá.
1984a Los cacicazgos Muiscas a la llegada de los conquistadores españoles. El caso del Zacazgo o 'Reino' de Tunja. Unpublished. Departamento de Antropología, Universidad de los Andes, Bogotá.
1984b Relación de una conquista prehispanica muisca y nuevas noticias sobre el Zaque de Tunja. Unpublished. III Congreso de Antropología en Colombia, Bogotá.
1990 Miguel de Ibarra, Memoria de los ritos y ceremonias de los muiscas en el siglo XVI. In *Revista de Antropología*, vol. VI, no. 1. Bogotá.

López Luján, Leonardo
1995 *The Offerings of the Templo Mayor of Tenochtitlan.* University Press of Colorado, Niwot.

McEwan, Colin and Maarten Van de Guchte
1992 Ancestral Time and Sacred Space in Inca State Ritual. In *Ancient Americas – Art from Sacred Landscapes*, ed. Richard F. Townsend. The Art Institute of Chicago.

Mauss, Marcel
1966 *The Gift*, trans. Ian Cunnison. Oxford University Press, Oxford.

Oliver, José R.
1989 The Archaeological, Linguistic and Ethnohistoric Evidence for the Expansion of Arawakan into North-Western Venezuela and North-Eastern Colombia. Ph.D. Thesis, University of Illinois.

Osborn, Ann
1985 *El Vuelo de las Tijeretas.* FIAN, Banco de la República, Bogotá.
1990 Comer y ser comido los animales en la tradición oral Uwa (Tunebo). In *Boletín Museo del Oro* 26.
1995 Las cuatro estaciones. Mitologia y Estructura social entre los Uwa. Coleccion Bibliografica, Banco de la República, Bogotá.

Perez de Barradas, Jose
1958 *Orfebrería Prehispánica de Colombia. Estilos Tolima y Muisca.* Texto y Laminas. Talleres Gráficos Jura. Madrid.

Pinch, Geraldine
1993 *Offerings to Hathor.* Griffith Institute, Oxford.

Plazas, Clemencia
1975 *Nueva Metodología para la clasificación de Orfebreria Prehispánica.* Jorge Plazas, Bogotá.

Reichel-Dolmatoff, Gerardo
1965 *Colombia, Ancient Peoples and Places.* Thames and Hudson. London.
1981 Things of Beauty Replete with Meaning – Metals and Crystals in Colombian Indian Cosmology. In *Sweat of the Sun, Tears of the Moon: Gold and Emerald Treasures of Colombia,* ed. D. Seligman, pp. 17–33, exh. cat., Natural History Museum of Los Angeles County. Terra Magazine Publications, Los Angeles.
1985a *Arqueologia de Colombia: un texto introductorio.* Segunda Expedición Botánica, Bogotá.
1985b *Los Kogi.* Nueva Biblioteca Colombiana de Cultura. Procultura. Bogotá.
1988 *Orfebreria y chamanismo. Un estudio iconográfico del Museo del Oro.* Editorial Colina, Medellin.

Rostworowski, Maria
1986 *Estructuras Andinas del Poder. Ideología religiosa y Política.* Instituto de Estudios Peruanos, Lima.

Silva Celis, Eliecer
1945 Investigaciones arqueológicas en Sogamoso, Departamento de Boyaca. In *Boletín de Arqueología,* vol. 1. Servicio Arqueologico Nacional, Bogotá.

Simon, Fray Pedro
1981 (1625) *Noticias Historiales de las conquistas de tierra firme en las Indias Occidentales*. Biblioteca Banco Popular. Bogotá.

Uricoechea, Ezequiel
1971 (1854) *Memoria de las Antiguedades Neogranadinas.* Banco Popular, Bogotá.

Van de Guchte, Maarten
1990 Carving the World – Inca Monumental Sculpture and Landscape. Ph.D. Thesis, University of Illinois at Urbana-Champaign.

Zerda, Liborio
1883 *El Dorado; estudio historico, etnográfico y arqueológico de los chibchas, habitantes de la antigua Cundinamarca y de algunas otras tribus.* Imprenta de Silvestre. Bogotá.

7

The Gold of Greater Zenú

Prehispanic Metallurgy in the Caribbean Lowlands of Colombia

Ana María Falchetti

Introduction

The Caribbean lowlands of Colombia have long been renowned for the range and quality of their prehispanic goldwork. The first Spanish expeditions to the Sinú and San Jorge rivers in the early sixteenth century found flourishing towns inhabited by the Zenú and obtained significant amounts of gold from the Indian graves.

The conquistadors observed vestiges of the past, including many earthern mounds, and referred to the former splendour of these populous lands. The chronicles of the period describe an extensive ancient territory, which was formerly divided into three 'provinces' – Finzenú, Panzenú and Zenufana – located along the Sinú, San Jorge, Cauca and Nechí rivers. This was 'Greater Zenú', the ancestral territory of the Zenú people (see maps p. 93 and Fig. 7.2).[1]

Archaeological research enables us to reconstruct the history of settlement in the San Jorge drainage and the development of the Zenú people and their ancestors during a period of more than 2,000 years. Through the centuries they gradually constructed an elaborate system of artificial canals which grew to embrace some 500,000 hectares of swamp lands, the largest prehispanic hydraulic system in the American continent. These populations reached their greatest prosperity around the years AD 500–1000. After this time the Zenú people gradually abandoned the seasonally flooded plains for the higher regions to the west, where they survived until the sixteenth century.[2]

The classification of the numerous metal objects found in the Caribbean lowlands and the study of their technical, morphological and iconographic characteristics have made it possible to define the diagnostic features of this metallurgy

and organize the abundant information provided by the objects themselves. This analysis, combined with archaeological data for the area, has facilitated the difficult task of matching subgroups to stages in a long development that lasted more than 1,500 years. The present study reveals the limitations of the evidence, but at the same time traces the principal metallurgical developments and establishes guidelines and priorities for future work.

The descriptions in the chronicles and early documents, as well as traditions preserved by present-day Zenú communities, can shed some light on the social and religious function of gold in ancient Zenú society and on the possible meaning of some elements of its rich iconography. Although the modern communities who inhabit the reserve of San Andrés de Sotavento in the northern Caribbean lowlands have lost their language and have adopted many non-traditional customs and beliefs, they still conserve elements of their ancient traditions and cosmology. Diverse influences have gradually modified the interpretations that this society makes of its own beliefs, but the essence of ancient myths survives as well as traditional components of social and ritual occasions, for symbolic systems are resistant to change. Surviving local traditions prove to be helpful in the attempt to find some explanations about the symbolism of gold in the past. Even the fragmentary remnants of the original system of beliefs can offer intriguing insights into the ancient cosmological order.

Based on the study of goldwork, together with archaeological, historical and mythological data, the following is an interpretation of the history of Zenú metallurgy and of aspects related to the symbolism of gold and of some iconographic representations.

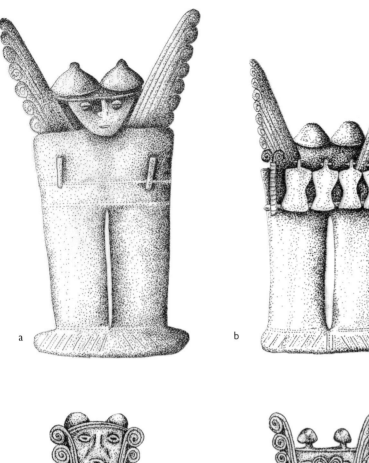

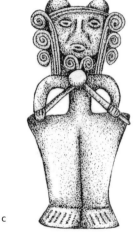

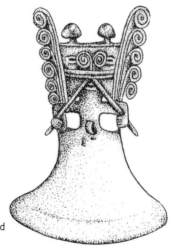

7.1 Regional interpretations of 'Darién Pectorals' have been found from Central Colombia to Yucatán (Mexico): (a) Lower San Jorge river, northern Colombia; (b) Sinú river area, northern Colombia; (c) San Carlos, Costa Rica; (d) Chichén Itza (Yucatán), Mexico.

Zenú goldwork and the development of metallurgy in northern Colombia and the Central American Isthmus

The development of prehispanic metallurgy in the Caribbean lowlands of Colombia must be understood in the context of a process which included an extensive area in central and northern Colombia and the lower Central American Isthmus. During the first centuries AD the transmission of metallurgical knowledge stimulated its adoption over the whole region. The technology emphasized casting techniques, gold-copper alloys (*tumbaga*) and depletion gilding, and shared forms and

iconographic attributes played a fundamental role in the development of northern regional styles.

The earliest metal objects produced in the Isthmus – conjoined animals, simple two-headed birds and double spiral pendants, among others – have been defined by Bray as the Initial Group, which developed during the early centuries after Christ.[3] Due to the homogeneity of the group, its sudden appearance and lack of technological antecedents in Panama and Costa Rica, Bray argues for the introduction from outside and looks to Caribbean Colombia through the Urabá region as a source of transmission of technological knowledge; this was a fundamental link in a very old pattern of relationships.[4]

Among the many prehispanic metal objects from northern Colombia housed in the Gold Museum of Bogotá, we can identify a number of items that are directly related to the Initial Group and form part of local metal assemblages in San Pedro de Urabá[5] and in the vicinity of the Sierra Nevada of Santa Marta, where they belong to the Early Tairona Group dating to a period prior to AD 900.[6] Some additional isolated finds of double spiral pendants and other items related to the Initial Group come from northern Colombia.

In the Isthmus the Initial Group merges into the assemblage defined by Bray as the International Group, produced prior to AD 900. It includes a number of anthropomorphic figures that have been found over an extensive area from central Colombia to Costa Rica; some items appeared as far away as Yucatán (Mexico) in Maya territory.[7] Human figures that have similar traits but are clearly local variants show similarities with the naturalistic personages depicted on Early Quimbaya metallurgy from Central Colombia.[8] These similarities indicate the importance of Quimbaya technology – which emphasizes lost-wax casting and gold-copper alloys – and of its characteristic shape and stylistic features, in the development of metallurgy in northern Colombia and the Isthmus.[9] Some of the 'International' figures mentioned above appear to be associated with schematic anthropomorphic representations known as 'Darién Pectorals' (Fig. 7.1) and with human figures with recurved headdresses, with which they frequently hybridize.[10]

'International' metal objects produced in the early centuries AD share a common iconography which could indicate that they were not originally tied to any local ideology or mythology.[11] However, the objects do have regional differences. Local adaptations of techniques that show the distant influence of Quimbaya metallurgy are evident,[12] as well as differences in morphological

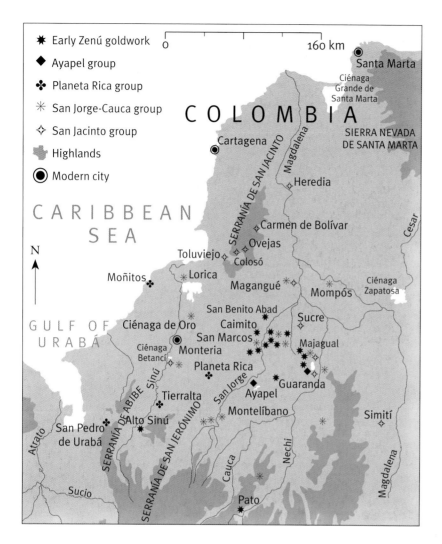

7.2 Map showing distribution of goldwork groups in the Caribbean lowlands.

and stylistic features and in particular hybrid figures. These regional preferences demonstrate the strength of the local cultures, which progressively absorbed different external influences, developing characteristic goldwork assemblages that anticipated the consolidation of regional styles in northern Colombia and the Isthmus. Each local style has unique features, such as a particular adaptation of technology, a series of forms tied to specific social functions and an iconography with themes, which express a local symbolic system.

Several forms included in the Initial and International Groups were incorporated in regional styles and adapted to the local technology, style and iconography. As will be mentioned later, Zenú metalwork of the Caribbean lowlands includes double-headed birds and other forms which have, however, a very local style. Additionally, the basic technology of Quimbaya metalwork and the naturalistic orientation of its iconography appear to have influenced Zenú goldwork in its early stages. As will be seen later,

local variants of forms related to the International Group, such as 'Darién pectorals', were in use during many centuries in northern Colombia.

During the first centuries AD, while Early Quimbaya gold was produced in central Colombia and objects related to the International Group were in use in many regions, Zenú goldwork had already developed as a local style, associated with an important cultural development in the Caribbean lowlands.

A definition of Zenú goldwork

The area of distribution of prehispanic Caribbean metallurgy covers the basins of the Sinú, San Jorge, Nechí, lower Cauca and lower Magdalena rivers, as well as the San Jacinto mountain range, with a total number of more than seventy recorded provenances. Related objects have been found in neighbouring areas, such as the Sierra Nevada of Santa Marta and Urabá (Fig. 7.2).

The study of more than 5,000 metal items has helped me to distinguish four forms that are particularly characteristic of Caribbean metallurgy:[13] staff heads, cast-filigree ear ornaments (Fig. 7.3), nose ornaments with elongations and breastplates decorated with raised bosses . Although they exhibit a great range of variation in technological, morphological and stylistic details, these forms always maintain a basic pattern, which shows they were made to fulfil the same special social functions. Their distribution covers part of the Greater Zenú territory described in the chronicles, but some of them – especially cast-filigree ear ornaments and breastplates with raised bosses – also spread to neighbouring areas.

These shapes are most distinctive of the metallurgy traditionally called 'Sinú'. However, this term could be misleading for it might be interpreted as restricting that widespread metallurgy to a single geographical setting: the Sinú river valley. We prefer to apply the term 'Zenú', to encompass a much wider tradition, for there are indications in the archaeological and historical data that those forms are associated with a long history of goldworking related to the Zenú people.

I have identified several groups of goldwork on the basis of repeated associations of specific types of objects in different finds. Each group includes one or more of the distinctive Zenú forms, as well as special shapes and traits. Analysis of morphological, technical, stylistic and iconographic features has allowed me to corroborate the association of particular types of objects with shared elements. The groups of goldwork are,

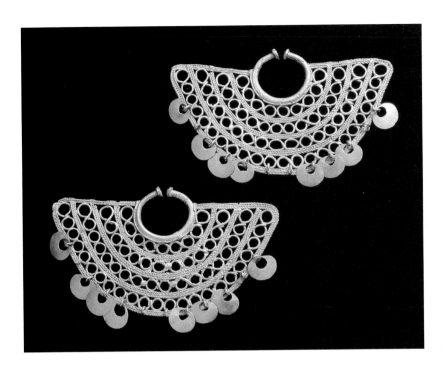

7.3 Cast-filigree ear
ornaments (width 13.6 cm)
typical of Zenú goldwork.

nization and frontiers of prehispanic communities, cultural, technological and even ideological traits have a diffuse distribution that varied through time. We cannot speak of groups of goldwork isolated in time and space, for they represent the precursors of a long and increasingly complex cultural process that we are just beginning to reconstruct.

The goldwork assemblages defined as 'Early Zenú', 'Planeta Rica Group', 'Ayapel Group' and 'San Jorge-Cauca Group' appear in funerary mounds built by communities who inhabited an extensive territory in the Sinú, San Jorge and lower Cauca drainages, and possibly part of the Nechí river area. These communities transformed the natural landscape with a system of artificial canals in seasonally flooded plains (Fig. 7.4), raised house platforms and burial mounds. They produced assemblages of gold and pottery objects with local traits, which at the same time are very closely interrelated through common shapes,

7.4 Artificial canals and
raised fields, lower
San Jorge river area.

however, related one to another, testifying to the presence of a common tradition.

Each group of goldwork can be defined as an assemblage that was produced and used by communities occupying a particular geographical setting during a specific period of time (Fig. 7.2). None, however, belongs exclusively to a geographical area: with the fragmentary information available, it is not possible to know the precise original distribution of the objects, and we should bear in mind that, due to the fluid territorial orga-

function, technology and iconography, showing that they belonged to a single 'great family'. Such is the case of the 'Modelled and Painted' pottery tradition – the characteristic cream-coloured wares with appliqué and modelled decoration or with geometric designs in red paint – which has an extensive geographical distribution in the San Jorge river basin and neighbouring areas.[14] The Modelled and Painted tradition is clearly related to pottery of the 'Betancí Complex' identified by Reichel-Dolmatoff (1957) for the Sinú river area.

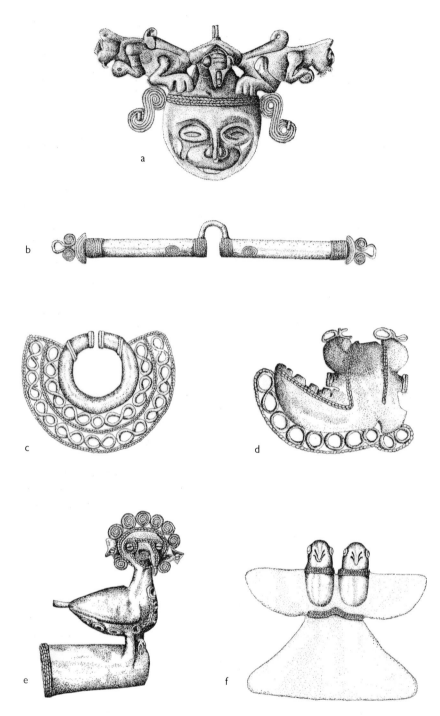

7.5 Early Zenú goldwork:
(a) pendant in the shape
of a human head; (b) nose
ornament with elongations;
(c) cast-filigree ear
ornament; (d) finial in the
shape of a crustacean's claw;
(e) staff head; (f) pectoral
with two-headed bird.

economic factors. This could partly explain the variety and abundance of gold objects and the existence of different groups of goldwork that show a strong 'Zenú identity' and belonged to a long-lasting tradition.

Towards the northern limits of the Caribbean lowlands different influences were responsible for the production of highly characteristic metalwork. The 'San Jacinto Group' shows not only the influence of Zenú goldwork but also changes in technology and a different context. In this area metallurgy seems to reflect the confluence of two ethnic groups: Zenú and Malibú.

Zenú goldwork through time

Early Zenú goldwork

Early Zenú goldwork (Fig. 7.5) was produced by communities who were heirs to a cultural tradition which developed in the Caribbean lowlands over a period of many centuries. In the lower San Jorge region the construction of artificial canals began as early as the ninth century BC. The earliest habitational site investigated in the area dates back to the second century BC, and the gradual development of the local communities reached its peak between the fifth and tenth centuries AD.[15] We know little about the initial stages of development of Early Zenú goldwork,[16] but the information shows that it was fully developed in the first centuries AD, and that it is associated with pottery belonging to the Modelled and Painted Tradition. Early Zenú objects have also been found to the east, towards the lower Cauca valley, and some items appeared in the Sinú valley.[17]

A relationship between Early Zenú goldwork and objects of the International Group mentioned in previous pages is suggested by the presence of local interpretations of pectorals in the shape of two-headed birds (Fig. 7.5f) and human figures with recurved headdresses. The technological influence of Early Quimbaya metalwork is apparent in the preference for casting techniques and in the use of *tumbaga* with a high gold content, depletion gilding and cast filigree as the principal decorative method. Some elements of the iconography, such as naturalistic representations and the traits and decoration of the human face, are also reminiscent of Quimbaya metalwork. Early Zenú goldwork also shows some links with Early Tairona metallurgy which developed, near the Sierra Nevada of Santa Marta, during the first centuries AD. The two assemblages share a basic technology and some forms, such as elongated laminar pendants and finials in the shape of a crustacean's claw (Fig. 7.5d). In the first centuries

We believe that these elements – goldwork and pottery assemblages – define a cultural complex belonging to related communities with local characteristics and a specific geographical setting, who shared dwelling and funerary patterns and a similar approach in their adaptation to the lowland environment.

Analysing the information provided by the gold itself, together with archaeological and historical data, we believe that this reflects the presence of different centres of manufacture whose importance fluctuated due to social, political and

7.6 Early Zenú staff head with representation of alligator, made from cast *tumbaga* with enriched surface and found in the lower Cauca area (width 15.4 cm).

AD Early Zenú metalwork was already an established style, while the Early Tairona assemblage is an initial phase of what was to become Late Tairona metallurgy which flourished after AD 1000.[18]

Besides the features that link it to neighbouring styles, Early Zenú metalwork has a number of highly characteristic features of its own. Although it includes hammered ornaments of high-grade gold, there is a noticeable preference for large heavy objects, cast in gold or *tumbaga* with a low copper content, and surface enriched. Distinctive shapes include large staff heads adorned with animal figures (Fig. 7.5e), nose ornaments with elongations (Fig. 7.5b) and pendants in the shape of human heads (Fig. 7.5a). These items are frequently decorated with cast filigree, a distinctive technique also used to make ear ornaments with thick cast wires (Figs 7.3 and 7.5c). Conical penis covers, pendants in the shape of felines, bells, barrel-shaped and bird-shaped beads, can also be added to the list of characteristic Early Zenú items.

Fauna typical of the lowland plains, swamps and neighbouring environments are depicted in a naturalistic style. The list includes egrets, various species of duck, ibis, owls (Fig. 7.5e), birds of prey (Fig. 7.5f), alligators, deer, felines and peccaries.[19] The symbolism of some of these animals and their association with a particular cosmological order have survived in the traditions of present-day Zenú communities who inhabit the San Andrés reserve.

These traditions, which have been compiled by Turbay and Jaramillo (1986, 1994, 1998), explain how the universe consists of three different layers with human beings living in the central, terrestrial 'world'; the upper and lower zones are inhabited by different 'spirits'. The lower world is associated with water and with spirits in the form of golden animals, which are the 'owners' of the paths and caves that exist under water. The most important of the lower world's water spirits is the golden alligator, which supports the world and protects humanity.[20]

The alligator, an animal which is common in the iconography of Early Zenú (Fig. 7.6) and other gold assemblages of the Caribbean lowlands, is associated, in contemporary Zenú tradition, with turtles, water snakes and amphibians. These animals are related to the lower world but at the same time they are classified in the category of animals that 'belong to different worlds' and provide balance between them, due to their ability to move on earth and in water.[21] Turtles are absent from the iconography of Early Zenú gold and amphibians are scarce. However, turtles are represented on a Modelled and Painted vessel from the lower San Jorge river and, as will be seen later, these animals sometimes appear in other gold assemblages of the Caribbean lowlands. Snakes are not explicitly depicted on Early Zenú iconography, although they were probably represented in a very schematic manner; cast-filigree earrings adorned with wire in the shape of rings and figures-of-eight (Figs 7.3 and 7.5c) are reminiscent

7.7 Early Zenú cast-gold staff head with representation of deer (height 12.9 cm).

these traditions, water birds do not seem to be as important as terrestrial and aquatic animals. We have to bear in mind that aquatic birds belong to the seasonally flooded lands, the former territory of the Zenú. Although the present-day reserve of San Andrés covers three different environments – the hills of the San Jerónimo mountain range and the adjacent savannahs and flood plains of the Sinú river – the central zone of the reserve is the mountainous area. This could partly explain the secondary importance, in contemporary Zenú beliefs, of some species endemic to the flood plains, the result perhaps of an adjustment to historical evolution and to changes in geographical location.

However, people from the San Andrés reserve affirm that they came from the Sinú river in the past, and in their traditions there seem to be remnants of an old system of beliefs related to the role of seasonally flooded lands as the 'heart' of ancient Zenú territory. The present-day Zenú attribute special importance to animals associated with the lower world and to the balance between earth and water. In the seasonally flooded lands earth and water mingle and must be kept in constant equilibrium to ensure people's survival, a balance which would be maintained, in a cosmological context, by golden animals that represent the powers of water and the lower world, and are capable of movement on earth and in water; such animals are characteristic of lowland environments. This might also explain why in contemporary Zenú tradition gold is closely related to the powers of the lower world, in contrast to the association, more common in other Indian mythologies, of gold with the upper world.

The iconography of Early Zenú gold shows the association of felines and birds with human beings. The pendants in the shape of a human head are adorned with headdresses which may include these animals (Fig. 7.5a). In some items it is possible to identify a bird of prey flanked by two bird's heads or by two felines in the act of springing. The human head accompanied by these powerful animals, a very important representation in Early Zenú metalwork, could reflect the idea of the transformation of human beings into animals whose powers they obtain in the supernatural world.

The Planeta Rica Group

This group of goldwork (Fig. 7.9) includes items found in large cemeteries of funerary mounds located in the area between the San Jorge river and the Sinú drainage to the west. Archaeological research is beginning to demonstrate the relation-

of some Tairona ear ornaments from the Sierra Nevada of Santa Marta, which have a similar pattern of cast-filigree decoration that represents the body of the snake, and include a clear representation of the head of the animal.

Terrestrial animals represented on Early Zenú gold, such as felines and deer (Fig. 7.7), also appear in the classification of mammals of present-day Zenú people, who distinguish three 'levels': the animals from above (air) such as bats, monkeys or squirrels, those from the earth – the 'world' of humanity – such as felines and deer, and those from below such as the armadillo,[22] which is sometimes represented on Betancí pottery objects from the Sinú river.

Water birds are very common in Early Zenú gold (Fig. 7.8, p. 140) and, in general, in Caribbean metalwork. These birds might be important because they can move in different environments, an ability that is emphasized in contemporary Zenú beliefs in the case of other animals which 'belong to different worlds'. Surprisingly, in

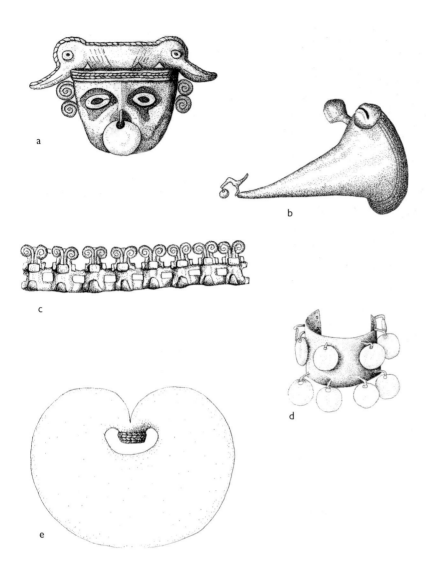

7.9 Planeta Rica Group:
(a) pendant in the shape of a human head; (b) penis cover; (c) pendant with multiple animals; (d) bracelet; (e) breastplate.

water birds and of some other animals which are not common in Early Zenú gold, such as frogs and a few bivalves. Frogs might be expected to play an important role in the mythology of the people of the lowlands; for the present-day Zenú they are associated with female sexuality and belong to the category of animals that can live on earth and in water.[25]

Planeta Rica metalwork shows a preference for geometric design. The group includes simple breastplates as well as nose ornaments, bracelets (Fig. 7.9d), pectorals and other ornaments frequently adorned with many danglers. Ornaments were added to some objects, joining several previously shaped pieces and using, probably, some type of soldering. The combination of metals and alloys of different colours in the same object is apparent in human heads cast in *tumbaga* of a reddish colour, which contrasts with the yellow tone of danglers of high quality, hammered gold.

The Ayapel Group

The Ayapel Group (Fig. 7.10) includes objects with particular shapes and associations found near the limits of the San Jorge flood lands with the higher savannahs to the west. A spectacular grave group, found in a tumulus in 1919 and now housed in the University Museum of Philadelphia,[26] has been used to define this group of goldwork. Related pieces have been found mainly to the east, in the lower Cauca basin.

Archaeological research in Ayapel is still at a preliminary stage and little is known of the chronology of cultural development in the area. However, we know that the region was inhabited by communities related to those of the lower San Jorge, who constructed similar dwelling and burial structures and produced related ceramic materials.[27] The area witnessed a long cultural development which lasted up to the Spanish conquest, when Ayapel was one of the principal towns of the Zenú people.

High-grade gold was hammered to make spectacular ornaments such as breastplates with raised bosses (Figs 7.10d and 7.11). Casting techniques were used to produce staff heads (Fig. 7.10a) and filigree ear ornaments (Fig. 7.10b) which are related to Early Zenú objects but have some different features. Ear ornaments are semi-circular and made of thin cast wires, and staff heads from Ayapel and similar objects found in neighbouring areas are smaller than Early Zenú items. Iconography shows naturalistic figures, but it also favours schematic representations such as the small birds which decorate cast-filigree ear and nose ornaments.

ship between Planeta Rica and contemporary developments in both the San Jorge and the Sinú regions by AD 1000.[23]

The presence in the Planeta Rica Group of a local type of pendant in the shape of two-headed birds, reminds us of the International Group, while other items show a relationship with Early Zenú goldwork. There are some common forms, cast in gold or *tumbaga*, such as anthropomorphic heads adorned with birds (Fig. 7.9a), nose ornaments with elongations and penis covers (Fig. 7.9b). Both groups show the same association between human beings and birds, which suggests a similar orientation in function and meaning. Objects belonging to the Planeta Rica Group have been found in a tomb on the Caribbean coast, to the west of the Sinú river; they were associated with ornaments that are reminiscent of Early Zenú gold, such as a staff head that has been dated, from charcoal in the casting core, to the thirteenth century AD.[24]

Planeta Rica gold includes representations of

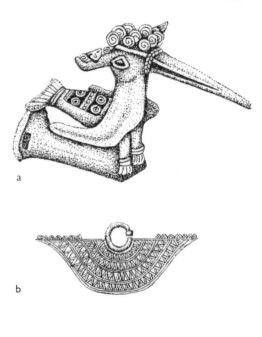

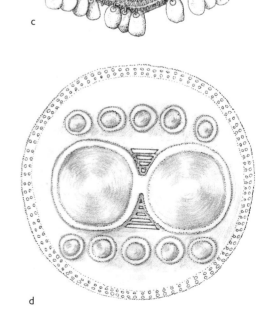

7.8 (above) Early Zenú
cast-gold staff head with
water bird (height 10.4 cm).

7.10 (right) Ayapel Group:
(a) staff head; (b) cast-filigree
ear ornament;
(c) cast-filigree nose
ornament; (d) breastplate.

which supports the world. At the same time, the beam that supports the roof of the Zenú houses – the protection of the social space – is called 'the alligator'.[29] These associations indicate that the space limited by the house is, in fact, an inversion of the lower world inhabited by the golden alligator. In this cosmological scheme, the presence of the alligator in the upper and lower spaces of the breastplates may well symbolize this powerful animal's ability to ensure the stability of the universe and the survival of the human race. The cos-

The iconography includes water birds (*Anhinga anhinga*) (Fig. 7.10a) and alligators (*Crocodylus acutus*),[28] as well as scenes such as the fight between a feline and a snake that decorates a large pectoral and could symbolize the confrontation of the powers of the terrestrial and lower worlds (Fig. 7.11). The body of the snake forms a zigzag and the markings on its skin are represented by rhomboids. The zigzag as a way of reproducing the snake's body is also found on Zenú Modelled and Painted vessels. It is interesting to notice that zigzags and rhomboids predominate in cast-filigree earrings of the Ayapel Group and of other assemblages from the Caribbean lowlands discussed later. Ear ornaments with these motifs are the most numerous and widespread metal items in the Caribbean area (Fig. 7.10b).

Some circular gold breastplates from Ayapel are decorated with alligators which follow the curvature of the upper and lower zones of the ornament. These designs remind us of the cosmological importance of the alligator in present-day Zenú beliefs as the 'spirit' of the underworld,

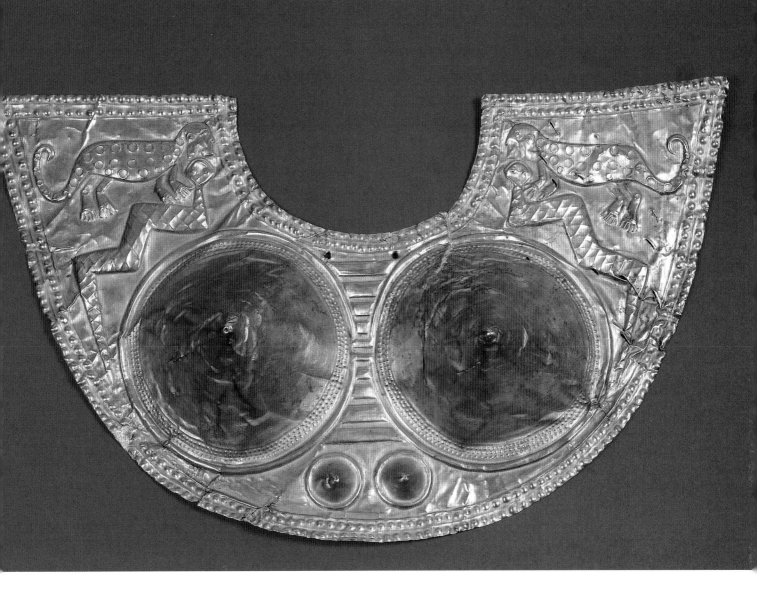

7.11 Hammered and repoussé gold, Ayapel breastplate with raised bosses and designs of jaguars and snakes (width 53.5 cm).

mological power of the golden ornaments would be transmitted to the Indian chiefs or priests, who used them while conducting the ritual activities that ensured the stability of the world and of human society, for in traditional societies the ritual occasions reproduce the acts of the mythical creators who gave origin to the ordered universe.[30]

The San Jorge-Cauca Group

Items belonging to the San Jorge-Cauca Group (Fig. 7.12) have been found over extensive areas of the San Jorge and neighbouring Cauca drainage. In the middle San Jorge river area they are found in large cemeteries of funerary mounds, one of them dated to the tenth century AD.[31] There, gold is associated with a local variety of Modelled and Painted pottery, including human figurines represented as wearing gold ornaments,[32] which match forms of the San Jorge-Cauca Group (Fig. 7.13).

Objects belonging to this group of goldwork also appeared in the Sinú river area where they could be associated with the Betancí Complex. It

is also evident that both the pottery from this complex and the settlement and funerary patterns relate to those of the San Jorge region mentioned above. The correlation of archaeological and historical data indicates that the cultural manifestations that define the Betancí Complex lasted up to the sixteenth century.[33] However, the period of Spanish contact and the definition of the archaeological remains belonging to this period deserve further study in the future.

The San Jorge-Cauca Group includes nose ornaments with elongations (Fig. 7.12f) reminiscent of Early Zenú gold, as well as cast-filigree ear ornaments (Fig. 7.12a) and breastplates with raised bosses (Fig. 7.12k) related to the Ayapel Group. It introduces new shapes and the mass-production of small items, such as a variety of nose ornaments, the majority hammered out of high-grade gold (Fig. 7.12b–h). Embossed decoration is simple and geometric, with a few stylized anthropomorphic or zoomorphic representations (Fig. 7.14). The numerous cast-filigree ornaments belonging to this group of goldwork are mostly decorated with the zigzag pattern. The

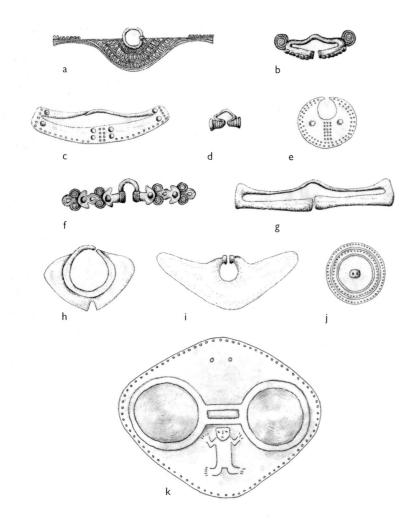

7.12 San Jorge-Cauca
Group: (a) cast-filigree ear
ornament; (b–i) nose
ornaments; (j) textile
ornament; (k) breastplate.

7.13 Modelled and Painted
pottery figurine with
representations of semi-
circular ear ornaments, nose
ornament with elongations
and breastplate, from the
San Jorge river area
(height 17.5 cm).

upper zone of these ear ornaments is usually adorned with small, schematic zoomorphic figures representing water birds, mammals – probably felines – and alligators.

We suggest that highly abstract animal representations are also present; for instance, a particular animal might be represented by the outline of its basic shape and some of its salient traits. Some hammered nose ornaments of high-grade gold may represent two bird's heads, with the beaks located on the upper zone of the nose ornaments on both sides of the suspension loop, and the eyes indicated by embossed circles at the sides. The nose ornaments with converging elongations belonging to the San Jorge-Cauca Group (Figs 7.12b and 7.12g) recall a design present in other regions, such as a pottery vessel from Parita (Panama) which includes more explicit animal features – a face and claws – suggesting a possible interpretation of the figure on the vessel as the front view of a turtle (Fig. 7.15).[34] Some of the Zenú gold nose ornaments mentioned above have protruding elements on both sides, which could represent the claws of the animal (Fig. 7.16), and are decorated with two small alligators; this reminds us that for the present-day Zenú turtles and alligators belong to the same category of animals which can move on earth and in water. Although this interpretation cannot be taken further, one would expect to find representations of the turtle in Zenú metalwork, an animal which is endemic to the seasonally flooded lands and which has been of such importance through the centuries for the local populations. In prehispanic habitational sites the remains of turtles are particularly abundant, and this animal still maintains its importance for the present-day Zenú and for other inhabitants of the Caribbean lowlands, who eat turtles especially at Easter, during social and religious activities.

The Ayapel and San Jorge-Cauca Groups of goldwork testify to a process that needs further study: the expansion and evolution of Zenú goldwork and the mass-production of some ornaments, such as semi-circular cast-filigree ear ornaments, which were used over extensive areas for many centuries and lasted up to the Spanish conquest.

In the sixteenth century the Zenú people maintained a strong metallurgical tradition. Specialized goldsmiths, such as those of Finzenú in the middle Sinú river area, produced items for internal use and for trade. They made objects of high-grade gold and *tumbaga*, using the techniques of hammering, lost-wax casting and depletion gilding. Some descriptions in the Spanish chronicles

7.14 Hammered and repoussé gold breastplate with representation of human face, San Jorge-Cauca Group from the San Jorge river area (width 24.8 cm).

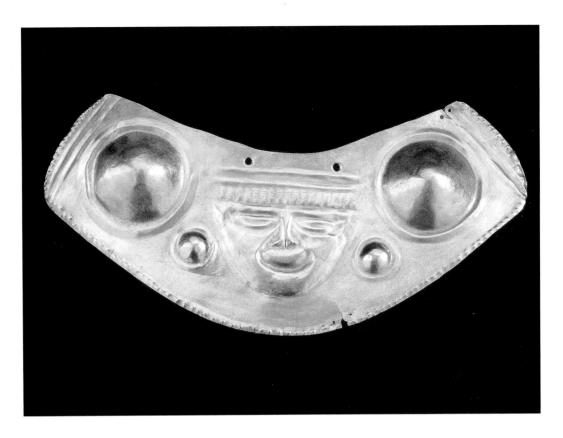

indicate that bells, sheet-metal items and objects in the shape of birds and of terrestrial and aquatic animals were still in use in the sixteenth century as ornaments and offerings, while breastplates with raised bosses were found in the graves looted by the Spaniards in Finzenú.[35]

7.15 Zoomorphic decoration on a vessel from Parita (Panama).

Gold in Zenú society

The combined analysis of historical and archaeological information allowed us to propose that the three ancient 'provinces', which, according to sixteenth-century Zenú tradition, made up Greater Zenú territory, had complementary functions: Zenufana was where the native gold came from, while Finzenú on the Sinú river was important as the land of various craftsmen, and Panzenú on the San Jorge river was the major food producer, especially fish and agricultural products cultivated intensively on the raised fields. Regional specialization and trade were at

7.16 Cast *tumbaga* nose ornament, San Jorge-Cauca Group, found in the lower Cauca river area (width 7.6 cm).

the basis of an economic organization which still survived in the sixteenth century.[36]

In sixteenth-century Zenú tradition, Zenufana – the land of gold – is identified as the most important of the ancestral 'provinces', and it was chosen by the mythical *cacique* Zenufana, who organized Greater Zenú territory, as his own centre of government.[37] Some documentary sources locate Zenufana on the Nechí river area, while others extend this territory to the Abibe mountain range and neighbouring areas where the conquistadors found a *cacique* and a town named Zenufana.[38] The well-known mining centre of Buriticá was located in the Abibe mountains and, according to the chroniclers, this was the source of much of the gold worked by Zenú goldsmiths. However, the mountainous area of Zenufana was not inhabited by the Zenú in the sixteenth century, and we do not know if these lands were once occupied by this ethnic group.[39]

Zenufana was in fact beyond the heartland of the Zenú which covered mainly the lowlands. The 'legendary' nature of this territory in the sixteenth century might be related to its characterization as land 'beyond the limits' of society, which could carry the connotation of distant and unknown lands as analysed by Eliade (1959) in the case of many ancient or non-Western societies: these territories are believed to be inhabited by non-human beings without social norms and are associated with supernatural and ancestral realms. This could explain why in the mythology of people from neighbouring areas, such as the present-day Embera, the 'gold owners' who seem to be related to the ancient gold miners of Zenufana, appear as supernatural beings with animal powers, who 'used their hands as reels to get the gold out of the veins'.[40] The ancestral and supernatural importance of Zenufana might be the reason why the Zenú people maintained trade relationships with these lands whose rich gold deposits supplied the metal for Zenú goldsmiths and whose name survived until the sixteenth century.

Zenú communities were linked by a shared cultural tradition, a system of religious beliefs and a regional political organization. Zenú towns of the sixteenth century, such as Ayapel in the San Jorge drainage (Panzenú) and Finzenú near the Sinú river, were ruled by *caciques* who had regional political control. Finzenú was then an important ceremonial centre inhabited by local chiefs, priests and goldsmiths, and its temple was sacked by the Spanish troops, attracted by the gold offerings it contained.[41] Other ceremonial centres in the Sinú and San Jorge areas had temples devoted to the same deity of Finzenú, testifying to the region-wide importance of a system of beliefs.

In Finzenú there was a necropolis where political and religious leaders were buried during ceremonies which strengthened the social links between communities spread over a large territory. According to sixteenth-century Zenú tradition, the legendary *cacique* Zenufana ordained that all the principal leaders of the Zenú territory should be buried in Finzenú. The mounds were built by the community, and the height reflected the social status of the deceased.[42] Archaeological information confirms this social difference. The mounds located near the edges of thousands of house platforms in the San Jorge area suggest that they were family tombs. There are cemeteries of small mounds which contain a few offerings and special concentrations of large tumuli, more than 6 m high, with multiple burials and hundreds of golden offerings.[43] Multiple burials remind us of the great tumulus of Finzenú – 'the Sepulchre of the Devil', according to the Spanish chroniclers – where many of the Zenú priests were buried.[44]

Present-day Zenú communities still conserve some of the funerary customs practised by their ancestors, such as the construction of artificial mounds. Building the earth mound – which symbolizes the 'roof of the house of the dead' – is a communal activity. Before the mound is constructed, the grave underneath is filled with three layers of earth which are compacted with cylindrical wooden instruments. They say that 'one male and two female instruments stamp on the grave' in a rhythmic dance that symbolizes the moment of fecundation. This ritual 'gives life' symbolically to the dead person and propitiates his 'birth' in another world – where he follows the paths of gold – preventing his spirit from wandering around the houses of the living.[45]

The analogy of the funerary mound with the roof of the house must include the idea of protection for the continuity of life, for the house is the space for social reproduction, and the grave is the 'house' where the process leading to the 'rebirth' of the spirit of the dead begins. Both the house and the funerary mound appear to represent a cosmological model, and the dead would enter that dimension when starting the journey, following the paths of gold in the golden alligator's realm of the lower world.

This cosmological scheme might be at the basis of former funerary practices. Gold objects were 'owned' by the *caciques* of different Zenú towns as one symbol of their sacred power, and these

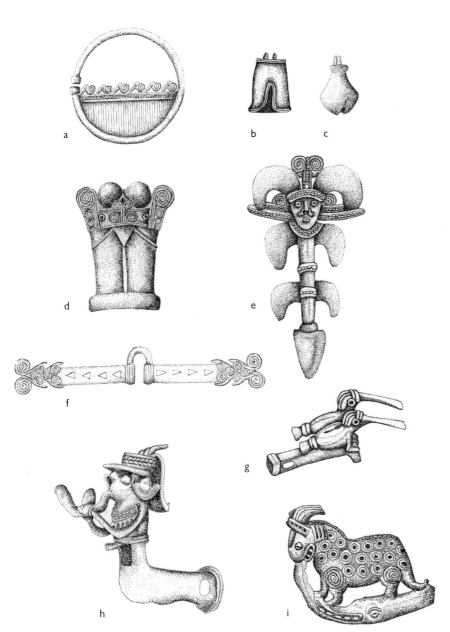

7.17 San Jacinto Group:
(a) cast-filigree ear ornament;
(b) bell; (c) tinkler;
(d) anthropomorphic pectoral
('Darién pectoral');
(e) anthropozoomorphic
pectoral; (f) nose ornament
with elongations;
(g–i) staff heads.

chiefs were supposed to be buried with their ornaments in special cemeteries, such as that of Finzenú. The Spanish chroniclers affirm that if a chief was not buried in Finzenú, half of the gold he had at the time of his death should be buried in the grave assigned to him in that necropolis.[46] In this context gold objects might be considered as a substitute for the powerful dead man and for his spirit in the journey to the underworld, and were imbued with cosmological powers as were the chiefs or the priests who might act as mediators between society and the supernatural world. The 'rebirth' of the spirit of the powerful dead person could symbolize the return of his energy – and that of the sacred golden objects – to an ancestral world, bearing in mind that in traditional societies, the political and religious leaders, who

maintain the equilibrium of human society, are usually identified with the ancestors who were responsible for the ordering of the world.[47] The process of the 'rebirth' of the spirit of former Zenú dead people started during the burial ceremonies in a particular necropolis imbued with ancestral power, such as sixteenth-century Finzenú, whose ancestral importance survived in the Zenú traditions recorded by the Spanish chroniclers.

In the past the work of the specialized Zenú goldsmiths, like those who lived in Finzenú, was linked to the rituals performed in major ceremonial centres. According to the chroniclers, they produced ornaments for people of the other Zenú 'provinces' or for burial during the funerary ceremonies, as did probably potters and other specialists.[48] This system of production involved a regional distribution of gold objects and other manufactured goods which could explain, in part, the wide distribution of some metal items, such as cast-filigree ear ornaments. Manufactured goods from different regions were carried considerable distances to be buried in special cemeteries, as confirmed by the finds in the Planeta Rica mounds which include pottery from both the Sinú and the San Jorge rivers.[49]

The role of the goldsmiths and of other skilled craftsmen would contribute to maintain the stability of Greater Zenú, an ordered territory with mythical origins, and might also have a supernatural character. Goldsmiths transformed a sacred metal which came from the rich deposits of Zenufana into objects with cosmological and social meaning. In fact, in traditional societies the role of the craftsmen is usually imbued with a supernatural character, for these people master powers of transformation. The artisans reproduce the cosmological ordering of the world from a previous indifferentiated natural existence, and reaffirm the essential order of human life and of social behaviour.[50]

To the east of Zenú territory

The San Jacinto Group

A unique metalwork assemblage was produced in the San Jacinto mountain range that separates the lowlands from the Caribbean coast and extended to the neighbouring lowlands of the Magdalena drainage. The San Jacinto Group (Fig. 7.17) shows the influence of Zenú goldwork in the many small staff heads (Fig. 7.17g–i), cast-filigree ear ornaments (Fig. 7.17a) and nose ornaments with elongations (Fig. 7.17f), the majority, however, with local features.

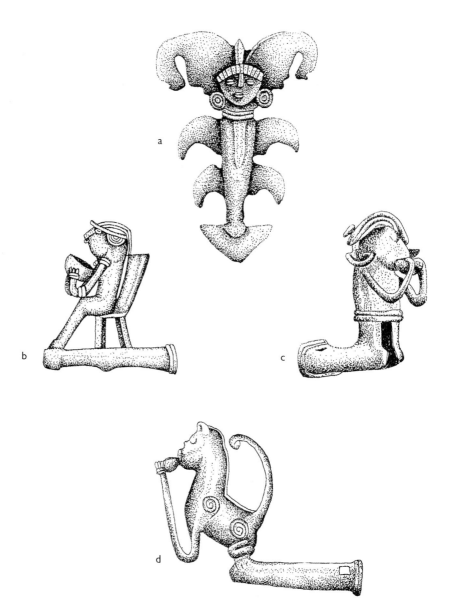

7.18 San Jacinto Group:
(a) anthropozoomorphic
pendant; (b) staff head
representing a man holding a
gourd vessel (height 4.8 cm);
(c) staff head with man
apparently playing a musical
instrument (height 3.2 cm);
(d) staff head with
representation of feline
playing a musical instrument
(height 4 cm).

The San Jacinto Group shows a special emphasis in the use of copper and *tumbaga* with a low gold content for lost-wax castings which were surface enriched. Many small, standardized and intensively used *tumbaga* ornaments appear to have been mass-produced for popular use, in contrast to the emblematic and spectacular gold of the Early Zenú and Ayapel assemblages, and the large-scale production of small high-grade gold items of the San Jorge-Cauca Group. The San Jacinto metal ornaments are also found in a different context: large cemeteries located on the natural hills of the mountain range, where such objects are buried in funerary urns or in simple shaft graves.

We do not know when San Jacinto metalwork was first produced, but the presence and continuity of forms related to the International Group, such as schematic human figures ('Darién pectorals') and anthropozoomorphic figures with recurved headdresses (Fig. 7.17d–e), should be noted. We know that these items were used even after the Spanish conquest, for there is a seventeenth-century date associated with a 'Darién pectoral',[51] and metal pieces have been found in graves together with glass beads and iron weapons of Spanish origin.[52]

In San Jacinto metalwork animal representations are numerous and diverse, and include species that are typical both of the mountainous environment and of the neighbouring lowlands. There are representations of egrets, ducks (Fig. 7.17g), birds of prey, parrots, owls, monkeys, felines, alligators, deer and frogs,[53] as well as scenes, such as groups of birds or a fight between a feline and an alligator (Fig. 7.17i).

The associations of men and animals are numerous, sometimes fused in a single being, such as those with a human face and an elongated body, possibly that of a crustacean (Fig. 7.18a). The iconography also shows the humanization of some animals, such as the felines adorned with headdresses (Fig. 7.17i). The human beings portrayed on San Jacinto staff heads include men with gourd vessels and musicians playing flutes, rattles and apparently a special type of whistle still used by present-day Zenú communities (Figs 7.17h, 7.18b–c). Similar personages appear on pottery vessels from the Sinú river area, and are reminiscent of the people participating in funerary ceremonies described by the Spanish chroniclers and of the funerals of contemporary Zenú communities. Nowadays, musicians still play an important role on these occasions and they are associated with the jaguar and with other animals which are also considered to be musicians. The origin of this association can be found in an old myth which describes the origin of some musical instruments in the 'world of the men with tails'.[54] This might refer to an 'ancestral world' without clear boundaries between human beings and animals. These associations of men and animals and their transformations, still alive in present-day Zenú beliefs, are evident in the iconography of prehispanic metalwork: some felines depicted on San Jacinto staff heads (Fig. 7.18d) appear to be playing musical instruments, in an attitude which is similar to that of some human beings portrayed on these ornaments (Fig. 7.18c).

The personages represented on metal staff heads of the San Jacinto Group, wear cast-filigree ear ornaments, necklaces and nose ornaments as well as diadems, visors or hats which appear to have been made in some sort of basketry technique (Figs 7.17h and 7.19). This tradition has survived and is represented nowadays by the Zenú hat, manufactured in the San Andrés reserve.[55] The distinctive designs of the hat, 'owned' traditionally by different towns, are abstractions of plants, animals and objects, whose names have survived, although their symbolism has gradually disappeared.[56] The contemporary hat designs recall the motifs of prehispanic Modelled and Painted ceramics, and the influence of textiles is also evident in ancient metal objects, for cast filigree, a metal weave, represents one of the most distinctive and long-lasting techniques of Caribbean metalwork.

The confluence of Zenú and Malibú cultures
Ornaments related to the San Jacinto Group have been found in the neighbouring lower Magdalena region where there is evidence of production after the Spanish conquest. Sixteenth-century docu-

ments describe centres for specialized goldsmiths on the lower Magdalena in the lands of the Malibú people. Descriptions refer to the manufacture of high-grade gold ornaments, the production of gold-copper alloys, the use of the techniques of smelting, hammering, annealing, burnishing and depletion gilding,[57] and the pro-

duction of bracelets, necklace beads and nose ornaments.[58]

Malibú settlements have been identified along the Magdalena river and neighbouring watercourses and lagoons by the presence of pottery of the 'Incisa-Alisada' tradition, which in the lower Magdalena was produced until a period later than the sixteenth century.[59] The Malibú expanded to neighbouring regions, entering the San Jorge river area where they were living in the fourteenth century,[60] and they influenced the inhabitants of the San Jacinto mountain range, where pottery related to the Incisa-Alisada tradition has been found both in dwellings and burials, sometimes associated with metal objects. The general distribution of this pottery tradition coincides with that of the metalwork of the San Jacinto Group, an indication that deserves future research.

7.19 Cast copper-rich *tumbaga* staff head with man wearing cast-filigree ear ornaments, necklace and hat, San Jacinto Group.

Although archaeological field work has distinguished between Zenú and Malibú settlements, we are still ignorant as to the type of contacts that may have occurred between these two ethnic groups. Productive fields for future research are suggested by the distribution of San Jacinto metalwork and Malibú pottery mentioned above and by the presence of hybrid traits in gold and pottery objects, which indicate a possible cultural confluence. The two cultural traditions may have influenced the historical evolution of the Zenú communities who have survived up to the present. The area occupied by the reserve of San Andrés was included in the past in the Mexión 'province'. Of considerable importance in the sixteenth century, this territory had strong cultural ties with the Zenú people of the Sinú and San Jorge drainages. In the Mexión 'province' Zenú culture could mix with eastern traditions, as is suggested by the influence in the area of San Jacinto metallurgy and of Malibú pottery.[61]

Iconography appears to shed some light on these relationships. As was mentioned in previous pages, representations of musicians and men holding hemispherical containers appear in Zenú gold and pottery, and are also a common theme in San Jacinto metalwork. The people portrayed on these objects are reminiscent of the musicians and other participants in Zenú funerary ceremonies, and of those who participated in Malibú rituals, as described by some sixteenth-century documents: caciques or shamans sitting on their benches, drinking maize beer from their gourd containers and wearing hats adorned with feathers, gold beads and nose ornaments, while musicians played wind instruments and rattles (Fig. 7.18b–c).[62]

Common beliefs could also be shared by the Zenú and the Malibú. The alligator of gold, for example, a central theme in a cosmological order that must go back to the ancient Zenú, is still a powerful being for present-day Zenú people and could be at the origin of popular widespread legends in the lower Magdalena area, the territory of the ancient Malibú. There, everybody knows about the alligator-man who tricks the fishermen and seduces women, and about the 'alligator spir-

its' living in golden palaces in the bottom of the rivers.[63]

The eastern part of the Caribbean lowlands was also an important centre of trade which specialized in the production and exchange of tumbaga and copper objects. The Malibú played an important role in this activity, and during the sixteenth century some of their towns controlled the exchange relationships on the river.

The symbolic value of both metals and objects was the essence of their power and an important reason for their use in trade. This value was directly related to the symbolism of the material they were made from, their technology and iconography. The structure, colour, shine and even the odour of metals were essential properties. The Malibú, for example, distinguished the provenance of tumbaga objects according to their shape, their colour and their odour, and used some of them, especially nose ornaments, during marriage ceremonies and in trade relationships.[64]

The association of gold with the energy of the sun is still alive in many mythologies, and for the present-day Desana of the north-western Amazon copper has the colour of blood, transformation and life, according to a myth analysed by Reichel-Dolmatoff. At the same time, metallurgical processes are compared to embryonic transformations symbolized by the sequence of coppery colours through which the Moon passes after being fertilized by the Sun. Metallurgical combinations would also be related to the rules of marriage exchange and to the manner in which male and female characteristics of different groups should be mixed to reach a balance.[65]

With these associations in mind, it seems possible that in particular contexts tumbaga – the gold-copper alloy – might represent the balanced mixture of male and female characteristics contained in gold and copper, which would be expressed by properties such as colour and odour. This might also explain, in part, the importance of the production of tumbaga objects over extensive areas, and their role during marriage alliances and in trade activities intended to reach a balance in inter-ethnic relationships.[66]

Notes

1 Cf. Falchetti 1996.

2 Plazas and Falchetti 1981; Plazas *et al.* 1993.

3 Bray1992, 1997; Cooke and Bray 1985.

4 Bray 1984, 1992.

5 Uribe 1988.

6 Falchetti 1987, 1993.

7 Cf. Balser 1966; Lothrop 1952; Bray 1992; Cooke and Bray 1985; Falchetti 1979, 1993; Coggins 1984; Uribe 1988.

8 Cf. Pérez de Barradas 1966; Plazas 1978.

9 Falchetti 1987, 1993.

10 Cf. Bolian 1973; Falchetti 1979.

11 Bray 1992.

12 Cf. Howe 1985.

13 Prehispanic metallurgy of the Caribbean lowlands of Colombia was studied for the first time by the Mexican archaeologist Carlos Margain (1950). He classified the collection of the Gold Museum of Bogotá – some 5,000 items in those days – which included objects from the Sinú and San Jorge river valleys. In 1966 José Pérez de Barradas studied the Gold Museum's collection, which numbered some 7,000 objects, and established the 'Sinú style', based on analysis of the pieces from the Sinú and San Jorge. In 1974–6 I analysed some 2,000 objects from the Caribbean lowlands, most of them housed in the Gold Museum and some in foreign collections (Falchetti 1976). Since then many new finds and archaeological research carried out in the Caribbean lowlands have produced more information about metallurgy and the prehispanic history of these lands. Both the area of distribution and the variation within Caribbean metalwork have broadened considerably since the first pioneering studies. I have incorporated all this new information in a recent study (Falchetti 1995). This paper provides a review of the results of this work and includes some preliminary information of a study on iconography and on the function of gold in ancient Zenú society.

14 Plazas *et al.* 1993.

15 Plazas and Falchetti 1981; Plazas *et al.* 1988; Plazas *et al.* 1993.

16 Recently the results of C14 analysis of the casting cores of Zenú metal objects have been published (Plazas 1997). The great antiquity of a few dates for Early Zenú items (i.e. eighteenth century BC) shows the need for further archaeological research into the distribution of this metallurgy, where information for that early period is non-existent.

17 Cf. Falchetti 1995: 197–212, 258–66.

18 Falchetti 1987. 1993.

19 Egrets (*Ardeidae*), ducks (*Ajaia ajaia, Dendrocygna automnalis, Mumenius phaeopus*), owls (*Strigidae*), birds of prey (*Cathartidae, Harpia harpyja*, probably *Vultur gryphus, Sarcoramphus papa, Coragyps atratus*), ibis (*Threskiornithidae*); alligators (*Crocodylus acutus* and *Caiman fuscus*); deer (*Odocoileus virginianus, Mazama sp.*); felines (*Felis onca*); peccaries (*Tayassu sp.*) (cf. Legast 1980: 54, 59–60, 65–6, 69, 72, 85, 95, 97).

20 Turbay and Jaramillo 1986; Turbay 1994: 233, 236.

21 Cf. Turbay 1994: 232.

22 Cf. Turbay 1994: 231.

23 ICAN 1993; Falchetti 1995.

24 Museo del Oro, Bogotá, no. 33459; Beta 82926: 670 ± 70 B.P; Plazas 1997. Cf. Falchetti 1995: 218–19.

25 Cf. Turbay 1994: 232, 249.

26 Farabee 1920.

27 Plazas *et al.* 1993: 111–13.

28 Cf. Legast 1980: 82, 97.

29 Cf. Turbay and Jaramillo 1998: 379.

30 Cf. Helms 1993: 168.

31 Plazas *et al.* 1993: 97–111; Falchetti 1995: 226.

32 Sáenz S. 1993.

33 Reichel-Dolmatoff 1957; Plazas and Falchetti 1981.

34 Labbé 1995: 44.

35 López de Gómara 1946 (1552): 199; Simón 1981 (1625), V: 106, 128; Castellanos 1955 (1601), III: 74.

36 Cf. Plazas and Falchetti 1981: 59–87.

37 Simón 1981 (1625), V: 98.

38 Aguado 1957 (1581), T. IV: 49; Robledo 1938 (1542); Cieza de León 1962 (1553).

39 Cf. Falchetti 1996.

40 Cf. Betania 1964; Falchetti 1996.

41 Simón 1981 (1625), V: 109. Friede 1956, VI : 216.

42 Simón 1981 (1625), V: 98, 105, 128.

43 Plazas and Falchetti 1981.

44 Simón 1981 (1625), V: 109.

45 Cf. Turbay and Jaramillo 1986: 299; 1998: 388–9.

46 Simón 1981 (1625), V: 98.

47 Cf. Helms 1993.

48 Cf. Falchetti 1995: 278.

49 Cf. ICAN 1994: 87–98, 169. Falchetti 1995: 215–16.

50 Cf. Lévi-Strauss 1988.

51 Museo del Oro, Bogotá, no. 28282; Beta 67954: 350 ± 60 B.P.; Plazas 1997.

52 Falchetti 1995: 241.

53 Monkeys (*Alouatta sp., Ateles paniscus*), felines (*Felis onca, Felis pardalis*), deer (*Mazama sp.*), egrets (*Ardeaidae*), ducks (*Ajaia ajaia, Phalacrocorax olivaceus*), birds of prey (*Cathartidae*), parrots (*Ara sp.*), owls (*Tyto alba*), alligators (*Crocodylus acutus*), frogs (*Bufonidae, Leptodactylidae*) (cf. Legast 1980: 50–51, 55, 72, 78, 82, 85, 97, 101).

54 Cf. Turbay 1994: 249.

55 Cf. Le Roy Gordon 1957: 304–41.

56 Turbay and Jaramillo 1986; Turbay 1994.

57 Oviedo 1944 (1548), V: 304; Archivo General de Indias, Sevilla, Justicia 587-A, f. 600–793, in Martínez 1989.

58 Medina *et al.* 1983 (1579): 186–7; Briones de Pedraza 1983 (1580): 165.

59 Reines 1979; Plazas and Falchetti 1981: 117–18.

60 Plazas *et al.* 1993: 117–25.

61 Falchetti 1995: 293, 1996: 21–5.

62 Briones de Pedraza 1983 (1580): 157, 163.

63 Cf. Fals Borda 1979: 34; Turbay 1994: 238.

64 Cf. Falchetti 1993.

65 Reichel-Dolmatoff 1981: 21.

66 Falchetti 1997.

References

Aguado, Fray Pedro de
1957 (1581) *Recopilación Historial.* Biblioteca de la Presidencia de Colombia, Bogotá.

Balser, Carlos
1966 Los objetos de oro de los Estilos Extranjeros de Costa Rica. *Actas y Memorias del XXXVI Congreso Internacional de Americanistas*, vol. 1: 391–8. Sevilla.

Betania, María de
1964 *Mitos, leyendas y costumbres de las tribus suramericanas.* Coculsa, Madrid.

Bolian, Charles
1973 Seriation of the Darién Style Anthropomorphic Figure. *Variation in Anthropology*: 213–32, ed. D. Lathrap and J. Douglas. Illinois Archaeological Survey, Urbana, Illinois,.

Bray, Warwick
1984 Across the Darien Gap: A Colombian view of Isthmian Archaeology. In *The Archaeology of Lower Central America.* F. Lange and D. Stone (Eds) University of New Mexico Press, Albuquerque.
1992 Sitio Conte Metalwork in its Pan-American Context. In *River of Gold: Precolumbian Treasures from Sitio Conte.* P. Hearne and R. J. Sharer (eds). University of Pennsylvania. University Museum of Archaeology and Anthropology.
1997 Metallurgy and Anthropology: Two Studies from Prehispanic America. *Metalurgia precolombina de América.* 49th International Congress of Americanists, Quito, Ecuador, 1997. *Boletín Museo del Oro* 42.

Briones de Pedraza, Bartolomé
1983 (1580) Relación de Tenerife II. *Cespedesia* nos 45–6, Suplemento no. 4. Cali.

Castellanos, Juan de
1955 (1601) *Elegías de Varones Ilustres de Indias*, Tomo III. Editorial ABC. Bogotá.

Cieza de León, Pedro
1962 (1553) *La Crónica del Perú.* Colección Austral no. 507. Espasa Calpe S.A. Madrid.

Coggins, Clemency
1984 The Cenote of Sacrifice: Catalogue. In *Cenote of Sacrifice: Maya Treasures from the Sacred Well at Chichén Itzá*, ed. C. Coggins and O. Shane. University of Texas Press, Austin.

Cooke, Richard and Warwick Bray
1985 The Goldwork of Panama: An Iconographic and Chronological Perspective. In *The Art of Precolumbian Gold: The Jan Mitchell Collection*, ed. J. Jones. Weidenfeld & Nicolson, London.

Eliade, Mircea
1959 *Cosmos and History: The Myth of the Eternal Return.* Harper & Brothers, New York.

Enciso, Martín Fernández de
1974 (1519) *Summa de Geografía.* Biblioteca Banco Popular, Bogotá,.

Falchetti, Ana María
1976 *The Goldwork of the Sinú Region,* Northern Colombia. M. Phil. Dissertation. University of London, Institute of Archaeology.
1979 Colgantes Darién: relaciones entre áreas orfebres del Occidente Colombiano y Centroamérica. *Boletín Museo del Oro*, Año 2.
1987 Desarrollo de la orfebrería Tairona en la provincia metalúrgica del norte colombiano. *Boletín Museo del Oro* 19.
1993 La Tierra del oro y el cobre: parentesco e intercambio entre comunidades del norte de Colombia y áreas relacionadas. *Boletín Museo del Oro* 34–5.
1995 *El oro del Gran Zenú. Metalurgia prehispánica en las llanuras del Caribe colombiano.* Colección Bibliográfica. Banco de la República, Bogotá.
1996 El territorio del Gran Zenú en las llanuras del Caribe Colombiano. Arqueología y Etnohistoria. *Revista de Arqueología Americana.* Instituto Panamericano de Geografía e Historia, no. 11. Mexico.
1997 La Ofrenda y la Semilla. Notas sobre el simbolismo del oro entre los Uwa. *Metalurgia precolombina de América.* 49th International Congress of Americanists, Quito, Ecuador, 1997. *Boletín Museo del Oro* 43.

Fals Borda, Orlando
1979 *Mompóx y Loba. Historia doble de la Costa.* Carlos Valencia Editores, Bogotá.

Farabee, W.M. Curtis
1920 Ancient American Gold. *The Museum Journal*, vol. XI, no. 3. Philadelphia.

Friede, Juan
1956 *Documentos inéditos para la Historia de Colombia*, vol. VI, Academia Colombiana de Historia. Artes Gráficas, Madrid.

Helms, Mary
1993 *Craft and the Kingly Ideal: Art, Trade and Power.* University of Texas Press, Austin.

Howe, Ellen G.
1985 A Radiographic Study of hollow-cast Gold Pendants from Sitio Conte. *Precolumbian American Metallurgy.* 45th International Congress of Americanists. Banco de la República, Bogotá.

ICAN (Instituto Colombiano de Antropología)
1994 COLCULTURA, Oleoducto de Colombia. *Arqueología de Rescate. Un viaje por el tiempo a lo largo del Oleoducto* (Archaeological Research directed by Alvaro Botiva). Bogotá.

Labbé, Armand
1995 *Guardians of the Life Stream: Shamans, Art and Power in Prehispanic Central Panamá.* The Bowers Museum of Cultural Art, Santa Ana, California. The University of Washington Press.

Legast, Anne
1980 *La fauna en la orfebrería Sinú.* Fundación de Investigaciones Arqueológicas Nacionales. Banco de la República, Bogotá.

Le Roy Gordon, Bruce
1957 *Human Geography and Ecology in the Sinú Country of Colombia.* University of California Press, Berkeley and Los Angeles.

Lévi-Strauss, Claude
1988 *The Jealous Potter.* University of Chicago Press.

López de Gómara, Francisco
1946 (1552) *Historia general de las Indias.* Biblioteca de Autores Españoles, Historiadores Primitivos de Indias, Tomo 22. Madrid.

Lothrop, Samuel K.
1952 Metals from the Cenote of Sacrifice, Chichen Itzá, Yucatán. *Memoirs of the Peabody Museum of Archaeology and Ethnology*, vol. X, no. 2. Cambridge, Mass.

Margain, Carlos
1950 *Estudio inicial de las colecciones del Museo del Oro del Banco de la República.* Imprenta del Banco de la República, Bogotá.

Martínez, Armando
1989 Un caso de alteración aurífera colonial en el Bajo Magdalena. *Boletín Museo del Oro* 23.

Medina, Rodríguez de, *et al.*
1983 (1579) Relación de San Miguel de las Palmas de Tamalameque. *Cespedesia* 4 (45–6). Cali.

Muñoz (Colección)
1884 *Colección de documentos inéditos relativos al descubrimiento, conquista y organización de las antiguas posesiones españolas de América y Oceanía, sacados de los Archivos del Reino y muy especialmente del de Indias*, Tomo 41. Imprenta de Manuel G. Hernández, Madrid.

Oviedo, Gonzalo Fernández de
1944 (1548) *Historia general y natural de las Indias, Islas y Tierra Firme del Mar Océano.* Asunción.

Pérez de Barradas, José
1966 *Orfebrería Prehispánica de Colombia. Estilos Quimbaya y otros.* Banco de la República, Bogotá.

Plazas, Clemencia
1978 Tesoro de los Quimbayas y piezas de orfebrería relacionadas. *Boletín Museo del Oro*, Año 1.

Plazas, Clemencia
1997 Cronología de la Orfebrería prehispánica de Colombia. *Metalurgia de América precolombina.* 49th International Congress of Americanists, Quito, Ecuador. *Boletín Museo del Oro* 44.

Plazas, Clemencia and Ana María Falchetti
1981 *Asentamientos Prehispánicos en el bajo río San Jorge.* Fundación de Investigaciones Arqueológicas Nacionales. Banco de la República, Bogotá.

Plazas, Clemencia, Ana María Falchetti, Thomas van der Hammen and Pedro Botero
1988 Cambios ambientales y desarrollo cultural en el bajo río San Jorge. *Boletín Museo del Oro* 20.

Plazas, Clemencia, Ana María Falchetti, Juanita Sáenz S. and Sonia Archila
1993 *La sociedad hidráulica Zenú. Estudio arqueológico de 2.000 años de historia en las llanuras del Caribe colombiano.* Banco de la República, Bogotá.

Reichel-Dolmatoff, Gerardo
1981 Things of Beauty Replete with Meaning –
Metals and Crystals in Colombian Indian
Cosmology. In *Sweat of the Sun, Tears of the
Moon: Gold and Emerald Treasures of Colombia*,
ed. D. Seligman, pp. 17–33, exh. cat., Natural
History Museum of Los Angeles County. Terra
Magazine Publications, Los Angeles.

Reichel-Dolmatoff, Gerardo and Alicia
1957 Reconocimiento arqueológico en la hoya del
río Sinú. *Revista Colombiana de Antropología*,
vol.VI. Bogotá.

Reines, León
1979 Una contribución a la arqueología del bajo
río Magdalena. Excavaciones en Guaiquirí.
Manuscript. Fundación de Investigaciones
Arqueológicas Nacionales. Banco de la
República, Bogotá.

Robledo, Jorge
1938 (1542) Descripción de los pueblos de la
provincia de Anserma. In Jacinto Jijón y
Caamaño, *Sebastián de Benalcázar*, vol. II
(63–80). Editorial Ecuatoriana, Quito.

Sáenz S., Juanita
1993 Mujeres de barro: estudio de las figurinas
cerámicas de Montelíbano. *Boletín Museo del
Oro* 34–5.

Simón, Fray Pedro
1981 (1625) *Noticias Historiales de las
Conquistas de Tierra Firme en las Indias
Occidentales.* Biblioteca Banco Popular, Bogotá.

Turbay, Sandra
1994 Los animales en la tradición Zenú. *Costa
Atlántica colombiana. Etnología e Historia.*
Departamento de Antropología, Universidad de
Antioquia, Medellín.

Turbay, Sandra and Susana Jaramillo
1986 La identidad cultural entre los indígenas de
San Andrés de Sotavento, Córdoba, Colombia.
Unpublished thesis. Universidad de Antioquia,
Departamento de Antropología, Medellín.
1998 Los indígenas Zenúes. *Geografía humana de
Colombia. Región Andina Central*, Tomo IV, vol.
3. Instituto Colombiano de Cultura Hispánica,
Bogotá.

Uribe, María Alicia
1988 Introducción a la orfebrería de San Pedro de
Urabá, una región del noroccidente colombiano.
Boletín Museo del Oro 20.

Vadillo, Johan
1884 (1537) Carta del Licenciado Johan de
Vadillo a su Magestad dándole cuenta de su visita
a la Gobernación de Cartagena. In Muñoz
(Collection).

Acknowledgements

I thank Clara Isabel Botero and Roberto Lleras of
the Gold Museum, Bogotá, for providing photographs for this paper. I am also grateful to Colin
McEwan and Marianne Cardale, who read preliminary versions of the manuscript, for their help and
stimulating comments.

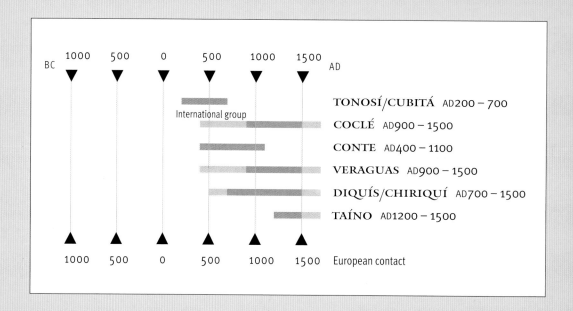

BC 1000 500 0 500 1000 1500 AD

International group

TONOSÍ/CUBITÁ AD200 – 700
COCLÉ AD900 – 1500
CONTE AD400 – 1100
VERAGUAS AD900 – 1500
DIQUÍS/CHIRIQUÍ AD700 – 1500
TAÍNO AD1200 – 1500

1000 500 0 500 1000 1500 European contact

SECTION III
CENTRAL AMERICA, THE CARIBBEAN AND BEYOND

NICARAGUA

CARIBBEAN SEA

COSTA RICA

GUANACASTE-NICOYA

San Jose

Guayabo de Turrialba

Panteón de la Reina

Rivas

El General

VERAGUAS

Chitra

DIQUÍS

CHIRIQUÍ

Diquís

PACIFIC OCEAN

N

0   200 miles
0   400 km

PANAMA

Panamá Viejo   Panama City   Bayano

Playa Venado   Miraflores

COCLÉ   Pearl Is

Natá   Sitio Conte

El Caño

La Mula-Sarigua   GULF OF PANAMA

Las Huacas   Cerro Juan Diaz

La Cañaza   El Cafetal

La India   El Indio

Búcaro

GULF OF URABÁ

Chucunaque

Tuyra

Atrato

San Pedro de Urabá

Cupica

COLOMBIA

Highlands

COCLÉ Culture

■ Archaeological site

◉ Modern city

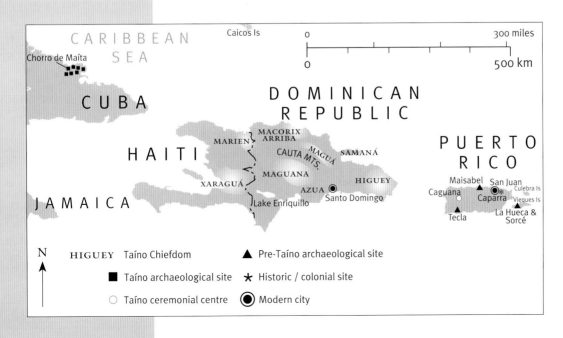

CARIBBEAN SEA

Caicos Is

0   300 miles
0   500 km

Chorro de Maíta

CUBA

HAITI

JAMAICA

DOMINICAN REPUBLIC

MACORIX ARRIBA

MARIEN

CAUTA MTS.

MAGUÁ

MAGUANA

XARAGUÁ

AZUA

Lake Enriquillo   Santo Domingo

SAMANÁ

HIGUEY

PUERTO RICO

Maisabel   San Juan   Culebra Is

Caguana   Caparra   Vieques Is

Tecla   La Hueca & Sorcé

N

HIGUEY Taíno Chiefdom

■ Taíno archaeological site

○ Taíno ceremonial centre

▲ Pre-Taíno archaeological site

✶ Historic / colonial site

◉ Modern city

8

Contextualized Goldwork from 'Gran Coclé', Panama

An Update Based on Recent Excavations and New Radiocarbon Dates for Associated Pottery Styles

Richard Cooke, Luís Alberto Sánchez Herrera and Koichi Udagawa

The 'Gran Coclé Semiotic Tradition'

The subject of this paper is the metallurgy of a region of Precolumbian Panama, which is well known for its mortuary artefacts decorated with distinctive combinations of abstract and figurative icons. These occur not only on goldwork but also on pottery, stone, bone, ivory and resin. When S.K. Lothrop first described these artefacts, he attributed them to the 'Coclé culture' because the Sitio Conte site where he discovered about sixty stratified graves is located in Coclé province (see map on previous page).[1] Lothrop proposed that the 'Coclé culture' flourished for 190 years before the Spanish settlement of the lowlands of central Pacific Panama, i.e. AD 1330–1520.[2] A few years later Alden Mason excavated additional graves at Sitio Conte, which represented the most recent part of Lothrop's sequence.[3]

In the 1950s and 1960s a few radiocarbon dates and analyses of stratified refuse middens induced Lothrop himself and other archaeologists to propose that the Sitio Conte funerary artefacts were older than originally thought.[4] These and subsequent investigations[5] identified three styles of painted pottery ('La Mula', 'Aristide' and 'Tonosí'), which are more ancient than the 'Conte'- and 'Macaracas'-style vessels that predominate in the Sitio Conte graves, and two that are more recent ('Parita' and 'El Hatillo').[6] Thus the Sitio Conte artefacts represent the middle rather than the end of a 1,500-year-old continuum.

The spatial dimension of Lothrop's 'Coclé culture' has also been revised. Although we do not know much about manufacture and exchange or about regional variability within styles, artefacts decorated with the characteristic 'Coclé' iconography were surely made (and used daily) outside Lothrop's original cultural epicentre.[7] In this part of the isthmus Spanish troops described small but well-populated territories in montane valleys, along major rivers and near estuaries. Each territory possessed its own 'language' and all interacted in both hostile and cooperative engagements. Political elites exchanged women.[8] This documentary information suggests that relationships among communities, material culture and imagery were so complex that archaeological data will never be able to reconstruct them satisfactorily.

A 'culture area' scheme with temporally and spatially immutable boundaries[9] now seems inappropriate.[10] This paper is not the place to discuss alternative schemes. Suffice the advancement of a proposal that three major 'interaction spheres' existed in Panama during the last 1,500 years of the Precolumbian period. Within each one, relations between larger and smaller settlements, 'cores' and 'peripheries' and purveyors and recipients of goods varied through time in response to poorly understood demographic and economic parameters.[11] The western and eastern spheres extended beyond Panama's current frontiers into Costa Rica and Colombia. Lothrop's 'Coclé culture' was not restricted to this province. Therefore, since the term 'Greater' or 'Gran Chiriquí' is now in general use,[12] it is appropriate to prefix the same adjectives to 'Coclé' and 'Darién' as well. Our paper refers, then, to the metal and ceramic components of the 'Gran Coclé Semiotic Tradition'.

Recent finds of Gran Coclé metalwork

Since the spectacular finds made at Sitio Conte, most archaeological research projects in Gran Coclé have addressed subsistence economy, human-land relationships and cultures that ante-

8.1 Gold artefacts from
'Gran Coclé', Panama:
(a) El Caño, 1974–6
excavations, uncertain
provenance;
(b–d) Miraflores, Tomb 2;
(e) El Cafetal;
(f) Las Huacas, Tomb 47;
(g) El Caño, Mound 3
(depth 2.9–3 m);
(h–i) El Caño, mound area,
unprovenanced;
(j) Cerro Juan Díaz,
Operation 3, Feature
(F.) 115; (k) Cerro Juan Díaz,
Operation 3, F. 2;
(l–m) Cerro Juan Díaz,
Operation 3, F. 1.

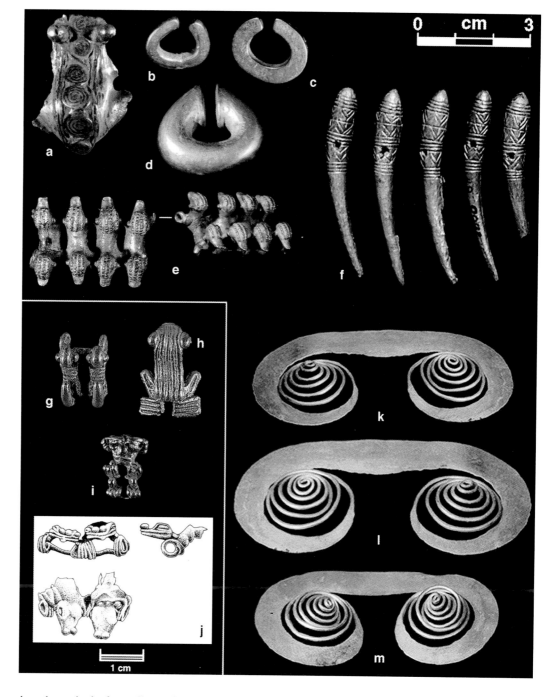

date the arrival of metallurgy from South America.[13] For this reason, archaeologists have added very few items to the inventory of 'contextualized' metal artefacts.[14] Some of these finds made after the Sitio Conte excavations in the 1930s and 1940s are important, however, because they represent the 'Initial Group', which in Bray's opinion is the earliest metallurgy in Lower Central America.[15] Other finds come from mortuary features approximately coeval with the Sitio Conte graves, but much less wealthy. And a few artefacts date to the beginning of the sixteenth century AD when the Spanish were colonizing the region.

The first goal of this paper is to reassess the nature and chronology of Initial Group metalwork. To assist us in this task, we shall summarize data from the Cerro Juan Díaz site (see map p. 153), where ongoing excavations have added useful details about gold-pottery associations and the radiometric dating of relevant pottery styles.[16]

The most recent syntheses of the Gran Coclé painted pottery sequence propose that the graves excavated by Lothrop and Mason represent the period AD 400/500–900/1000 in uncalibrated radiocarbon time.[17] Interestingly, though, only

Table 8.1 Radiocarbon dates associated with the major polychrome pottery styles of the Gran Coclé Semiotic Tradition.

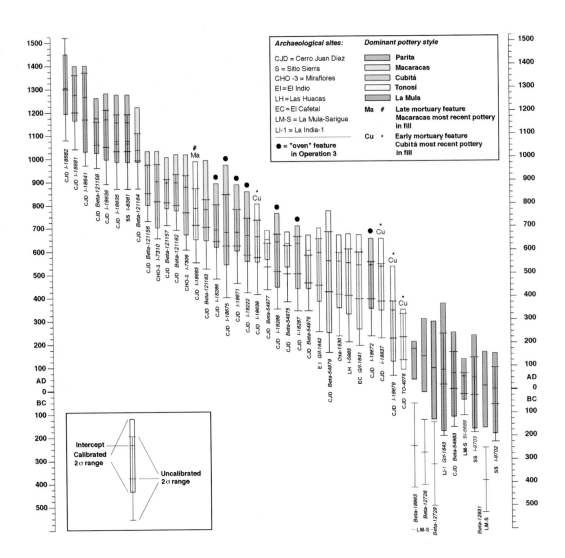

two radiocarbon dates have been associated stratigraphically with the characteristic four-colour polychromes of the Conte and Macaracas styles, and these come not from sites in Gran Coclé but from Miraflores (CHO-3), a large cemetery on the Bayano river in 'Gran Darién', where imported Macaracas sherds were found in tomb fills.[18]

Our second goal, then, is to present new information from Cerro Juan Díaz about the dating of the Conte and Macaracas styles. This will help specialists refine the chronology of the many kinds of metalwork that Lothrop and Mason found in the Sitio Conte graves.

Our third goal is to recapitulate what we know about metallurgy at Spanish contact. Some of the relevant artefacts have already been reported, but mostly in poorly illustrated Panamanian sources.[19]

We are archaeologists, not specialists in metallurgy. For this reason, we avoid guesses about metal content and manufacturing techniques. The new material from Cerro Juan Díaz is available for study by technical experts.

Initial Group metalwork

Contextualized finds of Initial Group artefacts indicate that they are synchronous with two painted pottery styles – Tonosí and Cubitá, whose manufacture we now believe spans the period cal (calibrated) AD 200/300–700 (Table 8.1).

The database is exasperating. Most of the relevant sites have not been completely published. Many lack field notes and catalogues. The relationship between artefact and archaeological context has often been mislaid or lost. An added complication is that Precolumbian people during this time period were accustomed not only to 'killing' mortuary artefacts, but also to reusing the same grave feature. This means that even careful excavation by natural stratigraphy does not guarantee that artefacts intentionally buried with the dead can be distinguished from others present in grave fills and not necessarily synchronous with the mortuary deposits.

Descriptions and illustrations are available for

the Tonosí style,[20] but not for Cubitá, which Sánchez described on the basis of a refuse feature in Operation 1 at Cerro Juan Díaz.[21] Sánchez's detailed *licenciatura* thesis in Spanish has not been published. If readers find the following typological and excavation details irksome, we apologize, but they are necessary for being objective about the antiquity of metallurgy in Gran Coclé. We have cross-referenced our observations as fully as possible with published illustrations.

Southern Azuero sites

Ichon, who first described the Tonosí-style pottery, did not find any metal items in forty-three

were often found in the same feature. There was evidence for two sequential funerary episodes. We have gleaned the following metal-pottery associations from González (1972):

1. The plaque with the dorsal fold was associated with a Tonosí-style Vase Double.
2. The 'necklace' and the hammered plaque with spirals (Fig. 8.2b) were found around the neck and under the mandible of a primary flexed burial. A bird-effigy jar, a red plate and fragments of a 'Culebra Appliqué-Incisé' pedestalled chalice[25] were associated with these remains. The conjoined bicephalous creatures (Fig. 8.1e) and the twisted ring (Fig. 8.2k) were buried with a secon-

8.2 Metal artefacts from the Azuero Peninsula and the site of Las Huacas, Veraguas:
(a) El Indio, second mortuary phase;
(b) El Cafetal;
(c) El Indio, second mortuary phase;
(d) La India-1;
(e) El Indio, second mortuary phase;
(f) La India;
(g) El Cafetal;
(h) La India-1;
(i) El Indio, second mortuary phase;
(j) La India-1;
(k) El Cafetal;
(l) Las Huacas, Tomb 8;
(m) El Indio, second mortuary phase;
(n) Las Huacas, Tomb 19;
(o) El Cafetal;
(p) El Indio, second mortuary phase.

burials in the earlier of two cemeteries at El Indio, in one burial at La India-1 and in another at Búcaro.[22] The eleven Tonosí-style funerary vessels belonged to his 'Vases Doubles' and 'La Bernardina à Bord Decoré' varieties.[23]

At neighbouring El Cafetal González (1972) recorded eight metal artefacts in five mortuary features (Figs 8.1e, 8.2b, g, k and o). He described the unillustrated items as (1) a gold 'necklace' (*collar*), (2) a plaque with a fold on the back for a string and (3) the head of a cast 'armadillo'.[24]

Stratigraphy at El Cafetal was complicated: primary flexed and secondary burials in packages

darily prepared skeleton, which formed part of the same mortuary unit. Between these two skeletons González found sherds of plain jars with lateral handles and an incense burner.[26]

3. The remaining metal pieces were associated with a complex group of interments, which included (a) a primary flexed skeleton, (b) a jumble of long bones, (c) an urn with jumbled bones and no crania and (d) an urn that contained a primary flexed burial. The cast gold spider (Fig. 8.2o) was found on top of a red plate buried with (b). The bicephalous bird (Fig. 8.2g) and the 'armadillo' head were found alongside (d). The

only decorated pottery vessel in this funerary group was a Culebra Appliqué-Incisé chalice.[27]

Mitchell and Heidenreich (1965) – members of the Archaeological Society of Panama (see note 1) – uncovered 'urn' and 'open' burials at La India-1. The latter comprised secondary 'bundle' and primary flexed skeletons. Some open burials had intruded upon urns. They report the following metal artefacts: (1) a double-animal *tumbaga* effigy inside an urn in which four Tonosí-style Vases Doubles had been placed, (2) a spiral nose-ring recovered on top of a legged *metate*,[28] (3) a frog-effigy pendant (Fig. 8.2d), (4) another effigy pendant depicting three curly-tailed animals and (5) a large double-headed bird effigy (Fig. 8.2f). In a letter to Bray Mitchell added to the above list: (6) fragments of a *tumbaga* sheet, (7) a second spiral nose-ring, (8) part of a bell-eyed creature, (9) a conical nose clip, (10) a monocephalous spread-eagled bird (Fig. 8.2j), (11) two *tumbaga* discs and (12) a cast pendant depicting four birds (Fig. 8.2h).[29] Mitchell informed Bray that item nos 3, 10, 11 and 12 were found inside a 'La India Rouge' urn.[30]

These metal-pottery associations at El Cafetal and La-India would be easier to evaluate if the ceramics had been adequately illustrated. Nevertheless, we can say with confidence that cast and hammered metal artefacts of Bray's Initial Group were associated in mortuary features with Tonosí-style Vases Doubles, bowls with expanded and everted lips that carry a painted decoration (La Bernardina à Bord Decoré), pedestalled chalices of the Culebra Appliqué-Incisé type and red-painted vessels of Ichon's 'Infiernillo' and La India Rouge types. Ichon assigned this group of vessels to his El Indio Phase, which he then believed spanned the period AD 200/250–550 (uncalibrated) with an 'apogee' at c.AD 400.[31]

Certain features of ceramic type distributions within the El Indio Phase led Ichon to propose that some of the El Cafetal graves were later than the ones he excavated in the early cemetery at El Indio. Sherd counts in stratified middens showed that the red-daubed Infiernillo type – present in the El Cafetal burials – appeared in the latter half of the El Indio Phase.[32] New data from Cerro Juan Díaz support Ichon's hypothesis: some of the El Cafetal painted vessels[33] share motifs and shapes with the 'Nance Rojo y Negro sobre Crema' type, which Sánchez (1995) includes in the Cubitá style. El Cafetal, then, may be intermediate in time between the first El Indio cemetery, which lacked goldwork, and the early mortuary phase in Operation 3 at Cerro Juan Díaz (to be described shortly), which contained metal artefacts.

Unfortunately, none of the southern Azuero Peninsula sites provided radiometric dates derived from organic materials recovered within mortuary features. The two radiocarbon dates that Ichon associated stratigraphically with Tonosí-style pottery were run on charcoal fragments scattered through habitation refuse.[34] To complicate the issue, these middens were excavated by arbitrary layers. The El Cafetal sample dated to AD 390 $\pm$ 100 (Gif-1641) and the El Indio sample to AD 450 $\pm$ 100 (Gif-1642). These calibrate respectively to cal AD 260 [535] 665 and cal AD 380 [590] 695.[35] Although their intercepts are in reverse order to Ichon's typological sequence, we shall see later that they overlap with dates from Cerro Juan Díaz strata that contained abundant Tonosí sherds.

Las Huacas

Another site at which Initial Group metalwork has been reported is Las Huacas on the Gulf of Montijo where de Brizuela (n.d.) excavated about forty-six tombs in 1971–2. She recovered 140-odd ceramic vessels and 30 *metates*. Cut through bedrock to a maximum depth of 4.7 m, these features were often used more than once. De Brizuela left Panama before she could write up her fieldwork. It is apparent from her field diary, however, that she found fourteen metal objects in the following features:

Tomb 8: A cast figurine in the form of two curly-tailed conjoined animals (Fig. 8.2l) found inside a red-and-buff collared jar with two biomorphs modelled on opposite shoulders (Fig. 8.3h). This is a most unusual vessel whose chronology is unknown.

Tomb 19: Five overlays for small beads (cf. Fig. 8.2n). We believe that a trichrome jar with a rampant quadruped was found in this grave.[36] Its design is similar to that of a vessel from Tomb 27, described on the next page.

Tomb 28: Fragments of a double-headed 'eagle' found on top of a three-legged *metate*. This feature did not contain whole mortuary vessels. Some Tonosí sherds were found in the fill.

Tomb 39: Fragments of a very deteriorated *tumbaga* object also found on top of a *metate* and associated with a fragmented Tonosí-style vessel.

Tomb 47: (a) Five canine-shaped pendants – these have clay/charcoal cores underneath gold leaf overlays with incised decoration (Fig. 8.1f); (b) fragments of a *tumbaga* 'eagle' found on top of a *metate* embedded into the grave floor. The major ceramic offering in this feature was a Tonosí Vase Double with painted human figures.[37]

Only one radiocarbon date was obtained at Las Huacas: cal AD 325 [545] 670 (I-5983). It came

8.3 Mortuary ceramics from
Operation 3 at Cerro Juan
Díaz and Las Huacas:
(a) Cerro Juan Díaz, F. 94,
Ciruelo Black-on-Red bowl
(Cubitá style) representing a
stylized crocodilian;
(b) Cerro Juan Díaz, F. 94,
Ciruelo Black-on-Red plate
representing a turtle;
(c) Cerro Juan Díaz, F. 68,
Macaracas (Pica-Pica) burial
urn (with rim broken off and
ground down);
(d) Cerro Juan Díaz, F. 94,
Guábilo Black-on-White
bowl (Cubitá style);
(e–f) Cerro Juan Díaz, F. 1,
Espavé Red incense burners;
(g) Las Huacas, Tomb 27,
plain ware collared and
bevelled jar with three strap
feet and two Atlantean
figures grasping the collar;
(h) Las Huacas, Tomb 8, plain
ware jar with two modelled
biomorphs.

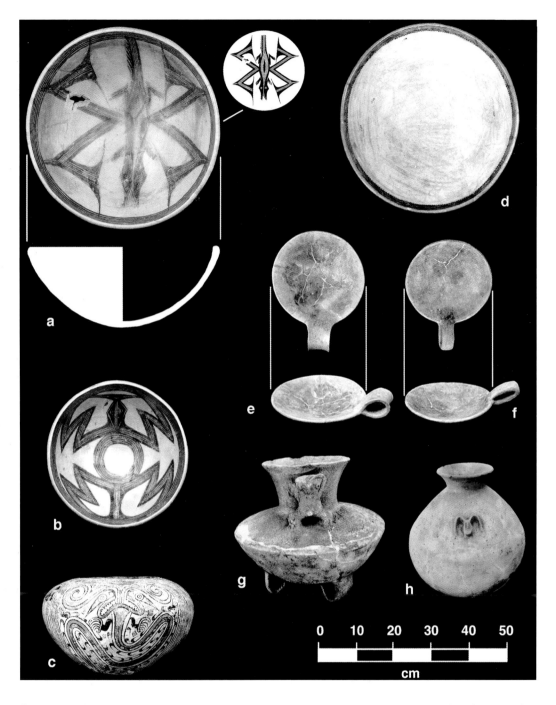

from Tomb 27, *which did not contain metalwork.* We are sure that this feature was used at least twice. It contained a plain collared jar with three strap feet, sharp median bevel and two human figures which hang on to the rim (Fig. 8.3g). This vessel is typologically analogous to Parita-style 'Atlantean' vessels.[38] The Parita style did not materialize until about cal AD 1000–1100.[39] In this feature de Brizuela also found a collared vessel with a saurian figure painted in red and outlined in black, which runs around the white-slipped shoulder (Fig. 8.9f). The background 'filler' motifs in black are called 'snail-shell scrolls' by Lothrop,

who considered them diagnostic of the earliest burials at Sitio Conte, e.g. Grave 32.[40] Similar vessels can be studied in Cooke and Labbé.[41] Labbé's inclusion of this material in a 'Montijo Transitional Style' accurately reflects the fact that it is stylistically intermediate between Cubitá and Conte. The radiocarbon chronology we propose in this paper suggests that these vessels were manufactured nearer cal AD 700 than cal AD 545. It is possible, then, that the Tomb 27 radiocarbon date represents older charcoal incorporated in the grave fill – a common occurrence in these kinds of features.

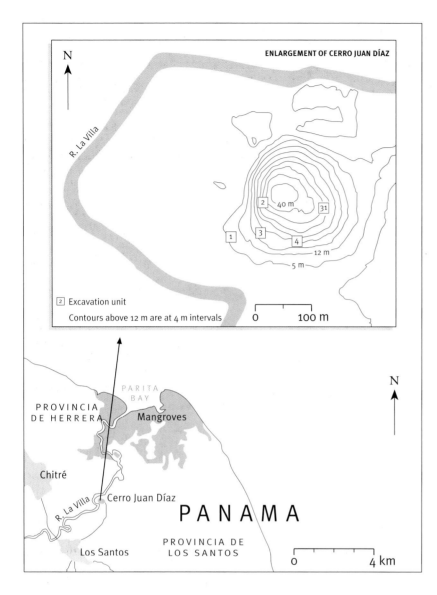

8.4 Maps of Cerro Juan Díaz showing (a) the location and (b) the contours of the site.

To sum up the situation at Las Huacas, it is rash to assume that the single and oft-quoted radiometric date is a sound temporal datum for all the metalwork at this site,[42] even though it is consistent with finds of Tonosí-style pottery in many of the graves. The beads, canine-shaped overlay pendants and cast bird figures are probably contemporary with Tonosí-style vessels (some of which bear zoomorphic designs akin to those illustrated in Labbé[43]) or with collared jars stylistically transitional between Cubitá and Conte. The antiquity of the cast conjoined animals (Fig. 8.2l) remains uncertain.

Rancho Sancho de la Isla
Cooke and Bray (1985) include the three *tumbaga* chisels found in a shaft tomb at this Coclé site in the Initial Group of metalwork. This is because the five painted vessels illustrated by Dade (1960) clearly represent the transition from the Cubitá

into the Conte styles upon which we have just commented. This feature appears to overlap chronologically with Graves 31 and 32 at Sitio Conte.[44]

Cerro Juan Díaz
The sixth Gran Coclé site that has provided information about Initial Group metalwork is Cerro Juan Díaz. Since the results of these excavations, which began in 1992, are not yet available in English, we preface our comments on ceramic chronology and gold-pottery associations with a brief description of this site's geography and salient cultural features.[45]

Cerro Juan Díaz is a 40 m-high hill with steep, stone-strewn flanks and a flattish summit. It is located landward of the southern shore of Parita Bay (Fig. 8.4a–b) along both banks of the La Villa river that divides Herrera and Los Santos provinces. On the southern flank is another flat area. Excavations directed in 1998 by Desjardins (Université de Montréal, Québec) indicate that this platform was modified as a special mortuary zone. Two excavations – Operations 3 and 4 – have uncovered about 200 human skeletons on the platform, buried in many kinds of graves with several primary and secondary treatments (Fig. 8.5).

Operation 3 burials
At the western end of the platform a 12 × 20 m cut exposed features initially revealed by emptying out looter pits.[46] Prominent among these is a circular arrangement of stone-lined oval pits, which may have been used as ovens (Fig. 8.6). When these large features were constructed, they disturbed graves. After they were abandoned, people were buried on top of them. Therefore, they act as a convenient stratigraphic division between an early and a late group of burials in Operation 3.

The early graves that were disturbed by the 'ovens' are Features (F.) 1, 2, 16, 17, 21, 26, and 94 (Fig. 8.6). F.1, 17 and 26 are less than 1 m deep and have sub-rectangular floor plans. F.2, 16, 21 and 94 are narrow straight-walled pits, with a depth of 1.5–2 m. F.2 cut through F.1, pushing its contents to one side. Likewise, F.16 disturbed F.26. F.94 was used at least twice. These disturbances – and the extremely tight packing of skeletons into multiple graves F.2 and F.16 – mean that it is not always possible to relate specific funerary goods to a particular grave, burial event or skeleton.

F.1 contained two ceramic incense burners (Fig. 8.3e–f), twenty-four jaguar and puma canines perforated through the roots, 400 elongated *Spondy-*

8.5 Mortuary features in Operation 4 at Cerro Juan Díaz: (a) F. 44, Individual 55 (adult female, 40–45 years) – the white arrow points to the polychrome vessel illustrated in 8.9e;
(b) F. 43, Individual 66 (unstudied) – the white arrow points to the polychrome vessel illustrated in 8.9d;
(c) F. 51, which contained several superimposed layers of burials, some primary (flexed) and others in urns;
(d1) F. 1, first level, containing an urn burial with the remains of an infant (0–2 months);
(d2) F. 1, second and third levels, containing a flexed adult, six juvenile crania and the dispersed remains of a second adult.

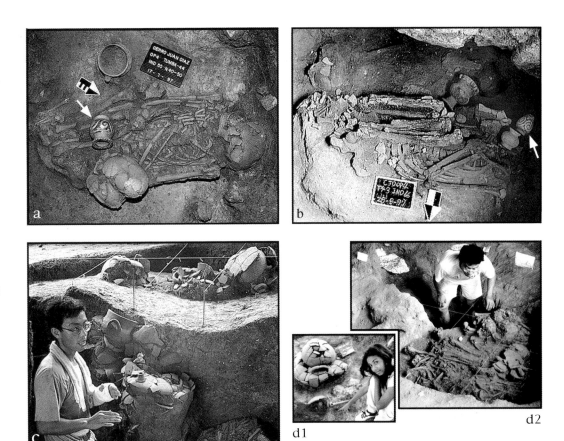

8.6 Archaeological features found in Operation 3 at Cerro Juan Díaz, Panama.

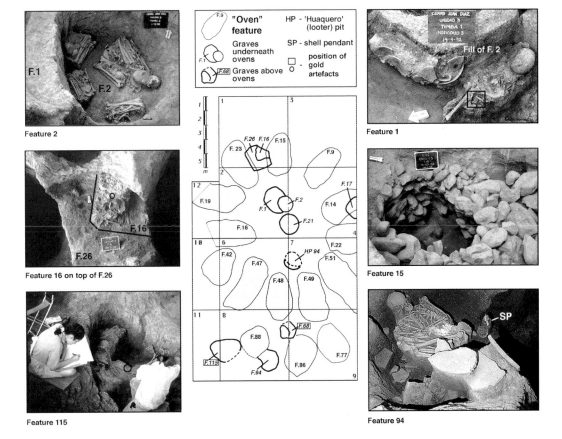

8.7 Small mortuary artefacts
from Operation 3 at Cerro
Juan Díaz:
(a–b) ocelot (*Felis pardalis*)
canines, F. 16;
(c) puma (*Felis concolor*)
canine, F. 2;
(d) jaguar (*Panthera onca*)
canine, F. 2;
(e–h) mother-of-pearl
pendants, F. 94, lower level;
(i–k) polished agate beads,
F. 2;
(l–t) *Spondylus* beads, F. 16;
(u) frog of marine gastropod
shell, F. 94 (see Fig. 8.6);
(v) polished bar of agate
with terminal perforations,
F. 16;
(w) polished bar of a bluish
stone with longitudinal
perforation, F. 16.)

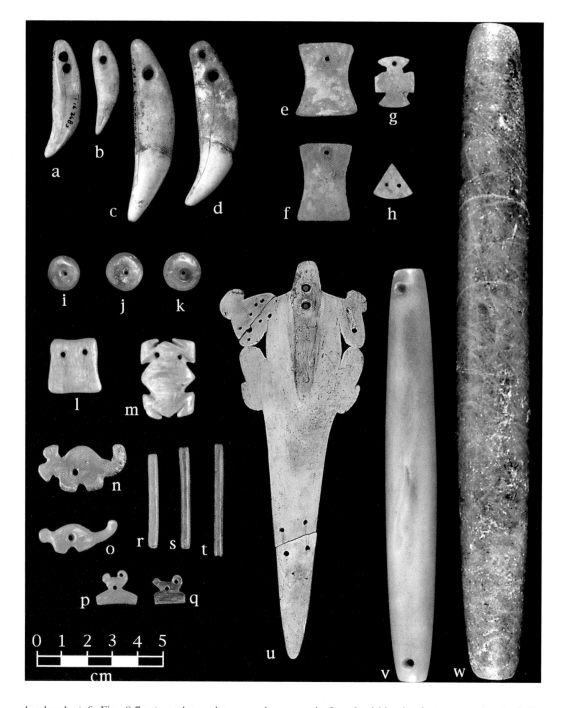

lus beads (cf. Fig. 8.7r–t), and two hammered gold plaques with double raised spirals (Fig. 8.1l–m). The black rectangle in the relevant photograph in Fig. 8.6 shows where the plaques were found – alongside the *Spondylus* beads and the felid teeth. This suggests that teeth, shell and metal belonged to a composite artefact – a necklace, perhaps, or a garment with the above items sewed onto it.

F.2 contained thirteen packages of human skeletons, most of which were already disarticulated when they were wrapped and deposited in the grave – on three different occasions.[47] Burial

goods found within the feature consisted of (1) five polished agate beads (cf. Fig. 8.7i–k), (2) one puma and four jaguar canines (cf. Fig. 8.7c–d),[48] (3) a worked marine gastropod (*Calliostoma sp.*), (4) thirty-four elongated *Spondylus* beads (cf. Fig. 8.7r–t) and (5) a gold plaque with raised spirals (Fig. 8.1k). The gold artefact was found at the top of the shaft near its junction with F.1. It is possible therefore that it was dislodged from F.1 when F.2 was dug through it.

F.16 contained at least eighteen individuals deposited very tightly in the shaft in bundles. As in F.2, no whole pottery vessels were found in the

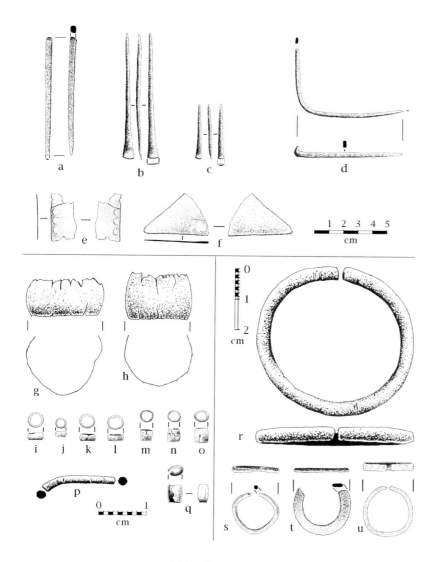

8.8 Metal artefacts from Cerro Juan Díaz:
(a) Operation 3, Level 4, 16S-11E; (b) Operation 3, surface shell feature; (c) Operation 3, underneath F. 68; (d) Operation 4, F. 43, Level 6, 10–15 cm; (e) Operation 3, F. 16, fill; (f) Operation 3, F. 16, fill; (g) Operation 4, F. 1, Level 5, 190–200 m; (h) Operation 4, F. 43, Level 4, 0–10 cm; (i) Operation 4, F. 51, bottom of Urn 26; (j) Operation 4, F. 44, Individual 55; (k) Operation 4, F. 51, between Urns 26 and 29; (l) Operation 4, F. 51, Individual 99; (m) Operation 4, F. 44, Level 40–50 cm; (n) Operation 4, F. 51, Individual 55; (o) Operation 4, F. 44, Individual 55, underneath polychrome vessel; (p) Operation 3, F. 16, fill; (q) Operation 3, F. 94, upper part of fill; (r) Operation 3, F. 16; (s) Operation 31, shell feature; (t) Operation 1B, F. 1; (u) Operation 31, Trench 1, 47.5 cm below datum.

grave. Mortuary artefacts consisted entirely of small objects made of marine shell (mostly *Spondylus*), pearls, stone, animal teeth and metal. Only one metal item was found intact: the ring illustrated in Fig. 8.8r. This was associated with a package that contained an adult and an infant, several *Spondylus* pendants shaped like mammals (cf. Fig. 8.7n), seventy-three perforated canine teeth (mostly puma and ocelot; cf. Fig. 8.8a–c)[49] and two polished stone bars (Fig. 8.7v–w). Seven other metal fragments were recovered from the clayey matrix of the tomb fill. It is feasible that these are fragments of artefacts originally buried in underlying F.26, which was all but emptied when F.16 cut into it. One is elongate and bent (Fig. 8.8p).[50] One thin and flat fragment exhibits small embossments (Fig. 8.8e), which suggest that it was broken off the wing of a bird effigy similar to the one found at La India-1 (Fig. 8.2j). Another thin fragment is triangular and has a raised edge (Fig. 8.8f). This could also be a piece of a bird-effigy tail. The remaining four fragments in F.16's fill are very thin gold overlays.

F.94 was used twice. In the bottom of the shaft were the scattered remains of an adult on the same level as ninety-odd pearl oyster pendants cut into geometric shapes (cf. Fig. 8.7e–h). Later, a primary flexed burial of a twenty- to twenty-five-year-old woman was put in the same shaft (Fig. 8.6).[51] She was placed on top of a broken legged *metate* and fragments of three ceramic bowls, which had been intentionally smashed before being deposited in the grave (Fig. 8.3a, b, d). A long-tailed shell anuran was placed alongside her (Fig. 8.7u). A single gold bead (Fig. 8.8q) was found in F.94's fill. Perhaps it was strung together with the mother-of-pearl ornaments.

F.16 and 94 were disturbed by 'ovens' F.23 and 88. Other field evidence suggests that F.1 and F.2 were also constructed before the 'ovens'.[52] The stones in the centres of the 'ovens' were laid into a 0.5 m-thick reddish clay lining. The spaces in between the stones were filled with ash, earth, burnt clay and sherds (see F.15 in Fig. 8.6). Five charcoal dates are available for the clay linings of F.15, 19, 23, 42 and 49 (Table 8.1) (I-18222 and 27, I-18671, 72 and 75). Their combined 2σ range is cal AD 350–970 and the average of their intercepts: cal AD 647. We do not know whether the soft fills within the central stones represent use or abandonment débris or both. Two dates obtained from the fills of F. 15 (I-18286) and F. 19 (I-18288) have a 2σ range of AD 435–890 and intercepts of cal AD 635 and cal AD 690.

Sánchez has analysed the sherds found in the red clay linings of F.15 and 23. No Conte-,

Macaracas- or Parita-style sherds were present. The most recent and predominant style is Cubitá, which represents 62% of painted sherds in F.15 and 74% in F. 23.[53] It is likely, then, that the construction of the 'ovens' coincided at *c*. cal AD 650 with the apogee of the Cubitá style.

Only five complete ceramic vessels were recovered in the graves stratified underneath the 'ovens'.[54] The two incense burners from F.1 are similar in shape to those recorded by Ichon and González at El Indio and El Cafetal.[55] This kind of burner with the ribbon handle was not reported at Sitio Conte where round or 'fish-tail' handles and nubbin feet prevailed.[56] Two of the plates from F. 94 belong to the 'Ciruelo Black-on-Red' type and one to the 'Guábilo Black-on-Cream' type, which are synchronous with Cubitá-style trichromes.[57]

Charcoal flecks from the fill material that enclosed the packages of bones in F.16 dated to cal AD 120 [340] 530 (I-18679). Larger chunks of wood charcoal found around the upper skeleton in F.94 – the one that was associated with the painted plates described above – dated to cal AD 550 [660] 800 (I-18638). A similar sample recovered at the level of the disturbed burial in F.94 returned cal AD 340 [530] 650 (18637).

To sum up, funerary ceramics and sherd distributions in fills suggest that the sub-'oven' grave features in Operation 3 were deposited when the Cubitá style was in vogue. They probably do not antedate the 'ovens' by very long (some of the charcoal samples could have derived from soils used to fill the tombs).[58] We now turn to two stratified refuse deposits elsewhere on the site in which Cubitá and Tonosí sherds were the dominant painted categories and in which no Conte or later materials were recovered.

Sherd and metal distributions in Operations 1 and 2

In 1992 two test pits (Operations 1 and 2) were excavated in stratified refuse. Sherd distributions and radiometric dates from two strata are relevant to the temporal relationship between the Tonosí and Cubitá styles and therefore to the antiquity of Initial Group metalwork. These are:

1. Macrostratum C in Operation 2: a 0.5 m–1 m thick layer of clayey burnt soil that runs circumferentially around the summit of the hill. In one 1 × 1 m section of Operation 2, this unit was divisible into an upper and lower member by a layer of ash.

2. F.1 of Operation 1: a shallow (0.2 m deep) refuse dump near the La Villa river, which was deposited over house features including postholes and clay floors. A broken flat metal ring –

probably for the nose – was found in this feature (Fig. 8.8t).

In Macrostratum C the lower member contained 78% Tonosí sherds, 18% Aristide, 3% Cubitá and 1% others in a sample of 188. In the upper member, the proportions were: Tonosí 48%, Aristide 27%, Cubitá 23%, and others 3% (n=181). In F.1 of Operation 1 the situation was reversed, with Cubitá dominant (87% of a sample of 143), Tonosí 8%, Aristide 2%, and others 3%. This sequence demonstrates that the Cubitá style gradually replaces Tonosí.[59] Some additional details are relevant to our discussion of gold–pottery associations: (1) no sherds of the 'Nance Red-and-Black on Cream' or Ciruelo Black-on-Red types of the Cubitá style were found in Macrostratum C, and (2) 93% of Tonosí sherds in both the lower and upper members of Macrostratum C were Vases Doubles and 2%, La Bernardina à Bord Decoré. We commented earlier that the majority of metal items associated with Tonosí-style pottery in graves at El Cafetal, La India-1 and Las Huacas were associated with Vases Doubles.

Two charcoal dates were recovered in Macrostratum C in Operation 2 (lower member): cal AD 435 [660] 635 (Beta-54976) and cal AD 530 [630] 680 (Beta-54975). Charcoal from the same Macrostratum elsewhere around the hill returned: cal AD 560 [645] 685 (Beta-54977) and cal AD 245 [555] 770 (Beta-54979). The average of the intercepts of these four dates is cal AD 623. The average of the intercepts of the two dates associated in the Tonosí valley with Tonosí-style pottery is cal AD 563 (Gif-1641, 42). If we ignore results with a standard deviation of >80, the 2σ range of charcoal samples associated with abundant Tonosí pottery in refuse lenses is cal AD 380–685.

The fact that no charcoal samples have been recovered in mortuary features with Tonosí vessels warns us against exaggerating the precision of the above group of dates. At Cerro Juan Díaz the presence of a few Cubitá sherds in the lower member of Macrostratum C could indicate that this layer was laid down synchronously with the 'oven' features and the early burial episode in Operation 3 and therefore that it represents an intentional fill that incorporated older cultural deposits. Even so, we have strong reasons to doubt the earlier contentions of the senior author[60] that the Tonosí style materialized as early as the period cal 350 BC–cal AD 50 and that, inferentially, metallurgy was correspondingly ancient in Gran Coclé. We do not think that the Tonosí style developed until cal AD 200–300.

This revised opinion receives indirect support

from a suite of date estimates for the La Mula pottery style, which has been isolated stratigraphically at Sitio Sierra and La Mula-Sarigua.[61] The characteristic La Mula vessel type is a large subglobular urn with cream or buff slip and a tall outflaring collar, which is decorated with groups of vertical black lines running from rim to neck.[62] At La Mula-Sarigua this pottery was found in features whose four uncalibrated shell dates have a range of 530–60 BC.[63] When these dates are calibrated, however, the 2σ range moves up to cal 160 BC–AD 310 (Beta-12728, 12729, 12931, I-8863) with an average intercept value of cal AD 105. This last estimate accords with four charcoal dates associated with the La Mula style and coeval red-painted wares. Two from Sitio Sierra came from refuse lenses associated with a circular structure: cal 170 BC [AD 50] AD 115 (I-9703) and cal 190 BC [AD 1] AD 155 (I-9702). One from La Mula-Sarigua returned cal 45 BC [AD 50] AD 130 (SI-5689) and another from La India-1 cal 180 BC [AD 85] AD 370 (Gif-1643). The combined 2σ range of the three dates with standard deviations of ≤80 is cal 190 BC–AD 230 and their intercept average cal AD 35. We infer from these data that the La Mula style materialized between about cal 200 BC and cal AD 200 with an apogee in the first century cal AD.

At least two La Mula style vessels were found by de Brizuela at Las Huacas, but we have not been able to identify their provenance.

Four-colour polychromy and the burgeoning of metalwork

Taking stock of Initial Group metalwork in Gran Coclé, we can reasonably infer that the following artefacts were being made between about cal AD 200/300 and 700, before the Sitio Conte burials were deposited: beads; incised and plain gold leaf overlays; cast figurines of (a) eagle-like birds with one or two heads, (b) frog-like creatures, (c) a spider, (d) an 'armadillo' and (e) the El Cafetal conjoined and crested animals (whatever these may be);[64] small hammered discs; hammered plaques with divergent raised spirals; circular, twisted and possibly spiral nose-rings; nose clips; and, perhaps, chisels.

The inventory is depauperate and mortuary artefacts are sparse. Where proper field records exist, no more than five items have been found in a single funerary feature.

When we turn the clock forward to Sitio Conte, the situation is radically different. Although we heed Briggs's observations that gold is not the only or even the primary correlate of rank and status at this site,[65] the record states quite clearly that some folks were buried with socially meaningful quantities of gold and with artefacts whose size and weight dwarf the Initial Group objects just summarized.

That this change occurred at the *beginning* of the Sitio Conte grave sequence is evidenced by Grave 32, in which six bodies represented three burial episodes. Lothrop remarked that in this grave 'most of the objects … whether of bone, ivory, metal or clay, differ markedly in style from other finds at the Sitio Conte'.[66] All the illustrated tri- and polychrome pottery is clearly Conte in style.[67] Some vessels, however, exhibit the snail-shell scroll, which, as we have already remarked, is a stylistic link with Labbé's 'Montijo Transitional Style' found at such sites as Rancho Sancho de la Isla, Las Huacas and Cerro Juan Díaz. A linkage with earlier times is also provided by the human effigy found in Grave 32's shaft[68] – the only vessel from Sitio Conte that clearly belongs to Sánchez's Cubitá black-and-red-on-cream group – and also by the black-on-red plate,[69] which conforms with the decorative criteria of the Ciruelo Black-on-Red type already discussed.

Sitio Conte's Grave 32 contained: three animal figurine pendants; one human figurine pendant; one animal figurine; one bar; 7,116 beads; a three-and-a-half-yard (3.2 m) string of tiny beads; three bells; four chisels; eight cuffs, some of these paired; seventeen embossed discs with zoomorphic designs; forty-one whole and six fragmentary small discs; one ear plug; four ear-spools; one head crest; two nose clips; two nose-rings; one nose pendant; twenty-seven overlays; two overlays for the tips of nose-rings; one plaque; two rings; twenty strips; eleven triangles; and three whistles (one of these a crocodile figure).[70] Notable by their absence in the above list are the two best-represented metalwork forms in the meagre Initial Group inventory: hammered discs with raised spirals (cf. Fig. 8.1k–m) and 'eagle' bird pendants with open wings.[71]

Does this contrasting situation really point towards a sudden burgeoning of metalwork and a rapid increase in wealth differentiation about cal AD 700? Has this situation been exaggerated by sampling vagaries? A little of both, we think. A key site to understanding the increasing importance of metallurgy in Gran Coclé is Playa Venado,[72] whose splendid cast figurines are well known in the international art market. Some of these are assigned to the Initial Group by Bray[73] and most to the 'Openwork Group'.[74] We pointed out in note 14 that we believe that most, if not all, the published metalwork was associated with mortuary vessels painted in the Cubitá or Conte styles (and intermediate forms). We hope at a later date to be able to identify particular metal-pottery associations, which are necessary for estimating objectively the antiquity and development of metallurgy at this important, but tragically mismanaged site.

Ironically, in spite of the size and typological importance of Lothrop's and Mason's grave samples from Sitio Conte, there are fewer radiometric dates available for their Conte- and Macaracas-style pottery than for the other subsequently defined styles. One temporal datum has been provided by two charcoal samples recovered on the floors of two rock-cut tombs at Miraflores (CHO-3) on the Bayano river: cal AD 700 [900] 1030 (I-7310) and cal AD 670 [875] 1015 (I-7309). Three gold nose-rings (Fig. 8.1b–d) were found in the largest tomb (no. 2),[75] which provided the latter date.

The mostly red-painted mortuary vessels at Miraflores are strikingly different from contemporary ceramic grave lots from Gran Coclé.[76] In the grave fills Cooke and Jacinto Almendra found a handful of Macaracas polychrome sherds.[77] Their surface finish and paste type point to manufacture in the eastern Azuero Peninsula. Grave fill associations do not, of course, guarantee synchrony of charcoal and artefacts. But the possibility that these particular dates really do identify the time span of the Macaracas style receives support from excavations in Operations 3 and 4 at Cerro Juan Díaz, to which we now turn.

The second mortuary phase at Cerro Juan Díaz
We pointed out earlier that the 'oven' features in Operation 3 at Cerro Juan Díaz provided a convenient stratigraphic hiatus for distinguishing between an early and a late group of burial features in this excavation unit. Many of the stratigraphic details of the second mortuary phase remained to be collated with excavation notes and artefact inventories. Some data on metal-pottery associations are at hand, however.

In the south-west corner of Operation 3, a sub-circular grave with about five individuals was identified intruding upon the edge of F. 88 (one of the 'ovens') (Fig. 8.6). Looters had damaged it so severely that some mortuary artefacts must have been damaged or removed. There were no whole pottery vessels in the feature, but the most recent polychrome sherds in the fill around the bodies are Macaracas. The grave was filled with a heterogeneous mixture of clays amid which a single dispersed charcoal sample dated to cal AD 650 [785] 985 (I-18683). Two cast-metal figurine pendants were recovered alongside one of the skeletons

amid a fibrous mass that included phytoliths from the tree family Moraceae. Since the Moraceae genus *Ficus* is frequently used in the Neotropics for making bark cloth, we presume that these remains belonged to such an artefact – for which Lothrop found ample evidence at Sitio Conte.[78] According to conservator Jacinto Almendra, one of the pendants was a conjoined animal figurine similar to the one from Las Huacas (Fig. 8.2l).[79] Someone stole it from the Restoration Laboratory of the Anthropology Museum in Panama City before Almendra had begun to clean it! The other artefact represents one half of a very small pendant that depicts twin, conjoined crocodilians (Fig. 8.1j). Organic fibres adhering to this artefact were identified by Emilia Cortés (Metropolitan Museum of Art, New York) as strands of twisted cotton.

The only other metal artefact associated stratigraphically with the second burial phase in Operation 3 is a small chisel (Fig. 8.8c). This was recovered underneath a large Macaracas polychrome urn (Fig. 8.3c) decorated with the frontal version of the plumed crocodilian icon, which will figure prominently in later pages. Inside the urn we found the burnt remains of a baby.

Stratified above these and other burial features is a 0.3 m lens of habitation refuse in which the predominant polychrome style is Parita. Three charcoal fragments scattered throughout this matrix (I-18635, I-18636 and I-18641) have a combined 2σ range of cal AD 905–1400 and an intercept average of cal AD 980. The chisel illustrated in Fig. 8.8c was recovered in this stratum.

A few other gold items turned up in refuse lenses in Operation 31 excavated at the eastern edge of the summit of Cerro Juan Díaz. A ring with a round cross-section (Fig. 8.8s) was stratified within a small shell mound in which the predominant decorative style was Macaracas. A chisel-like artefact (Fig. 8.8a) and another ring with a rectangular cross-section (Fig. 8.8u) were found in refuse lenses that accumulated over the shell mound, in which the majority of painted sherds belong to the Parita style.

Burials in Operation 4
At the opposite end of the platform at Cerro Juan Díaz project archaeologists investigated a complex series of interlocking burial features.[80] The age-sex profiles of the skeletons and the continual reuse of features (Fig. 8.5c, d1, d2) suggest that we are dealing with a community cemetery. Several skeletons of very young infants have been found, whereas at Sitio Conte Lothrop reported only one 'baby' burial.[81] The dead are treated in

8.9 Macaracas-style vessels from Cerro Juan Díaz and a 'Montijo Transitional Style' jar from Las Huacas:
(a) Cerro Juan Díaz, Operation 4, F. 4;
(b) Cerro Juan Díaz, Operation 4, F. 51;
(c) Cerro Juan Díaz, Operation 4, F. 48;
(d) Cerro Juan Díaz, Operation 4, F. 43 (see Fig. 8.5b);
(e) Cerro Juan Díaz, Operation 4, F. 44 (see Fig. 8.5a);
(f) Las Huacas, Tomb 27.

many different ways and more than one interment mode is frequently evident in the same feature: e.g. primary flexed skeletons (Fig. 8.5a, b), urn burials (Fig. 8.5d1), multiple burials (Fig. 8.5d2), ossuaries with jumbled bones and intentional burials of detached crania with other skeletons (Fig. 8.5d2). Some features are shallow with a single skeleton and others are 1–4 m deep with several bodies (Fig. 8.5c).

To date, the only tri- and polychrome vessels that have been recorded in this mortuary zone represent the stage at which Conte designs are evolving into Macaracas, when one of the commonest and most distinctive icons was a running or standing crocodilian with plumes. The vessels illustrated in Fig. 8.9b, c and e, for example, have close parallels in Sitio Conte graves 5, 6, 24, 25 and 74.[82]

The plate illustrated in Fig. 8.9b was found in F.51,[83] for which three radiocarbon dates are available. Carbonized (food?) residue adhered to sherds from red-painted urns dated to cal AD 800 [975] 1030 (Beta-121156) and cal AD 785 [895] 1005 (Beta-121157). Charcoal recovered alongside Individual 98 dated to cal AD 640 [780] 990 (Beta-121163). The small jar with the decorated rim (Fig. 8.9e) was recovered in F.44 associated with a charcoal date of cal AD 775 [895] 1015 (Beta-121162). The combined 2σ ranges, then, for F.44 and 51 in Operation 4 span cal AD 640–1030 while the average of the intercepts is cal AD 883. This is remarkably close to the average of the intercepts of the Miraflores tomb fills with the Macaracas sherds (cal AD 886).

A globular vessel, whose rim was removed before burial (Fig. 8.9a), represents the Cuipo variety of Macaracas polychrome.[84] The zoomorphic figure stands out in the pale slip colour highlighted by black. Significantly, we think, no Macaracas vessels with this *en negatif* treatment of icons were found at Sitio Conte. A charcoal sample from the deep feature in which it was buried (F.4) predictably returned a slightly more recent date: cal AD 985 [1035] 1220 (Beta-121164).

A few small metal items were recovered in burials 43, 44 and 51 in Operation 4: a thin bent object (Fig. 8.8d), overlays (perhaps for subspherical ceramic beads, which are frequent at this site) (Fig. 8.8g, h)[85] and several beads (probably also overlays) (Fig. 8.8i–o). The maximum number of beads in a single context was eleven.

Very little metallurgy has been reported from other sites coeval with four-colour polychromes elsewhere in Gran Coclé since the Sitio Conte excavations. Ichon found four metal items in burials of the second mortuary phase at El Indio, which produced several vessels of the Joaquín variant of the Conte and Macaracas styles. A cast quadruped figurine pendant with human features (Fig. 8.2p) and a figurine pendant representing two frogs (Fig. 8.2e) were found in a burial urn. A nose clip (Fig. 8.2m) was found in Grave 7 along with two Joaquín polychrome pedestal plates.[86] A bracelet or nose-ring (Fig. 8.2a) turned up during general digging. A cast frog-effigy figurine (Fig. 8.2c) and a cast spread-eagled bird figurine pendant (Fig. 8.2i) were found by looters but are surely from this site and period. In addition to these illustrated pieces, Ichon records a *tumbaga* pendant and a small plaque.[87]

This paltry inventory of contextualized metallurgy during the period cal AD 700–1000 stands in stark contrast with the lavish late tombs at Sitio Conte. According to Briggs, Grave 74 (excavated by Mason) contained 3,496 beads; 188 'ear rods'; ninety-one stone and gold 'ear rods'; forty-five gold appendages for 'ear rods'; eighty-seven bells; twenty-nine 'medallions' (repoussé discs with geometric designs); seventeen chisels; thirteen plaques (repoussé discs with figurative designs); four cuffs; two pendants; twenty-three overlays for bone, resin and ivory objects; six wristlets or anklets; thirty miscellaneous overlays; four nose ornaments; two nose clips or ear-rings; one bar; and a copper bell.[88]

Grave 74's metalwork inventory is similar in sheer quantity to that of Grave 32, which should be about 200 years older. But differences between them in icon and artefact popularity are probably significant chronologically and socially. Grave 32's repoussé discs, for example, exhibit a greater variety of icons – a pair of spotted long-tongued quadrupeds, two pairs of seahorses, a felid face, an abstract human (?) face, a frog with legs shaped like pelicans and a toothed mouth,[89] and a representation of the standing humanized crocodilian flanked by two laterally depicted brethren.[90] The last-named personage dominates the Grave 74 large repoussé disc assemblage.[91] Some of these grim saurians sport long ear rods. This feature suggests that they were of equivalent rank to the human occupants of this grave, who owned large numbers of these artefacts.

Metalwork, then, exhibits the same trend as painted pottery during the period cal AD 700–1000: the variety of icons diminishes as a humanized crocodilian image with plumed clothes and headdresses and belts that end in *alter egos* becomes ascendant. An enigma is why this particular icon should also prevail in burial grounds reserved for much poorer sectors of Gran Coclé society represented by the people buried in the late mortuary phase in Operations 3 and 4 at Cerro Juan Díaz and in the cemetery excavated by Lleras and Barillas at El Caño.[92] Perhaps the plumed crocodilian *per se* is relevant to social affiliation – tribe, clan, etc. – while sartorial detail – ear-spools, weapons, etc. – identifies rank or status on a real and supernatural plane.

Contact-period metalwork

Panama was the first region in the New World where the Spanish encountered plentiful gold ornaments. Soldier Espinosa's 1519 description of the mortuary accoutrements of *cacique* Antatará and two other principals in a house near Cerro Juan Díaz bears witness to the fact that mortuary practices recorded archaeologically at Sitio Conte continued until contact. Stripping off several layers of cordage and cloth to get to the desiccated bodies, Espinosa uncovered a golden casque, four or five necklaces, cuffs, large discs, a belt, bells and greaves.[93]

In 1973 earth-moving operations for a cane field at El Caño eliminated eight mounds and damaged two out of a total of twelve.[94] In one of the damaged mounds (no. 3), four burial urns contained European and Native American artefacts. In Urn 1 the bones of a single adult were associated with two twisted and three elongate glass beads (Fig. 8.10a–c), five elongate pendants of a hard blackish stone (Fig. 8.10d–f), about eight shell beads and pendants shaped like the stone ones (Fig. 8.10g) and the dorsal spine of a marine catfish (Ariidae: *Sciadeichthys dowii*).

Inside Urn 2 were the remains of an adolescent and a child, fragments of shell beads, a perforated gold disc (Fig. 8.10h), a cast frog-effigy pendant (Fig. 8.10i) and a miniature cast human effigy pendant (Fig. 8.10j).

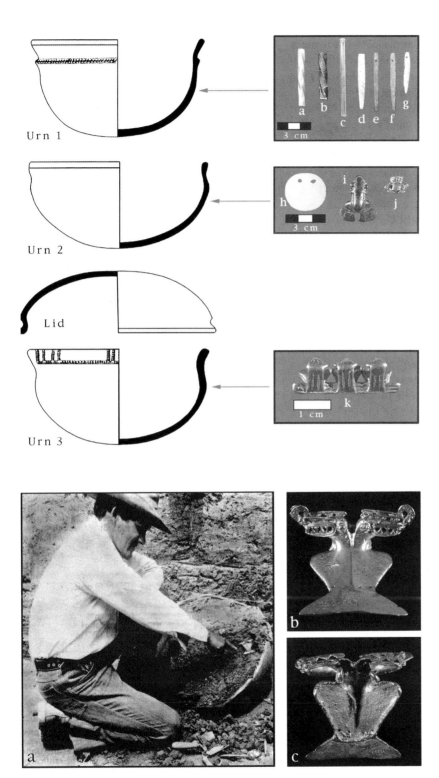

8.10 Burial urns from Mound 3 at El Caño, which contained small ornaments of European and Native American manufacture: (a–c) glass beads; (d–f) elongate pendants of an igneous stone; (g) elongate pendant of *Anadara grandis* shell ; (h) gold disc with perforations; (i) gold frog; (j) gold human effigy; (k) three conjoined frogs.

8.11 El Caño, Mound 3:
(a) Jacinto Almendra points to the bicephalous gold figurine illustrated in (b) and (c).

Urn 3, whose skeletal remains were probably removed by the bulldozer, contained a cast effigy pendant of three conjoined frogs (Fig. 8.10k). It was capped by a shallow bowl. The fourth urn did not contain funerary remains.[95]

The ethnohistoric environment of these urn burials is intriguing. At the end of 1502 and beginning of 1503 Columbus founded an ephemeral settlement at the mouth of the Belén river on the windswept Caribbean coast, whence he sallied in search of a probably mythical 'king' (the Quibián). Spanish penetration of the Pacific slopes opposite Santa María de Belén began in 1515. Espinosa established a provisioning centre at Natá – a few kilometres from El Caño – in 1516. This town became the operational base for the conquest of Veragua to the west. It received its charter in 1522. Since it is unlikely that native people would have practised traditional funerary rites after Spanish priests were in residence at Natá, we assume that these urns were deposited between late 1502 and 1516–22.

Soon after these fortuitous finds in 1973 the National Institute of Culture conducted larger excavations in three altered mounds.[96] These were not directed by professionals. Although stratigraphy was very complex, strata were removed by horizontal 10–20 cm layers. Underneath the fill of Mound 2 the incisors, molars and partial post-cranial of a horse were found near twelve monochrome pots. (These were originally identified as *Equus caballus* by A.S. Rand [STRI, Panama]; the identification of the teeth was confirmed in 1999 by M. Jiménez.) Two undescribed *tumbaga* fragments were found in this excavation.

In Mound 3 nine funerary features were located in strata accumulated underneath the four urns salvaged by Cooke. One burial at 2.1–2.2 m depth was associated with a miniature human-effigy figurine (Fig. 8.1i).[97] One metre below this, a monochrome burial urn (Fig. 8.11a) contained a miniature gold *vasija* (ceramic pot) and an open-backed effigy of the crocodilian creature with two heads (Fig. 8.11b–c).[98] We could not find the urn to determine its typological affiliations. A small gold bead and a thin *tumbaga* plaque were associ-

8.12 Bajo Chitra (CL-4), Veraguas: (a) hammered gold plate with circumferential embossments; (b) find spot of (a); (c) rim sherds of panelled red plates.

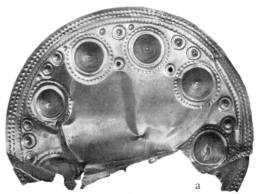

a

b

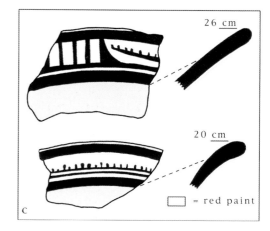

26 cm

20 cm

□ = red paint

c

ated with an extended supine burial at unspecified depth. A small rectangular plaque[99] was found at 1.9–2.0 m below surface, a tiny cast effigy pendant shaped like two armadillos (Fig. 8.1g) at 2.9–3 m and a 5 cm-long chisel at 3.0–3.1m.

In Mound 4, where Arosemena and González reported eight burials, a small gold plaque with a hole and a 4 × 0.4 cm chisel were found unassociated with burials (see note 92).

The co-occurrence of European and native artefacts in the salvaged urns and the horse remains should not be taken as evidence that the sub-mound gold artefacts at El Caño are necessarily coeval with contact. We have not encountered field drawings or catalogues of artefact-burial associations for the 1974–6 excavations. The 1983–5 excavations directed by Lleras and Barillas in deposits stratified underneath Mound 4 unearthed several Macaracas style vessels (see note 92). A temperate inference, therefore, is that the El Caño double-headed crocodile dates somewhere between cal AD 850 and AD 1502 rather than to AD 1300–Conquest as proposed by Bray (1992). Iconographically, it exhibits parallels with a cast bell found in Grave 74 at Sitio Conte[100] and with the 'Parita Assemblage'.[101] The 'Parita Assemblage' is a group of uncontextualized hammered plaques and cast figurines, which includes 30-odd artefacts discovered in a hoard at El Hatillo or Finca Calderón by a looter who 'leased the site' from the owner in 1962![102] Mortuary pottery found at El Hatillo during the Smithsonian-National Geographic excavations of 1948 belongs to the Macaracas, Parita and El Hatillo styles.[103] Bray mentions that an 'eagle in Veraguas style' was found by Stirling and Willey who directed these excavations.[104] But it is not mentioned in Ladd's (1964) monograph and we have never seen it.[105]

Several sites near Natá and El Caño have produced sherds of trichrome pedestal plates, which are decorated with designs painted in black or black-and-red on a white ground. These are arranged either in a circumferential panel just below the interior rim or are spread over the entire interior surface.[106] Some designs emphasize a stylized and rectilinear form of the humanized crocodilian icon.[107] A sherd of this kind of pottery was found at Belén (where Columbus founded his ill-fated settlement),[108] and a complete vessel was excavated in 1998 at Spanish Panamá La Vieja.[109] The stylized crocodilian is one of the design elements of the last of the Gran Coclé polychrome styles, El Hatillo.[110]

Plate sherds like those we have just described represent the only polychrome pottery found at CL-4 (Bajo Chitra), a nucleated village located in the mountains of eastern Veraguas. Surveys and test excavations conducted in 1985 found no sign of earlier occupations. Cooke (1993) equates Bajo Chitra with the contact-period chieftain Esqueva or Esquegua, who defeated one of Espinosa's captains in 1517. In 1987 he recovered a damaged embossed gold plaque in a vertical exposure in front of a private house (Fig. 8.12a, b).[111] Although it lay in a redeposited stratum, we presume it is synchronous with panelled plates (Fig. 8.12c). It also suggests that somewhere at this site there are burials of high-rank personages who resisted the Spanish – maybe even Esquegua himself!

This repoussé plaque was stolen from the Anthropology Museum on the night of the US invasion of Panama (19 December 1989).

Conclusion

Many paradoxes surround the study of Native American metallurgy. With modern techniques it is possible to date metal pieces sitting in museums using charcoal in clay cores or fibres preserved by copper salts. Such radiometric sophistication gives a much-needed temporal context to this technology and its semiotic content, but it tells us nothing about its social dimension. This can only be reconstructed by the careful excavation of intact archaeological features. Museums all over the world are full of Precolumbian gold artefacts, but only a minute percentage of these was found in controlled excavations.

When the Harvard and Pennsylvania teams excavated at the famous Sitio Conte in the 1930s and 1940s, they found most of the grave features intact. Replication and re-analysis are essential features of archaeology as they are of any investigative endeavour. The context of Sitio Conte metalwork was recorded with enviable detail and precision by Lothrop (1937). But once studied, the collections were split up: some were sent back to the landowners and some were dispatched to other museums. Woe betide the researcher who wishes to re-study everything that came out of a particular feature at this important site.

Since the Sitio Conte excavations, few academic archaeological projects in Gran Coclé have concentrated on recovering material culture from mortuary sites synchronous with metalwork. In those instances where excavations have been undertaken at village-cum-cemetery sites these have generally focused on time periods that pre-date the degree of wealth differentiation that is evident at Sitio Conte. The record, though, would be much more complete were it not for illicit excavations. A perusal of items exhibited in foreign museums or at international exhibitions underlines the fact that looting and collecting continue unabated. Two very important sites, Playa Venado and El Hatillo (or Finca Calderón), were systematically exploited by people covering as archaeologists. They paid lip-service to the requisites of modern fieldwork, but kept for themselves the proceeds of sale abroad, cynically using the export opportunities provided by the existence of the US-administered Canal Zone. Recent confiscations of archaeological material by Panamanian Institute of Culture officials indicate that this cynicism is still rife. Our excavations at Cerro Juan Díaz have determined empirically that about 60% of the site has been damaged by looting.[112]

In spite of these sampling difficulties, our inventory of contextualized gold artefacts found in Gran Coclé (Panama) since the Second World War demonstrates that the earliest-known metal artefacts are associated with a distinctive trichrome style of pottery (Tonosí). We strongly doubt that this style materialized as early as cal 350 BC–cal AD 50,[113] because a different and ancestral style (La Mula) was at its apogee about then. A more temperate estimation is cal AD 200/300–cal AD 500/600. Some aspects of pottery distribution suggest that the introduction of gold artefacts occurred during this period and not at the beginning, i.e. about cal AD 300–400. But the nature of the radiocarbon-date record makes this a weak inference, which requires substantiation.

The artefact inventory associated with Tonosí pottery and its stylistic successor, Cubitá (probably manufactured between cal AD 500/600 and 700) comprises cast figurine pendants shaped like birds and animals, solid and overlay beads, overlays on top of clay cores, rings, nose clips, small hammered discs and hammered plaques with divergent raised spirals. Finds of pendants of spread-eagled birds on top of legged *metates* point towards a symbolic relationship between these icons and agriculture, fertility or similar concepts. Several authors have remarked that the hammered plaques with spirals are very similar to uncontextualized examples found in the vicinity of San Pedro de Urabá in northern Colombia[114] and at Guácimo in Atlantic Costa Rica.[115]

The former region probably is the *fons et origo* of the Initial Group metallurgy. However, it is clear from the record of contextualized artefacts that, soon after the introduction of metallurgy, very close correspondences developed among the geometric and naturalistic icons, which are utilized on much of the metalwork from Lower Central America and also on Gran Coclé painted pottery. These are not limited to the humanized crocodilian with its plumes and belts. Frogs, turtles, curly-tailed creatures, crocodilians, double-headed birds, spread-eagled birds and double spirals figure prominently on the Tonosí and Cubitá styles of pottery and also on coeval artefacts made of *Spondylus* and pearl oyster (*Pinctada*) shell.[116] Many of these icons continue to be painted in different guises for the rest of the Precolumbian period. We do not believe that such close iconographic parallels among the different media used to display a symbolic system can be demonstrated for other culture areas in the 'Chibchan realm'. In other words, Gran Coclé was in some way intellectually nuclear.

We intentionally refrained from discussing Playa Venado because we do not have enough data on metal-pottery associations at this important site. We will present some bona fide data on metal-pottery associations in a future publication. We exhort museum curators to verify whether cast pieces from Playa Venado and other important looted sites contain residues of clay cores whose charcoal could be AMS-dated.[117]

The four-colour polychromes of the Conte and Macaracas styles, which were found by Lothrop and Mason in the Sitio Conte graves with abundant and heterogeneous gold artefacts, do not seem to have materialized until cal AD 700 at the earliest. New radiocarbon dates for the Cubitá style (of which only one vessel was present in Sitio Conte graves) and for the Macaracas and later Parita styles suggest, in fact, that the graves excavated by these two researchers span the period cal AD 750–950. These dates, then, seem to signal diversification of artefact types, increasing size of individual pieces (especially embossed plaques) and much larger numbers of metal items in individual graves. Some people during this time period were able to amass and show off a lot of wealth. The ascendancy of a particular icon – a humanized crocodilian – is evident on both metalwork and painted pottery. This obviously has very interesting implications for the study of the relationship between imagery and social organization. We pointed out, on the one hand, that this personage is not restricted to rich folks' graves and, on the other hand, that some representations depict it with symbols of high social rank such as long ear rods.

Was Sitio Conte the burial ground of important people from a small 'chiefdom' like that of the contact-period chieftain Natá? Or was it the central necropolis of Gran Coclé, to which certain dignitaries from a number of socioculturally related territories were taken? As far as we know, only at the contiguous archaeological site of El Caño has evidence been found for some kind of ritual space in Gran Coclé – lines of columns with carved and plain statues and other monoliths.[118] So it could be true that the territories that the

archaeologists and ethnohistorians are wont to call 'chiefdoms' – Natá, Parita, Escoria and the like – were just groups of villages within the Gran Coclé macroterritory, sometimes in alliance with each other and sometimes at each others' throats.

Finds made by looters of spectacular gold figurines and embossed plaques at the El Hatillo or Finca Calderón site (the Parita Assemblage) suggest that here – as at Sitio Conte – the very influential and very wealthy were laid to rest, but only during the last six or seven centuries of the Precolumbian era. Colonial documents suggest that chief Antatará, or París, who may well have resided here,[119] was, in regional terms, a particularly influential and respected person – a paramount chief or *Dux Bellorum*. In the context of the macroterritory hypothesis, did El Hatillo replace Sitio Conte as the top-rank necropolis for Gran Coclé (because its headmen became more influential than Sitio Conte's)? In the context of the alternative small chiefdom hypothesis, have the vagaries of archaeological sampling prevented us from finding a site synchronous with Sitio Conte in the neighbouring 'chiefdom' of Parita? These are interesting questions for future research projects.

Finds of metal artefacts at El Caño and, with less temporal precision, Bajo Chitra in the Veraguan cordillera, provide archaeological corroboration for Spanish soldiers' observations of contact-period metallurgy. Chitra lies on the other side of the cordillera from the Belén valley where Griggs has found good evidence for a large Native American population at and probably after contact.[120] It took the Spanish nearly forty years to establish themselves in this inhospitable and defensible part of Panama. We assumed that native goldwork was stifled in the Pacific lowlands by AD 1522. An interesting research project would be to determine whether and for how long Precolumbian traditions of figurative polychromy and metallurgy continued in areas that remained outside colonial military and political control.

Notes

1 Lothrop 1937, 1942.

2 Lothrop 1942: 198.

3 Briggs 1989; Hearne and Sharer 1992; Mason 1941, 1942.

4 Baudez 1963; Ladd 1957, 1964; Lothrop 1959; Willey and Stoddard 1954.

5 Cooke 1972; Hansell 1988; Ichon 1980; Isaza 1993; Sánchez 1995.

6 Cooke 1985; Labbé 1995.

7 Lothrop 1942: fig. 486.

8 Cooke 1993; Helms 1979; Linares 1977.

9 Cooke 1976b, 1984.

10 Bray 1984; Cooke 1998a; Cooke and Ranere 1992.

11 Cooke 1998a; Cooke and Sánchez 1998.

12 Haberland 1976, 1984.

13 Cooke 1984, 1998c; Cooke et al. 1996; Cooke and Ranere 1992; Piperno and Pearsall 1998; Ranere and Cooke 1995, 1996; Willey and McGimsey 1954.

14 'Contextualized': recovered in a stratum or feature that permits association with other artefacts and/or datable organic materials. During the 1950s and 1960s the local Archaeological Society of Panama conducted excavations at many metal-bearing sites, authorized by the director of the National Museum of Panama. Some of the mostly foreign members of this society were honest and did their best to record and publish their finds. Others were not: they did not mention the most complete metal objects in their reports and sold some to local and foreign collectors and museums (the double bird pendant from La India-1 [Fig. 8.2f] ended up in a German museum!). Gladys de Brizuela told Cooke [1998] that Neville Harte requested a painted vessel (de Brizuela 1972: fig. 12) as 'payment' for his assistance. This double standard is not only socially reprehensible, it has also been a tragedy for scholarship. For example, Archaeological Society members worked at El Hatillo or Finca Calderón (He-4) (Ladd 1964), arguably one of the principal villages of the contact-period chieftain París or Antatará (Cooke 1993). They found a remarkable collection of cast figurines (Biese 1967), which Bray (1992: 45) groups in the 'Parita Assemblage'. Their reports on this site only mention two metal plaques (Bull 1965). Another site that produced goldwork of remarkable quality is Playa Venado where Lothrop worked at the invitation of the Archaeological Society. Once again, finds were selectively published and most of the metalwork ended up in foreign museums. In 1996 Luís Alberto Sánchez studied the collections from Playa Venado at Harvard and Dumbarton Oaks. He determined that most of the painted pottery unearthed here belongs to the Cubitá and Conte styles. At a later date he will report on his findings in the light of the Cerro Juan Díaz excavations. We have excluded Playa Venado metalwork from this paper in the belief that unsubstantiated remarks would confuse an already complicated chrono-spatial situation.

15 Bray 1996; Cooke and Bray 1985; Ichon 1980: 176–8.

16 Cooke and Sánchez 1998; Cooke et al. 1998; Sánchez 1995.

17 Bray 1992; Isaza 1993; Labbé 1995; Sánchez 1995.

18 Cooke 1998a.

19 E.g. Cooke 1976c, 1993.

20 Ichon 1970, 1975, 1980.

21 This is not the place to discuss minutiae of ceramic classification. Suffice the comment that we are unsatisfied with current treatments and we are revising concepts and categories. The seven tri- and polychrome Gran Coclé 'styles' – La Mula, Tonosí, Cubitá, Conte, Macaracas, Parita and El Hatillo – were described on the basis of grave groups and/or sherd collections from stratified middens (Cooke 1972; Hansell 1988; Ichon 1980; Isaza 1993; Ladd 1964; Lothrop 1942; Sánchez 1995). The radiocarbon dates summarized in Table 8.1 confirm that they represent a progression. This contemplates intermediate stages that have not yet been isolated stratigraphically, such as the Zahina and Montevideo polychromes (Ichon 1980: 212–30), the 'Montijo Transitional Style' (Labbé 1995) and vessels from the latest graves at Sitio Conte, which represent the transition from Conte into Macaracas. Some regional variation is also apparent. Joaquín polychromes appear to be a variant of the Conte and Macaracas styles, which was manufactured in the southern half of the Azuero Peninsula (Ichon 1980: 230–68). The status of the bichrome Aristide 'style' is uncertain. It comprises a large number of vessel forms and decoration modes. Some of these are synchronous with the La Mula and Tonosí styles. At Cerro Juan Díaz, Tonosí-style sherds co-occur in Macrostratum C (see p. 164) with two types of black-on-red plates – Cocobó (Cooke 1985) and Jagua (cf. Lothrop 1942: fig. 470) – while Cubitá trichromes are associated in Feature 1 of Operation 1 with the Ciruelo type.

22 Briggs 1989: 24; Ichon 1980: 467–9.

23 Ichon 1975: figs 6, 8b, 10b, 10d, 11, 12c, 13, 15d; 1980: pls 16, 19b, 21a; Labbé 1995: figs 17, 22, 127.

24 González 1971: 165–7, 171; Ichon 1980: 176.

25 Cf. Ichon 1980: pl. 36a.

26 Cf. Ichon 1980: fig. 23e.

27 González 1971: fig. 14; cf. Ichon 1980: fig. 49 a, pl. 36 a.

28 Mitchell and Heidenreich (1965) referred this object to Lothrop 1937: fig. 40. This plate illustrates about forty metal items from Tolita Island, Esmeraldas, Ecuador. Eight of these are spiral nose-rings shaped like springs. If the La India-1 example really were like them, it would be unique in Panama. But perhaps it is the broken spiral of a hammered plaque like Fig. 8.1l–m.

29 Cooke and Bray 1985: 41.

30 Cf. Ichon 1980: 88–92.

31 Ibid: 200–203.

32 Ibid: fig. 21.

33 I.e. Ichon 1980: fig. 3a and pl. 20b.

34 Ichon 1980: 200.

35 We report radiocarbon dates in calibrated form (using the convention: lower 2σ value [intercept] upper 2σ value, followed by the lab. no.). We do this for two reasons. Firstly, when marine-shell dates are calibrated, they approximate charcoal dates obtained for similar cultural materials. This particularly affects the chronological position of the La Mula painting style, whose dating is important for understanding when metallurgy appeared in Panama. Secondly, some Gran Coclé metalwork has been associated with European artefacts, which can be related to historical events. The calibrations were provided by Darden Hood and Ron Hatfield of Beta Analytic in November 1998, and are based on the Pretoria Calibration Procedure programme. Marine carbonates that were not corrected for have been adjusted by an assumed $\partial13C$ value of 0‰. A local marine reservoir effect was

not calculated. Where $\partial13C$ was not determined empirically for terrestrial carbonates a value of –25.0 was assumed unless otherwise stated in the text. The calibrated 2σ ranges and intercepts of all dates have been arranged in Table 8.1 along with their uncalibrated 2σ ranges.

36 De Brizuela 1972: 134, fig. 14.

37 Cf. Ichon 1980: pl. 28; Labbé 1995: 29, fig. 17.

38 E.g. Ladd 1964: fig. 26 g, pl. 5a.

39 The following dates in the Appendix are associated stratigraphically with Parita polychromes and coeval red wares at Cerro Juan Díaz and Sitio Sierra: I-18635, I-18636, I-18681, I-18682, Beta-121158, I-8381. Taken as a group, their 2σ range is cal AD 985–1450 and the average of their intercepts: cal AD 1150.

40 Lothrop 1942: 74, fig. 132.

41 Cooke 1976d: pls 12, 13; Labbé 1995: 34, fig. 26.

42 Contra Bray 1992; Cooke and Bray 1985.

43 Labbé 1995: 31, fig. 22.

44 Cf. Dade 1960: fig. 19c (left) with Lothrop 1942: fig. 226g.

45 For additional details consult Cooke et al. 1998; Cooke and Sánchez 1998; and Sánchez 1995.

46 Cooke 1997.

47 Sánchez 1995.

48 Cooke 1998b: fig. 4.8.

49 Ibid.

50 Perhaps it is a fragment of a wire nose ornament (cf. Lothrop 1937: fig. 117e, from Sitio Conte grave 16).

51 Cooke and Piperno 1993: fig. 4.1.

52 Cooke et al. 1998; Sánchez 1995.

53 Cooke and Sánchez 1998: fig. 10.

54 The contents of F.17 and 21 were removed by the activities responsible for the ovens and/or by looters.

55 Ichon 1980: fig. 23e.

56 Tschopik 1942.

57 Sánchez 1995.

58 An attempt was made to AMS-date human bone fragments from F.1 and F.2. The results are equivocal. The only sample that had acceptable proportions of purified collagen (0.5%) (TO-4078) gave the only date that is consistent statistically with stratigraphy and artefact distribution. The Toronto AMS facility used a 13C value of –25, which is unrealistic for human bone from a maize-consuming coastal population such as this. If a $\partial13C$ value of 19 is used, this sample calibrates to cal AD 135 [370] 435 and, if a $\partial13C$ value of 12 is preferred, to cal AD 85 [225] 345. Technically, we advocate the latter calibration because $\partial13C = 12$ approximates the values that Norr (1990) determined empirically for human bones from Parita Bay coastal agricultural sites of similar age. Nevertheless, since F.1's fill contained Ciruelo Black-on-Red sherds, we believe the human bone date overestimates the real antiquity of this feature.

59 Summarized in Cooke and Sánchez 1998: fig. 10.

60 Cooke 1985; Cooke and Bray 1985: table 2.

61 Hansell 1988; Isaza 1993.

62 Cooke 1976: pl. 14; Ichon 1980: fig. 13d; Isaza 1993: figs 17–21; Labbé 1995: 26, fig. 10.

63 Hansell 1988.

64 Lothrop (1937: fig. 174a) illustrates an unprovenanced piece from Sitio Conte, which depicts

four conjoined monocephalous animals with similar characteristics.

65 Briggs 1989, 1993.

66 Lothrop 1942: 289.

67 Ibid: figs 1*, 16, 30a, 32*, 33*, 58a*, 59, 64, 85, 88, 94d, 95, 97a, 106a*, d, f, 109a*, b, c, d*, e*, f, g, h, i*, 277c, 311a–c, f*, g, i, 377, 382a* (asterisks indicate vessels with the snail-shell scroll).

68 Ibid: fig. 122.

69 Ibid: 227b.

70 Ibid: 283–9.

71 The only two 'eagle' figurine fragments from Sitio Conte were found digging trenches (Lothrop 1937: fig. 176).

72 Lothrop 1954.

73 Cooke and Bray 1985: fig. 15.

74 Bray 1992: fig. 3.7, top; Emmerich 1977: fig. 108 and Emmerich 1965; Helms 1979: fig. 12 b; Lothrop 1956: figs 5–7; Lothrop et al. 1957: no. 266; Museum of Primitive Art 1958: fig. 30; Wardwell 1969: 103.

75 Cooke 1998a: fig. 8.7.

76 Ibid: fig. 8.8.

77 Ibid: fig. 8.9.

78 Lothrop 1937: 108–9.

79 Almendra, pers. comm. to Cooke, 1995.

80 These excavations were directed by Koichi Udagawa and Claudia Espejel, assisted by Diana Carvajal, Eric Fournier and Benoit Desjardins.

81 Lothrop 1937: 24.

82 E.g. Lothrop 1942: figs 148, 192c, 225d, pl. 2b.

83 A plate very similar to the one in Fig. 8.9b was excavated by Neville Harte at Río de Jesús, Golfo de Montijo, Veraguas and sold to the Museum of the American Indian (Metropolitan Museum of Art 1973: 20, fig. 85). Another similar example in the British Museum is illustrated by Bushnell (1965: fig. 226).

84 Ladd 1964: 113-120; cf. Labbé 1995: 43, fig. 45.

85 Cf. Lothrop 1937: fig. 135a (Grave 26).

86 Cf. Ichon 1980: pl. 43a.

87 Ichon 1980: 470, 472.

88 Briggs 1989: 201–2. Some of these objects are illustrated in Hearne and Sharer 1992: 69–121.

89 Lothrop 1937: figs 84, 88, 96e, f, 99a, b.

90 Ibid: fig. 95.

91 Hearne and Sharer 1992: pls 1–6, 9.

92 At El Caño near Sitio Conte, to which we will refer shortly, Lleras and Barillas (1985) excavated sixteen graves. They contained but one metal item (an animal pendant which we have not been able to locate in the Institute of Culture). Four of the seven illustrated Macaracas vessels that have zoomorphic icons represent the anthropomorphic crocodilian.

93 Lothrop 1937: 46.

94 Lleras and Bartillas 1985:16.

95 Cooke 1976c.

96 Arosemena and González, n.d.

97 Arosemena and González (n.d.) record a second human figurine, which measured 4 × 4.5 cm, at an unspecified depth. We have not been able to find it. A cast frog effigy with spirals on the back (Fig. 8.1a) and a tiny frog effigy (Fig. 8.1h) were found in the mound area, but there are no field data for them.

98 See also Bray 1992: fig. 3.12; Cooke 1998b: fig. 4.5c.

99 Illustrated in Cooke and Bray 1985: fig. 18.

100 Hearne and Sharer 1992: pl. 43.

101 Cooke and Bray 1985: 44.

102 Biese 1967: 207; cf. Easby and Scott 1970: fig. 230; Galerie Mermoz 1986: item 36.

103 Ladd 1964: 243–55.

104 Bray 1992: 30.

105 According to the artefact inventory from El Hatillo (He-4) (Ladd 1964: 243–55), the following metal items were identified in these excavations: (1) Find 346 – nine gold beads associated with a Macaracas (Pica-Pica) vessel; (2) Find 361 – several pieces of copper without ceramic associations; (3) Find 381 – a few fragments of 'gold-plated copper' and 'gold disks with perforations'; (4) Find 358 – fragments of 'gold-plated copper'; (5) a small fragment of 'gilded copper'; and (6) Find 376 – two 'copper fragments'.

106 Cooke 1976d: figs 1–7; Cooke 1993: 19; Labbé 1995: 48, fig. 51.

107 Cf. Cooke 1985; Cooke 1998c: fig. 4.5e.

108 Griggs 1993: 53.

109 Jacinto Almendra, personal information.

110 Cf. Ladd 1964: figs 9a and 13.

111 Cf. Galerie Mermoz 1986: item 40.

112 Cooke 1997.

113 Cooke and Bray 1985

114 Falchetti 1995; Uribe 1988.

115 Stone and Balser 1965: fig. 23a.

116 Sánchez and Cooke 1998.

117 Bray (1992: 42) illustrates an unprovenanced cast double-headed crocodile with spiral designs down the spinal chord. Charcoal from the casting core inside the body gave a radiocarbon date of 1540 BP ± 90 (OxA-1530), which calibrates at cal AD 350 [550] 665 with an assumed ∂13C value of –25. This date places this item chronologically in the Initial Group.

118 Cooke 1976c; Torres and Velarde 1980.

119 Cooke 1993.

120 Griggs, pers. comm., 1998–9.

References

Arosemena, Marcia A. de and Raúl González Guzmán
N.d. Resumen de las Actividades Realizadas por la Dirección Nacional del Patrimonio Histórico para la Habilitación del Parque Arqueológico de Coclé. Dirección Nacional de Patrimonio Histórico, Panama City.

Baudez, Claude
1963 Cultural development in Lower Central America. In *Aboriginal Cultural Development in Latin America*, ed. Betty J. Meggers and Clifford Evans. *Smithsonian Miscellaneous Collection* 146(1). Washington DC.

Biese, Leo P.
1967 The gold of Parita. *Archaeology*: 202–8.

Bray, Warwick M.
1984 Across the Darién Gap: a Colombian view of Isthmian Archaeology. In *The Archaeology of Lower Central America*, ed. Frederick W. Lange and Doris Z. Stone, pp. 305–38. University of New Mexico Press, Albuquerque.
1992 Sitio Conte metalwork in its pan-American context. In *River of Gold: Precolumbian Treasures from the Sitio Conte*, ed. Pamela Hearne and Robert J. Sharer, pp. 33–46. University of Pennsylvania Museum of Archaeology and Anthropology, Philadelphia.
1996 Central American influences on the development of Maya metallurgy. In *Los Investigadores de la Cultura Maya*, no. 4, pp. 307–29. Universidad Autonóma de Campeche.

Briggs, Peter S.
1989 Art, Death and Social Order: the Mortuary Arts of Pre-Conquest Central Panama. *British Archaeological Reports International Series 550*, Oxford.
1992 La diversidad social de Panamá central: los restos mortuorios del sitio El Indio, Los Santos. *Revista Patrimonio Histórico* (Panamá), Segunda Época 1: 74–104.
1993 Fatal attractions: interpretation of prehistoric mortuary remains from lower Central America. In *Reinterpreting Prehistory of Lower Central America*, ed. Mark Miller Graham, pp. 141–168. University of Colorado Press, Niwot CO.

Bull, Thelma H.
1965 Report on archaeological investigations, Azuero Peninsula, Province of Herrera, Republic of Panama. *Panama Archaeologist* 6: 31–64.

Bushnell, Geoffrey H.S.
1965 *Ancient Arts of the Americas*. Thames and Hudson, London.

Cooke, Richard G.
1972 The Archaeology of the western Coclé province of Panama. Ph.D. dissertation, 2 vols. University of London.
1976a Informe sobre excavaciones en el sitio CHO-3 (Miraflores), río Bayano, febrero de 1983 *Actas IVo Simposium Nacional de Antropología, Arqueología y Etnohistoria de Panamá*: 369–426.
1976b Panamá, Región Central. *Vínculos* 2: 122–40.

1976c Rescate arqueológico en El Caño (NA-20), Coclé. *Actas del IVo Simposium Nacional de Arqueología, Antropología y Etnohistoria de Panamá:* 447–82.

1976d Una nueva mirada a la evolución de la cerámica de las Provincias Centrales. *Actas IVo Simposium Nacional de Antropología, Arqueología y Etnohistoria de Panamá:* 305–65.

1984 Archaeological research in central and eastern Panama: a review of some problems. In *The Archaeology of Lower Central America,* ed. Frederick W. Lange and Doris Z. Stone. University of New Mexico Press, Albuquerque, pp. 263–302.

1985 Ancient painted pottery from central Panama. *Archeology* July/August: 33–9.

1987 El motivo del ave de las alas desplegadas en la metalurgia de Panamá y Costa Rica, pp. 139–153. In *Metalurgia Precolombina,* ed. Clemencia Plazas. Banco de la República, Bogotá.

1992 Preliminary observations on vertebrate food avoidance by the Precolombian Amerinds of Panama, with comments on the relevance of this behaviour to archaeozoology and palaeoenvironmental reconstruction. In *Archaeology and Environment in Latin America,* ed. Omar Ortiz-Tronocos and Thomas van der Hammen, pp. 59–107. Instituut voor Pre- en Protohistorische Archeologie Albert Egges van Giffen, Universiteit van Amsterdam.

1993 Alianzas y relaciones comerciales entre indígenas y españoles durante el período de contacto: el caso de Urracá, Esguegua y los vecinos de Natá. *Revista Nacional de Cultura* 25: 111–22.

1997 Huaquería y coleccionismo en Panamá: reflexiones en torno a un patrón de conducta antihistórico y antinacionalista. *Revista Nacional de Cultura, Nueva Época* 27: 50–66.

1998a Cupica (Chocó): a reassessment of Gerardo Reichel-Dalmatoff's fieldwork in a poorly studied region of the American tropics. In *Recent Advances in the Archaeology of the Northern Andes,* ed. J.Scott Raymond and Augusto Oyuela, pp. 91–106. UCLA Institute of Archaeology, Los Angeles, Monograph 39.

1998b The Felidae in Pre-Columbian Panama: a thematic approach to their imagery and symbolism. In *Icons of Power: Felid Symbolism in the Americas,* ed. Nicholas J. Saunders, pp. 77–121. Routledge, London.

1998c Subsistencia y economía casera de los indígenas precolombinos de Panamá. In *Antropología Panameña: Pueblos y Culturas,* ed. Aníbal Pastor, pp. 61–134. Editorial Universitaria, Panama City.

Cooke, Richard G. and Warwick M. Bray
1985 The goldwork of Panama: an iconographic and chronological perspective. In *The Art of Precolumbian Gold: The Jan Mitchell Collection,* ed. Julie Jones. Weidenfeld & Nicolson, London, pp. 35–49.

Cooke, Richard G., and Dolores R. Piperno
1993 Le peuplement de l'Amérique Centrale et de l'Amérique du Sud et les adaptations aux forets tropicales avant la colonisation européenne. In *L'Alimentation en Foret Tropicale: Interactions Bioculturelles et Perspectiuves de Développement,* vol. 1. *Les Resources Alimentarires: Production et Consommation,* ed. Claude Marcel Hladik, Annette Hladik, Hélène Pagezy, Olga F. Linares, Georgius J.A.. Kjoppert and Alain Froment, pp. 71–96. UNESCO, Paris.

Cooke, Richard G. and Anthony J. Ranere
1992 The origin of wealth and hierarchy in the Central Region of Panama (12,000–2,000BP), with observations on its relevance to the history and phylogeny of Chibchan-speaking polities in Panama and elsewhere. In *Wealth and Hierarchy in the Intermediate Area,* ed. Frederick W. Lange. Dumbarton Oaks, pp. 243–316. Washington DC.

Cooke, Richard G., and Luís Alberto Sánchez
1998 Coetaneidad de metalurgia, artesanías de concha y cerámica pintada en Cerro Juan Díaz, Gran Coclé, Panamá. *Boletín Museo del Oro* 42: 57–85.

Cooke, Richard G., Lynette Norr and Dolores R. Piperno
1996 Native Americans and the Panamanian Landscape. In *Case Studies in Environmental Archaeology,* ed. Elizabeth J. Reitz, Linda A. Newsom and S.J. Scudder, pp. 103–125. New York, Plenum Press.

Cooke, Richard G., Luís Alberto Sánchez H., Ilean Isaza A., and Aguilardo Pérez Y.
1998 Rasgos mortuorios y artefactos inusitados de Cerro Juan Díaz, una aldea precolombina del 'Gran Coclé' (Panamá central). *La Antigua (Panamá)* 53: 127–96.

Dade, Philip L.
1960 Rancho Sancho de la Isla, a site in Coclé province, Panama: a preliminary report. *Panama Archaeologist* 3:66–87.

De Brizuela, Gladys Casmir
N.d. [1970–71] Field notes, Las Huacas. On file at the Insituto Nacional de Cultura (Panama) and the Smithsonian Tropical Research Institute.
1972 Investigaciones arqueológicas en la provincia de Veraguas. *Hombre y Cultura* 2(3): 119–37.

Easby, Elizabeth Kennedy and John F. Scott
1970 *Before Cortés: Sculpture of Middle America (A Centennial Exhibition at the Metropolitan Museum of Art from September 30, 1970 through January 3, 1971).* Metropolitan Museum of Art, New York.

Emmerich, André
1965 Master Goldsmiths of Sitio Conte. *Natural History* 74: 19–25.
1977 *Sweat of the Sun and Tears of the Moon.* Hacker Art Books, New York.

Falchetti, Ana María
1995 *El Oro del Gran Zenú: Metalurgia Prehispánica en las Llanuras del Caribe Colombiano.* Banco de la República (Museo del Oro), Santa Fé de Bogotá.

Galerie Mermoz
1986 *Art Precolombien.* XIIe Biennale Internationale des Antiquaires, Stand 24, Grand Palais, Paris, 25 Sept.–12 Oct.

González Guzmán, Raúl
1971 Informe preliminar sobre las investigaciones arqueológicas realizadas en El Cafetal, Distrito de Tonosí, provincia de Los Santos, Panamá. *Actas del II Simposium Nacional de Antropología, Arqueología y Etnohistoria de Panamá:* 143–73.

Griggs, John C.
1995 Archaeological Survey and Testing in the Belén River Valley, Panama. M.A. Thesis, Graduate Faculty, Texas Tech University.

Haberland, Wolfgang
1976 Gran Chiriquí. *Vínculos* 2: 115–21.
1984 The Archaeology of Greater Chiriquí. In *The Archaeology of Lower Central America,* ed. F. W. Lange and D. Z. Stone, pp. 233–54. Albuquerque, University of New Mexico Press.

Hansell, Patricia
1988 The Rise and Fall of an Early Formative Community: La Mula-Sarigua, central Pacific Panama. Ph.D. dissertation, Temple University, Philadelphia.

Hearne, Pamela and Robert J. Sharer (eds)
1992 *River of Gold: Precolumbian Treasures from the Sitio Conte.* University of Pennsylvania Museum of Archaeology and Anthropology, Philadelphia.

Helms, Mary W.
1979 *Ancient Panama: Chiefs in Search of Power.* University of Texas Press, Austin.

Ichon, Alain
1970 Vases funéraires d'El Indio, District de Tonosí, Panama. *Objets et Mondes* 10: 29–36.
1975 *Tipos de Sepultura Precolombina en el Sur de la Península de Azuero.* Publicación Especial de la Dirección Nacional de Patrimonio Histórico, Instituto de Cultura. Editora de la Nación, Panama City.
1980 *L'Archéologie du Sud de la Péninsule d' Azuero, Panama. Études Mésoamericaines – Serie II.* Mexico City: Mission Archéologique et Ethnologique Française au Méxique.

Isaza Aizuprúa, Ilean I.
1993 Desarrollo Estilístico de la Cerámica Pintada del Panamá Central con Énfasis en el Período 500 a.C.–500 d.C. Undergraduate thesis, Universidad Autónoma de Guadalajara, México (available through the Smithsonian Tropical Research Institute, Panama).

Labbé, Armand J.
1995 *Guardians of the Life Stream: Shamans, Art and Power in Prehispanic Central Panamá.* Bowers Museum of Cultural Art, Los Angeles.

Ladd, John
1957 A stratigraphic trench at Sitio Conte. *American Antiquity* 22: 265–71.
1964 *Archaeological investigations in the Parita and Santa María zones of Panama.* Smithsonian Institution Bureau of the American Ethnology, Bulletin 193. Washington DC.

Linares, Olga F.
1977 Ecology and the Arts in Ancient Panama: on the Development of Rank and Symbolism in the Central Provinces. *Dumbarton Oaks Studies in*

Precolumbian Art and Archaeology 17. Trustees of Harvard University, Washington DC.

Lleras, Roberto and Ernesto Barillas
1985 *Excavaciones Arqueológicas en el Montículo 4 de El Caño.* Instituto Nacional de Cultura and Centro de Restauración OEA-INAC, Panamá.

Lothrop, Samuel K.
1937 Coclé: an archaeological study of central Panama, Part 1. *Memoirs of the Peabody Museum of Archaeology and Ethnology,* 7.
1942 Coclé: an archaeological study of central Panama, Part 2. *Memoirs of the Peabody Museum of Archaeology and Ethnology,* 8.
1954 Suicide, sacrifice and mutilations in burials at Venado Beach, Panama. *American Antiquity* 19: 226–34.
1956 Jewelry from the Panama Canal Zone. *Archaeology* 9: 34–40.
1959 A re-appraisal of isthmian archaeology. Amerikanistische Miszellen. *Mitteilungen aus dem Museum für Völkerkunde in Hamburg* 15: 87–91.

Lothrop, Samuel K., W.F. Foster and J. Mahler (eds)
1957 *The Robert Woods Bliss Collection of Precolumbian Art.* Phaidon, New York.

Mason, J. Alden
1941 Gold from the grave: Central American Indian cemeteries yield exquisite ornaments of almost pure gold. *Archeology* 165: 261–63.
1942 New excavations at the Sitio Conte, Panamá. *Proceedings of the 8th Scientific Congress (Anthropological Sciences),* pp. 103–7.

Metropolitan Museum of Art
1973 *Masterworks from the Museum of the American Indian: An Exhibition at the Metropolitan Museum of Art, October 18 to December 31, 1973.* Metropolitan Museum of Art, New York.

Mitchell, Russell H. and James F. Heidenreich
1965 New developments on the Azuero Peninsula, Province of Los Santos, Republic of Panama. *Panama Archaeologist* 6: 13–17.

Museum of Primitive Art
1958 *Pre-Columbian Gold Sculpture.* New York.

Norr, Lynette
1990 Nutritional Consequence of Prehistoric Subsistence Strategies in Lower Central America. Ph.D. Thesis. Department of Anthropology, University of Illinois, Urbana.

Piperno, D.R. and D.M. Pearsall
1998 *The Origins of Agriculture in the Lowland Tropics.* Academic Press, San Diego.

Ranere, Anthony J. and Richard G. Cooke
1995 Evidencias de ocupación humana en Panamá a postrimerías del Pleistoceno y a comienzos del Holoceno. In *Ambito y Ocupaciones Tempranas de la América Tropical,* ed. Inés Cavelier and Santiago Mora, pp. 5–26. Fundación Erigaie, ICAN, Santafé de Bogotá.
1996 Stone tools and cultural boundaries in prehistoric Panama: an initial assessment. In *Paths to Central American Prehistory,* ed.

Frederick W. Lange, pp. 49–77. University Press of Colorado, Niwot CO.

Sánchez Herrera, Luís Alberto
1995 Análisis Estilístico de Dos Componentes Cerámicos de Cerro Juan Díaz: su Relación con el Surgimiento de las Sociedades Cacicales en Panamá. Práctica dirigida presentada ante la Escuela de Antropología y Sociología para optar al Grado de Licenciado en Antropología con Enfasis en Arqueología. Universidad de Costa Rica, Facultad de Ciencias Sociales, Escuela de Antropología y Sociología.
In press Panamá: Arqueología y Evolución Cultural. In *Catálogo de Arte Precolombino de América Central.* Museo Barbier-Mueller, Barcelona.

Sánchez Herrera, Luís Alberto and Richard G. Cooke
1998 ¿Quién presta y quién imita?: orfebrería e iconografía en 'Gran Coclé', Panamá. *Boletín Museo del Oro* 42: 87–111.

Stone, Doris Z. and Carlos Balser
1965 Incised slate disks from the Atlantic watershed of Costa Rica. *American Antiquity* 30: 310–29.

Torres de Arauz, Reina and Oscar A. Velarde B.
1980 El Parque Arqueológico de el Caño: un Proyecto en Ejecución. *Revista Patrimonio Histórico* 2: 201–21.

Tschopik, Marion Hutchinson
1942 Incense Burners. In *Coclé: an Archaeological Study of Central Panama, Part 2. Memoirs of the Peabody Museum of Archaeology and Ethnology,* 8, pp. 174–7.

Uribe, María Alicia
1988 Introducción a la orfebrería de San Pedro de Urabá, una región del noroccidente colombiano. *Boletín Museo del Oro* 20: 35–53.

Wardwell, Allen
1969 *The Gold of Ancient America.* New York Graphic Society and Museum of Fine Arts, Boston.

Willey, Gordon R. and Theodore Stoddard
1954 Cultural stratigraphy in Panama: a preliminary report on the Girón site. *American Antiquity* 19: 332–43.

Willey, G.R., and C.R. McGimsey III
1954 The Monagrillo Culture of Panama. *Papers of the Peabody Museum of Archaeology and Ethnology* 49(2). Harvard University Press, Cambridge.

Acknowledgements

The authors wish to thank the following persons for helping us locate metal artefacts in various Panamanian institutions and for giving us unpublished details about them: Gladys de Brizuela, Jorge Schmidt, Arsenio González and Jacinto Almendra. J. Almendra and Aureliano Valencia were responsible for cleaning and restoring many of the illustrated artefacts. The fieldwork at Cerro Juan Díaz was funded by two Smithsonian Institution 'Scholarly Studies' grants, two National Geographic research grants, a National Geographic contingency grant and a personal subvention provided by Sr. Ronaldo Pérez. The Panamanian National Institute of Culture provides funds for security guards and a housekeeper. Other institutions and organizations who have provided welcome assistance are: Universidad Autónoma de Chiriquí, Centro Regional Universitario de Azuero, Instituto Enrico Fermi, Universidad de Costa Rica, London Institute of Archaeology, Université de Montréal and Arcillas de Chitré. In addition to the authors, the following persons worked as project archaeologists during the 1992–8 seasons: Adrián Badilla, Aguilardo Pérez, Ilean Isaza, Olman Solís, Claudia Espejel, Claudia Díaz, Diana Carvajal, Benoit Desjardins, Eric Fournier, Aline Magnoni, Isabel Anderton, Clara Bezanilla and John Griggs. Special thanks are due to our long-time field assistants Luís Barría C. and Luís Barría Q.

9

The General and the Queen

Gold Objects from a Ceremonial and Mortuary Complex in Southern Costa Rica

Jeffrey Quilter

Introduction

In an article entitled 'Bootleg Archaeology in Costa Rica', written in 1973, Dwight B. Heath (1973) decried the looting he had witnessed in that country: 'During my year of research, the illicit trade in artifacts totaled, by my estimate, at least a half-million dollars—an intake matched only by one tenth of the country's manufacturing establishments.'[1] His despair was perfectly reasonable for one who cares about the importance of context and provenance of archaeological remains. He was swimming against the tide, however. Looting, or *huaquerismo,* has been common for a long time in Costa Rica. For small-scale subsistence farmers digging for artefacts, especially gold, provides a ready means of cash. In early days such activities also increased the general wealth of the country. For collectors illegal excavations produce a bonanza of fine pieces at relatively cheap prices.

Although there were attempts to pass legislation to halt looting as early as 1899, it was not until 1923 that *huaquerismo* was officially outlawed in Costa Rica.[2] Nevertheless, it continues to be a lucrative activity. Thus, although many hundreds of Costa Rican gold pieces are found in museums and private collections throughout the world, we have very little knowledge of the origins of these objects. Only a handful of gold pieces can be said to come from a particular region of the country, and designation as to the site from which they were removed is even rarer. C.V. Hartman identified five pieces that probably came from the site of Agua Caliente,[3] and single or small finds have continued to be made at various locales in the country.[4] Except for Lothrop's (1963) report on pieces from Palmar Sur, however, we have few descriptions of grave lots or even many pieces from a single site in Costa Rica.

Richard Cooke's work at Cerro Juan Díaz, Panama (see previous article), is providing valuable information on gold and other high-status objects in mortuary contexts, but, along with the Sitio Conte excavations in Panama,[5] it is one of the few professional archaeological projects in Lower Central America to retrieve such information.

The lack of secure provenance for gold objects from Costa Rica presents fundamental problems in advancing studies of the ancient peoples of the region, especially since gold objects were a principle means for expressing religious concepts and sociopolitical rank and hierarchy. Theoretical questions, such as Mary Helms's (1979) claim that gold objects were widely dispersed by seekers of esoteric knowledge in distant lands, cannot be adequately tested until local, regional and international styles are securely identified. Issues concerning the introduction and spread of metalworking technologies, together with local innovation, similarly cannot be addressed without basic information on provenance of objects. No attempts at beginning to unravel the complex mix of spatial, temporal and regional variability will be successful until a corpus of information is produced in which specific pieces can be linked at least to regions and, preferably, sites and specific locales in them. Fortunately, recent investigations resulting from archaeological research at the Rivas site[6] and museum studies by the author have identified a great number of gold objects as having most probably come from the Panteón de La Reina cemetery adjacent to the Rivas site proper or from similar cemeteries close to it.

The general and the kings

The river that runs from the foothills of Costa Rica's highest mountain, Cerro Chirripó, is long by regional standards but at 132 km it is quite short on a global scale. Nevertheless, this is one of the longest river courses in Lower Central America. The valley must have served as a major communication route in ancient times and appears to have been the key factor in linking the late prehistoric peoples of southern Pacific Costa Rica with those of Panama. This cultural unity is described in archaeological terms as the Chiriquí style. Chiriquí ceramics are yet to be seriated in detail, so the period is only divided into two parts, which span the time from AD 700 to 1600.[7] The people represented by this archaeological culture carried on and elaborated the practices of goldworking, and in some areas stone carving, that began late in the preceding Aguas Buenas phase. While cultural distinctions are in evidence in the drainage system, there is an overall sense of unity in the late prehistoric occupation of the valley.

Despite its short run, the river has many names. Today, in its upper reaches, as it wildly tumbles down a narrow gorge, it is called the Chirripó del Pacífico. Joined by the Río Buena Vista, it becomes the El General, passing through the wide valley named after it. As it swings towards the Pacific it is joined by a major tributary, the Coto Brus, and is thereafter called the Térraba which slowly works its way through the Diquís Delta before entering the Pacific.

Part of the reason for the plethora of names for the river may be the fact that its extent was not well known until relatively recently. The high mountains of the Talamanca range blocked easy access from the population centre of the Central Valley. E.G. Squier (1858) makes no reference to the General. His map, quite detailed for many areas of Central America, shows the southern Pacific coast in only vague outline and a river, possibly the Térraba/Diquís, running in a straight line to the mountains. C.V. Hartman (1901), active in Costa Rican archaeology at the turn of the century, also depicts a similar, ill-defined 'R[ío] Grande de Terraba'. By 1911, however, the map in George MacCurdy's *A Study of Chiriquian Antiquities* only includes a small section of Costa Rica but depicts the section of the river visible on it fairly accurately.[8] While the river was known to H. Pittier as early as 1892, it is likely that the relationship of the upper portion of the stream and its lower course was not well known, with the connection finally made close to the turn of the century or slightly later.

Before the advent of the Panamerican highway, the principal route of foot travel between the Central Valley and the Pacific slope was by a pass through the mountains, a route travelled by the

eminent botanist, Alexander Skutch (1992), in the mid-1930s. The juncture of the Buena Vista and the Chirripó del Pacífico is a significant point in this trail,[9] marking where the traveller has a sense of coming out of (or heading into) the mountains from the more open terrain of the valley. The upper reaches of the river thus would have been well known to early travellers while the lower stretches of the river would have been encountered early on by mariners. Thick forests would have created a formidable barrier to reaching the middle section of the river, however, for quite some time.

The 'General' for whom the river was named has been lost from memory. A hundred years ago the term was used not only for the river but for the entire upper region of the valley. The population appears to have been dispersed with clusters of habitations casually referred to as districts, which is how Alexander Skutch alludes to Rivas, in the upper valley. Even in the mid-1930s, when Skutch lived there, Rivas was known for its remnant Indian population. A second concentration of settlement was General Viejo, near where the valley opens up. The third was in the area of modern San Isidro de El General and was called Quebrada de los Chanchos, when first settled.[10] These three areas were recognized by the 1880s, although outside settlers, of whom little is known, entered the valley from the 1850s onwards.

Judging from the writings of both Pedro Pérez-Zeledón and H. Pittier, the term 'General' may have been first applied to the greater geographical region and only later to the river, which was called the Térraba even in its upper reaches.[11] In fact, the discovery of the course of the river may have been made, eventually, by travellers moving from Panamá northwards, rather than in a downstream direction. Since the 'gold rush' which originated in Panamá was gathering momentum at the turn of the century the search for gold may have contributed to a better understanding of the geography of the region.

Overlooking the meeting point of the two rivers and projecting out from the foothills is a long tongue of land rising 75 m above the valley floor. Today, this ridge is known as the Panteón de La Reina (Fig. 9.1). 'Panteón' is a local term referring to any cemetery, including modern ones, while the 'Queen' in question, like the General of the town and river, is unknown.

On the Chirripó del Pacífico river terraces immediately below the Panteón lies the Rivas site. A long-term field project at Rivas indicates that the two sites were contemporary and part of a single complex, with the lower component serving as a combined residence and ceremonial stag-

9.1 Map of the Rivas-Panteón de La Reina area, Costa Rica.

ing area for mortuary rites leading to the interment of the high-status dead on the ridge top above.[12] There are multiple and conclusive lines of evidence to suggest that a hundred years ago, the Panteón was called by a slightly different name, however.

The term *huacal* is derived from the Quechua *huaca*, which signifies any sacred object in its original, Andean, sense. Costa Rica and southern Nicaragua mark the northern limit of the use of the term as it applies to ancient cemeteries, usually those containing treasure. In his 1911 publication on Chiriquian antiquities George MacCurdy wrote, regarding certain styles of gold ornaments (Fig. 9.2):

> Two of the finest examples of what we shall henceforth call the parrot-god were recently acquired by Mr. Keith and like the two alligator-gods in the Keith collection form part of the golden treasure of the Huacal de los Reyes in the valley of the Rio General, Costa Rica, discovered some three years ago, and almost rivaling in richness the Chiriquian huacal of Bugavita.[13]

There are many reasons to believe that the site to which MacCurdy refers is the Panteón de La Reina. He calls the site the Huaca of the Kings, which apparently was the original name, and some local *huaqeros* refer to the ridge near Rivas as the Panteón del Rey y la Reina. At some point it seems that the 'King' part was omitted to give the modern rendering as the Panteón de la Reina. The only puzzling aspect of his statement is his remark that the site was discovered 'three years ago'. With MacCurdy finishing his writing in 1908/9 and a publication date of 1911, the 'discovery' might fall some time between 1905/6 and 1908, perhaps slightly earlier, by this account. As early as 1892, however, Pittier reported that the cemetery at the junction of the two rivers had been severely looted.[14] It is quite possible that the 'discovery' is defined in terms of the era of Minor Keith's purchases in Costa Rica which seem to have occurred in the southern zone in about 1907, near the end of Keith's collecting.

If there were any doubt as to the location of the 'General' site, Alden Mason, who published the Minor Keith collection of stone sculpture, stated, in referring to stone work: 'The northern-most [site], El General, near the sources of the river, is well known, but the specimens in the Keith Collection from this locality consist entirely of pottery and gold.'[15] To this day, the Rivas-Panteón de La Reina complex is the northernmost large site in the valley, as confirmed by Robert Drolet's (1986, 1988, 1992) surveys in the region in the 1980s.

9.2 Drawing by MacCurdy of object K669 (an alligator god) in the Keith collection (see Fig. 9.8).

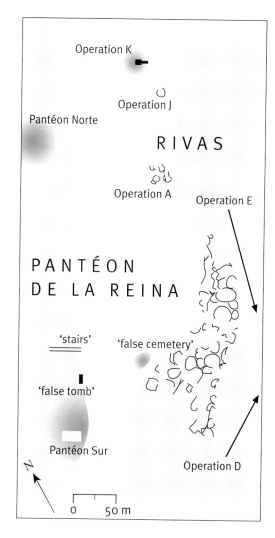

Operation K

Operation J

Pantéon Norte

R I V A S

Operation A

Operation E

P A N T É O N
D E L A R E I N A

'stairs'

'false cemetery'

'false tomb'

Pantéon Sur

N

Operation D

0   50 m

Further confirmation of the Panteón de La Reina as the site of El General can be found in Eduard Seler's discussion of a collection of gold and other pieces given to the Royal Museum in Berlin by Frau Dr Alice Mertens: 'The place of discovery is a location by the name of Buenos Aires and another one, situated somewhat higher, in the mountains, named El General.'[16] Once again, the reference to the 'higher' location, in the mountains, suits the locale of the Rivas site and the Panteón de la Reina.

Given Pittier's statement of early looting, the isolated nature of the southern zone of Costa Rica, the great wealth of the Panteón and its location close to a major communication route, it may be that much of the Chiriquí gold from Costa Rica that made its way into collections at the turn of the century came from the Huaca de los Reyes, especially given the fact that Pittier stated that 'almost all' (*casi todas*, see note 14) the graves had been looted. This statement is also of particular importance in fully verifying the Panteón de La Reina as the site referred to by early explorers and scholars. Many of the ridges overlooking the junction of the river have gold cemeteries but none, apart from the Panteón de La Reina, show signs of early looting. The La Reina cemetery, however, has huge numbers of looter holes many of which are now overgrown with large trees while the back dirt from illegal excavations is consolidated, suggesting that the burials were disturbed some time ago. Such looting can be found all along the La Reina ridge top but pillaging elsewhere shows signs of much more recent activity. Even if we take Pittier's statement that almost all the burials had been looted as undocumented hyperbole, it still suggests that extensive looting had occurred at the site by the 1890s.

Given the strong indications that the El General cemetery and the Panteón de La Reina are one and the same, the study of objects cited as originating from El General may be used to develop an archive of pieces from a known locale that can be dated. This will contribute to the identification of the temporal, spatial and formal variables necessary for further investigation of the cultural forces at play in the development of gold technology and its associated cultural attributes in Lower Central America.

Collections and objects

Some of the earliest purchases of La Reina gold were probably made by José Ramón Troyo, whose collection was eventually donated to the National Museum of Costa Rica. About 3,000 pieces, of which 140 were gold objects, constituted this collection at the time of Troyo's death in the mid-1880s, after which his wife added a thousand more objects to the collection.[17] A precise accounting of pieces that may be from La Reina remains to be done, however. Forty gold objects are listed as from 'El General' in the catalogue of the collection of the Banco Central.[18] Seven pieces are listed as from San Isidro ('Sn. Isidro Gral.') perhaps indicating the place of purchase. These objects may be from La Reina but they could have been brought from elsewhere.

A few objects were acquired by the Royal Ethnographical Museum of Berlin.[19] But the single largest collection of gold outside of Costa Rica that presently can be documented as having come from La Reina is that of Minor Keith, who first collected as a surveyor for railroads while establishing the United Fruit Company.[20]

The bulk of Minor Keith's collection consists of materials from the Mercedes site on a plantation he owned in the Santa Clara Valley in the Atlantic watershed region. Other pieces were apparently bought through agents or made when Keith travelled to different parts of Costa Rica. The organization of the catalogue of the collection at the American Museum of Natural History suggests that Keith's collecting efforts in the southern zone were relatively late in his career and done in a somewhat rushed manner. Whereas there is a piece-by-piece listing of the Mercedes assemblages, no listing is given of the ceramics collected from El General, even though Mason, who studied and published the stone sculptures, noted that El General pottery was part of the Keith collection.[21]

With initial acquisitions beginning in 1872, the Keith collection swelled to 16,308 specimens by 1914. Of these, 881 objects were recorded in a special catalogue of gold and jade. Some of the collection went to the Museum of the American Indian, Heye Foundation, but 874 of the ornaments stayed at the American Museum. In the special ornaments catalogue the entries for items from 'Rio General' are the last to be listed, beginning at number 661 and ending at 881. A total of 200 metal ornaments are in this list with the remaining score of objects consisting of stone and miscellaneous materials.

A portion of the original collection was purchased from the Minor Keith estate by John Wise, a New York art dealer, and eventually presented to the Brooklyn Museum. These transactions resulted in a total of 115 objects at the Brooklyn Museum and 81 pieces at the American Museum of Natural History. The remaining four pieces appear to have been kept and possibly sold later by Mr Wise.

To the objects in New York and Brooklyn may be added the gold discussed by Seler in his 1909 article. Thirty-nine gold pieces are depicted in two photographic plates.[22] This brings the total number of gold pieces from El General to 239. Adding the thirty-seven objects identified as from El General in Carlos Aguilar's (1972) Museo de Oro catalogue produces a grand total of 276.[23]

As the identification of El General as the Panteón de La Reina has been made only recently, it will be quite some time before a detailed study of all of the known gold from this cemetery can be made. At this point, however, a general presentation of the nature and variability of the collection, particularly in terms of iconography, can be done. Before doing this, I will discuss the character of the Rivas site and the Panteón de La Reina, because it is the larger archaeological context and the inferences for social organization and other ethnographic matters that make the Panteón de La Reina collection of such great scholarly value.

The Rivas site and the Panteón de la Reina

While earlier scholars may or may not have been aware of ruins at the base of the Panteón de La Reina, the Rivas site was first identified by Robert P. Drolet in an archaeological survey conducted in the 1980s.[24] Although Drolet mapped and carried out some test excavations at Rivas, full-scale research began in 1992 in work supervised by myself and Aida Blanco (1995). Continuing field investigations have identified an occupation dating to between AD 1000 and 1300. With tropical conditions affecting preservation, the most common archaeological remains are those of fired clay and stone.

Ceramics are in the Chiriquí style that was popular in an area from Rivas, close to its northernmost limit, to central Panama as its southern boundary. This Chiriquí phase was the time when gold objects became the most prized status markers for the people of the region, replacing an earlier preference for jade and, quite probably, shell objects (see Cooke, this volume).

The remains of stone objects at Rivas consist mostly of a rather poorly developed core and flake industry and some well-made ground stone adzes and celts. The moving and placement of large numbers of unmodified stones, however, left the most impressive archaeological record of human activity at the site. These were deployed to create pavements and circular rings, which formed walking and living surfaces for the ancient inhabitants of Rivas. Stone cobbles ranging in size from small plates (c.15 cm in diameter) to huge boulders weighing over a ton were placed to form paved areas for seated work; short causeways and longer paths to connect different parts of the site; benches and stairs; and perimeter rings around perishable houses to catch rain water as it poured off thatched roofs. Cobble pavements were also used simply to delimit space and as grave coverings. While the perishable remains of ancient structures have vanished, an expansive area of cobble architecture, covering at least 2 sq. km at its core, is preserved. Outside this core area are more dispersed and smaller stone rings.

While the core area contains large stone rings tied to patio-like extensions and other large spaces defined by cobbles, the smaller rings appear to be the remains of simple household clusters. We thus interpret the core area as a place where high-status families lived and participated in ceremonial activities in the large public architecture, while the smaller, household clusters were residences of lower-status families.

Although we are still investigating the Rivas population's social organization, there is evidence in mortuary remains that there were at least two distinct social ranks or strata. The members of one group, in the clusters of small houses, were buried on the same river terrace on which the Rivas site was located, in cemeteries not too distant from their homes. We have excavated two such cemeteries and both contain burials with ceramic offerings of plainware or simply decorated pottery vessels, which probably contained food. In contrast, the residents of the core area of the site were buried on the Panteón de La Reina.

We have a number of lines of evidence for the burial of site core residents on the Panteón. First, throughout the entire 2 km-square area of the monumental site we have found no evidence of the presence of a cemetery. Signs of such use should have been easily observable as most of the area is in short grass in which cobble pavements are visible, and we have also scraped clear or excavated about half the monumental area. Second, and even more convincingly, we have a direct connection between the monumental sector and the Rivas site that links the two as a unit and also helps shed light on Chiriquí high-status burial ceremonialism.

A series of distinct, sharp terrace edges demarcate the monumental sector. The first one of importance for our purposes defines the eastern edge of the site, and on the level area of this terrace is found much of the large-scale architecture. In the northern part of this area the architecture consists of large circular and oval stone rings. Excavations along the edge of one of the largest of such structures, Operation E, revealed dense accumulations of pottery including complete, though broken, vessels in non-local styles, indicating contact with the Atlantic Watershed and Central Valley regions. Also found were fragments of large open-mouthed bowls.

Either a secondary, minor terrace system or deliberate human modification of the ground surface created another, higher level in the southwestern area of the monumental sector. Large circular structures are oriented with patios facing towards the flanks of the Panteón and a stair and causeway system link the lower architectural complex to the higher one. From this somewhat higher level, a sharp terrace edge rises another 3 m. On this level, close to the edge, are elaborate cobble pavements with associated large stone pillars. This pavement and pillar architecture resembles a cemetery, but excavation below the cobbles revealed no signs of burials (Fig. 9.3). Heading towards the Panteón, the modern site visitor encounters coffee plants that make it difficult to

9.3 The 'false cemetery' on the western edge of the Rivas site. Note the pillars and pavements, similar to a real cemetery.

observe the ground, and details remained obscure even after an archaeological shovel test-pit survey. At about 80 m west of the 'false cemetery', however, there is a cobble stairway that rises to the Panteón summit. Interestingly, the Panteón de La Reina ridge is slightly lower here than in other parts and its sides are more sloped. To what degree the hillside was modified is difficult to say, but the organization of the complex suggests that a dramatic ascent by the stairs would have been accentuated by the steep slope of the Panteón on either side.

The stairway may be part of elaborate cemetery architecture first reported by Pedro Pérez-Zeledón (1907–8) and later discussed by María Eugénia Bozzoli de Wille (1966).[25] Both accounts describe modifications of the ground surface of the Panteón in the form of three levels: the highest, central one, at 18.5 m and the lower, flanking sections 7.5 m high. Burials were arranged in three rows in the high, central section and in two rows, each, in the lower ones. These artificial mounds or terraces were defined and divided by cobblestone walls. Bodies are reported to have faced east, but no details of grave furniture are mentioned in the reports.[26]

A recent inspection of the Panteón de La Reina by the author failed to identify any levels that even closely approached those described by Pérez-Zeledón. Even though looting has been intensive, the remnants of mounds as high as 18.5 m and 7.5 m should be evidence. Pérez-Zeledón's wording is vague and perhaps he was referring to the widths of burial platforms rather than their heights. Alternatively, if the sides of the Panteón had been set with cobble stones, they might have given the appearance of raised areas. Future field work may clarify this issue.

We have not been able to study the stairs or the ridge top architecture in detail, to date. It seems reasonable to suggest, however, that much of the monumental architecture close to the Rivas false cemetery was associated with mortuary activities and that the latter architectural feature was a staging area for funeral rites before the dead were carried up the stairs for burial on the Panteón.

Some recent work has noted several interesting aspects of the arrangement of burials on the ridge top. Once the summit of the stairs is reached, burials are concentrated in an area stretching about 120 m, southward, towards the end of the ridge. This area of greatest concentration of burials covers about 6,000 sq. m. North of the top of the stairs, there are no looter holes, and no reports of graves, for a distance of about 310 m, after which looters' holes begin again and continue for 200 m or more northwards. Examination of pottery sherds from the two cemetery areas indicates that the Chiriquí style is found in each, but there are differences that may represent temporal phases, regional variations, or other distinctions in the two cemetery populations. The southern sector, close to the stairs, seems most securely associated with the Rivas site.

Analysis of the Keith collection[27]

The following discussion and analysis of the El General gold represent a preliminary step towards a more comprehensive study. At the time of writing it has only recently become apparent that the portion of the Keith collection marked as from El General in the original catalogue is, in fact, from the site now known as the Panteón de La Reina or the vicinity. These pieces are divided between the American Museum of Natural History and the Brooklyn Museum, and while staff members at each institution have been generous in allowing me access to the pieces, various constraints have limited a full and detailed study. Many of the more spectacular objects are on display and are not easily accessible for examination. There have been issues of variations and inconsistencies in catalogue numbers, including many that apparently were made when the collection was still in the hands of the Keith estate. The large size of the collection has also limited the amount of analysis that can be accomplished in half a year's time. Furthermore, those pieces in Costa Rica and Germany that probably come from the Panteón de La Reina are still to be documented and studied in detail.

A number of considerations about the possible original contexts of the El General pieces need to be addressed. For example, although we can say with some confidence that more than two hundred objects come from a single cemetery, how many grave lots are represented by these pieces? It is possible that this many objects could have come from a single grave, as *huaqueros* have reported that as much as a full coffee bag of gold was found in a single burial.[28] The same reports, however, indicate that some graves had very few or no gold objects at all. If only a few graves yielded the Keith gold from El General, then the range of variability in iconography and goldworking techniques may be under-represented in this collection. Given the variety of forms and the number of large and small pieces, there is a sense that the collection represents more than one or two tombs, although this is purely speculative.

The cemetery at the very end of the ridge and securely tied to the Rivas site by the stairs certainly suggests that objects found on that part of the Panteón will be contemporary with activities that occurred at the site below. Still, if looting on the ridge top occurred in a relatively random pattern, the Keith El General gold may consist of pieces from different phases during the era of gold jewellery in Costa Rica. This possibility is increased by the fact that two spatially discrete cemetery areas with somewhat different Chiriquí-style ceramics were recently identified at the Rivas site (Operations C and K). It is thus possible that both the Rivas-site cemeteries and those on the Panteón de La Reina represent two or more temporal phases, although the Rivas cemeteries are likely to be close in date, if not contemporary. Despite these caveats, the opportunity to comment on a large body of gold objects known to come from a single locale which probably contains contemporary pieces or closely dated ones has not occurred before.

To begin with, several broad statements about the Keith collection from El General can be made. While most of the objects in this and other gold collections from Lower Central America were worn as jewellery, those depicting anthropomorphs and other creatures are more easily recognized today as loaded with iconographic significance than pieces formed of flat sheets. It seems reasonable to suggest that, for the most part, the sheet-work which usually has little adornment was designed to impress from a distance by maximizing the surface area of the metal. Although these pieces are often very thin (0.3–0.1 mm), they covered a great amount of the body or clothing surface of the wearer, providing a large area to reflect light.[29] In a similar manner plain tubular beads would have shone brilliantly when great numbers were massed together in necklaces, while even a single strand glowed against dark skin.

Some figures of 'eagles', frogs and other creatures could also be seen from afar, especially when planar surfaces were emphasized or when they were grouped together in strands, as is documented in a photograph of the last *cacique* of Talamanca.[30] Nevertheless, the finer points of iconography of such objects could only be seen at fairly close range, within several feet, a conversational range. These figures thus operated on at least two levels, one that consisted of an impressive display from several metres or more, which might demonstrate that the wearer had the right or the means to wear particular symbolic forms, and a closer range at which the specific symbolism became manifest.

A third category of gold objects are small pieces generally 40 mm or less in maximum dimension. These include bells and beads that could have made impressions from afar, the former as much through sound as sight,[31] and a host of small but elaborate figures. So, too, small miscellaneous pieces could have been used for particular ceremonial purposes that highlighted the details of their iconography within an intimate setting.[32]

9.4 A selection of objects from the Keith collection encompassing metal bands, small and large discs.

5 cm in width (Fig. 9.4: K820–22). Another pair of narrower bands (Fig. 9.4: K853–4) each measure 11 cm in length and about 3 cm wide. These sets tend to have two widely spaced holes at each end, presumably for tying to arms or legs, although there are slight variations in the numbers and arrangements of holes.

Discs are of two principal sizes: large ones ranging from 90 to 292 mm in diameter and small ones, 19 to 27 mm in diameter, with occasional mid-range examples between about 50 and 60 mm in diameter. There are twenty-two discs listed in the Keith catalogue of which fourteen large discs and five small ones are available for study through photographs or collections. Two discs fall between the large and small varieties (Fig. 9.4: K845 & 847) while K846 (Fig. 9.4), a simple form, is slightly oval in shape (93 × 88 mm). There are also some fragments of discs in the collection, at least some of which belong to larger, almost complete examples.

All of the large discs, a small one (Fig. 9.4: K849) and one of the two mid-sized discs (Fig. 9.4: K845) have bevelled or flanged edges so that they resemble thin-rimmed modern lunch plates with slightly convex centres. Some have double bevels. Ten of the fourteen large discs have punctates near their edges. Seven of these have punctates or dimples on both the extreme outer edge and the interior bevel edge, while two others only have punctates on the exterior edges, four are plain, and one is elaborately decorated. These punctates would have added strength to the thin metal as well as slightly increased the reflective properties of the edges of the discs. Two large discs (Fig. 9.4: K830 and Fig. 9.4: K843) are crumpled throughout while a third (Fig. 9.4: K838) is slightly crumpled. We cannot determine when this crumpling occurred, whether before or after burial. The only disc with extensive decoration is K832 (Fig. 9.4) which not only has a double line of punctates around its edge but also a central boss, defined by a double ring, surrounded by five somewhat smaller bosses and eleven smaller bosses, double-ringed.

Large discs commonly bear two punched holes near the edge of the exterior flange, if present. These holes tend to be spaced so that an acute angle is described by radii from the centre of the disc. If these holes were used for suspension or attachment it is remarkable that such thin objects were rather poorly anchored as some have the consistency of foil. Small discs tend to be without decoration, only occasionally having flanges and dimples. They commonly have two holes in the same arrangement as the large discs.

The following descriptions are organized according to the iconographic loads they bear, beginning with sheet-metal objects, followed by bells and then beads and small figures.

Sheet-metal jewellery

Six metal bands that may have served as bracelets or other limb adornments are in the Keith collection. Four of these appear to be roughly the same in their length-to-width ratios, with two (K820–21) measured at 14 cm in length and about

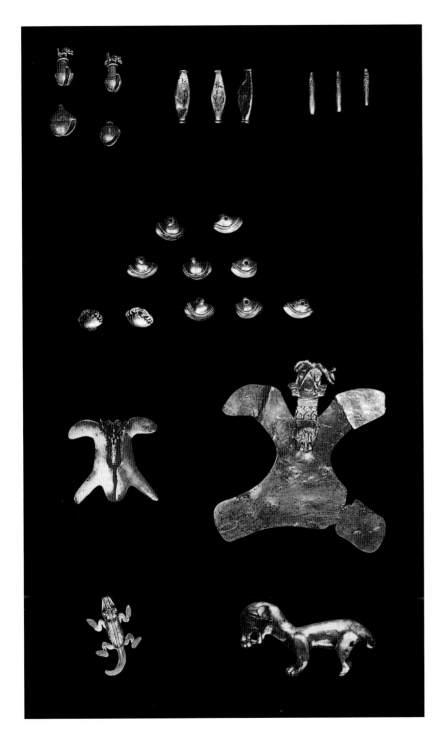

9.5 A selection of objects from the Keith collection encompassing bells, beads and clam-shell beads.

lip jewellery known from the assemblage. It seems quite likely that other objects, such as bells or beads were suspended from the labret.

Bells

At almost half the total inventory, 121 bells constitute the largest single object category in the collection. There are three principal types of bells (Fig. 9.5: K765–6, 775–6): spheroid, conicospheroid and figural. Many small beads were probably also made to produce sounds.[33]

As the term suggests, spheroid bells are round in shape. Holes for suspension occur on the wall of the bell itself, well above the equatorial line. What may have been a set of four such bells at the American Museum had long, linear sound holes that cut across the equatorial line with expanded, rounded ends. These are fashioned in gold with a distinct reddish hue, lack clappers and are all close to 13 mm in diameter while other examples are somewhat smaller.

Conicospheroid bells approximate tear-drop shapes. They commonly consist of an upper, slightly convex, cone-shaped section, at the top of which are suspension holes. There is usually a sharp line demarcating the spherical section of the bell. The straight-edged sound hole approaches or reaches this line. Of those studied in the Keith collection there is a high consistency in size; ten were measured, yielding an average height of 19.8 mm and an average diameter of 16.3 mm for the spheroid section.

These two basic bell forms were sometimes modified by flat proximal ends with small animal figures as finials. Birds and bird-quadrupeds are the preferred creatures to serve as such adornments. Some beads conforming to the general conicospheroid shape and probably made as sound producers may vary slightly in form and be surmounted with a suspension ring instead of holes.

Bells in figural forms are rare in the collection. A frog whose round body served as the sound chamber, with hind legs shaped to form a suspension loop, is at the American Museum. What appears to be a match to this frog is at the Brooklyn Museum. These are the only two examples of figural bells known for the Keith collection.

Beads

Two kinds of beads in the collection, cylindrical and lenticular, were probably made more for visual effect rather than to convey sounds. The former are usually about 3 cm in length and sometimes finished on their ends by smooth, raised edges encircling them, although some are simple

The only example of sheet-metal work that is not clearly intended to be worn around a limb or neck and is not a disc is a flat, slightly flaring trapezoidal piece (Fig. 9.4: K852/B 35.250) 49.7 mm in maximum width and 44.7 mm in height. Its edges are decorated with punctates, a central raised dimple is present, and two holes are found at the upper, narrower edge.

Although technically not sheet metal, a single labret of 'fish hook' style is in the collection (Fig. 9.4: K712). This is the only identifiable piece of

9.6 Gold tube (K713), tapered with ridged ends, that possibly served as a bead.

9.7 Gold pendant in the form of a spider (K688).

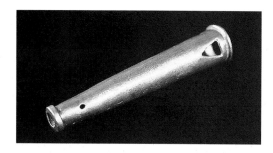

photographs: both left and right valves are present, holes are present near the apex of each object, and one or two raised ridges run near and parallel to the distal end of each object. Each of those examined also bore thin, concentric circles centred in the middle of the interior side of the shell. The central hole probably served to string these gold shells, as the beads were highly standardized in size, between 2.2 and 2.5 cm in maximum width and 1.7 and 1.9 cm in height, judging from those examined.

An interesting object that might have served as a bead but probably had another use is K713 (Fig. 9.6). This is a tapered tube with ridged ends, 64.6 mm in length and 13.3 mm in diameter on one end and 8.0 mm on the other. Just below the wide end is a small triangular notch with its apex pointed down the tube. Perhaps this was a bead or hair ornament that doubled as a whistle.

Figures

Other than bells, the dominant form in the El General gold is an erect or upright figure depicting either an anthropomorphic or composite supernatural being, often in therianthropic form, combining human and animal characteristics.[34] There are a little more than three dozen of this kind of figure and most are large (60–100+ mm), although a few others are mid-sized (40–60 mm). Almost all of these objects have suspension rings on their dorsal surfaces, indicating they were worn as jewellery.

About a third of the figures are avian forms commonly referred to as 'eagles' but, in reality, made up of features combining a number of bird and sometimes other characteristics.[35] Variation is great enough in this category that the style of the 'wings' of one figure (Fig. 9.5: K683) encouraged the compiler(s) of the Keith catalogue to refer to it as a 'butterfly', while the sharply bent wings and facial features of another recall those of a bat. These figures are generally fairly flat in the treatment of their bodies. They almost all have circular bosses on their chests where the planes of wings and tail meet, creating a three-dimensional effect that is only found elsewhere in the beak or snout area of the depicted creatures. This protrusion suggests the puffed-out breast of a bird. In some examples of Chiriquí gold this rounded area is a bell while in others it is only a bulge.

The largest avian figure in the collection (Fig. 9.5: K696) is somewhat different than the others. A representational rendering of distinct wing and tail sections has been discarded in favour of a single expanse of flat metal with three curved negative spaces to create the illusion of wings and tail, all of which have rounded ends as opposed to

tubes. Three examples (Fig. 9.5: K715–17) of what appear to be these rounded-edge beads were deliberately flattened into diamond-like shapes, probably by a sharp application of pressure.

Lenticular beads have length-wise cross-sections that resemble rounded diamonds with flat ends, while their transverse cross sections are circular. Four examples studied ranged from 13.3 to 15.2 mm in length and 7.7 to 8.7 mm in maximum diameter. A single bead (Fig. 9.5: K718), 35.3 mm in length and 8.2 mm in maximum diameter, was intermediate between the two forms: a cigar-shaped tube that gently sloped from its centre to smooth, round ends. Two others, not examined (Fig. 9.5: K719 and K720), seem to also have this form, judging from the photograph available.

Shown in photographs (Fig. 9.5: K726–35) are ten beads resembling small clam shells, four of which were examined directly. These appear to duplicate the general forms that are in the

9.8 A selection of
anthropomorphic figurines
from the Keith collection.

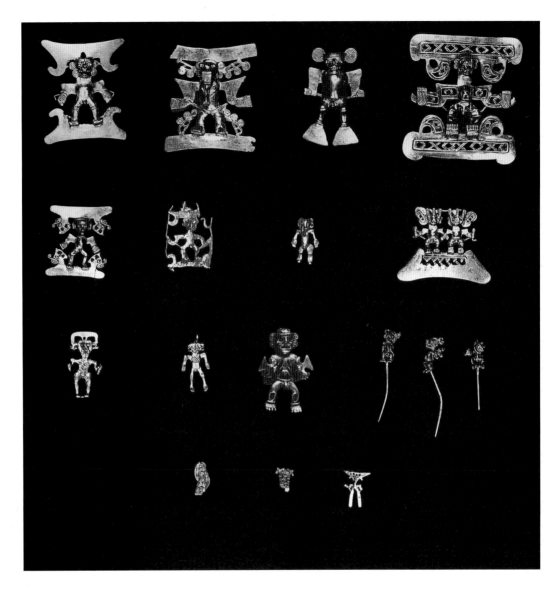

the more common, pointed tips of other avians. In contrast to what appears to be a rather simple execution of the body, the upper part of the figure is elaborately rendered with a fantastic head, false filigree decorated neck, and a boss transformed into a (feline?) head. Whether this figure falls within the corpus of a local gold style cannot be determined at present, but its distinctiveness suggests that further research is warranted. Aguilar identifies a similar piece as of the Jalaca type, distinct from his Dikis type.[36]

Other large figures with strong animal characteristics in the collection are relatively few in number especially those found in 'naturalistic' poses. These include a complete crocodilian (Fig. 9.5: K701) and a fragment of a larger one. There are also a large feline-like creature, not available for study (Fig. 9.5: K686), and a very large pendant of an arachnid (Fig. 9.7: K688). As will be discussed, below, the more representational forms

of animals, as well as particular classes of 'monsters', seem to be more frequently found among the smaller objects in the collection.

After avian creatures, anthropomorphic forms are most numerous and are seemingly the most approachable ones for iconographic interpretation. These tend to fall within the medium range of sizes and consist of nude figures almost always sexed as male with wide, bowed legs. Arms are commonly shown as parallel to, but away from, the body, with open hands or bent at the elbows with hands raised to shoulder or head height and often clenched. A repeating feature of these figures is one or a pair of spiral designs on either side of the head, resembling a form of hair treatment, ear-spool or perhaps the ear itself.

Variability within the anthropomorphic forms includes twin figures (five examples); figures hidden by square, dangling plaques on projecting rods (three examples); and figures with rays or hair

9.9 (above) Gold anthropomorphic figure (K693) with bent elbows and outstretched hands.

9.10 (top right) Gold 'alligator god' figure (K664) with raised shoulders and hands clenched into a fist.

9.11 (above right) Gold figure with 'monster'-like features (K665). This piece features openwork.

projecting from their heads. The twins often have crossed arms or hands held at shoulder height. The figures behind dangling plaques seem to range between human-looking beings to more monstrous forms. There are also the occasional unique forms. One of these (Fig. 9.8: K675) has a projection extending out of its chest area ending in a hook similar to the labret mentioned above. Presumably this hook also held additional danglers of some sort, as may have the labret. Another small anthropomorph (Fig. 9.8: K679) is distinguished by wristlets and the rendering in small detail of a pectoral suspended from a band around his neck.

It is difficult to know if figures with cranial rays or projections are iconographically connected in some meaningful way or are simply the product of the process of categorizing objects. One figure (Fig. 9.8: K678), which has suffered crushing to

the face and torso, holds its hands up, close to the shoulders, while a device springs from the centre of its head and divides in two with each end terminating in open-mouthed serpent or feline heads in the area of the figure's ears. Another anthropomorph (Fig. 9.9: K693) has squared shoulders with bent elbows and hands out and up, again, near the shoulders. The feet are barely defined with the legs flattened and marked by thin, parallel vertical grooves. A central element on the head resembles that of K678 if the serpents were removed, but the most prominent feature is a pair of long, flat, ray-like projections, also grooved, that run at about a 45-degree angle from the sides of the head. What appears to be a small version (Fig. 9.8: K737; 33.35 mm high) of this individual shares all of the main features of the larger one but also has a horizontal bar connecting the two ends of the projec-

9.12 Detail of a finial depicting a 'monster'-like figure (see also Fig. 9.8: K710).

tions. This bar would have served to strengthen the projections on this small object, no matter what its specific symbolic reference, and the similarities between the two figures suggest that they represent the same deity or other being.

Another anthropomorphic figure of interest is a large individual with a grimacing mouth and snout-like face (Fig. 9.8: K670). His sharply defined shoulders are raised while his hands have folded fingers and slightly project to the sides. A large spiral is placed on each side of a head adorned only with a band, and instead of feet the figure has large flippers. There are few other human-like figures of this size in the collection. The other humanoid almost as big (Fig. 9.8: K690) has two small spirals on each side of the head and an open mouth. Tab-like devices projecting from the arms are the only distinctive features in what otherwise appears to be

a quite human representation, including life-like feet. Cavities on the figure may have served to contain jewels or cut shell.

The 'alligator god' figures are highly variable in the degree to which they range between humanoid and zoomorphic forms. They also differ in the degree of elaboration of the coronas on top of their heads, and the pedestal-like forms on which they commonly stand. Some, such as K664 (Fig. 9.10), look quite approachable. It has a closed mouth and fairly human features, shoulders raised high and hands in a distinctive clenched fist, with fingers flat against outward turning palms and thumbs to the side of the hand. The corona and pedestal are smooth, scroll or wave-like planes. A somewhat more imposing figure is K672 (Fig. 9.8). Here, the human form is similar to the previous example but the ends of the scrolls on the upper and lower elements surrounding the humanoid are now depicted as the profiles of snarling, close-mouthed monsters. In K665 (Fig. 9.11) and K669 (Figs 9.3 and 9.8), however, a monster is revealed. In the former the snout-like mouth of the creature is opened, and the corona and pedestal and the monsters that they bear are elaborated with openwork. In K669, while the corona and pedestal are plain bands, they serve to frame the wild scene they contain. The monster shows an unusual snout and its mouth either grasps or spews a serpent, while the accompanying monster profiles are now elaborated with spirals, one set projecting directly out of the head of the main figure and the other falling from a belt he wears. Sharp, pointed shoulders and flat hands concentrate attention on the monstrous aspect of the figure.

The largest anthropomorphic figure (Fig. 9.8: K671 [B35.148]; 104.7 × 97.5 mm) is elaborately decorated with openwork resembling basket weave.[37] No other object in the collection resembles this piece in its technical execution nor in the distinct treatment of the upper limbs and hands, suggesting that this may be a non-local piece. A pair of anthropomorphs on a fan-shaped pedestal (Fig. 9.8: K676) have similar kinds of openwork immediately below them in the fan itself, but this is the only piece that resembles K671. Perhaps the basket-weave style was an influence in the crafting of the twins because, except for this small section, the object generally resembles the rest of the pieces in the Keith collection.

Small objects

There are a great many small objects in this collection, which seem to replicate iconographic themes seen in larger pieces. Twin anthropomorphs and frogs appear, for example. But, in general, there seems to be a somewhat different emphasis in the subjects of these small pieces. This difference does not appear to be due to any limitations in the technical capabilities of the artisans who created these pieces for some are skilfully rendered in great detail. Rather, the choices made were probably due to deliberate decisions and beliefs about what was appropriate for different scales, if the Keith collection is representative of the goldworking tradition of the region, in general. For example, although the presence of a small avian was previously mentioned, this is the only example. Therianthropic forms are virtually absent among the small pieces.

Feline-like creatures are frequently found among the small objects, and this is also true for objects resembling finger-rings. Careful inspection suggests that they are not simply felines, however, but composite quadrupeds, while others resemble monkeys. One such creature (Fig. 9.8: K756) measures only 27.1 mm in height and 18.5 mm in maximum width, and shows a quadruped or monkey apparently eating a rainbow or a tail resembling one. Another (Fig. 9.8: K760: 22.7 × 17.7 mm) holds a bicephalous serpent above its head.

Three masterpieces in miniature (Fig. 9.8: K709–11) consist of intricately rendered beings on the proximal ends of rods. One (Figs 9.8 and 9.12) that was examined in detail had an overall length of 97.4 mm with a maximum width (on the figure) of 13.5 mm. The finial consists of a long-snouted monster with mouth partly open and flared-back ears. It stands on two legs, leaning backwards, with what appear to be tiny snake-like elements thrust behind and away from its body. The Keith Catalogue lists this and the other objects as pins, but the soft gold and relatively blunt ends, at least as these appear today, would have not been very effective. They could have served as hair pins or to wrap other soft material around them. While southern Costa Rica is not usually considered to be a coca-chewing province, these objects nevertheless could have served as spatulas to ingest lime by which to release the psychoactive substances in coca or perhaps some other kind of leaf.

Many of the quadruped monsters that appear in the small objects seem to share features with the profile heads found as rays or appendages on the monstrous larger figures, including snouts with raised nostrils, distinctly defined brows and ears flared to the rear. Perhaps the small objects served as vehicles to celebrate the supernaturals of secondary importance or manifestations of those beings depicted in larger pieces. Alternatively, if,

among the social group that had the privilege or ability to wear gold objects, different social ranks wore gold objects of greater or smaller size based on their relative rank in the social hierarchy, then it is possible that the differences in iconography could signal differential access to the spiritual realm, perhaps with lesser deities more closely tied to lower-ranking members, while only high-ranking individuals were associated with the highest rank of gods.

Discussion

It may be that much of the variability among the objects just discussed simply reflects chronological and spatial variation in their production. Even with the reasonable assurance that these gold pieces come from the Panteón de La Reina, and are presumably contemporary with the Rivas site, dates for the latter span some three hundred years (c. AD 1000–1300), during which changes in technology, styles and beliefs would impinge on the range of objects produced. Furthermore, both our research and the statement by Pérez Zeledón that the Panteón was divided into three units suggest the possibility that variation among grave goods could be due to status differences manifest in three areas within the overall cemetery complex. Indeed, local 'retired' *huaqueros* state that there was considerable variability in the grave lots that they found. Some graves contained only ceramics, some only gold, and some had both pottery and gold. We may further surmise that the number of gold objects also varied among the graves that had such ornaments according to status within the community of those who were entitled to be buried with these kinds of goods. But the El General gold is a rare example of a large group of objects probably originating in a single cemetery complex. The temporal and spatial dimensions of the objects are among the best known and most narrowly defined of any examined and encourage further study.

The La Reina objects bear the distinctive hallmarks of Diquís goldwork from both technological and iconographical perspectives. The mid- to large-sized figures are open-back castings primarily designed to be worn as pendants, as indicated by suspension loops. The splayed, trapezoidal feet and rendering of flat closed hands of anthropomorphs are distinctly Diquís in style, as is the preference for the use of spirals.[38] Interestingly, while false-filigree technique is present, it is not abundant and 'braided-rope' elements in costume or as borders around figures are almost entirely absent. The El General figures tend to have plain, thin bands in places where other Diquís gold objects have 'braided rope'. This suggests that braided decoration as in 'Carbonera' figures[39] may represent a regional variation, a temporal phase in the development of Diquís goldworking or combined temporal and regional stylistic factors. The single Carbonera-like figure (Fig. 9.8: K 674) in the Keith collection is surrounded by a rectangular frame of plain rods rather than braided decorations. While the simplicity of execution may be due to factors other than temporal or spatial ones and its distinctiveness could be due to the 'luck of the draw' of the sample provided by the Keith collection, it seems quite possible that this object represents an early stage in the evolution of the treatment of the Carbonera style. Given that the radiocarbon dates for the Rivas site tend towards the early end of the Chiriquí phase, I suspect that the braided decoration is indicative of Diquís goldwork somewhat later than the Panteón de La Reina examples and that the Keith collection represents goldworking later than the suspected earliest-known pieces but earlier than the late, highly elaborate styles, such as Carbonera.

The range of forms of the La Reina assemblage is fairly restricted, including composite beings with a small percentage of representations of natural forms, most of which are predatory creatures. The composite figures might comprise any one of a number of sets of beings. They might represent several different deities, culture heroes or other beings, or they could represent only one or a few such creatures. At present, there is no way to champion a single, clear means by which to begin to make such distinctions. To begin to approach an understanding of these figures, two considerations must be discussed, the first concerns how we view the objects themselves, the second, how we view the objects within the context of what we may reasonably assume about the cultural contexts in which these objects were worn and used for social purposes.

MacCurdy (1911) and others of his generation referred to figures by the dominant, recurring characteristics that they recognized in groups of pieces. Given the fact that the objects did not depict creatures found in nature, they assumed that they represented particular deities consisting of composite beings. From this were born such terms as 'Alligator God', 'Parrot God', 'Eagle' and so forth. Each group in the taxonomy was distinguished from the others by its most salient animal characteristic, even though it soon became clear that these animals were often combinations of different creatures.[40] Furthermore, there is a high degree of variability in the elaborateness of representation: some figures appear fully human, others have selective 'fantastic' attributes and still others have only vestigial human elements. If viewed from the perspective of a single corpus, however, the forms appear to metamorphose, as hunched shoulders become more sharply defined, turning into the wings of other figures. Human faces transform into monstrous ones with increasingly menacing visages and toothed maws. Even the coronas surrounding the heads and pedestals on which some figures stand start to swirl with emanating rays and serpent-like heads; these elements also adorn the bodies and heads of the main figures.

We do not have many details on religious beliefs and their relations to systems of social and economic organizations in late prehistoric Costa Rica and Panama. We do know, however, that when the direct descendants of the late prehistoric Bribri and Cabecar peoples were contacted after the conquest, they supported a hierarchy of religious orders,[41] which were involved in curing and the maintenance of human and agricultural fertility in elaborated forms of shamanism. Among bellicose peoples, marshalling supernatural forces against enemies was also an important shamanic duty. Indeed, much of native religion practised in the ancient American world was based on similar shamanic principles. A common *modus operandi* of shamans is their transformation into animals, often through the use of hallucinogenic substances, flights to supernatural realms, battling with demons, retrieving souls and sustaining the world order through their supernatural powers. Shamans gained status by their transformational powers; the high regard in which goldsmiths were held in many cultures in the Intermediate Area[42] was very probably due, at least in part, to the manifestation of powers to turn the ordinary into the extraordinary.[43]

Given the shape-changing features represented in the gold figures of Lower Central America and what we know of the religious lives of the people who made them, it seems reasonable to suggest that the figures represent either shamans or gods themselves undergoing transformations from human to monstrous forms. While this is probably not the case for all times and places in the Intermediate Area, it seems to hold true for most of the La Reina collection and the broader tradition of which it is a part. Gerardo Reichel-Dolmatoff (1988) suggested that the animals commonly represented in Colombian gold were representations of the mystical death and symbolic rebirth of the shaman, while Carlos Aguilar (1996) has recently emphasized this point for Costa Rican gold as well. Obviously, some pieces, such as gold discs, bracelets and beads, were not iconographically laden with these messages and probably served simply to impress the viewer with the allure of shining objects. Perhaps they also referred to general concepts such as the plane of the earth or the disc of the sun. But many pieces were designed to signal vital symbolic meanings, and it appears that the information they carried was often related to the process of transformation, whether specifically related to shamans or partaking in more general transformative properties of gods or the world in general.

A human, demigod or god in anthropomorphic form, or a pair of gods or humans, stands as the transformation begins (Fig. 9.4: K690). Perhaps the transformation occurs while dancing, the varying arm positions representing the motions of rhythmic movement. As the transformation or manifestation begins we witness a number of signs of a changed state of being, depicted in the separate gold objects as distinct phases, but probably seen as a continuing flow of change by participants or witnesses to such transformations of shamans or priests.

In all representations are embedded the sense of expansion, brilliance and ecstasy, as might be expected in a drug- or dance-induced state. The gold itself glistens like a separate source of divine light and heat, or a piece of the sun itself.[44] From the head sprouts a brilliant fan of light, curling like smoke, transforming into two snake-like creatures or a single, bicephalous monster. Not only a celestial monster manifests itself but a terrestrial one as well. Less frequently depicted as the monstrous corona, pedestals sometimes also show snake-like monster heads. But these are not independently brought into being; rather, they are expressions of the changed state of the main figure, as is clearly shown in the monster-headed belt of K669 (Figs 9.3 and 9.8). There are obvious variations and inconsistencies if the figures are viewed as a group. For example, K664 (Fig. 9.10) and K672 have much more human-like faces than K666, which has a monster-like face with a similar corona and pedestal to K664 but less elaborate than K672 (see Fig. 9.8). Until such time as fine distinctions can be made, we may assign this variability to the different skills and preferences of craftsmen and their patrons; minor spatial and temporal differences must also be taken into account.

As the transformation gains full force, the main figure takes on a different aspect. The face assumes animalistic characteristics with a snout and bared fangs. While the legs rarely change

position, they remain bent, containing the incipient power of flexed muscles, ready to spring. At the same time, the shoulders are hunched, also taut with power, while the arms and hands assume the rigid posture of the full trance or numinous condition. In the full glory of the transformed state the being can completely expose his vital parts, assured of his omnipotence. This glorified state may not always be the apogee of transformation, in some cases. The figure may change completely into a zoomorphic form, as is common among such religious practitioners, perhaps to carry out some special role in the parallel world of animals, be they of this or another cosmological plane of reality. So, too, the sequence might be read backwards, although it seems more likely that emphasis would be placed on the transformation origin point to another state of being rather than the reverse.

Concepts of transformation are ubiquitous in Native American thought and art, including shamanic practice.[45] Given this consideration, the transformations seen in the gold objects perhaps do not necessarily refer simply to a shamanic sort but equally to other transformative acts, including the gods themselves in some mythic tale. Matthew Looper using ethnohistoric and ethnographic parallels has suggested, however, that larger gold ornaments with greater iconographic detailing were probably worn by elite members of society and perhaps referred to their owners' roles in society.[46] Gold objects, perhaps above all other artistic expressions, came to express transformative capacities and powers – in how they were manufactured, how they were displayed and what they represented – in the late prehistoric cultures of ancient Costa Rica, Panama and Colombia. Directly or indirectly, transformation lies at the core of this constellation of meanings and activities.

The interpretation of Diquís goldwork offered above is an example of the potential to discuss individual pieces from a perspective that may help elucidate finer points of religious thought and action among the prehistoric peoples of Lower Central America. In addition, while the peoples of the region surely had their own traditions and their own variations on larger patterns of belief and practice, the fact that they may have drawn upon ancient, fundamental principles that were and are found over a large area of America can at least provide plausible proposals for closer examination, using a combination of ethnographic sources as well as iconographic analyses of specific traits and characteristics (see Oliver, this volume).

An example of such an analysis may be found in the image of the serpents, especially the bicephalous variety. Bicephalous serpents are common in the Andes, Intermediate Area and Mesoamerica. The Andes and the Intermediate Area both frequently depict individuals wearing bicephalous snake belts. Even more common is the bicephalous sky serpent.

Karl Taube (1995, 1996) has convincingly argued for the shamanic basis of Olmec art and religion: practices and beliefs that were focused on the assurance of agricultural fertility and particularly concerned with maize and the essential ingredient needed to produce it, water. As part of this argument, he presents the case for the interpretation of serpents, including bicephalous ones, as sky imagery in a theology that interrelated sky, earth and the underworld in a complex way. While serpents do not simply represent the celestial realm, it is a key aspect of their symbolic power, and Taube believes that the common Olmec theme of a jaguar biting the Avian Serpent may 'portray the Olmec Rain God as the pivotal, cosmic mountain integrating the regions of the underworld, earth, and sky'.[47] It does not seem unreasonable to suggest that the bicephalous serpent held above the head or snakes springing from the crania of some Diquís figures may be closely related to the same set of ideas, and the serpent in the mouths of some creatures could likewise refer to the jaguar who bites the snake (Fig. 9.3). Looper (1997) explores this image in Tairona gold pectorals and recent Kogi myth. He sees bicephalous serpents linked to concepts of communication between different realms of the universe. Whatever the specific symbolism in Costa Rica, it is likely that the image was associated with a separate plane of reality, probably a celestial one linked to concepts of fertility.[48] The widespread presence of bicephalous serpents in ancient America suggests that these images had a basic common reference that varied in specifics depending on local and historical circumstances.

The high-ranking shamans and warriors who wore and were buried with gold jewellery such as found in the La Reina assemblage must have claimed command of cosmic forces as part of their rights to power, especially in what appears to be the absence of state political institutions. Burial of such quantities of wealth meant that more had to be made and circulated, and that too may have been either closely supervised or monopolized by the most powerful members of these societies. While certain styles of goldwork were widespread, this does not mean that power itself was necessarily diffuse. Rather, the procurement of gold, its transformation into objects of social value and its distribution and circulation among people who valued it were themselves subject to complex processes of political and economic change that probably included times of relatively easy access to precious metal objects and the rights to wear them, while at other times restrictions may have been in place. Rivas appears to represent a time when only a certain segment or class of society had such rights.

Until now, we have not been able to approach documenting changes in the production, distribution and use of gold in the Intermediate Area very well because the lack of provenance of so many looted pieces has impeded even a rudimentary understanding of variations in the formal styles or their symbolism. The materials from the Panteón de La Reina offer one of the first large, significant collections that can be so studied. If the ages and places of origin of more collections are identified in museums or through excavations, we will be able to add substantively to our understanding of the prehistory of particular regions of Lower Central America, the region itself and beyond.

Notes

1 Heath's figure was an estimate. He suggested it was a conservative one.

2 Van Horne 1965: 142–3.

3 Hartman 1901: 190.

4 See Bray 1981.

5 Hearne and Sharer 1992; Lothrop 1937, 1942; Mason 1942.

6 Quilter and Blanco 1995.

7 Snarskis 1981. Chiriquí A: AD 850–1200; Chiriquí B: AD 1200–1600. These span late Period V (AD 500–1000), Period VI (AD 1000–1500) and the contact era in Snarskis' chronology.

8 MacCurdy's map incorrectly shows a tributary of the main stream as running parallel to it, near Buenos Aires. The general course of the river is correct, however.

9 See Pérez-Zeledón 1907–8.

10 Aida Blanco, pers. comm. to Quilter, 1996.

11 Pérez-Zeledón 1907–8. Pittier (1892: 71): 'El nombre de "El General" se aplica indiferentemente á la región que comprende la cuenca colectora del Río Grande de Térraba, al curso superior del mismo rio, desde su formación por la unión de los rios Buena Vista y Chirripó…'; Pittier (1903: 74): 'Algo y mucho parecido á eso sucede á los actuales pobladores de El General: ocupan un territorio incomparablemente bello y feraz, en la margen izquierda del alto río de Térraba…'

12 Quilter and Blanco 1995.

13 MacCurdy 1911: 218–19.

14 'En el ángulo que resulta de la junta de los ríos Chirripó y Buena Vista, existía un vasto cementerio, cuyas tumbas had sido abiertas casi todas. De ellas se sacaron muchos muñecos de oro y piezas de alfarería.' (Pittier 1892: 72.)

15 Mason 1945: 283.

16 'Als Fundorte werden hier eine Lokalität Namens Buenos Aires und eine andere etwas höher im Gebirge gelegene El General genannt.' (Seler 1909: 466; translation by Jerry Goldberg.) According to Dr Manuela Fischer of the Museum Für Völkerkunde, Berlin (pers. comm., 1997) thirty-five objects were given to that museum by Walter Lehmann. Dr Fischer also reports that a letter from Lehmann to Seler states that the former was only able to buy his collection in San José, because Minor Keith was out of town!

17 Aida Blanco, pers. comm. to Quilter, 1997.

18 Aguilar 1972.

19 MacCurdy states that (at least two) objects from El General had recently been given to the Berlin museum by Dr Frau Mertens (MacCurdy 1911: 200, 219). Aida Blanco (pers. comm. to Quilter) notes that a German Consul named Frederik Lahmann is also reported to have collected gold from the region in the 1870s. More research must be done to investigate the whereabouts of that collection.

20 Stewart 1964.

21 Mason 1945: 283.

22 At the time of writing I only have a photocopy of the journal article available. The count of thirty-nine is based on attempting to distinguish between gold and jade objects in the article's reproduced plates.

23 Six pieces in that catalogue are listed as from San Isidro de El General. Perhaps this was the place of purchase and the objects are from El General. Given the uncertainties, I have not included or considered them as from the Panteón de La Reina.

24 Drolet 1986, 1988.

25 Cited in Stone 1977: 109.

26 Some of the Bozzoli de Wille description, as reported by Stone, may have been adapted from that of Pérez-Zeledón, as they are quite similar.

27 With the occasional exception, catalogue numbers reported here – preceded by a 'K' – are those in the 'Keith Catalogue' on file at the American Museum of Natural History. These have been retained at the American Museum. In some cases these numbers are no longer found on pieces at the Brooklyn Museum, although identification of the original numbers can be made through reference to photographs. When Brooklyn Museum catalogue numbers are cited they are preceded with a 'B'. Precise measurements are usually given in millimetres, while general ranges and 'guesstimates' for objects not accessible for study are given in centimetres.

28 Aida Blanco, pers. comm. to Quilter, 1996.

29 See Saunders 1998.

30 See Ferrero 1981: 95, fig. 34.

31 See Hosler 1994.

32 See Fernandez E. 1995.

33 Twenty-four beads were examined in detail. Others were seen on exhibit and examined in photographs. Since the complete inventory has not been seen directly, and some reliance on photographs has been necessary, the cited numbers of objects in different categories is approximate as the photographs do not always allow precise counts.

34 See DeBoer 1996.

35 Bray 1981: 160.

36 Aguilar 1996: 26, fig. 8.

37 This piece is illustrated in Bennett's (1954: 169 [fig. 198]) *Ancient Arts of the Andes*, where it is identified as coming from Nicoya. The poor state of knowledge of the prehistory of the region is in evidence in the volume, including the misidentification of the locations of Costa Rica and Panama in the end paper maps.

38 Bray 1981: 166.

39 Ibid.

40 E.g. Cooke 1985.

41 Pittier 1938.

42 See Bray 1978: 26.

43 Quilter 1998.

44 Saunders 1998.

45 For a critique of modern scholarly use of 'shaman' and 'shamanism' see Kehoe 1996.

46 Looper 1997: 121.

47 Taube 1995: 98.

48 See Snarskis 1985. The exact significance of bicephalous or other serpents in various Andean symbolic systems remains to be fully explored. See articles in Urton 1985 for some approaches. Snarskis (1985) provides insights into attitudes about snakes that do not necessarily contradict the interpretation presented here but enrich it.

References

Aguilar, Carlos
1972 *Colección de Objetos Indígenas de Oro Del Banco Central de Costa Rica*. Ciudad Universitaria Rodrigo Facio (Universidad de Costa Rica), San José.
1996 *Los Usékares de Oro*. Fundación Museos Banco Central, San José.

Bennett, Wendell C.
1954 *Ancient Arts of the Andes*. The Museum of Modern Art, New York.

Bozzoli de Wille, María Eugénia
1966 Observaciones arqueológicas en los valles del Parrita y del General. *Boletín de la Asociación de Amigos del Museo*, 19. San José.

Bray, Warwick
1978 *The Gold of El Dorado*. Times Books, London.
1981 Gold Work. In *Between Continents/Between Seas: Precolumbian Art of Costa Rica*, ed. E. P. Benson, pp. 153–66. Harry N. Abrams, New York.

Cooke, Richard
1985 The 'Spread Eagled Bird Motif' in the Goldwork of Panamá and Costa Rica. In *Precolumbian American Metallurgy*, pp. 154–68. 45th International Congress of Americanists, Bogotá. Banco de La República, Bogotá.

DeBoer, Warren R.
1996 *Traces behind the Esmeraldas Shore, Prehistory of the Santiago–Cayapas Region, Ecuador*. University of Alabama Press, Tuscaloosa.

Drolet, Robert P.
1986 Social Grouping, Domestic Centers, and Residential Activities within a Late Phase Polity Network: Diquís Valley, Southeastern Costa Rica. *Journal of the Steward Anthropological Society* 14 (1–2): 325–38 (1982–3). University of Illinois, Urbana.
1988 The Emergence and Intensification of Complex Societies in Pacific Southern Costa Rica. In *Archaeology and Art in Costa Rican Prehistory*, ed. Frederick W. Lange, pp. 163–88. University of Colorado Press, Boulder.
1992 The House and the Territory: The Organizational Structure for Chiefdom Art in the Diquís Subregion of Greater Chiriqui. In *Wealth and Hierarchy in the Intermediate Area*, ed. Frederick W. Lange, pp. 207–42. Dumbarton Oaks Research Library and Collection, Washington, DC.

Fernández E., Patricia
1995 Ofefrería Precolombina: Formas de Utilización e Interpretación Iconográfica. *Vínculos* 21 (1–2), pp. 59–78. Museo Nacional De Costa Rica, San José.

Ferrero A., Luis
1981 Ethnohistory and Ethnography in the Central Highlands-Atlantic Watershed and Diquís (trans. M. J. Snarskis). In *Between Continents/Between Seas: Precolumbian Art of Costa Rica*, ed. E.P. Benson, pp. 93–111. Harry N. Abrams, New York.

Hartman, C.V.
1901 *Archæological Researches in Costa Rica.* The Royal Ethnographical Museum in Stockholm. Ivar Hæggstroms Boktryckeri A. B.

Hearne, Pamela, and Robert J. Sharer (eds)
1992 *River of Gold: Precolumbian Treasures from Sitio Conte.* The University Museum of Anthropology, University of Pennsylvania.

Heath, Dwight B.
1973 Bootleg Archaeology in Costa Rica. *Archaeolog* 26(3): 217–19.

Hosler, Dorothy.
1994 *The Sounds and Colors of Power: The Sacred Metallurgy of Ancient West Mexico.* MIT Press, Cambridge.

Helms, Mary W.
1979 *Ancient Panama: Chiefs in Search of Power.* University of Texas Press, Austin.

Kehoe, Alice B.
1996 Eliade and Hultkrantz: The European Primitivism Tradition. *The American Indian Quarterly* 20 (3 & 4): 377–92.

Looper, Matthew G.
1997 The Iconography and Social Context of Tairona Gold Pectorals. *Journal of Latin American Lore* 19 (1–2): 101–28.

Lothrop, Samuel Kirkland
1926 *Pottery of Costa Rica and Nicaragua* (vols I & II). Contributions from the Museum of the American Indian, Heye Foundation, New York, vol. VIII.
1937 Coclé: An Archaeological Study of Central Panama, Part 1. *Memoirs of the Peabody Museum of Archaeology and Ethnology,* 7. Harvard University, Cambridge.
1942 Coclé: An Archaeological Study of Central Panama, Part 2. *Memoirs of the Peabody Museum of Archaeology and Ethnology,* 8. Harvard University, Cambridge.
1963 Archaeology of the Diquís Delta, Costa Rica. *Papers of the Peabody Museum of Archaeology and Ethnology,* 51. Harvard University, Cambridge.

MacCurdy, George Grant
1911 A Study of Chiriquian Antiquities. *Memoirs of the Connecticut Academy of Arts and Sciences,* vol. III, March 1911. Yale University Press, New Haven.

Mason, J. Alden
1942 New Excavations at the Sitio Conte, Coclé, Panama. In *Proceedings of the Eighth American Scientific Congress,* vol. 2, pp. 103–7. Washington, DC, Department of State.
1945 Costa Rican Stonework, The Minor C. Keith Collection. *Anthropological Papers of the American Museum of Natural History,* vol. 39, part 3. New York.

Pérez-Zeledón, Pedro
1907–8 Las llanuras de Pirrís y Valle del Río General ó Grande de Térraba. Informe presentado a La Secretaría de Fomento. Tipografía Nacional, San José.

Pittier, H.
1892 Viaje de exploración al Río Grande de Térraba. *Anales del Instituto Físico-Geográfico y del Museo Nacional de Costa Rica,* Tomo III-1890. Tipografía Nacional, San José.
1903 Buenos Caminos. *Boletín del Instituto Físico-Geográfico y Organo de La Sociedad Nacional de Agricultura de Costa Rica,* Año III, no. 28: 74–80.
1907–1908 *Informes presentados a la Secretaría de Fomento acerca las llanuras de Pirrís y Valle del Río General ó Grande de Térraba.* Tipografía Nacional, San José.
1938 Apuntaciones etnológicas sobre los indios Bribri. *Serie Etnológica,* vol. I, part I. Museo Nacional, Imprenta Nacional, San José.

Quilter, Jeffrey
1998 Metallic Reflections. *Science* 282: 1058–9.

Quilter, Jeffrey, and Aida Blanco Vargas
1995 Monumental Architecture and Social Organization at the Rivas Site, Costa Rica. *Journal of Field Archaeology* 22 (2): 203–21.

Reichel-Dolmatoff, Gerardo
1988 *Orfebrería y chamanismo.* Editorial Colina, Medellín, Colombia.

Saunders, Nicholas J.
1998 Stealers of Light, Traders in Brilliance: Amerindian Metaphysics in the Mirror of Conquest. *RES* (Spring) 33: 225–51.

Seler, Eduard
1909 Vorlage einer neu eingegangenen Sammlung von Goldaltertümern aus Costa Rica. *Zeitshrift für Ethnologie,* XLI: 463–67. Berlin.

Skutch, Alexander F.
1992 *A Naturalist in Costa Rica.* University Press of Florida, Gainesville.

Snarskis, Michael J.
1981 The Archaeology of Costa Rica. In *Between Continents/Between Seas: Precolumbian Art of Costa Rica,* ed. E. P. Benson, pp. 15–84. Harry N. Abrams, New York.
1985 The Comparative Iconography of Metalwork and Other Media in Precolumbian Costa Rica. In *Precolumbian American Metallurgy,* (No editor given), pp. 120–36. 45th International Congress of Americanists, Bogotá. Banco de La República, Bogotá.

Squier, Ephraim George
1858 *The States of Central America.* Harper Brothers, New York.

Stewart, W.
1964 *Keith and Costa Rica.* University of New Mexico Press, Albuquerque.

Stone, Doris
1977 *Pre-Columbian Man in Costa Rica.* Peabody Museum Press, Cambridge, MA.

Taube, Karl A.
1995 The Rainmakers: The Olmec and Their Contribution to Mesoamerican Belief and Ritual. In *The Olmec World, Ritual and Rulership,* ed. Jill Guthrie, pp. 83–103. The Art Museum, Princeton University, Princeton.
1996 The Olmec Maize God: The Face of Corn in Formative Mesoamerica. *RES* 29/30: 39–81.

Urton, Gary (ed.)
1985 *Animal Myths and Metaphors in South America.* University of Utah Press, Salt Lake City.

Van Horne, Willard C.
1965 An Ethnographic Study of the Huaquero, Digger of Pre-Columbian Graves in Costa Rica. Manuscript on file at the offices of the Associated Colleges of the Midwest, San José.

Acknowledgements

Luis Ferrero first put me on the track of gold from the Panteón de La Reina through a telephone conversation he had with Aida Blanco and me. I thank him and her profoundly. Aida also has provided useful commentary and suggestions throughout our association in work at the Rivas site.

This paper is a substantial reworking and expansion of a talk given at the symposium. I have many people to thank for its development. First and foremost, I am grateful to Colin McEwan and the staff of the British Museum, Department of Ethnography, for inviting me to attend the meeting and for help in many ways during my stay in Britain and afterwards, including very helpful commentary on the penultimate draft of this paper. Warwick Bray provided a wealth of information and support and a generous spirit in the development of this project. Robert P. Drolet was crucial in providing hard-to-find documents on early explorations of the General Valley and John Hoopes was also very kind in doing the same. Nick Saunders was a delight in discussing brilliance in ancient America and other issues. At the American Museum of Natural History Charles Spencer, Andrew Balkansky and Paul Beelitz were vital in allowing me to see objects and files. Craig Morris and Sumru Arincali, as Andeanists, went out of their way to supply additional help. Dr Manuela Fischer of the Museum für Völkerkunde, Berlin, was very kind in sharing information. At the Brooklyn Museum Diana Fane and Lauren Ebin were equally generous and efficient in allowing me access to materials and notes. At Dumbarton Oaks Jerry Goldberg, docent, was most helpful in the translation of German while my assistant Janice Williams was her usual masterful self in helping to finalize the document. All are most heartily thanked.

10

Gold Symbolism among Caribbean Chiefdoms

Of Feathers, *Çibas*, and *Guanín* Power among Taíno Elites

José R. Oliver

Introduction

While considerable advances have been made in archaeometallurgy, particularly in colourimetry, far less has been accomplished in the study of the classification and meaning of metals from an 'emic' perspective.[1] The rich sixteenth-century ethnohistoric documentation for the Antilles provides a valuable opportunity to exploit the full potential that a 'native' perspective can add to scientific archaeometallurgy studies. However, the poverty of secure prehispanic and even colonial contexts has severely limited our ability to make such inferences about the historical, behavioural and cognitive significance of metal artefacts in the Antilles.

Systems of Amerindian classification and meaning are often quite different to the western taxonomic (Linnean) approach, as Gerardo Reichel-Dolmatoff (1981, 1996) has elegantly demonstrated for the Tukano of Colombia's tropical rainforest. Native taxonomies and classifications of a perceived and/or imagined world proceed under different assumptions than that of the Western scientific tradition. The Western scientist begins by dividing the natural world into kinds of physical matter (animal, mineral, vegetal, down to genus and species). Not so with Amerindians and other popular, non-scientific systems of classification and hence meanings. Thus, among the historic Taíno the *tagua-tagua* plant (*Passiflora foetida*) with its pungent smell, the *guanina* (*Cassia occidentalis*) plant with its golden smelly flower, the iridescent feathers of the Cuban *guaní* humming-bird, the *caguamo* turtle, the island of *Cayguaní* and the copper-gold-silver alloy, *guanín*, form a single class of materials that are all *guanín*. Such a class of materials would rarely be found in archaeological and

archaeometallurgical reports grouped and quantified under the same list or 'type'.

Such materially diverse items lumped into a single 'class' are only rarely treated as a bounded taxon for analysis by archaeologists, save for that special circumstance we designate as a 'cache' (burial, votive, etc. caches). Treating diverse material remains as a *bounded* category through a contextual archaeological approach is one of the few practical means at our disposal that can provide a 'window' for the interpretation of the cognitive and symbolic meanings and attitudes that Amerindians had about a range of phenomena and their objects, such as metals. The analysis of the Templo Mayor caches in Tenochtitlan, Mexico City, by López Luján (1994) is a case in point.

This essay is a study of such a multifarious but bounded class of materials that come under the cognitive aegis of *guanín*. A corollary aim is to discuss the symbolism and power that gold and other metal alloys, particularly *guanín*, held for the Taíno in the Greater Antilles (see map p. 153). To accomplish this, I will have to rely almost entirely upon the data provided in the sixteenth-century chronicles and upon linguistics. I shall explore some of the ways 'golden' metals (in a generic sense) were understood and displayed by the Taíno elites. I will also consider how the *caciques* (chiefs) appropriated and deployed 'golden' metals to justify the divine origin of their political and religious power on Earth.

Golden metals, and *guanín* in particular, were held in special esteem by the Taíno, but to understand how and why demands that we first address the relationship between golden metals and several other prestige items. The regalia worn by *caciques* and *nitaínos* ('nobles'), and the objects they surrounded themselves with, form a sort of symbolic grammar that requires an understanding of word order and semantic function; golden metals are but one class of elements in this total ensemble. We shall discover that together all of these things are *guanín* and, more importantly, we shall attempt to find out why should this be so. It will be, I hope, clear enough that 'things *guanín*' are not just in the ethereal mental realm but are rooted in praxis and concrete life as well.

Precolumbian gold poverty: facts and fiction

When one thinks of Precolumbian gold, the West Indies is usually not the first place that comes to mind. The reasons for the limited number of gold artefacts on display in museums and reports are

10.1 A jade pendant of a raptorial bird holding in its talons a 'trophy head'. The bird is probably the king vulture (*Sarcoramphus papa*).

not difficult to explain. For the greater part of Antillean prehistory, some four and a half millennia, neither gold nor other metals were particularly ubiquitous or sought after.

The earliest confirmed pre-Taíno metal comes from the site of Maisabel on the north coast of Puerto Rico (see map p. 153). It is a *guanín* metal-sheet fragment (55% copper, 40% gold, 5% silver) recovered from the lowest cultural stratum of Midden 1 at Maisabel; a charcoal sample obtained near the guanín yielded a date of 140±60 bp or cal AD 70–375 at 2σ, and is associated with Hacienda Grande style (Saladoid) ceramics.[2] Nevertheless, the focus of these early pre-Taíno societies appears not to be on metals but rather on exquisite micro-lapidary work consisting of aventurine, serpentinite, nephrite/jade(?), turquoise,

amethyst and a variety of other gemstones, many of which were imported from outside the islands in a far-reaching circum-Caribbean trade network (Fig. 10.1).[3] Originating in the Orinoco Valley and the Guayanas,[4] these early societies, archaeologically known as Cedrosan Saladoid (500 BC–AD 300), were essentially egalitarian, with leadership probably based upon ranked lineages and politically autonomous village organization.[5] With just one documented fragmented metal sample, it is premature to interpret its symbolic role and economic function among the early pre-Taíno societies. What is important is that such alloy was already present within the first four centuries AD, especially since metal-smelting techniques were most likely unknown to them. This and all *guanín* alloys probably had to be imported from mainland South America (more on this later).

By around AD 900 chiefdoms, or *cacicazgos*, which were characterized by social stratification and hierarchical leadership with varying degrees of political integration and centralization, had already developed in the Greater Antilles.[6] The historic Taíno and their immediate ancestors, archaeologically known as Chican Ostionoid (AD 900/1000–1500), represented the climax of this process of increased sociopolitical complexity. Gold and other metal items for the later period are more ubiquitous, but nonetheless still infrequent in the archaeological record.

However, the apparent rarity of gold artefacts in the later proto-Taíno and historic Taíno times is not consistent with the many well documented sixteenth-century Spanish descriptions. The lack of gold was certainly a direct result of the plundering of the Taíno gold 'reserves' by the Spanish. Of the 180 tons of legally exported gold between 1500 and 1650 from the New World, the Caribbean contributed 50 tons (20%) and in a mere five decades.[7] This gold came almost entirely from Hispaniola, Puerto Rico, and Cuba in that order of importance. While some, perhaps most of this gold came from the Spanish-enforced mining and panning activities, the sheer volume indicates that the loss of Taíno gold artefacts must have been quite large and significant.[8]

Another important factor in the apparent poverty of Precolumbian gold from the Caribbean is that a significant portion of the prestige/sacred materials was not interred with the deceased elites.[9] The royal chronicler, Gonzalo Fernández de Oviedo y Valdés, noted that when a *cacique* died in Hispaniola:

[He] was wrapped with very long cotton bandages
… from head to feet tightly and completely
wrapped in a bundle. Then they dug a hole, like a

silo, and there they buried him. They laid him *with his jewels* and those *things he needed most.* To bury him in the hole, where he was to be placed, they built an abode with [wood] beams and then they sat him on a beautifully sculptured *duho* (which is a seat) and then covered the sepulcher with soil.[10]

After the deceased *cacique* was buried with the jewels and grave furniture 'he needed most', the funeral festivities began. Locals and peoples from further afield gathered to perform the *areíto* dances and sacred chants, an affair that lasted from 15 to 20 days. Most important, Oviedo specifically told us that foreign *principales caciques* were also invited and that it was 'among these foreign *caciques* that the wealth was distributed'.[11]

Thus, a significant proportion of the *cacique's* wealth, including pure gold *(caona)* and *guanín* objects, was not interred but rather redistributed to the political allies of the deceased *cacique.* This mechanism of wealth inheritance 'obliged' the foreign *principales caciques* to reiterate their allegiance to the new successor to the office of *cacique.*[12] In sum, many gold objects, among other prestige items, were to remain in circulation among the elites and were thus visible to and accessible for Spanish bartering or plundering.

These facts alone go a long way to explain why over the years so few archaeological Taíno golden metal objects, such as pure gold *(caona),* have been recovered either by archaeologists or looters. But, the scarcity of *guanín* artefacts is still not fully accounted for.

The Taíno classification of metals

The Spanish chroniclers mentioned five types of metals in reference to the Taíno:[13] gold, silver, *guanín* or *oro de baja ley* (gold-copper-silver alloy), brass or *latón* (copper-zinc), and bronze or *bronce* (copper-tin). The term *alambre* or *arambre* also occurs in the Spanish documents. Today it means 'wire' made of any metal, but in the sixteenth century it was a generic term for copper, brass, and bronze artefacts. Of all these copper, brass and bronze were undoubtedly introduced by the Spanish. Silver, gold and copper occur naturally in the Greater Antilles, whereas all other metal alloys were introduced either from Europe or Central-South America.

At this juncture it is useful to first understand how the Taíno themselves recognized and classified the various kinds of materials that Westerners classify as *metales.* Bishop Bartolomé de Las Casas stated that: 'Anything made of *latón* [brass] was esteemed more than any other [metal]... They

called it *turey,* as a thing from the sky, because their name for sky was *turey* [or *tureyro, tureygua*]; they smelled it as if by doing so they could sense it came from heavens...'[14] Brass, or *latón,* which was certainly introduced by the Spanish from Europe,[15] was conceived by the Taíno as coming from a remote, divine place, from another cosmic domain. It received the name of *turey* in reference to its remote origin, which they metaphorically linked to and placed in the 'sky'. The Taíno term *turey* translates more properly as 'the *bright* part of the sky', excluding the clouds. It is yet another clue: its resplendence is a fundamental quality added to its colour, smell and remoteness. The former three have their Western metallurgical specifications, if indeed there are central or normal tendencies for all metals designated *turey* by the Taíno, but they did include a fourth non-physical quality: remoteness, 'skyness'. It is likely that bronze, brass and other European alloys would fall under this class of smelly, remote and resplendent 'things' from 'heaven'.

The other important metal, pure gold, received the name of *caona*/kaona. It is not always clear whether this classificatory term also included *guanín* (gold-copper-silver alloy), brass and/or other gold-like metals. Unlike *guanín,* bronze and brass, *caona* was not imbued with the same value or highly charged symbolism. Nevertheless *caona* does relate to the sacred. The metaphorical chains relating to *caona* are of a different sort to those relating to *guanín,* as we shall see later when we examine the Guahayona journey myth cycle.

Silver is only mentioned once (a nose-ring) in the *Diario* of Columbus's first voyage, while he was in north-eastern Cuba.[16] No silver artefacts have yet been recovered archaeologically. According to Las Casas, silver seemed to require a mining technology that was beyond the means of the Taíno and even exceedingly difficult for the Spanish to exploit.[17] Next to nothing can be said about the function and meaning of prehispanic silver in the Antilles.

Guanín was unquestionably the most valued and symbolically charged of all native metals among the Taíno. It is a copper-gold-silver alloy, with the highest proportion found on the first element. Bishop Las Casas noted: 'The [Taíno] smelled from [this metal] such an odor that they held it in great value, and so they made a kind of *oro de baja ley* [low-grade gold] that had a reddish-purplish color, which they called *guanín...*'[18] Bishop Las Casas further explains that the Taíno:

> valued certain sheets of *guanín,* which was a
> certain kind of low grade gold that they smelled
> and used as jewels to wear dangling from the

ears… In their language, they called these sheets and jewels on their ears, *taguagua*… They had such regard for this *guanín* … that they … gave it to the daughter of some *cacique* or to the *señor* of the bride so that the *señor* would give them what they wanted [i.e. a bride]… [19]

In contrast to the Spanish, what the Taíno valued was not the weight or mineralogical purity of gold, or its mercantile exchange value, but its peculiar smell, its reddish-purplish colour, and its resplendent, shiny quality. It was this *guanín* that held numinous power for the Taíno as distinct from that held by the pale yellowish-white, odourless and pure *caona* gold. It could be said to be a contrast between the 'sacred' *guanín* and the 'pro-

10.2 Oviedo engraving showing sixteenth-century Taíno panning for gold in a river.

fane' and naturally available *caona,* but this would be an oversimplification. I suspect that what is involved are different degrees of remoteness and sacredness. *Turey* indeed came from a most remote cosmic plane: Spain! The Spanish-imported brass/bronze *(turey),* which the Taíno also said they could recognize by its odour, seemingly was given a classification by the natives different from that of *caona. Turey* metal was conceptualized as a far and remote, heavenly matter imbued with sacredness, just as *guanín* also originated from afar and was pregnant with numinous qualities. *Turey* and *guanín,* the two Taíno-recognized exotic metal classes (alloys), are contrasted with the native pure gold *(caona).*

These different native cognitive classifications of metal partly explain why the Taíno had eagerly

bartered *caona* for *guanín,* brass, bronze and even for shiny-coloured glass beads and iridescent red and black felt garments brought by Columbus to exchange with *cacique* Guacanagarí in the Marién Chiefdom.[20] Brass *(turey)* also had the reddish-purplish, deep yellow qualities that they coveted from *guanín.* It also explains why the Spanish had little compunction in smelting *guanín* artefacts and extracting its gold component, or trading *oro de baja ley,* or low-grade gold, for *caona.*[21] For the Spanish, the value of gold largely resided in its circumscribed and limited availability, and in its physical properties attached to monetary value (i.e. what goods it could buy). But for the Taíno the exotic alloys were worth far more than pure gold. As Bray noted, the inflated exchange rate of *guanín* to *gold* reached extraordinary levels: 'Commercial documents of the Colonial period repeatedly state that the Taíno … valued both guanín and brass above pure gold, and were willing to trade at what – in Hispanic terms – were inflated prices. In the early years of contact the exchange rate reached 200:1 in favour of guanín over gold.'[22] *Guanín,* because it still has a percentage of pure gold, was the one metal that would have probably moved through barter in both directions, depending on the supply-demand and availability of pure gold vs. *guanín.* In the last analysis the near invisibility of *guanín* in the archaeological record is probably related to the collapse of the gold mining enterprise in the Antilles,[23] creating a local high demand for even this *oro de baja ley.*

Guanín and gold: technology and sources for the Antilles

Precolumbian Caribbean gold was not shaft-mined but extracted as nuggets and gold dust from major gold-bearing rivers (see Fig. 10.2). Hammering gold into thin sheets directly from nuggets and occasional repoussé goldwork were the only techniques known among Taíno metal smiths; casting, smelting, gilding, and other sophisticated technologies were apparently unknown to the Taíno.[24] Bishop Las Casas noted that *caona* objects were made from single nuggets, which evidently placed constraints on size, volume and overall character of the finished product:

Gold sheets were not smelted, nor were they welded from many nuggets, because the Indians of this island [of Hispaniola] did not know how to smelt. Instead the gold nuggets they found were hammered between two stones, and in this way the nuggets were widened and flattened from single large nuggets or gold pieces found in the rivers.[25]

10.3 A nose-ring (above) of hammered *caona* (pure gold) from Tecla-1 site (*c*. AD 700–1100), Guayanilla, Puerto Rico, and (below) a hammered sheet of metal (*guanín*?) from the site of Sorcé, in Vieques Island, associated with late Saladoid to very early Monserrate ceramics (AD 500–800; width 3.5 cm).

10.4 A gold (*caona*) sheet from Montecristi, Dominican Republic. The specimen shows repoussè designs that duplicate those found in typical Taíno (Chican Ostionoid) ceramics.

adoid or possibly a transitional Elenan Ostionoid (*c*. AD 500–900) midden context at the site of Sorcé on Vieques Island.[28] Due to its 'softness' Chanlatte has suggested that the nose-ring specimen is pure gold, whereas the latter 'reddish' colour may suggest a high content of copper, perhaps a *guanín* specimen. Thus far, the only scientifically confirmed prehistoric *guanín* artefact in Puerto Rico is the sheet fragment from the Maisabel site.[29]

Bernardo Vega reported exactly twenty-nine (stylistically) Taíno metal artefacts found at various localities in Hispaniola (Haiti and the Dominican Republic) up to 1978–9 (see map p. 153): Sabana Yegua yielded eleven crescent-shaped bronze/brass specimens (*media lunas*); Barrera in the province of Azua produced three rounded and trapezoidal bronze sheets; Anadel site in the province of Samaná yielded a single 'spatular-triangular' bronze sheet; three pure gold or suspected *caona* specimens (all hammered sheets) came from Cadet and Limonade in Haiti, and seven from Montecristi and La Cucama Taíno cemetery in the Dominican Republic (Fig. 10.4). However, only one specimen from Montecristi was confirmed to be 99% pure gold. A high copper-content artefact has been reported from each of La Cabuya in His-

Fernández de Oviedo independently echoed Las Casas's statement, noting that 'the Indians did not know how to [mine], but only [how] to collect it [gold] from the surface of the land'.[26]

In the absence of smelting technology, any Taíno gold-copper-silver alloy artefacts had to be imported from elsewhere, since it does not occur in nature.[27] Yet, given the Taíno over-valuation of *guanín* (in practice and as well as in ideology), it is curious that so very few artefacts thus far recovered in the Caribbean have been determined to be *guanín*. This fact coupled with the absence of a native smelting and casting technology raises the issue of whether *guanín*, and its associated symbolic values, developed before or after the Spanish arrived. Where is (are) the source(s) of *guanín* gold and how did it reach the Greater Antilles? Let us briefly examine some of the archaeologically recovered artefacts.

In addition to the definite Cedrosan Saladoid *guanín* fragment (AD 70–375) from the Maisabel site mentioned above, a pure gold nose-ring and several nuggets have been recovered from Ostionan Ostionoid (AD 700–1100) contexts at Tecla site, Puerto Rico (Fig. 10.3), and a copper-gold(?) elongated sheet piece with small perforations, possibly sewn into other objects (cotton textile?), was recovered from a terminal Sal-

paniola, Maniabón region in Cuba, and Jamaica (undetermined site). In summary, not one single confirmed specimen of *guanín* has yet been recovered from Hispaniola or Jamaica.[30]

But even lacking secure contexts or precise metallurgical identification, there are a few *guanín* artefacts reported, most notably two artefacts recovered from Cuba (see map p. 153). These merit special attention because they provide clues about the ultimate origin of *guanín* in the Carib-

10.5 (right) The Yaguajay statuette, in a style reminiscent of the Gran Zenú gold region in Caribbean Colombia, was found in the 1950s at the Chorro de Maíta necropolis.

10.6 (below) Necklace found in Burial 57 at El Chorro de Maíta, Eastern Cuba. The bird pendant is a gold, copper and silver alloy weighing 3.5 g (10 carats); the four trapezoidal hammered plaques are also made of *guanín*. The beads are made of calcite.

necropolis also located in the region of Banés (Fig. 10.6).

Up to 1987 the excavations at El Chorro de Maíta have yielded twelve hollow, cylindrical pendants of hammered copper sheet and one large (36.5 mm diameter) copper disc covered by four layers of cotton cloth, stitched with a technique identified as *zancaraña*.[33] A set of five cylindrical, hollow copper rods hang from this disc, thought to have functioned as a 'medallion' (?). The tubular pendants were secured to the disc by means of a thread or string sewn in the disc's cloth cover passing through the cylindrical pendant, with a knot at its distal end. This object is unique among Taíno artefacts, perhaps the result of contact with the Spanish. Ten of the twelve copper pendants were found resting in the neck, thorax or abdominal areas of seven individuals while the copper disc was located between the tibia and fibula of another individual (Fig. 10.7).

One of the cylindrical, hollow rods (pendants) was analysed using a

> micro spectral laser analyser LMA-10… [This] determined, through the [analysis of the] various spectra obtained, a predominance of copper, in addition to other components not yet determined, among which it is possible that gold is found. This preliminary analysis did not achieve conclusive results because of the fear that a [further] increase of the laser power would damage the specimen.[34]

Up to 1987 the burials comprised a total of ninety-five Taíno individuals (only thirty-eight analysed) and one Spanish skull identified among them.[35] That only eight of the thirty-eight analysed Taíno burials included metal artefacts is an indication of its prestige value, and possibly a confirmation of the hypothesis that many such items were not interred with the deceased. At the Chorro de Maíta site the most important and unusual indigenous burial was no. 57, belonging to a nineteen- to twenty-one-year-old woman (Fig. 10.7). It yielded a necklace of calcite beads (called *çibas* in Taíno) that included four plain, trapezoidal to triangular-shaped metal-sheet danglers (Fig. 10.6). The four sheets weighed 0.3 g each and were made of *guanín* with metal alloys in the following proportions: Au 43–37%, Ag 6–13% and Cu 54–48%. This necklace included a *guanín* pendant in the shape of a bird, weighing 3.5 g (10 carat),[36] which almost certainly came from somewhere in Caribbean Colombia.[37]

The same burial (no. 57) also yielded a tear-drop-shaped 'jingle bell' (Au 52.8%, Ag 22.6% and Cu 24.4%), which, according to Guarch (1996), is of a type found in Monte Albán (Oaxaca, Mexico) and reminiscent of other jingle

bean. One of these, described as a 10-carat gold (thus, most likely *guanín*) statuette of northern Colombian-Isthmian origin, was recovered from the Banés region (Yaguajay) in the province of Holguín in Eastern Cuba (Fig. 10.5).[31] The statuette's style is reminiscent of a type found in the Gran Zenú region of Caribbean Colombia.[32] The other is a possible *guanín* pendant inserted in a necklace recovered from excavations at El Chorro de Maíta, a protohistoric to historic Taíno

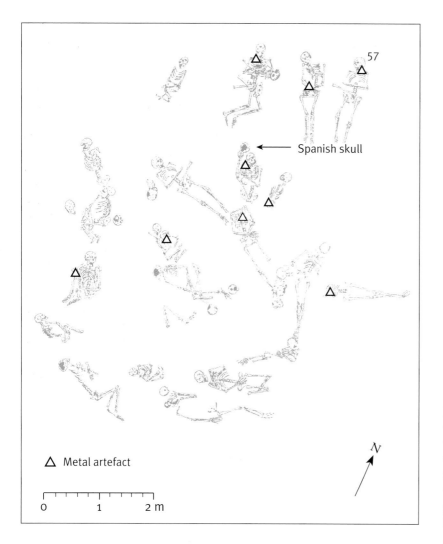

57

← Spanish skull

△ Metal artefact

0   1   2 m

N

10.7 Part of the excavations at El Chorro de Maíta, a Taíno necropolis in Eastern Cuba. Burial 57 (a 19- to 21-year-old woman) included a necklace of calcite beads with *guanín* trapezoidal separators and a *guanín* bird pendant of possible Colombian origin. The Spanish or European skull (Burial 22) is indicated with an arrow.

bells from Mesoamerica and Central America, while near the pelvic area a tubular copper dangler was found. In association with this necklace (or maybe part of it) were also found three pearl beads; twenty-three white discoidal micro-shell beads; eighteen reddish-pink cylindrical coral beads; four micro-beads of calcite, one made of a black stone (basalt?); and one spherical bead with two tubular danglers made of *guanín*.[38]

The Yaguajay statuette and the above-noted *guanín* bird pendant belong to the Taíno culture, as Dacal and Rivero (1996) suggested, but only insofar as they were adopted, readapted and incorporated into the Taíno material cultural inventory. Both the Yaguajay *guanín* cast statuette and the hollow birdlike finial from El Chorro de Maíta were undoubtedly imported from the mainland and ultimately derived from the Caribbean Colombia-Isthmian region.

Because the Chorro de Maíta Taíno necropolis chronologically straddles the contact period (i.e. associations with Columbia Plain majolica and pig [*Sus scrofa*] bones), it is entirely possible that

the Spanish themselves were responsible for importing Colombian *guanín* and bartering for pure Taíno gold and/or other valuables.[39] As Bray recently discussed:

> European brass items are easily identifiable and are not uncommon on Colonial Taíno sites (Vega 1979), but the status of the few guanín objects from the islands is difficult to assess. Given the unequal exchange rate [of 200 *caona* for 1 *guanín*], the Spanish found it worthwhile to import native guanín gold from the mainland … to barter for Taíno [pure] gold in Hispaniola and Cuba. Documents in the Casa de Contratación, in Seville, describe eagles and frogs of guanín, and explain that these items were accumulated in storehouses in Santo Domingo to be exchanged with the Indians for gold dust and nuggets (Sued Badillo personal communication). Since we know that the Spanish term *oro de rescate* referred to artefacts taken from looted archaeological cemeteries as well as from living Indians (Bray 1973: 12–13), it is likely that the guanín objects brought to the Antilles had diverse origins and were of many different styles and ages.[40]

Bray goes on to ask whether the *guanín* artefacts from Cuba, as well as the famous Mazaruni pectoral, a suspected Caribbean Colombia import to Guyana,[41] are all 'indicators of a poorly documented prehispanic trade' from Colombia to Cuba, via Guyana, or whether they were exclusively Hispanic period imports, to which he answered: 'We have no way of knowing.'[42] Given the presence of *guanín* in Maisabel, Puerto Rico, around cal AD 70–375, it is more than likely that the trade of *guanín* artefacts was in place well before the Hispanic contact period, and that it had always carried a high exchange rate value for the proto- and pre-Taínos. The instant effect that Spanish imported brass/bronze (*turey*) had upon the Taíno supports the evidence of early *guanín* at Maisabel. I say 'instant' because almost all the pertinent early sixteenth-century documents, including Taíno myths and legends (recorded by Pané in 1495–6), had bestowed on *turey* a value that was the same as, if not greater than, *guanín*. Yet it is *guanín*, rather than *turey*, that had a much more prominent role in myth, language and other areas of Taíno life. It also seems to me, from reading the chroniclers, that the comparison is always about how brass and bronze (*turey*) have similar qualities to *guanín*, rather than the other way around; *guanín* preceded in time the *turey* alloys. In sum, the argument that the *guanín* alloy could *only* be attributed to Spanish (colonial) exchange for gold is falsified both by archaeological evidence and by how the terms *guanín* and *turey* were employed in the Taíno myths.

Table 10.1 Columbus's Treasure List
'Account of the gold, jewels and other things that the Admiral obtained after the "receiver" Sebastian de Olaño left this island (Hispaniola) for Castille, from 10 March of year '95 [1495]'*

A. Guaízas (carátulas, or 'masks') and plaques (hojuelas, or sheets)

Region	Cacique	Guaízas	Cotton	Stone/Çibas	Gold
Maguana	Caonabo	11	11	11	1
Maguana	Caonabo	3	3	3	7
Maguana	Caonabo	2	–	–	–
Maguana	Caonabo	2	–	–	10
Maguana	Caonabo	1	–	–	4
Maguana	Caonabo	1	–	–	7
Hispaniola	?	5	–	–	8
Hispaniola	?	1	–	–	3
Hispaniola	?	3	–	–	11
Hispaniola	?	1	–	–	10
Hispaniola	?	5	–	–	15
Hispaniola	?	1	1	–	9
Hispaniola	?	4	–	–	21
Hispaniola	?	2	–	–	9
	TOTAL	**42**	**15**	**14**	**115**

B. 'Espejos', or mirrors (burnished metals)

Region	Cacique	Mirrors	Cotton	Gold	Copper
Hispaniola	?	3	3	3	–
Hispaniola	?	16	–	16	–
Maguana	Caonabo	1	–	–	1
	TOTAL	**20**	**3**	**19**	**1**

C. Various prestige materials (Hispaniola-Cuba)

Object	Quantity	Cacique	Comments
guaízas	42	various	see A above
mirrors	20	various	see B above
cinto/belt	1	Caonabo	belt with 'green face' + 2 gold sheets
figure (wood?)	1	Behechío	gold-covered
figure	1	Guacangarí	gold frog ('7.5 oz')
tablets	4	?	gold-covered
cohoba tubes	4	?	gold-covered ('11 pints')
hojas/sheets	36	?	gold
hojas/sheet	17	Caonabo	gold
torteruelos	6	?	suelos de oro ('soles of gold')
torteruelos	2	Caonabo	latón (turey), brass
torteruelos	2	?	amber
cañutos/tubes	5	?	amber
cañutos/tubes	2	Caonabo	gold
cañutos/tubes	8	?	gold
tiraderas/atlatl	3	Caonabo	gold-covered
tiraderas/atlatl	1	?	gold ('9 pints')
purgadera	1	Caonabo	gold (vomiting spatula?)
taos	1	?	gold?
taos	1	?	gold
taos	5	Caonabo	gold
media luna	1	?	madejita (gold wire wound round a stick)
media luna	1	?	gold-covered pectoral, crescent shaped
bonete/cap	1	?	gold-covered cotton
amber beads	101	Caonabo	amber
brass beads	several	?	latón (turey), strewn brass beads

*Relación del oro é joyas é otras cosas que el Almirante ha rescibido despues que el receptor Sebastian de Olaño partió desta Isla (Española) para Castilla, desde 10 de marzo de '95 años' (Alegría 1994; Chanlatte Baik 1977; Vega 1979).

I suspect that, while *guanín* and gold may have always been associated with 'power' (since the arrival of the first agrarian and egalitarian Saladoid groups), it was not until the early appearance of ceremonial centres in Hispaniola and Puerto Rico around AD 900 that powerful golden metals, particularly *guanín*, were appropriated by chiefly lineages (*caciques, nitainos*) and converted into 'sacred political capital'.[43] By way of contrast, the early emphasis by the Saladoid on microlapidary personal adornments of gemstone quality ceased around AD 500,[44] and were replaced by larger and seemingly ordinary stone (*çibas*) and shell beads/pendants.

To summarize, the more malleable pure gold, *caona,* was locally available in the form of nuggets and gold dust from river sources. The absence of smelting technology in the Greater Antilles, on the other hand, required the importation of *guanín* from the mainland, which explains why it was regarded by the Taíno to have come from a remote place, 'from the sky', as brass or bronze certainly did in colonial times. One might argue that the relative value of metals for the Taíno was measured in terms of real as well as symbolic distance from its source of origin and by it being thoroughly exotic. It seems that they valued the unnatural metal admixtures above the natural and available pure metals.

The use of golden metals among the Taíno

Metals among the Taíno were used in three basic ways: (1) as an object that stood all on its own (e.g. the Yaguajay statuette), (2) as one element of body decoration (e.g. nose-ring) or (3) as an element affixed to and in tight coordination with other materials. Most of the known examples are of the latter two kinds.

Solid gold (*caona*) items, all hammered from single gold nuggets, as well as *guanín* objects, were largely used as body decorations: nose-rings (Fig. 10.3), ear plugs and lower lip plugs. Occasionally, jewellery pendants, such as the frog noted in Columbus's 1495 'treasure list', were also manufactured in solid gold (Table 10.1). Hammered gold sheets (or *hojuelas, media lunas*) of various shapes, often highly polished (called *espejos* by the Spanish), were sewn into cotton textiles, caps and belts. T-shaped brooch-like objects and other objects reminiscent of the shape of the *Papilionaceae* plant, respectively called *taos* and *torteruelos* by the Spanish, were also entered in Columbus's treasure list. Hammered gold sheets and pendants were combined with *çibas*, or stone (or shell) beads, to make bracelets

Metal sheets appear in a range of items other than body adornments. These objects are most closely associated with elite ritual and ceremonial paraphernalia. For example gold is attached to elaborate *guayacán* (lignite-wood) seats or *duhos* (Fig. 10.8), to *çemí* wooden or cotton idols, and to snuffing tubes used during the *cohoba* ceremony, which involved the intake of hallucinogens (*Anadenanthera peregrina*). It is also affixed to elaborate, quasi-cylindrical anthropomorphic wooden caskets; to wood, shell or bone vomiting spatulas used for ritual purging; and to stone, wood and shell three-pointed objects known as *çemí*. It is worthwhile noting that very often marine shells were used instead of, or in combination with metal-sheet encrustation on eyes, mouth, ears and limb joints. The possible symbolic meanings of shell (white) in contrast or coordination with metal (yellow or reddish yellow) encrustation has yet to be fully explored in the Caribbean. The potential for such an analysis can be seen, for example, in Mester's studies of the significance of worked white and red (e.g. *Spondylus*) marine shells, the iridescent and multicoloured mother-of-pearl materials, and resplendent (white) pearl beads recovered from Los Frailes, a Manteño cultural complex on coastal Ecuador.[48]

Gold and metals are never far from those in authority and always attached to objects that mediate between the supernatural and the ordinary worlds. Moreover, golden items, either worn by humans or by biomorphic ritual objects, are often affixed to points of articulation between 'inside-outside' (mediation, liminal space) such as the eyes for vision, the mouth for ingestion/vomiting, the ears for sound and even the navel for alive/dead.[49] It is evident that *caona* and *guanín* allowed access or interaction between contrasting domains, such as the sacred and profane or the visible and invisible cosmic domains. Likewise, *caona* and *guanín* are placed at liminal points of anatomical division: at the wrist, neck, ankle and elbow or at the middle (navel, belt) to separate the upper and the lower body segments. These spatial-anatomical landmarks are highly charged with symbolic meaning.[50]

As the Chorro de Maíta necklace shows, the important thing to be kept in mind is that Taíno gold and *guanín* objects were almost invariably one element in a more complex and materially diverse visual code of prestigious and highly charged numinous items, including feathers, necklaces and shell-beaded belts. Gold and *guanín* accentuated and complemented rather than constituted the focus of Taíno body attire and free-standing (portable) material objects.

10.8 *Duho*, or seat, from the Dominican Republic made from *guayacán* hardwood (*Guaiacum officinale*). Gold sheet encrustations are placed to mark articulators and orifices: joint marks, eyes, mouth and ears.

or necklaces (Fig. 10.6). The gold and some brass/bronze sheets thus far recovered also come in circular, ovoid, trapezoid, rectangular and crescent or 'half-moon' shapes *(media lunas)*.[45]

These hammered metals were attached with a tar-like resin *(betún)* to other raw materials, principally made of stone, shell and wood. Affixed *guanín* sheets or plaques *(hojuelas)* were used to fill the eyes, mouth, ears and noses of sculptured masks, known as *guaízas* and made of green stone, shell or wood. The above-mentioned *guaíza* 'masks', also called *carátulas* by the Spanish, were worn by the elites on ceremonial beaded belts[46] on their foreheads, or as *guaízas* on the chest among principal *caciques*. The term *guaíza*, meaning both 'face/*rostrum*' and 'soul of the living', contrasts with the term *mapiye/[m-]opía*, or 'soul of the non-living'.[47]

Items like ear-spools, metal discs on foreheads, and *guaíza* pectorals strung with *çiba* (stone/shell) beads are also visible in Taíno representational art, such as in the iconography of Caguana, Puerto Rico, and numerous wood, bone and ceramic figurines.

The Taíno social and political structure

At the time of European contact the Taíno of Hispaniola and Puerto Rico had developed into non-egalitarian societies.[51] The degree and complexity of political and economic centralization and territorial integration under a paramount *cacique* varied from region to region. Certainly not all *cacicazgos* (chiefdoms) and their *caciques* were on an equal footing. Xaraguá in Hispaniola (see map p. 153) was undoubtedly the most powerful *cacicazgo* in the Antilles.[52] At least six or seven other sizeable chiefdoms were reported for Hispaniola, Puerto Rico and Jamaica. But no single paramount leader was able to politically coerce an entire island, let alone rule several islands, suggesting a scenario of several polities with varying degrees of complexity.[53]

The Taíno had developed a three-tier social system, with *caciques* at the top of the pyramid, followed by the *nitaíno* elite or nobility and with the *naboría*, or commoners, at the base.[54] The shaman *(behique* or *buhuitihu)* also held power, but his did not normally extend to political affairs.[55] The primary function of the *behique* was similar to that of a tribal medicine-man.[56] The *cacique,* also regarded as a great shaman, ruled over the political and religious matters pertaining to the *cacicazgo,* and was aided in implementing the affairs of government by *nitaíno* elite.

The *caciques* themselves were further divided into three levels of prestige. *Guamiquina* is a vocative term that glosses as 'unique' or 'first lord', while *baharí* ('lord of the house/lineage') and *guaherí* ('our [lord] 'gatherer or joiner of people') were used to address second-order chiefs. *Caciques* and principal men also bore several honorary titles, aside from personal names that made reference to their bravery and qualities of leadership. Also, these honorary titles and names almost invariably contained a reference to precious metals, celestial bodies, and their shiny qualities. For example, Behechío, the most powerful, paramount *cacique* of Hispaniola (Chiefdom of Xaraguá), received the honorific title of *Tureygua Hobin,* which can be translated as 'Brilliant [as] Sky-Brass'.[57] Other personal names of first-order chiefs frequently enough made references to pure gold *(caona),* as in the cases of Caonabo and Anacaona in Hispaniola. The toponyms in Cuba, Hispaniola and Puerto Rico are replete with 'places of gold', the best known of which is the Caonao region in Hispaniola, where the Taíno of Hispaniola believed humanity originated (see Appendix, pp. 215–16). In sum, golden metals were appropriated by the Taíno elites as divine symbols of chiefly power.

Two other facts should be noted. First, the *caciques* extracted tribute in the form of *naboría* labour service, including panning for gold in the rivers (Fig. 10.2) and, second, gold was also 'offered to the idols', known as *cemí.* The term *semí* or *çemí* is a cognitively complex term that literally means 'sweet-sweetness' and relates to the religious concepts of 'honey' and 'tobacco', and to shamanism, throughout South America and the Antilles.[58] Lacking honey, the Taíno substituted it with *guayaba,* a fruit that is associated with the sacred night-world; a sexually alluring yet dangerous domain of darkness where the *çemí* spirits and *opías* reign supreme.[59] Guava is sweet and also the fruit that the spirits of the dead feed on when they leave the domain of the dead at night and roam through the forests. The domain of the dead (*Coaybay* or *Coabey*) is portrayed as an island and a distant place (*Soraya*) ruled by the Cacique of the Dead named *Máquetauire* ('lord of the absent ones') *Guayaba.* The myths collected by Pané in the Chiefdom of Maguá indicate that the lake and island were located to the west in Hispaniola, precisely where there is a real brackish yet landlocked lake, Enriquillo, with a concrete island that bore, according to Las Casas, the sixteenth-century toponym *Cayguaní* (today Isla Cabritos; see map p. 153). The morpheme *cay-* means 'island' ('kay' or 'key' in English is borrowed from Taíno language), while *-guaní[n]* is the same term given to the metal alloy, *guanín.* The significance of this Guanín Island will be explored later.

The display of chiefly power: *guanín,* *çiba* beads and iridescent feathers

The accoutrements of the Taíno elite, when dressed in full regalia, are of particular interest, since these are evident displays of their political prowess and of their unique ability to mediate between the profane world and the supernatural forces, particularly with the ever-present *çemí* spirit deities.

Principal or paramount *caciques* were the only ones that had a right to wear a *guanín*-covered pectoral (or *guaíza*) on their chest, tied to a necklace of *çiba* (stone) beads (Fig. 10.9). Second-order *caciques* and *nitaíno* elites wore distinct attires that distinguished them from the paramount chiefs. None of the pectorals recovered have their gold sheet covers preserved, but their iconographic representations can be appreciated in a petroglyph from the ceremonial centre of Caguana, Puerto Rico (c.AD 1000–1400). Interestingly, this petroglyph is the representation of a *cacique* engraved on a lithic slab *and* is found at the centre of an ensemble of petroglyphs in the central, quadrangular plaza of the ceremonial centre (Fig. 10.10). It is framed by a pair of high-ranking personages (ancestors) and a pair of young, low-ranking ones (descendants), each engraved in an igneous monolith. These two pairs are presented frontally and relate to the classic *Hockerfigur* theme.[60] They are in turn flanked by ornithomorphic petroglyphs portrayed laterally, in profile, each in its own monolith. In different styles the central, frontal, displayed anthropomorphic figure flanked or surmounted by birds (often in pairs and fours) is found in gold and *guanín* artefacts elsewhere in the Americas, such as Colombia's Tairona (Zuidema 1992). Just as the iconographic *cacique* of Caguana is placed at the central axis of the row of engraved monoliths, so is the golden *guaíza* pectoral he wears placed at the centre of his chest.

Sixteenth-century chroniclers have described the attire of Taíno elites in a number of instances,[61] but the most impressive description comes from Jamaica. The occasion was the approach of several canoes carrying an important (unnamed) Taíno *cacique* and his retinue of *nitaíno* nobles towards Colombus's caravel. This encounter, richly captured by Bernáldez, goes as follows:

> The *Cacique* brought in his canoe an *alférez* who was by himself standing at the prow, bedecked with a *sayo* [garment] of red feathers, decorated like a coat of arms; a large feathered crown surmounted his head, and on his hand he held a white banner without any [embroidered] designs. Two or three men had their faces painted in colors [red *Bixa* and black *Genipa*], all in the same style. These had on their heads great crowns of feathers … and on their foreheads each had a round tablet as large as a *plato* [dish, plate], both similarly painted … and on their hands they held a toy-like instrument that they played [*maracas?*]. Two other men with different painted bodies each held a wooden trumpet [*botuto*] sculptured with birds and other intricate designs. The wood was very fine and very black [*Guaiacum officinale* or *guayacán*]. Each of the [two] individuals had a beautiful *sombrero* [hat, cap?] decorated with thick and bright green feathers [cf. Fig. 10.11]; six others wore white feathered *sombreros,* and all were guarding [or flanking] the *Cacique.*[62]

In contrast, the *cacique's* attire bore the crucial and unique symbols of chiefly power:

> The *Cacique* had on his chest a very fine jewel of *alambre*[63] [that came] from an Island located in the region known as Guanique [perhaps the same as the mythical *Baneque* mentioned by Columbus?]. It is so fine that seemed to be of an eight karat gold piece [probably *guanín*], in the shape of a *Fleur-de-Lis,* as large as a plate. The plaque was strung with thick and large marble-like beads [diorite *çibas*], whom the Taíno also valued much [cf. Figs 10.9–10]. On his head he wore a large *guirnalda* (or danglers) made of minute green and red stones placed in order and interpolated with larger white-colored beads [shell?], where they seemed [to look] better. And [he] had a large jewel on his forehead, and on his earlobes he had two large gold tablets [known as *taguaguas* in Taíno] from which dangled minute green stone beads. Although naked, he wore a beaded belt made of same minute green stones.[64]

The accoutrement of this Jamaican Taíno *cacique* is a good example of how intricately woven were the arrangements of colour-coded feathers (Fig. 10.11), multicoloured shell and *çiba* beads (Fig. 10.9), body paints (black/red), and the gold and *guanín* adornments. I have already remarked on the further association of these decorative materials and the personal as well as the honorific titles accorded to them. I have also commented on how *guanín* and *turey,* in particular, linguistically correlate with and allude to the quality of iridescence that was imputed to a divine and remote origin: the sky and celestial bodies. This is in stark contrast to the 'nakedness' and simplicity of the commoner's attire.

From a pragmatic viewpoint this display of

10.9 A Taíno stone (calcite) necklace from the Dominican Republic. Such necklaces (*çibas*) were bestowed by the magical Guabonito on the primordial *cacique*, Guahayona.

10.10 Taíno iconography at the ceremonial centre of Caguana, Puerto Rico (c. AD 1000–1400). The central petroglyph represents a *cacique* with *guaíza* pectoral and necklace; he is framed on his right by the icons of a pair of powerful, high-ranking ancestors and on his left by a pair of low-ranking descendants.

'heavenly' objects, including gold, underscored the separation of a paramount chief from the rest of the people (i.e. social inequality and status ranking). Indeed, the term *naboría*, or commoner, literally translates as 'the remainder' or 'what is left'. But while this display of status is about separation and division, it is also about coordinating the disparate parts that form a social whole. *Caciques* cannot exist without *naborías* and vice versa. The display of feathers, gold, necklace of *çibas,* and body paints literally 'dress' and also invest the *cacique* with the power to access the numinous and to mediate between the sacred and the profane. Thus the chiefly regalia – as much as the chief himself – visually signal the mediation and coordination of the opposite domains of the profane and sacred. In sum, like rituals and ceremonial centres, the *cacique's* accoutrements, including *guanín,* serve to coordinate and articulate disparate parts. The entire ensemble and its bearer, the *cacique,* constitute the pivot or axis through which different social strata are coordinated and through which distinct cosmic 'layers' are linked.

This theme of 'union with separation' reminds me of the old Spanish saying that states *estamos juntos pero no revueltos* ('we are together but not mixed'). Gold and sacred materials displayed by

the elite are as much about separating them from *naboría* commoners as they are about coordinating the commoners with the elites as a whole society. Coordination is what is emphasized when the full regalia is worn by elites on important ceremonial events since, I suppose, on everyday occasions the *caciques* and *nitaínos* were literally dressed-down, and perhaps only such items as the ear-spools would be a sufficient signal of status. This seems to be the case for the *caciques* and *principales (nitaínos)* involved in the construction of Caparra, the first Spanish settlement in Puerto Rico: the gold decorations were ear-spools and nose-rings. Andrés López, a witness, declared:

> This witness saw the said Juan González … with
> many *caciques* and *principales* Indians that were
> there, where they gathered gold, because they
> were worn by all the most principal men and
> *caciques,* dangling from their ears and noses …
> that the Indians told him that if he wanted gold,
> they would take him to the rivers and *arroyos*
> where they collected gold for their feasts and
> jewels, and to offer it to their idols.[65]

But the above observations and inferences are, to my mind, rather obvious and perhaps less interesting. I am much more curious as to what such elaborate visual grammar of feathers, shell and *çiba*

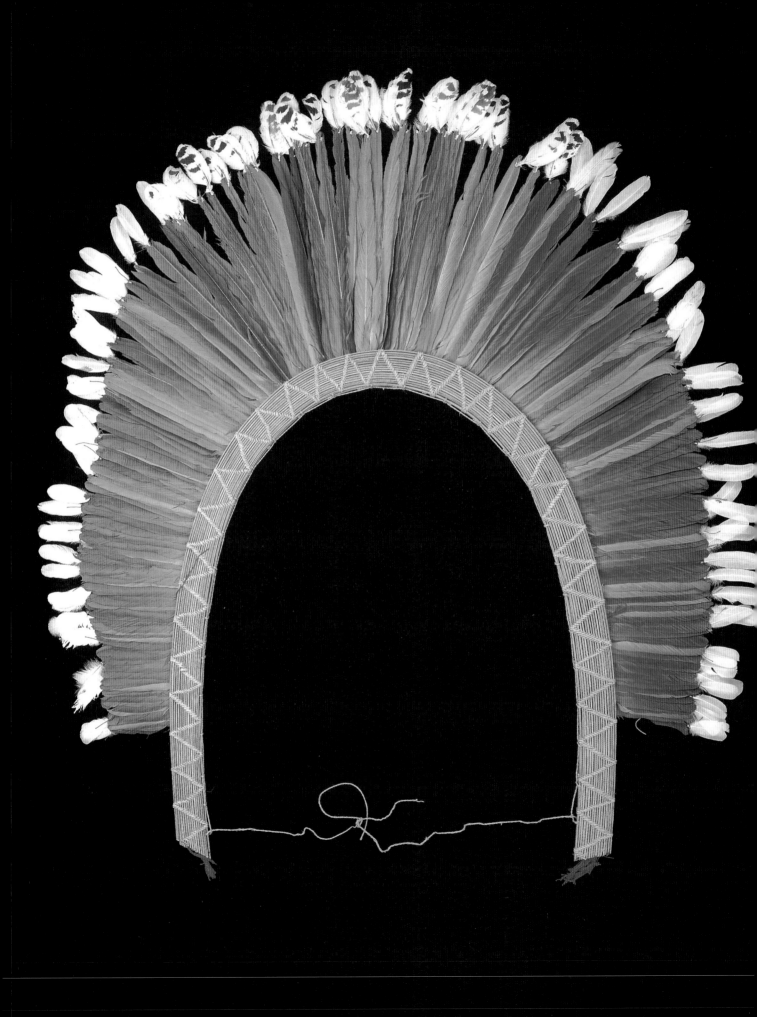

10.11 (left) Amazonian headdress from Cayapó, Brazil. Resplendent feathered caps similar to this one were part of the emblems of power associated with the concept of *guanín* ('golden').

necklaces, *guanínes*, red- and/or black-coloured body pigments and other elite regalia might have meant to the average Taíno. Why there are, for example, incessant linguistic allusions to brilliance, sky, heavens, and stars embedded in anything that contains *çibas*, feathers, gold, *guanín*, and even the names of *caciques*? After all, these could not be more different kinds of materials. What sort of images did such chiefly attire evoke for his people?

The answers to these questions can be rescued from Taíno mythology, specifically from a cycle that refers to what I will call 'Guahayona's journey'. This mythical cycle contains the information that helps to unravel the symbolism of the Jamaican *cacique's* attire. It also holds clues as to why *guanín* gold, shiny metals, colour-coded

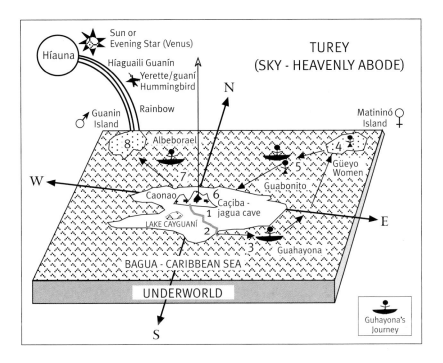

10.12 (above) Map of Guahayona's journey to Guanín Island. The numerals refer to the numbered stages of the journey discussed in the text.

feathers and multi-coloured *çiba* and shell necklaces form a sort of 'syntactic' unity with the heavens and stars, and ultimately with the source of political power (symbolic capital/wealth) wielded by the *cacique* and elites on earth.

Guahayona's journey to the heavens

The mythical cycle relating Guahayona's journey was recorded by Fray Ramón Pané in 1495–6 in Hispaniola on the orders of Christopher Columbus.[66] In the Appendix (pp. 215–16) I have provided an English version (with numbered paragraphs for reference) of a Spanish translation made by Arrom (1974); he, in turn, based his work on Ulloa's 1571 Italian translation of the text by Ferdinand Columbus who had copied

Pané's lost original. In some parts the order in which Guahayona's journey is presented has been purposefully altered from Pané's arrangement, since I believe it to be more in keeping with the sequence of events experienced by Guahayona.

What follows is a synthesis of the most important events of the Guahayona myth cycle, and comment on their relevance to the symbolism of the *cacique's* attire, and specifically to *guanín* gold and celestial bodies. As an aid to Guahayona's journey, a map is provided in Fig. 10.12, with the Arabic numerals (1 to 8) representing the crucial stages of the journey discussed below.

Stage 1: In Illio Tempore

Guahayona's journey takes place *in illio tempore*, in sacred time. The scenario is set in the Cauta Mountains in the region of Caonao ('Place of Gold') in Hispaniola (App. A1). Guahayona, like the rest of the Taíno proto-humanity, emerged from the mythical Cave of Caçibajagua, a compound word that means Cave (*ka-çiba*) of Darkness, where *jagua* is the *Genipa americana* tree whose sap yields the black pigment used in body decoration. It is a time when nature and culture and the seasons of time were indistinguishable, a time of social chaos when the extraordinary and numinous ruled. It is a place where everything was done at the inverse time and in the opposite way to how it was done in the ordinary, 'present' cosmos. Thus it is at night, in the absence of light, that the numinous and sacred become manifest and activated. It is a domain where animals act as humans, humans become animals or stones, and speech is onomatopoeic.[67] In this domain exogamy is unknown and incest is, in fact, permitted. In sum, social order, the Taíno way of life, has yet to be established. But it should be remembered that it was this extraordinary world that held all the knowledge and objects of power necessary for the creation and maintenance of the social and cultural order. These secrets and the sacred materials, including *guanín*, had to be stolen or wrestled from this domain by culture heroes.

While several of these pre-human personages from Caçibajagua attempted to establish cultural order, all failed to perform the duties as *caciques* (App. A2), as *naborías* (App. A4), and as shamans (App. A5). Each was punished and permanently immobilized in this primordial pre-social universe; they were transformed respectively into a stone, a *jobo* tree (*Spondias* sp.) and a singing bird – in essence the three primary constituents of nature: mineral, vegetal and animal. These transformations were expressed in terms of being 'captured by the Sun'. Their attempt to conduct activity in broad daylight and thus emulate ordinary Taíno social behaviour failed. The imagery is clear: sacred creatures can be no more ordinary humans than ordinary humans can be of the sacred and light-less cosmos. Mutual exclusion and separation of the sacred and profane is emphasized. What remains to be accomplished is the mediation and coordination between these two opposite, yet complementary domains. This is precisely what Guahayona, the hero of this myth cycle, accomplished in his quest to become the first leader and *cacique* of the Taíno.

This passage also illuminates Taíno principles of social behaviour expected from each social stratum: (1) the primordial *cacique*, named Mácocael, 'Son of the One Without Eyelids', failed in his duties to watch over his subjects, and command and distribute labour (App. A3); (2) the *naboría* fishermen's social sin was their failure to share the catch with their brethren upon their return to Caçibajagua (App. A4); and (3) the failure of the *behique* or shaman *Yahubabael*, a 'Spirit-bird-son', was to steal and betray the magic secrets of the *digo* herb used in ritual cleansing (App. A5).[68] Each bears a message of the consequences of failing to follow the strictures of the social contract.[69]

Stage 2: Guahayona establishes the rule of exogamy

Guahayona, a consummate trickster, is apparently immune to punishment (App. B1). He leaves the Cave of Jagua in broad daylight without the grievous consequences (immobility) experienced by the others who did. Before embarking on his journey, Guahayona established the separation of the sexes, the rule of exogamy, and the taboo of incest.[70] That all these proto-humans were born from the same cavernous uterine symbol meant that all women and men were too closely related; they were siblings. Consequently, incestual relations, while permissible in this primordial world, could never lead to Taíno social reproduction and order.

Guahayona accomplished the separation of sexes by luring these proto-women with the magical *güeyo*, a herb whose species remains unidentified. He kidnapped all the Caçibajagua women and abandoned the children next to a river, where they were transformed into toads *(tona)*, but this time the rainfall and springtime, rather than the Sun, are the transforming agents. Ordinary time, the rhythm of seasons, is established (App. B2).

Unlike his fellow Caçibajagua brethren, Guahayona does not suffer immediate punishment (transformation, immobilization) for abandoning

the Caçibajagua Cave in broad daylight. The Sun, so to speak, lets him go. Nevertheless, in the long run, he did pay for his daring defiance of the law of the primordial cosmos. Ultimately, that is why, like the others who attempted to leave the darkness of Caçibajagua, he was transformed into a numinous and extraordinary essence, a brilliant star, bedecked with *guanín* gold, *çiba* necklaces and metallic-coloured feathers. But in the process Guahayona wrestled from the divine the basic tenets of social order and the secrets of the numinous, sacred emblems of chiefly political power: *çibas, guanín,* and metallic feathers. This was his legacy: the revelation of world order, guaranteed under the watchful guard and power of the *cacique*.

Stages 3 and 4: Guahayona goes to Matininó Island

Upon leaving the children-frogs in Cauta (Hispaniola), Guahayona 'navigated' towards the mythical island Matininó where he abandoned all the women-sisters of Caçibajagua (App. B3). Matininó, translates as 'Without Fathers'. This act accomplished the complete separation of the sexes.

Numerous references in Columbus's *Diario* suggest that Matininó was symbolically found to the east of Cuba, where he was told – and took literally – that there was much gold, *caona*.[71] Again, gold seems to occur in association with an extraordinary, numinous and remote place. But, perhaps more significant, *caona* and Matininó can now be correlated with the east, sunrise and possibly the feminine principle of cosmos.

Stage 5: Guahayona finds Guabonito

Guahayona departed from Matininó Island, presumably towards the west, with the intention of reaching his ultimate destination, the mythical island of *Guanín*. It follows that Matininó, symbolically found to the east and associated with the feminine and *caona* gold is contrasted with Guanín Island, the west, the masculine principle and, of course, *guanín* gold. But Guahayona's journey to Guanín Island takes an important detour. Along the way he realized that there was one woman, Guabonito, left at the bottom of the ocean (App. B3). In my view, Guabonito was the same woman Guahayona kidnapped or stole from Ananacuya ('Centre Star'), who was identified as his brother-in-law. Thus, Ananacuya's wife, Guabonito, was in fact Guahayona's (real or classificatory) sister.

The correlation of (1) women/sisters (2) abandoned on the Matininó island to the east and (3) also below at the bottom of the ocean presents a symbolic contrast with (1) men/brothers (i.e. Guahayona), (2) Guanín Island to the west and (3) also *guanín* above in the sky. The structural relationships can be synthesized as follows: *guanín* is to the west, above and masculine, just as *caona* is to the east, below and feminine. *Caona* and *guanín* are manifestations of a dual opposite yet complementary system. What is interesting is that the separation of *caona* and *guanín* is a metaphor for the separation (incest, marriage prohibition) between brothers and sisters, between Guahayona and Guabonito (and vice versa). Yet, the incestual relation (violation) between the latter pair is precisely how *guanín* is generated later in the myth. (*Guanín* is the product of a fusion or the 'incest' of 'sibling' metals!)

In sum, the iridescent 'metallic' birds, celestial stars and odorous, sweet-smelling *turey-guanín* gold go hand in hand with masculinity, chiefly investitures, ceremonial objects and the upper stratum of the cosmos, whereas the duller *caona* gold, toads, rainfall and the depths of the ocean are connected with femininity and, generally, a profane, colourless and odourless lower stratum of the cosmos. In the ordinary Taíno world only the male sits on the *duho* above the ground, while women sit on the floor or on mats, a seating convention that is fairly widespread among lowland South American Indians today[72] and is also well represented in Boca Chica-style (Taíno of eastern Hispaniola) ceramic figurines.[73]

Stage 6: Guahayona becomes a cacique

Guahayona rescued the magical Guabonito, his own sister, and took her back to the Cauta Mountains, to Caonao, the place of gold, in Hispaniola. There he had a sexual encounter (incest) with Guabonito, which immediately resulted in the first step of the transformation of Guahayona into a *cacique* (App. B4). He contracted a skin disease, which Pané equated sometimes with scabies and at other times with syphilis.[74] While one might think this to be a penalty for violating a sexual taboo, the consequences of his act were far from being a simple punishment: the skin disease was metaphorically used by the Taíno to express an extraordinary, numinous condition intimately associated with gold! Gold, then, allowed Guahayona to 'grasp' the emblems of chiefly office, including *guanín*.

This extraordinary condition allows those who possess it – such as *Deminán Caracaracol,* the smart one of the twin pairs of Taíno culture heroes – to immobilize and grasp that which is fugitive and under ordinary circumstances unattainable,

because it pertains to an extraordinary domain that is otherwise unreachable by any ordinary means. The Taíno name given to this extraordinary condition is *caracaracol,*[75] a word that has survived as *caracoli,* meaning 'gold', among the Eyerí (Island Carib) and Lokono (Arawak), and other Maipuran-speaking groups in South America.[76]

In Guahayona's case this *caracaracoli* or golden condition enabled him to grasp the sacred emblems of chiefly power, including the metallic *guanín,* from the magical Guabonito woman/sister. Upon committing the sexual act, Guabonito takes Guahayona into isolation *(guanara)* where the latter undergoes ritual cleansing (bathing with *digo* herbs) and healing (App. B5) as part of his *rite de passage* ceremony. Upon completion of the isolation period *(guanara)* and ritual, Guabonito presented to Guahayona *guanín* ear-spools and a necklace of marble-like *çibas* (Figs 10.6, 10.10), which, implicitly, secured the *guaíza* pectoral on Guahayona's chest (App. B7). Moreover, the *guanín* ear-spools designated as *taguagua* (tawa-wa) share the same morpheme as the pungent flower *tagua-tagua,* the alliteration possibly reflecting a superlative form (i.e. very pungent). To the *guanín* (recognized by its odour) metaphorical chain we now can add the pungent tagua-tagua flower. The same may be said of the smelly yellow flower, *guanin[a]* (see Bray 1998). All of these are *guanín,* including Guahayona, ear-spools, plants and flowers: all exude the sweet *(çemí)* and pungent smell of the sacred *(guanín).*

The initiation into the office of *cacique* is also marked by name-changing (App. B6). Henceforward, he shall be known as *Albeborael* Guahayona, 'Son of Albebora Guahayona' (the suffix *-el* means 'child of'). His former namesake Guahayona already contains the stem 'haíuna' (metathesis of 'íau/o' into 'aíu/o'), which glosses as 'star' (in Lokono *[w]-íwa)* and possibly refers to the Sun itself.

The status change of Guahayona into a *cacique* is further underscored by the submission of the magical Guabonito, who asked for his permission to proceed in her journey, which Albeborael Guahayona granted (App. B5).

Stages 7–8: Guahayona ascends to the sky and reaches Guanín Island

Guahayona has already accomplished his tasks of segregating the sexes, establishing the rule of exogamy and acquiring the knowledge and sacred items of chiefly power. In achieving these goals, he had to commit social sins that, up to this point, did not result in the expected punitive transformations. Incest is a social sin that must be punished in this world but could only be condoned in the context of an extraordinary world where everything is done in the inverse of the ordinary Taíno world. And that is why, with his tasks accomplished, Guahayona is about to be transformed one last time into, of course, a celestial body of *guanín*. Like his brethren from Caçibajagua (App. A) Guahayona is ultimately also 'captured by the Sun' and condemned to permanently remain (immobilized) in an extraordinary world above in the skies (App. B8). It is only then that he reached his final destination, the mythical Guanín Island of the western celestial abode, an objective announced on numerous occasions during his journey (e.g. App. B1c).

Earlier, reference was made to the existence in western Hispaniola of an island in Lake Enriquillo that was known in the sixteenth century by the name of Cayguaní (mentioned by Las Casas), a compound of *cayo* (cay or key) plus *guanín*. This lake also happens to be rather unusual: it is highly brackish and salty, like the Caribbean Sea. The analogy is irresistible: there is a western celestial Guanín Island amidst a heavenly salty body of water, just as there is an earthly (below) western ocean-lake with a Guanín Island (today, Isla Cabritos). The Taíno expressed 'otherworldliness' and the separation of domains by means of vast bodies of water, and by the inversion of day-light (profane, earthly) to night-light (sacred, otherworldly). Guanín's reddish-yellow iridescent colour (evening, sunset) is a quality shared with the period of transition from day to night-time, when the numinous becomes manifest. *Caona*, on the other hand, seems to relate to sunrise and the east, a time when numinous becomes latent and when the ordinary wakes up (i.e. lacks iridescence and is pale yellowish). I suggest that it is because *guanín* is the quality associated with the awakening of the sacred (at sunset) that it, rather than pure *caona* gold, is prominent in mythology, but the real flesh and blood *cacique* is of this world and therefore possession of *caona* is as crucial as *guanín* (or bass/bronze). Recall that it is *caracaracoli* (another word for pure gold) that allows any being (mythical or otherwise) to grasp that which is numinous and fugitive (like the waning sunlight).

That *caciques* received honorific titles and personal names alluding to *guanín*, to shining stars and to brilliant colours in connection with *guanín* gold only makes sense in the context of Guahayona's journey. Needless to say, and in keeping with socially stratified societies like the Taíno, the gifts of chiefly power were for the elites. But so were the obligations that went with chiefly authority: to guard, command and distribute people (App. A3).

The apparel worn by the Jamaican *cacique*, by the second-order chiefs and *nitaíno* elite was visually woven into a single tapestry that encoded the numinous power and sacred nature of the accoutrements entrusted to them by the divine Guahayona. The intricate tapestry of *guanín, caona*, feathers and multicoloured beads are all of the sky, *turey*, and are all celestial and largely associated with sunset and sunrise, with the times of day/night inversion.

The careful reader will have noticed that my interpretation of these elements, especially the metallic, iridescent feathers in connection with *guanín* and *caona*, seems to extend beyond the factual data provided by Pané. To buttress the argument and, indeed, to demonstrate the strong plausibility of my thesis, it is necessary to include two other related myths that supply the missing clues.

The metallic feathers of the hummingbird Yerétte

Guahayona's ascension to the western sky and transformation into a celestial body, however, brings to the forefront the symbolic connection of feathers, for the latter are also intimately correlated with the metallic, iridescent qualities of *guanín* and, as I will argue, with (possibly) the multicoloured celestial phenomenon, the rainbow. This symbolic connection ultimately provides the linkage, the mediation, between the sacred and the profane, the ordinary world below and the heavens above. This mediating, liminal position is entrusted to the *cacique* and is symbolically represented by a feathered birdlike creature named Yerétte the Hummingbird. The name given to hummingbirds survives today in Cuba as *guaní*;[77] once again, there is an allusion to the numinous power of that which is brilliant as *guanín*, symbolized by the iridescent, quasi-metallic colours of the feathers of hummingbirds. Today, hummingbirds in the Spanish Caribbean are also known as *colibrí*, a noun of Taíno origin. *Colibrí*, in fact, is cognate to the modern Lokono (Guyana-Surinam) name for birds of all species, *kodibío* (App. C–D), a term also found among several northern Maipuran languages (Arawakan stock).

At the end of Pané's account of Guahayona's journey he stated in no uncertain terms that Albeborael Guahayona (the primordial *Cacique*) and his sister (the magical healer Guabonito) were responsible for the origin of *guanín* gold. But he also added that Albeborael Guahayona (Wahaíona) had a 'father' named Híauna (metathesis of 'aío' into 'íau') (App. B8). The two names are clearly related: both contain the morpheme 'hí[w]a', which refers to 'star'. Pané, however, failed to grasp the kinship relationships among these personages, since apparently the myth – as written down by Pané – did not mention the crucial creature, Yeréttê the Hummingbird.

Fortunately, the omission can be rescued by comparison with two myths that essentially tell the same story. These come from the Island Carib (or Eyerí) and the Kali'na of Dominica (both speakers of the Maipuran subfamily). The two versions presented in Appendix C and D were originally recorded by Breton in the 1660s and three centuries later by the linguist Douglas Taylor (1952). In addition to supplying the hummingbird as the agent of Guahayona's final transformation into an iridescent star, the myths from Dominica Island also clarify the confused kinship relationships muddled by Pané. The meaning of the names of the personages also becomes clearer, as do the celestial bodies they relate to. Last, but not least, body pigments – particularly black *jagua* – are added to the list of celestial gifts to the Taíno. In summary, the myths supply the connection between iridescent feathers and the rainbow with *guanín* gold and celestial bodies.

Once the noted missing elements are supplied, the Taíno myth from the Maguá Chiefdom would go as follows. After committing incest with his sister Guabonito, undergoing curing rites and receiving the gifts of chiefly power (*çiba* necklace, *guanín* gold), Albeborael Guahayona journeyed to his father, named Híaguaili (= 'brilliant star'). This last journey was also marked by a second change of name and status: Albeborael Guahayona was to be called henceforth as *Híaguaili Guanín,* literally 'The One Who Had Turned Brilliant *Guanín* Star'.[78] I am willing to bet that this 'star' is none other than the Sun, although Venus in its vespertine cycle (or Evening Star) is another strong possibility.[79] *Híaguaili* (Taíno) is cognate to *Híali* (Island Carib), meaning 'He Who Turned Brilliant'. In the Lesser Antillean myth Híaguaili Guanín is the same personage as the illicit child, Híali, who journeyed to meet his 'father', the Moon. If so, then the father of Guahayona (alias Híaguaili Guanín) is also, quite probably, the Moon. In other words, since Híaguaili Guanín – formerly Albeborael Guahayona – cannot be the Moon, then it is most probably either the Sun or the Evening Star, Venus.

In contrast to the Eyerí/Island Carib myth, however, Híaguaili Guanín was not the child of the incestuous relationship between the father Híali-Moon and the woman. Instead, in the Taíno myth it was between Guahayona (alias Híaguaili) and his Guabonito (brother-sister incest). And it was Guahayona, not the child born of incest (Híali in the Island Carib/Eyerí myths), that rose to heavens. Such variations, however, are to be expected. In any event, in both cases brother-sister incest prompted the 'banishment' into the sky of the male culprit. As a primordial and successful *cacique,* Híaguaili Guanín, alias Guahayona, in every sense of the word was the founder of the Taíno nation, just as Híali was for Island Carib-Eyerí. Híaguaili Guanín was the celestial tailor who sowed the golden *guanín* garments of power for the future generations of Taíno *caciques* and elite. Thus, while pure gold dust and nuggets could be recovered from rivers, *guanín* only could be made in heaven.

The Lesser Antillean myths further explained the ascent and transformation of Albeborael Guahayona into Híaguaili Guanín (i.e. Híali) by means of Yeréttê the Hummingbird, who took him to the sky (*turey*) to join his father (Moon). In recompense for this service the Hummingbird was given the multicoloured, iridescent metallic feathers in the form of a crown. Unfortunately, none of the myths is clear about who gave the metallic feathers: the 'father' Moon or the Sun/Evening Star? (App. C & D, last sentences) Though without solid proof, I suspect that it was Híaguaili Guanín, either as Sun or as Evening Star, who bestowed the iridescent, metallic feathers on the Hummingbird and thence on *caciques* in the ordinary world. It is possible that green, red and yellow parrot feathers also had a celestial origin, perhaps different from the *guanín*-related feathers of Yeréttê, but nevertheless still a powerful element of chiefly regalia. Undoubtedly, some of the feathered crowns or caps, and iridescent garments *(sayos)* worn by the Jamaican Taíno elite find the meaning of their numinous origin in Yeréttê Hummingbird.

While the name of this hummingbird in the Lesser Antilles could be roughly translated as 'benign spirit' (from *ya-* or *ia-*) 'father' (-*ette* or -*itti*), the Taíno name in Cuba for their hummingbird is, not surprisingly, *guaní.* The crown of feathers worn by the *caciques* is, therefore, also *guanín* gold as a result of its iridescent metallic colours. Thus, *guanín* is not merely a metal of a particular physical composition but primarily a metaphor for that which is sacred, divine and celestial, and which announces its 'presence' by its pungent-sweet odour. It is because of this linguistic evidence that I vote for Híaguaili Guanín being the giver of iridescent, metallic feathers, rather than Híauna, the father.

The flight of the hummingbird, with its iridescent, feathered crown, taking Híaguaili Guanín to his father, Híauna, in the sky evokes the image of the multicoloured rainbow. The Taíno crescent-shaped *guanín* plaques – or sometimes a circle with two crescents in opposition (mirror image) – provide the bridge between the sky and the earth, and thus between Híaguaili Guanín, Yeréttê the Hummingbird, and the *cacique*. The iridescent and multicoloured feathers of the *cacique's* attire, as much as the crescent-shaped *guanín* plaques, signal the ability and power of the *cacique* to bridge, or mediate between, the sacred and the profane (see Figs 10.11 and 10.13).[80]

Multicoloured iridescence, brilliance and reddish-purple sweet-odour are all part of a semantic string or coda enveloped by the broader concept of *guanín*. It is the total ensemble of the *cacique's* attire and the ritual, ceremonial objects that invest him with sacred authority. This ensemble is analogous to a musical score, where each note, in its proper place and sequence, when played together, results in a 'divine' symphony. The musical notes are individually recognizable, but it is the patterned and ordered sequence that produces a symphony, much as *guanín* the metal is a note in the symphony of feathers, stars, *çibas* and all those golden things.

I would also add to this ensemble the pigments used for body (skin) decoration, red (*Bixa orellana*) and black (*Genipa americana*), as these were among the gifts that resulted from the actions of Guahayona and his counterpart in the Lesser Antilles, the father-Moon-Híali: the 'charcoal' stains used to identify the incestuous offender (Híali-Moon) and smeared on its face (App. D, first paragraph). If black *Genipa* relates to the Moon, it is likely that red *Bixa* relates to Híaguaili Guanín (Sun or Evening Star).

Guanín, an assault on the senses

The chain of metaphors associated with things imbued with *guanín* (not just the metal alloy) all suggest that its referent objects are meant to stage a veritable assault on the neural senses of the ordinary Taíno: it is viewed with awe, smelled pungently, tasted strongly and distinctively, and touched in order to be able to grasp and sense the power and knowledge that comes from what is esoteric and remote. And it 'talks' or, better, 'speaks' of sacred power. This assault on the senses is meant to overwhelm and overtake, just as power does.

The example of Jamaican chiefly attire, the accoutrements, is a sensorial 'text' to be 'read'

and experienced by the Taíno in terms of the total power exuded by these numinous and diverse emblems of authority (the so-called symbolic 'capital' of chiefly elites). All these were once inaccessible and remote, but thanks to Guahayona they were made available to the ordinary human Taíno. That *guanín* as a metal alloy is but one element that makes sense only in connection with all other accoutrements is made evident in the Guahayona myth. It is more than likely that, upon viewing the royal regalia, the Taíno would invoke the images and subtle sub-texts drawn from the Guahayona myth. The awesome display of the chiefly attire would be a certain reminder not only of the sacredness of the event but also of the divine origin that the *cacique's* power had. The possession of *guanín* and the rest of the chiefly emblems endowed the *cacique* with knowledge and power; *caona* allowed him to grasp and retain such numinous power. In the last analysis, without such accoutrements, there would be no *cacique*, and without *caciques* there would be no Taíno social order. This was established since the beginning of time, *in illio tempore,* by the extraordinary creatures of the primordial world, of which Guahayona Guanín is its chief protagonist.

In conclusion, *guanín* is not merely an object of metal but a complex concept for the numinous, as all the feathers and all things iridescent and colourful also qualify as golden and celestial. The class of phenomena that is *guanín* extends in a metaphorical chain that includes the vespertine stars (Sun[set] or Venus), a sacred and real but unique island, pungent plants and yellow flowers, iridescent hummingbird feathers, and ear-spools. These items, rescued during Guahayona's journey, relate to the quest for civilization, the separation of sexes, exogamy, incest rules and the achievement of the ultimate social order: the establishment (justification) of a society ruled by *caciques* or chiefs.

The incorporation of brass/bronze (*turey*) into this metaphorical chain is still tenuous in the colonial Taíno myths collected by Pané in the Chiefdom of Maguá, and this is likely to be an indication of its recent arrival. I would suggest that *turey* (brass, bronze) was of the same 'class' as *guanín,* and likewise was contrasted with *caona. Caona,* the locally available pure gold, partook in this relation of 'divine' and celestial chiefly power. I interpret *guanín* and *turey* (and metallic feathers) to be instrumental in bestowing numinous knowledge, whereas things *caona* (and *caracoli*) allow the numinous to be attained, reached or grasped. Pure gold, rather than *guanín,* is the dominant metal for the encrusted 'eyes' of the *çemí* figures, as in the magnificent *guayacán*

10.13 Reconstruction of a petroglyph from Barrio Caguana, Puerto Rico. The triangular projections above the head suggest the representation of feathers from the caps, as noted in the Bernáldez description (p. 206) of the Jamaican *cacique*.

(lignite wood) seat, or *duho*, shown in Fig. 10.9. These golden 'eyes' permit the sculptured *çemí* to access the invisible and extraordinary, and the seat (*duho*) allows those who sit on it to grasp the unseen and to be literally at the centre or seat of power. Allusions to astral bodies, such as the Sun, Venus or the Moon, in connection with *duhos* with encrusted golden eyes are but one variant of a common theme that relates thrones/seats to the essence of political/sacred power and to solar or stellar bodies (esoteric, remote knowledge), also noted in other prehispanic cultures of Central and South America.[81]

The *cacique* had the knowledge and ability to access and master the extraordinary domain of the sacred. This was achieved through the *cohoba* ceremony over which he presided, involving the snuffing of the charred seeds of *Anadenathera peregrina* (*cohoba*) mixed with lime (burnt, grounded shells) in the privacy of the *caney* (chief's house). The *cacique* sat on his *duho*, surrounded by the *nitaíno* councilmen and the shaman, bedecked with multicoloured *çiba* beads, *guanín* gold pectoral, large *caona* ear-spools *(taguaguas)*, resplendent metallic rainbow of Yeréttê/*guaní* feathers, and black *Genipa* and red *Bixa* body decorations. He then snuffed the hallucinogenic *cohoba*, reaching into the sacred and extraordinary realm. While in a state of ecstasy, the *cacique* and noble *nitaíno* consulted the numinous powers *(çemí)* about all the important political-economic affairs of the 'state' and divined what laid in the future. To be the *cacique* or an elite *nitaíno*, literally invested with *guanín*, surrounded by 'golden metals' and possessing the quality of *guanín*, was to be powerful and knowledgeable. The *cacique* not only wore things *guanín*, but was *guanín*, just as the primordial *cacique* Guahayona/Híaguaili was *guanín*.

Appendix: Guahayona's journey and Yeréttê the Hummingbird – Taíno, Island Carib and Eyeri/Kali'na myths

(Arrom 1974, 1975; Breton 1892 (1665); Taylor 1952)

A. The Origin of Humankind

1. Hispaniola has a province named Caonao ['gold'], where there is a mountain called Cauta [a tree species] that has two caves, one named Caçibajagua [Cave of Jagua], the other Amayaúna ['Worthless' Cave]. From Caçibajagua emerged most of the people that populated this island.

2. Failure of Mácocael as *Cacique*
These people, while inside the cave, were guarded at night by someone called Mácocael ['Without Eyelids'], whom they [the Taíno] say was overtaken by the Sun, because he was late in returning to the door. Hence, having seen that the Sun had taken him as a result of his failure as a guard, they closed the [cave's] door [or entrance], and in this manner he was transformed into stone near the door.

3. Rights and Duties of the *Cacique*
The reason why Mácocael ['Without Eyelids'] watched over and stood guard was to see [and determine] to which part he would order [and] distribute the people.

4. Failure of the Fishermen-Commoners
Afterwards, they said, that others who had gone fishing were also captured by the Sun and had been transformed into trees called *jobos* [*Spondias lutea* or *S. mombin*]…

5. Failure of Yahubaba, the Shaman
As it happened, one who was named Guahayona [Wahaíuna?] said to another named Yahubaba [Lord Spirit 'Baba'] to go and fetch this herb called *digo* [species?], which they use to cleanse their bodies. He [Yahubaba] left before sunrise, and was [also] overtaken by the Sun and transformed into a 'bird that sings in the morning' … and is [now re-] named Yahubabayael.

B. Guahayona's Journey

1. Guahayona Kidnaps the Women
(a) Guahayona, upon seeing that the one he sent to collect the *digo* herb [Yahubaba] did not return, resolved to come out of the Caçibajagua cave.

(b) And [before leaving the cave] he said to the women: 'Leave your husbands, and let us go to other lands, and let us take a lot of *güeyo* [algae used for chewing like tobacco?]. Leave your children and only take the herb with us, that later we will return for them.'

(c) Guahayona left in search of other lands, and arrived to Matininó [mythical island, 'Without

Fathers'] where immediately he left all the women, and [eventually] he left for another region called Guanín [*tumbaga* gold, mythical island].

2. The Children are Abandoned in Cauta
And, thus, they [Guahayona and the women] had abandoned the children next to a creek. Later, when hunger began to pain them, it is said that they wept and called out for their mothers who had gone away, and their fathers could not relieve the children who called out for their mothers, crying 'mama, mama', trying to speak, but really asking for the breast. Thus they cried out 'toa, toa', as when one asked something with great desire, and very slowly they were transformed into small toad-like [or frog] animals, called *tona,* because they cried for breast feeding. (Ever since, the frogs retained this voice during springtime [in Martyr D'Anghiera's version only]). In this way all men were left without women.

3. Guahayona Tricks Ananacuya
When Guahayona – the one that took away all the women – left, he also took away the women [wives] of his *cacique,* whose name was Ananacuya ['Centre Star'], by tricking him as he tricked the others. Ananacuya, who was Guahayona's brother-in-law, went into the sea with him. While on the canoe, Guahayona said to his brother-in-law: 'Look what a beautiful *cobo* [marine gastropod] there is in the water!' And when his brother-in-law [Ananacuya] looked down to see the *cobo* sea-shell, Guahayona grabbed him by the feet and threw him into the ocean. And so this was how Guahayona took all the women for himself and left them in Matininó ['Without Fathers' island], where it is said that today it is inhabited only by women.

And [eventually] he set off to[wards] another island named Guanín [*tumbaga* gold], so called on account of what he took there with him [i.e. *çibas* and *guanín* gold].

4. The Incest of Guahayona
Guahayona returned to Cauta [mountain in Hispaniola] from where he had taken the women [and where Caçibajagua cave was located]. While Guahayona was in

this land [Cauta], he realised he had left a woman in the sea. He went down to fetch this beautiful woman he saw at the bottom of the sea. He had great pleasure [sex] with her and immediately sought purification to bathe himself, for he was full of [skin] sores* (which we call 'the French Disease' [syphilis]). The woman's name was Guabonito [etymology undeciphered].

* The mythical personages possessing the magical condition of skin disease (sores or scabies) were named *caracaracolis. Caracoli* or *karakoli* in Eyerí (Island Carib) and Lokono (Arawak) languages translates as 'gold' (see Stevens-Arroyo 1988: 192). This was the name of the mythical Taíno hero, 'Deminán Caracaracol'.

5. The Rite of Curing and Purification
She [Guabonito] placed him in a *guanara* (which means a place apart, in isolation). Thus, while he was there, he was cured of his sores. Afterwards she asked him for permission to continue her journey and he granted it to her.

6. Guahayona the *Cacique*: First Transformation
[Once initiated and purified] Guahayona changed his name, calling himself from thenceforward, Albeborael Guahayona ['Son of Albebora Guahayona-Wahaíuna?].

7. Guahayona Receives the Symbols of Chiefly Power
The woman Guabonito gave Albeborael Guahayona many *guanines* and many *çibas,* so that he could wear them attached to his arms … neck … and ears.*

* Pané explained: 'In these lands, the *çibas* are stones, which look very much like marble [diorite] and they wear them attached to the arms and neck. The *guanines* they wear on their ears, making openings when they are young, and are made of metal like *florín.*'

8. Guahayona is Transformed into a Brilliant Star-Sun/*Guanín,* or the Origin of Guanín
(In Pané's own explanatory words)
The origin of these *guanines* was Guabon-

ito, Albeborael Guahayona [Wahayuna or Wahaíuna] and the father of Albeborael.

Guahayona stayed in the land of his father, Híauna [*híali* = 'he who was made brilliant']. His son [meaning Albeborael] by his father [meaning Híauna] was [re-] named Híaguaili Guanín, which means 'Son of Híauna'. Henceforward and to this day he was always known as Guanín.

9. Fray Ramón Pané's Apology
And since they have no writing knowledge and cannot relate well their fables, I cannot write them well. As a result I think that I wrote first what should have been last, and the last, first. But all I wrote is how they narrated it, as I wrote it; thus, I here leave it as I understood it from the people of this country.

C. The Myth of Yeréttê and Híali
(Island Carib; Breton 1892 [1665])

Ieréttê or Yeréttê, hummingbird. The caribs [who actually spoke Eyerí, or Island Carib, an Arawakan language] imagine that the Moon (whom they believe to be a man) saw a sleeping woman and got her pregnant, forcing the woman's mother to place a person to guard her, to trap him and blacken him with *jagua* [*Genipa americana* sap] so as to recognize the culprit [the Moon]. According to them, these are the stains today still visible on the star [the Moon]. The child born from that woman was named Híali, whom they believe to have been the founder of this [Island] Carib Nation. The bird [Ieréttê, the Hummingbird] was chosen to transport this child [Híali] to his father [the Moon]. Having done so with great fidelity, it [Ieréttê] was rewarded with a beautiful 'crown' bedecked with feathers of many diverse colours, making him a marvel of nature (Taylor in Arrom 1974: 156).

D. Ieréttê's Myth – Dominica
(Dominica Caribs; Taylor 1952)

The Moon is a man with a dirty face. In the old times there was a young woman who became pregnant from a lover who surreptitiously visited her at night. The woman's mother stood guard. When the lover came again, she smeared his face with her hands full of ashes. This is why henceforth his face was stained with ashes. One morning they discovered that he [Moon] was the young woman's brother [incest]. The people laughed at him so much that he ran to the sky in shame, where he can still be seen with a dirty face. The child was given the name of Híali ('The-One-Who-Turned-Brilliant'), and was the founder of this Carib Nation.

When Híali was still a child, Iorotto – the hummingbird – took him to the sky so that his father could see him. In reward for his services, he received the beautiful feathers and the crown that he still has to this day (Taylor in Arrom 1974: 156).

Notes

1 See Hosler 1994; Bray 1997.

2 Siegel and Severin 1993: 71, 77

3 Boomert 1987; Oliver 1999.

4 Rouse 1992.

5 Siegel 1992; Curet and Oliver 1998; Oliver 1998: 28 *passim*.

6 Oliver 1998: 33–49.

7 Sued Badillo 1978, 1995: 62–3.

8 See also Fisher and Bray 1987: 24–6.

9 Oliver 1998: 70–71.

10 Oviedo y Valdés in Oliver 1998: 70 (my translation, emphasis and clarification in square brackets).

11 Ibid. (my translation).

12 Oliver 1998: 71.

13 Vega 1979.

14 Las Casas in Arrom 1975: 154.

15 Vega 1979.

16 Dunn and Kelley 1989: 126.

17 See Vega 1979: 29.

18 Las Casas in Arrom 1975: 154.

19 Las Casas in Chanlatte Baik 1977: 26 (my translation and clarification in brackets).

20 Wilson 1990.

21 See also Bray 1997.

22 Bray 1997: 49–50

23 See Cassá 1995: 207–8, 237–8.

24 See Vega 1979; Bray 1997.

25 Chanlatte Baik 1977: 29.

26 Ibid: 31.

27 Bray, pers. comm. 1996.

28 Chanlatte Baik 1977; pers. comm. 1997.

29 Siegel and Severin 1993.

30 Vega 1979: Cuadros 1–3.

31 Alonso 1950: 340–41; Dacal and Rivero 1996: 49, col. pl. 15.

32 Cf. Falchetti 1995: fig. 45.

33 Guarch *et al.* 1987: 29–30, fig. 3.

34 Ibid: 31 (my translation and clarification in brackets).

35 Rivero de la Calle *et al.* 1989.

36 Dacal and Rivero 1996: col. pl. 16; Guarch 1996: 24.

37 Bray 1997. Juanita Saenz of the Museo del Oro, Bogotá, confirmed that this piece formed part of a Tairona pectoral where the finial birds come in groups of four (pers. comm. 1999).

38 Guarch 1988: 162–83; see also Cassá 1995: 312.

39 Vega 1979: 28.

40 Bray 1997: 9 (my clarification in square brackets).

41 See Whitehead 1990.

42 Bray 1997: 51.

43 Oliver 1998.

44 Oliver 1999.

45 Vega 1979.

46 Cf. Taylor *et al.* 1997: fig. 126.

47 Oliver 1997, 1998.

48 Mester 1985, 1986, 1989.

49 Taíno mythology explained that the only way to recognize the *opía* or spirits of the dead that roamed the ordinary forests at night from the living humans was by the absence of a navel in the former.

50 See Zuidema in Oliver 1998: ii–iii; Schuster 1951.

51 Moscoso 1986; Wilson 1997; Oliver 1998.

52 See Wilson 1990, 1997; Oliver 1998.

53 There are disagreements on whether or not at the time of contact Puerto Rico *(Boriquén)* was ruled by a single paramount chief (the Agueybana chiefly lineage) or by several *caciques* of variable status (see Oliver 1998 and Moscoso 1986 for detailed discussion). Also note that historian Roberto Cassá (1974, 1995) stands alone in his insistence that the Taíno did not conform to the anthropologically defined 'chiefdom' type of society, insisting on their essentially egalitarian organization. This contradicts all of the Spanish chroniclers' observations on the Taíno sociopolitical organization (cf. Oliver 1998).

54 Oliver 1998: 64–5.

55 Ibid: 72–3.

56 Cassá 1974.

57 Arrom 1974, 1975.

58 Lévi-Strauss 1974, 1975; Stevens-Arroyo 1988; Oliver 1998: 68–9, 72.

59 Oliver 1998: 182–3; García Arévalo 1997.

60 Zuidema 1992; Fraser 1966.

61 E.g. Wilson 1990: 63, 85; Alegría 1994.

62 Oliver 1998: 67; see also Alegría 1994: 71, and Cassá 1974: 134. An *alférez* (from the Arabic *al faris*, or horseman) in Spain was the official who carried the banner *(estandarte)* for the cavalry or the flag for the infantry. Obviously the chronicler was establishing an analogy with the Spanish military officials.

63 In the sixteenth century the terms *alambre* or *arambre* referred to any object of copper and its alloys bronze and brass. It should not be confused with its modern usage as 'metal wire'. In fact, *alambre* was also used to refer to a set of strung cowbells, jingles, etc. worn by cattle (*Diccionario de La Real Academia de La Lengua Española*, Madrid,

1992, p. 56). Thus this pectoral may have been either made of a copper alloy, like *guanín*, or perhaps of brass or bronze, since it was still possible that such European alloys reached Jamaica some years before Columbus 'discovered' the Island.

64 Oliver 1998: 67; see also Alegría 1994: 71, and Cassá 1974: 134.

65 *Probanzas de Juan González* (1532), cited in Moscoso 1986: 366 (my translation).

66 Arrom 1990: 22.

67 Oliver 1997, 1998.

68 *Ya* = spirit being; *-hubaba* may be glossed as 'harbinger of bad fortune'. However, I think that this term simply refers to portentous circumstances that may bring (or give) as much good as evil.

69 Stevens Arroyo 1988.

70 See also López Baralt 1985.

71 Dunn and Kelley 1989.

72 Roe 1987.

73 See Oliver 1998: figs 50, 53.

74 Arrom 1974.

75 See Stevens-Arroyo 1988: 192; Pané in Arrom 1974: 29–31.

76 See words for 'gold' in Payne 1991; Taylor 1977; Bennett 1989.

77 Arrom 1975: 153.

78 'Star' in Lokono is *w-íwa*, hence the Taíno *h-í[w]a-ili* for 'star' (see Bennett 1989).

79 Robiou-Lamarche 1985, 1990; Oliver 1998: 160–64.

80 Stevens-Arroyo 1988: 191–4.

81 E.g. see McEwan 1998, 2000.

References

Alegría, Ricardo
1994 Christophe Colomb et le trésor des Indiens Taïnos D'Hispaniola. *L'Art Taïno,* ed. J. Kerchache, pp. 68–75. Paris Musées, Editions des Musées de la Ville de Paris, Paris.

Alonso, Orencio M.
1950 Discovery of a Pre-Columbian Gold Figurine in Cuba. *American Antiquity,* 15(4): 340–341.

Arrom, José J.
1974 *Fray Ramón Pané: Relación acerca de las antigüedades de los indios.* Siglo XXI Editores, Mexico, D. F.
1975 *Mitología y artes prehispánicas de las Antillas.* Siglo XXI Editores, Mexico, D. F.
1990 *Fra Ramón Pané: Relació sobre les Antiguitats dels Indis. Nova versió amb notes i apèdixs per José Juan Arrom.* [Traducció: Nuria Pi-Sunyer] Generalitat de Catalunya. Comissió Amèrica i Catalunya, 1992, Barcelona.

Bennett, John P.
1989 An Arawak-English Dictionary with an English Word-list. *Archaeology and Anthropology,* Vol. 6 (1–2). Walter Roth Museum of Anthropology, Georgetown.

Bercht, Fatima, Estrellita Brodsky,
John A. Farmer and Dicey Taylor (eds)
1997 *Taíno. Pre-Columbian Art and Culture from the Caribbean.* El Museo del Barrio-The Monacelli Press, New York.

Boomert, Aries (Aad)
1987 Gifts of the Amazons: 'Green Stone' Pendants and Beads as Items of Ceremonial Exchange in Amazonia and the Caribbean. *Antropológica* (67): 33–54.

Bray, Warwick
1997 Metallurgy and Anthropology: Two Studies from Prehispanic America. Proceedings of the Symposium 'Metalurgia prehispánica de América'. *Boletín Museo del Oro* 42: 37–55.

Breton, Raymond (Abbate)
1892 *Dictionaire caraïbe-français.* Leipzig (original edn 1665, Auxerre)

Cassá, Roberto
1974 *Los taínos de la Española.* Publicaciones de la U.A.S.D, Colección Historia y Sociedad no. 11, Santo Domingo.
1995 *Los Indios de las Antillas.* Ediciones ABYA-YALA, Serie Pueblos y Lenguas Indígenas no. 10, Editorial MAPFRE, Quito.

Chanlatte Baik, Luis
1977 *Primer adorno corporal de oro (nariguera) en la arqueología indoantillana.* Co-ediciones Museo del Hombre Dominicano – Fundación García Arévalo. Santo Domingo.

Curet, L. Antonio y José R. Oliver
1998 Mortuary Practices, Social Development, and Ideology in Precolumbian Puerto Rico. *Latin American Antiquity* 9(3): 217–39.

Dacal Moure, Ramón
and Manuel Rivero de la Calle
1996 *Art and Archaeology of Pre-Columbian Cuba.* University of Pittsburgh Press.

Dunn, Oliver and James E. Kelley (eds)
1989 *The Diario of Christopher Columbus's First Voyage to America, Abstracted by Fray Bartolomé de Las Casas.* University of Oklahoma Press. Norman, Oklahoma.

Falchetti, Ana M.
1995 *El oro del Gran Zenú: Metalurgia prehispánica de las llanuras del Caribe colombiano.* Museo del Oro-Banco de la República, Bogotá.

Fisher, John and Warwick Bray
1987 His Highness Has Need of Gold: Spaniards, Indians, and Gold in Colonial Latin America. *Terra,* vol. 25, pp. 19–26.

Fraser, Douglas
1966 The Heraldic Woman: A Study in Diffusion. *The Many Faces of Primitive Art,* ed. D. Fraser, pp. 36–9. Prentice Hall, Englewood Cliffs, New Jersey.

García Arévalo, Manuel A.
1997 The Bat and the Owl: Nocturnal Images of Death. *Taíno. Pre-Columbian Art and Culture from the Caribbean,* ed. F. Bercht, E. Brodsky, J. A. Farmer and D. Taylor, pp. 112–23. El Museo del Barrio-The Monacelli Press, New York.

Guarch Delmonte, José M.
1988 Sitio arqueológico Chorro de Maíta. *Revista Cubana de Ciencias Sociales.* Año VII, no. 17: 162–83. La Habana.
1996 La Muerte en las Antillas: Cuba. In *El Caribe Arqueológic*o, vol. 1: 12–25. Publicaciones Casa del Caribe & Taraxacun S.A., Santiago de Cuba-Washington DC.

Guarch Delmonte, José M.,
César Rodríguez and Roxana Pedroso
1987 Investigaciones preliminares en el sitio El Chorro de Maíta. *Revista de Historia,* Año II, no. 3: 25–40. Holguín.

Hosler, Dorothy
1994 *The Sounds and Colors of Power: The Sacred Metallurgical Technology of Ancient Mexico.* MIT Press, Cambridge, Massachusetts, and London.

Las Casas, Fray Bartolomé de
1929 *Historia de Las Indias* [y capítulos selectos de la *Apologética Historia de Las Indias*], vols I–III. Editorial M. Aguilar, Madrid.

Lévi-Strauss, Claude
1974 *From Honey to Ashes.* Harper-Torchbooks, New York.
1975 *The Raw and the Cooked.* Harper-Colophon Books, New York.

López-Baralt, Mercedes
1985 *El mito taíno: Lévi-Strauss en las Antillas.* Ediciones Huracán, Río Piedras.

López Luján, Leonardo
1994 *The Offerings of the Templo Mayor of Tenochtitlan* (trans. B. R. Ortíz and T. Ortíz). University Press – Colorado, Niwot.

McEwan, Colin
1998 Seats of Power: Palaces, Seating and Rulership. Paper presented at the Dumbarton Oaks Conference 'Ancient Palaces in the New World'. Washington, DC.
2000 And the Sun Sits in His Seat: Creating Social Order in Andean Culture. Ph.D. Dissertation. Department of Anthropology, University of Illinois at Urbana-Champaign.

Mester, Ann M.
1985 Un taller manteño de la concha madre perla del sitio Los Frailes. *Miscelánea Antropológica Ecuatoriana* 1: 136–54. Guayaquil.
1986 Pearl Divers of Los Frailes. Manufacture and Trade in Manteño Chiefdoms. Paper presented at the 51st Annual Meeting of the Society for American Archaeology, New Orleans.
1989 Marine Shell Symbolism in Andean Culture. *Proceedings of the 1986 Shell Bead Conference,* ed. C. F. Hayes III, L. Ceci and C. Cox Bodner, pp. 157–67. Rochester Museum Science Center. Rochester New York.

Moscoso, Francisco
1986 *Tribu y clases en el Caribe antigüo.* Universidad Central del Este, vol. 63. San Pedro de Macorís.

Oliver, José R.
1997 The Taíno Cosmos. *The Indigenous Peoples of the Caribbean,* ed. Samuel Wilson, pp.

140–53. University of Florida Presses, Gainesville, Florida.
1998 *El Centro ceremonial de Caguana, Puerto Rico. Simbolismo iconográfico, cosmovisión y el poderío caciquil taíno de Boriquén.* British Archaeological Reports, International Series, No. 727. Archaeopress, Oxford.
1999 The 'La Hueca Problem' in Puerto Rico and the Caribbean: Old Problems, New Perspectives, Possible Solutions. *Archaeological Investigations on St Martin, Lesser Antilles,* ed. C. Hofman and M. Hoogland. Archaeological Studies Leiden University no. 4. Leiden, Holland.

Oviedo y Valdés, Gonzalo Fernández de
1944 *Historia general y natural de la Yndias, Yslas y Tierra Firme del Mar y Océano.* Editorial Guaranía, Asunción del Paraguay.

Payne, David L.
1991 A Classification of Maipuran (Arawakan) Languages Based on Shared Lexical Retentions. *Handbook of Amazonian Languages,* ed. D. C. Derbyshire and G. K. Pullum, pp. 355–499. Mouton, The Hague.

Reichel-Dolmatoff, Gerardo
1981 Things of Beauty Replete with Meaning – Metals and Crystals in Colombian Indian Cosmology. In *Sweat of the Sun, Tears of the Moon: Gold and Emerald Treasures of Colombia,* ed. D. Seligman, pp. 17–33, exh. cat., Natural History Museum of Los Angeles County. Terra Magazine Publications, Los Angeles.
1996 *The Forest Within: The World-View of the Tukano Amazonian Indians.* Themis Book, London.

Rivero de La Calle, Manuel,
César Rodríguez and Minerva Montero Díaz
1989 Estudio del cráneo europoide encontrado en el sitio aborigen de El Chorro de Maíta, Yaguajay, Banés, provincia de Holguín, Cuba. *Revista de Historia.* Año III, nos 2–3. Holguín.

Robiou-Lamarche, Sebastián
1985 Ida y vuelta a guanín, un ensayo sobre la cosmovisión taína. *Myth and the Imagery in the New World,* ed. E. Magaña and P. Mason, pp. 459–98. Latin American Studies CEDLA 34. Foris Publications, Dordrecht-Rhode Island.
1990 Island Carib Mythology and Astronomy. *Latin American Indian Literatures Journal* 6(1): 36–54.

Roe, Peter G.
1987 Village Spatial Organization in the South Amerindian Lowlands: Evidence from Ethnoarchaeology. Paper presented at the 52nd Annual Meeting of the Society for American Archaeology. Toronto.

Rouse, Irving B.
1992 *The Taínos: The Rise and Fall of the People Who Greeted Columbus.* Yale University Press, New Haven and London.

Schuster, Carl
1951 Joint Marks: A Possible Index of Cultural Contact between America, Oceania and the Far East. *Adelfing Culturele en Physische Anthropologie,* No. 39. Amsterdam.

Siegel, Peter E.
1992 *Ideology, Power, and Social Complexity in Prehistoric Puerto Rico.* Doctoral thesis. Department of Anthropology, State University of New York at Binghamton. University Microfilms International no. 9219121. Ann Arbor, Michigan.

Siegel, Peter E. and Kenneth P. Severin
1993 The First Documented Prehistoric Gold-Copper Alloy Artefact from the West Indies. *Journal of Field Archaeology* 20: 67–79.

Stevens-Arroyo, Antonio M.
1988 *Cave of the Jagua: The Mythological World of the Taínos.* University of New Mexico Press, Albuquerque.

Sued Badillo, Jalil
1978 *Los Caribes: realidad o fábula.* Editorial Antillana, Río Piedras, Puerto Rico.
1995 The Island Caribs: New Approaches to the Question of Ethnicity in the Early Colonial Caribbean. In *Wolves from the Sea*, ed. Neil L. Whitehead, pp. 61–89. KITLV Press, Leiden.

Taylor, Dicey, Marco Biscione and Peter G. Roe
1997 Epilogue: The Beaded Zemi in the Pigorini Museum. *Taíno. Pre-Columbian Art and Culture from the Caribbean,* ed. F. Bercht, E. Brodsky, J. A. Farmer and D. Taylor, pp 158–69. El Museo del Barrio-The Monacelli Press, New York.

Taylor, Douglas MacRae
1952 Tales and Legends of the Dominica Caribs. *Journal of American Folklore,* vol. 65: 269.
1977 *Languages of the West Indies.* Johns Hopkins University Press, Baltimore and London.

Vega, Bernardo
1979 *Los metales y los aborígenes de la Hispaniola.* Ediciones del Museo del Hombre Dominicano, Santo Domingo.
1980 *Los Cacicazgos de La Hispaniola.* Ediciones Museo del Hombre Dominicano, Santo Domingo.

Whitehead, Neil
1990 The Mazaruni Pectoral: A Golden Artifact Discovered in Guyana and the Historical Sources Concerning Native Metallurgy in the Caribbean, Orinoco and Northern Amazonia. *Archaeology and Anthropology,* 7: 19–38. The Walter Roth Museum of Anthropology, Georgetown.

Wilson, Samuel M.
1990 *Hispaniola: Caribbean Chiefdoms in the Age of Columbus.* The University of Alabama Press, Tuscaloosa and London.
1997 The Taíno Social and Political Order. *Taíno. Pre-Columbian Art and Culture from the Caribbean,* ed. F. Bercht, E. Brodsky, J. A. Farmer and D. Taylor, pp. 46–55. El Museo del Barrio-The Monacelli Press, New York.

Zuidema, Tom R.
1992 The Tairona of Ancient Colombia. T*he Ancient Americas: Art from Sacred Landscapes,* ed. R. F. Townsend, pp. 245–58. The Art Institute of Chicago. Chicago, Illinois.
1998 Presentación. In José R. Oliver, *El Centro ceremonial de Caguana, Puerto Rico. Simbolismo iconográfico, cosmovisión y el*

poderío caciquil taíno de Boriquén, pp. ii–iii. British Archaeological Reports, International Series. Archaeopress. Oxford, England.

Acknowledgements

This essay would not have been conceived without Colin McEwan challenging me to participate in the conference that he organized at the Museum of Mankind in 1996. I am most grateful to my colleagues Luis Chanlatte Baik and Yvonne Narganes Storde of the Centro de Investigaciones Arqueológicas, Universidad de Puero Rico, for sharing with me information and photographs of their gold and precious stone collections. I am indebted to Juanita Saenz Samper (Museo del Oro, Bogota) for pointing out the probable provenance of the *guanín* bird dangler found in Cuba. Last but not least, the cross-pollination of ideas in the course of many conversations with Warwick Bray has also been instrumental in refining what is presented here. I am sincerely grateful to all, although any errors and shortcomings are my responsibility.

11

Diversity of Goldsmithing Traditions in the Americas and the Old World

Susan La Niece and Nigel Meeks

Gold has been prized throughout the world for its colour, lustre and resistance to corrosion, and goldsmiths of all cultures have exploited its unique working properties. It is found in the metallic state and is easily hammered to form ornaments as well as being suitable for casting into complex shapes. In most societies gold has been valued above other metals and was particularly the domain of deities and the elite classes, but cultural attitudes towards gold in Europe and Asia appear to have developed along significantly different lines from those of South and Central America. The first Europeans who landed in the Americas melted down almost every gold item they could lay their hands on and felt aggrieved that there was less gold in the alloys than they had expected from surface appearances. The indigenous peoples found this obsession with pure gold for its monetary value incomprehensible and they prized the copper-rich gold alloys, which the Spanish called *tumbaga,* for more complex reasons than as mere tokens of wealth. It is this difference in attitude which is the key to the divergence in the development of goldsmithing technologies.

In South America the earliest evidence for metal use has been traced to at least as early as 1500 BC in the central Andes, though there is still insufficient archaeological evidence to pinpoint the origins accurately.[1] The assumption that gold was the earliest metal to be worked is based on the excavation of a goldworker's tool kit and small pieces of gold foil at Waywaka in the south-central Peruvian Andes,[2] but the early date of the site is disputed.[3] Elsewhere in the world, including North America, native copper (copper found in its metallic state rather than as a copper mineral), not gold, was the first metal to be exploited.[4] In south-east Turkey a large number of

hammered copper items, some annealed, from the early Neolithic settlement of Cayönü Tepesi are dated to the eighth millennium BC.[5] Gold was certainly being exploited on a significant scale during the fifth millennium BC at Varna in Bulgaria;[6] before this the production of hammered gold trinkets in Eurasia was sporadic, presumably reliant on the chance discovery of a large nugget. After the initial ventures into sheet metalworking, all the familiar techniques of the goldsmith, including soldering, casting and gilding, followed rapidly, and goldworking was well established in much of the world many centuries before its first beginnings in South America.

Although metallurgy in South and Central America developed very much later than in most of the rest of the world, it grew independently and progressed in stages from the use of native metals, through the exploitation of copper minerals, to alloying.[7] This sequence would have been unnecessary if metallurgy had been imported directly by contact with the relatively advanced metal-using peoples of Asia. Metallurgy spread both north and south from its origins in the central Andes,[8] perhaps by sea as well as overland. Quite distinct regional traditions and styles evolved. Compare, for example, the fine castings of the Quimbaya in what is now Colombia, and the complex sheet-metal technology of the cultures of northern Peru. This individuality was probably fostered by the formidable geographical barriers of the Andes. Before the arrival of Europeans in the early sixteenth century AD, smelting, alloying and a whole range of metalworking techniques had been developed and flourished. Gold, silver, copper (including arsenical copper), platinum, tin and lead were all used by one or more of the cultures of South and Central America.[9] The drive to devise ever more effective weapons stimulated significant metallurgical development elsewhere in the world, but in South and Central America, the substitution of metals for stone and wood, either for weapons or utilitarian items, was far less common. Iron does not feature at all in the indigenous metallurgy of South America, and steel and brass were unknown anywhere on the American continent until introduced by Europeans. Meteoric iron can be found in both North and South America, but there is no suggestion that interest was shown in it any further south than Mexico, where a broken copper chisel of unknown date has been found embedded in an iron meteorite.[10] On the other hand, platinum was used by the indigenous smiths of the Tumaco-Esmeraldas region of the Pacific coastal plains,[11] yet did not feature in the metallurgical repertoire of the rest of the world until samples were sent as curiosities back to Spain. Even then platinum grains were merely considered a hindrance to the extraction of gold.[12]

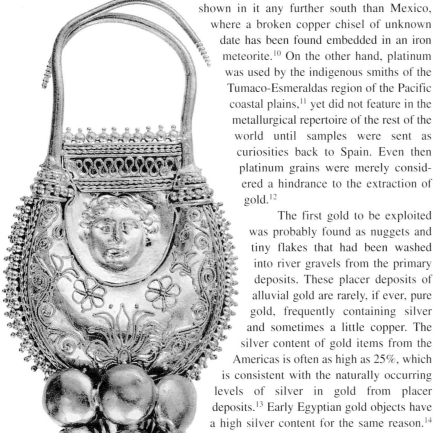

The first gold to be exploited was probably found as nuggets and tiny flakes that had been washed into river gravels from the primary deposits. These placer deposits of alluvial gold are rarely, if ever, pure gold, frequently containing silver and sometimes a little copper. The silver content of gold items from the Americas is often as high as 25%, which is consistent with the naturally occurring levels of silver in gold from placer deposits.[13] Early Egyptian gold objects have a high silver content for the same reason.[14] Modern concepts of 'pure' metals, of course, did not exist. In the past, metals were classified by their colour, by properties such as hardness and corrosion resistance, and by their source: references to gold found in Mesopotamian cuneiform tablets contain terms for different types of 'gold' and the purposes to which these were suited.[15] The colour and properties varied because the gold contained other metals, principally silver and a little copper. The earliest evidence for the knowledge of how to remove copper and silver from gold alloys has been identified on a group of low-gold alloy (c.40% gold) tools and weapons dated to the third millennium BC at the site of Ur, on the flood plain of the Euphrates in what is now Iraq.[16] However, this gold purification technology was only applied to the surfaces of the objects and it does not seem to have been used for true purification of the

metal until the advent of coinage in Lydia in the seventh century BC.[17] In the Americas there was no demand for purified gold, in the sense that we understand it today, until the introduction of coinage by the Spanish. This should not be surprising, as gold only takes on an importance above other precious commodities when it is linked to an economy in which gold coinage is issued by the state, and confidence in the value of a coin implies the ability to test and control the standard of metal in it. It does, however, highlight the difference in attitude to gold between the indigenous Amerindian peoples and their Spanish conquerors.

Metallurgical development depends not only on the availability of metals but also on having a stable social structure with surplus food production to support full-time specialized artisans. The development of a complementary ceramic technology was necessary to provide the refractory furnace, crucible and mould materials with which to handle the high temperatures of molten metal. A prerequisite of lost-wax casting is a suitable quality and quantity of wax. It has been suggested that the reason for the scarcity of castings amongst the metal finds from Peru is that there were no native species of bees in the highlands and west coast valleys of the area to provide the wax.[18]

Cultural factors have strong and often unpredictable (to us) influences on technological developments. The colour, lustre and reflective properties of metal alloys would have enhanced their allure and value, and it is reasonable to surmise, for example, that the transformations involved in melting and casting might have held some mystical significance.[19] There will have been many more cultural pressures and constraints that we cannot even guess at. All these factors must have affected the choice of different technological solutions that we find between cultures in their use of gold for the same design problem The archaeological record shows that these solutions differed not only between the independent metallurgical traditions of the Americas and the Old World but also between the many and diverse cultures of the Americas. It is this aspect of prehispanic metallurgy which is addressed in this paper, illustrated by objects from the collections of the British Museum.

Fine metalwork, from whatever part of the world, has certain design features in common. One such feature is the use of thin strands of metal which for the sake of simplicity we will call 'wire'. Wire has two main functions in goldsmithing: it is used structurally, for example as the

11.1 Greek earring from Taranto, 340–320 BC, one of a pair showing wire used for the suspension loop and filigree decoration. The body and spheres are hollow sheet halves soldered together. (Length of earring 65 mm)

loops for suspending earrings and it is also used decoratively, especially as filigree (Fig. 11.1; cf. Falchetti, this volume). From the beginnings of metalworking, throughout most of the Old World, wire has been made by working a piece of metal into a long thin strand. There are many ways of doing this, from simple hammering, to twisting and rolling rods or strips of sheet metal, through to the method used since the Middle Ages of pulling strips through a series of holes of decreasing diameter in a draw plate.[20] The early hand-working methods all have the advantage that the simplest of equipment is needed, together with a

relatively low-temperature fire for annealing. No gold is wasted in making the wire and its thickness and length can be adjusted at any stage. Presumably because of these factors, wire making by hand-working has developed along similar lines in most cultures (Fig. 11.2). However, by contrast, in some areas of Central and South America 'wire' was cast, not worked. Fig. 11.3 shows a detail of a pendant from Panama. The features of this lost-wax casting were all modelled in wax; the lips were modelled from thin wax 'wire', the teeth from wax strip and the eyes from small wax spheres, fused to the face with a drop of molten

11.2 Central European (Hungarian) Late Bronze Age gold wire jewellery in spiral forms, 11th–9th century BC. (Four-arm spiral piece 119 mm wide)

11.3 SEM details of the cast face of a figure on a pendant from Panama, AD 500–1000, showing the original 'wire' lips, 'strip' teeth and other facial features that were all modelled in wax, before casting the gold.
(Scale marker 1.5 mm)

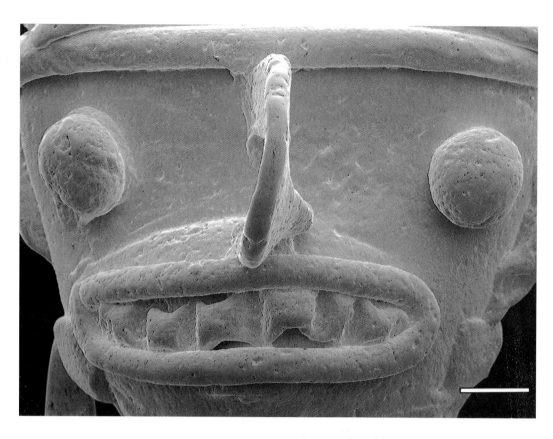

11.4 (below) SEM detail of the worked, decorative sheet face of the Greek earring from Taranto, Fig. 11.1. The sharp definition of the facial features and the dimensional similarity between this and its pair indicates the use of a die.
(Scale marker 1.5 mm)

11.5 (above right) SEM detail from Fig. 11.1. The individual wire, granulation and sheet components were soldered together. The fineness of the joints suggests that the copper-salt reduction process was used.
(Scale marker 0.9 mm)

wax. In contrast, a pendant earring with similar design features, but by a Classical Greek goldsmith, was made directly in metal from individual worked gold components soldered together (Figs 11.1, 11.4–5).[21]

The metal artefacts of the Zenú (cf. Fig. 7.3) and Tairona, as well as Tairona-style Muisca artefacts (Fig. 11.6; cf. Figs 6.4, 6.6, 6.10), are notable for their extensive use of filigree decoration, but it is well known that the 'wire' was cast as an integral part of the whole object. All the components of these artefacts, including the wires, were modelled in wax and assembled before casting.[22] The skill required to cast such complex shapes as the Zenú earrings with all their intricate detail is extremely impressive, not least for the ability to produce and manipulate the minute beeswax components and to add the

11.6 SEM detail of a Muisca *tunjo*, AD 700–1500, showing the dendritic surface of the cast-gold 'wire' and 'sheet' background.
(Scale marker 1.5 mm)

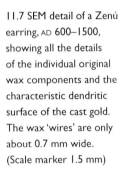

11.7 SEM detail of a Zenú earring, AD 600–1500, showing all the details of the individual original wax components and the characteristic dendritic surface of the cast gold. The wax 'wires' are only about 0.7 mm wide.
(Scale marker 1.5 mm)

11.8 Openwork wire-mesh ear-spool from Chancay, Peru (diam. 36 mm): (left) view showing the continuous zigzag lengths of wire running right across the ear-spool and the neat soldered joints where wires touch; (right) SEM detail of some of the soldered joints between the zigzag, rectangular section wires. (Scale marker 1 mm)

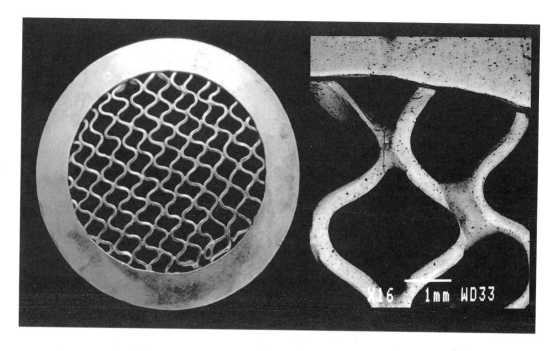

appropriate runners and risers to control the flow of the molten metal, so that it filled every part of the mould (Fig. 11.7). The craftsmanship of wax modelling, together with the ability to cast fine surface detail, essentially replaced the need to develop many goldworking techniques. There are several factors which would seem to have assisted in producing such delicate castings, including the refractory properties of the mould material, a fine-grained clay mixed with crushed charcoal, which was also instrumental in preventing porosity in the cast metal,[23] and also the fluidity of the copper-rich gold alloys when molten. One of the most significant differences between prehispanic American and Old World metallurgy is the extent of alloying. In South and Central America gold alloys, known as *tumbaga* or *guanín* gold, often contained up to around 60% copper. In the Classical world, under Greek and Roman influence, gold for wire and jewellery was characterized by relatively low additions of copper to the gold, generally less than 5%.[24] These higher gold-content alloys are more malleable and easily worked than *tumbaga*, whereas *tumbaga*, with its lower melting point, is better suited to casting. Furthermore, the complex filigree work of the Classical world was made up of many components, which needed to have a high melting temperature to avoid damage during soldering, and the high gold alloys fulfilled this criteria.

Not all wire from South and Central America is cast, for example amongst a group of gold fish hooks found in the Río Cauca, some are made from hammered wire and others from cast wire.[25] Hand-formed wires are also a feature of the sheet metalwork of La Tolita (on the borders of Ecuador and Colombia). Scott (1991) examined several fragments of wire from Colombia and found that some were made by careful hammering, for example a small coil of wire of the type used in the Calima region for the suspension of beads showed evidence in the microstructure that it had been shaped by cycles of cold-working and annealing. He also identified the block-twisting technique and possibly strip-twisting on two fragments of wire from the Tairona and Calima regions. Both these methods had also been developed and used extensively in the Old World for the manufacture of wire.[26]

A pair of gold and silver ear-spools from Peru are decorated with an openwork mesh of gold wires (Fig. 11.8a). The rectangular sectioned wires (approximately 0.5 × 0.25 mm) are hammered and had been bent, zigzag fashion. The corner of each zigzag was soldered to the corner of the adjacent wire (Fig. 11.8b). The gold alloy of the solder is considerably richer in silver (28%) and copper (27%) than the gold wire (which has only 18% silver and 6% copper), thereby lowering its melting point. This gave a safety margin of about 140°C between the melting point of the solder and the temperature at which the wire would also have melted. Another solution to the same design problem is the cast-gold mesh of a bell from a burial mound at Tampacayal, Mexico, in Fig. 11.9. Such openwork patterning was also achieved from a quite different starting point by the Byzantine goldsmiths of the early Christian era, who pierced solid gold sheet (Fig. 11.10).[27]

America is not the only continent on which fine

11.9 Back of a cast mesh openwork bell from a burial mound at Tampacayal, Mexico (height 33 mm).

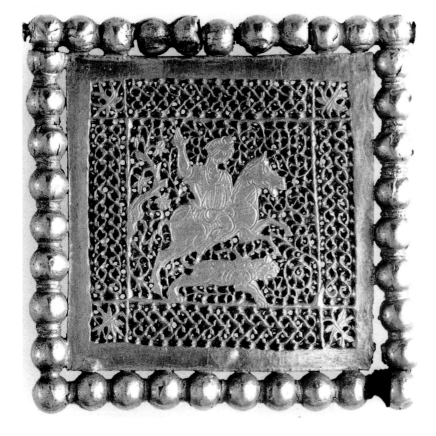

11.10 (above) Openwork gold plaque depicting a mounted huntress and a lion, from Asia Minor, 4th century AD (53 x 52 mm). This openwork was created by piercing a solid sheet of gold.

11.11 (right) Ashanti lost-wax cast filigree wire ornament, AD 1700–1800 (diam. 64 mm).

filigree work was cast by the lost-wax method. In Africa, too, casting is found alongside hammered and worked gold, though, interestingly, in some areas of Nigeria latex is in modern times substituted for wax. The material cannot be easily made into sheets like beeswax, and instead is pulled into fine threads, which are wound around the core.[28] A plant latex from one of the many spurges (*Euphorbia*) native to Mexico, for example *Euphorbia antisyphilitica*, also known as the wax-plant, could have been used to make some of the distinctive castings of Central America, which have a surface texture of fine, spirally wound wire. By the ninth century AD the Igbo of eastern Nigeria were casting fine bronzes by the lost-wax method and it has been argued by Craddock *et al.* (1993) that this technology had been developed independently in the West African rainforests before this date. Between 1700 and 1900 AD the kingdom of the Ashanti dominated the central area of the Gold Coast (modern Ghana) with its vast gold resources, and adopted the lost-wax method for making fine filigree castings in gold (Fig. 11.11). Only the king and important officials were allowed to wear gold, and the goldsmiths operated under strict government control. Casting requires more metal than will end up in the finished object, as allowance has to be made for casting sprues, etc., which will be trimmed off. They can of course be melted down and reused in the next casting, but it does require the goldsmith to have access to more metal than will end up in the commissioned item. This is more likely to be the case where the gold supply is centrally controlled, as amongst the Ashanti, than where individual patrons are taking their own gold to the jeweller to be made up into a particular item, as was done, for example, in medieval Europe.

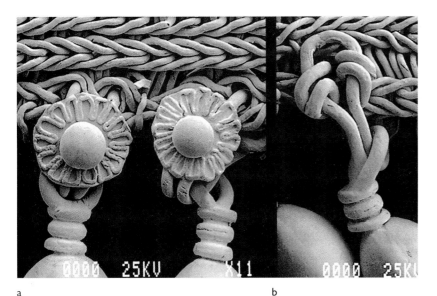

a b

11.12 SEM details of part of a Greek gold loop-in-loop chain necklace with suspended amphora-shaped pendants, from Capua, 4th–3rd century BC, viewed from the front (a) and the back (b). The strip-twist wire is hollow, and thousands of individual loops of wire form the chain links of the necklace. Each rosette is 3 mm in diameter and comprises sheet backing, wire and granule soldered together. The reverse side shows that the pendants are suspended by wires which pass through both the chain and the soldered wire loop on the pendant neck, and the ends of the wires are looped round themselves to hold the components together. Some chain links display the characteristic diagonal seams of strip twist wire. (Scale marker 1 mm)

A feature of many gold adornments is the flexible suspension of pendants and danglers which catch the light and jingle during movement. Chains of hand-worked wire were made for this purpose in the Classical world. Fig. 11.12a illustrates a detail of the loop-in-loop wire of a Greek necklace, from which rows of amphora-shaped pendants are suspended by strip-twisted wire bent through the chain (Fig. 11.12b).[29] This strong, flexible chain is elegantly simple to make from oval hoops of wire, each looped through the next.[30] While there was no similar hand-made wire chain in Central and South America, the equivalent flexible chain from the Mixtec of Mexico was cast (Fig. 11.13). This pendant has four chains, each made up of three cast loops and a bell. The entire assembly was cast, yet all the components are free to jingle with movement, producing a pleasing sound. All sixteen articulated components show evidence of the original wax modelling and the dendritic, cast-metal surface (Fig. 11.14). In this case there are no miscast joins, but there are examples of other objects where the links have fused together because of defects in the mould. To cast this pendant, including the head assembly with its false filigree wire, each component had to have its own runner and riser in the mould and the mould material had to isolate each link from the next. There is no equivalent technology in Classical Europe to the skills

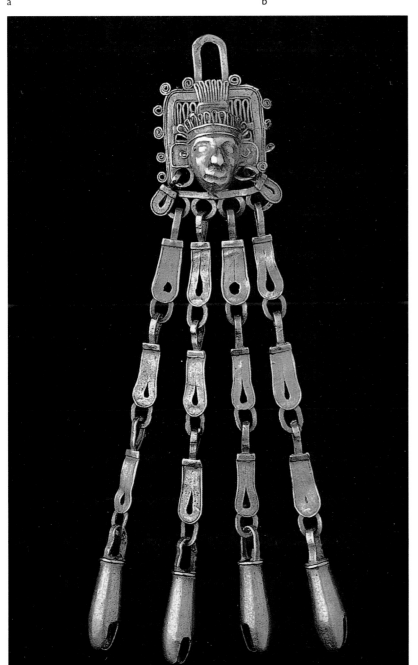

11.13 Mixtec cast-chain components and bells suspended from a mask, AD 1000–1521 (total length 135 mm). The individual components are all free to move.

11.14 SEM detail of the cast proper-left earring on the bell/mask, Fig. 11.13, showing the cast loop of the earring passing through the cast ear loop. The details of the original wax components that formed the individual earring are preserved in the metal along with the dendritic surface. (Scale marker 1.5 mm)

11.15 SEM detail of an earring from Crete, c.350–300 BC, showing the field of decorative granulation, and other wire components. (Scale marker 1.5 mm)

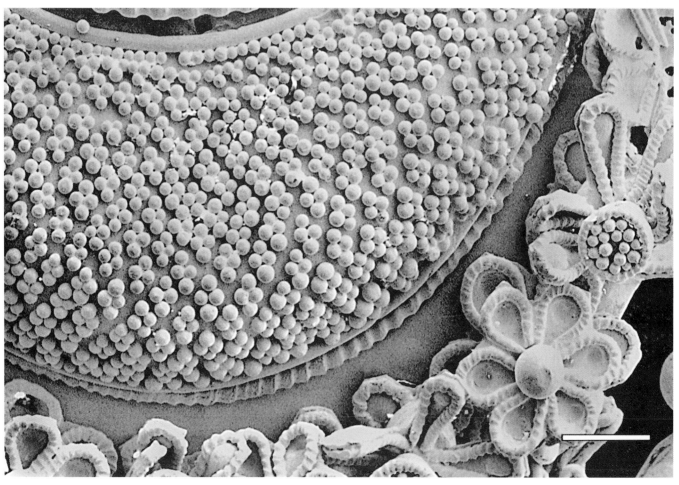

involved here, but the very different practical solutions to the same design problem are equally effective.

Granulation, the application of small spheres of gold at a single point, in rows or in fields, is another decorative feature of gold jewellery. The technique became widespread in the Middle East and Mediterranean regions,[31] spread into Europe and was known as far as India and China.[32] The earliest examples of granulation are from the Royal tombs at Ur about 2500 BC, with a granule size of 2 mm,[33] but some of the finest granulation work comes from areas of Greek influence (Fig.

0000 25KV   X220 100μm WD48

11.16 SEM detail of a group of four granules on the earring in Fig. 11.15. The fine solder joint is formed by *in situ* copper-salt reduction, and the granules are about 0.2 mm in diameter. (Scale marker 0.1 mm)

11.15). In northern Italy the Etruscans, 750–250 BC, were using hundreds or thousands of tiny granules, the smallest about 0.15 mm, to decorate the surface of a single piece of jewellery.[34] In South America, where the technique developed independently, there are examples from the La Tolita culture[35] and from Peru amongst Vicús,[36] Lambayeque and Chimú goldwork.[37]

True granulation requires the manufacture of tiny gold spheres or granules and a means of fixing them to a gold surface. The granules can be made by cutting small pieces of gold from a length of wire, placing them without touching each other in layers of charcoal or on a charcoal block, and then melting, to allow surface tension to turn them into spheres.[38] A fired clay plate, containing spheres of gold in rows of small, round depressions, from the Calima region of Colombia appears to be a mould for casting granules.[39] There are several methods by which it is possible to fix the granules to goldwork and there is much

debate about which were used in antiquity.[40] However, the finished appearance and analytical composition of the join differs very little between these methods of granulation when done by a skilled goldsmith.

The finest granulation was applied by a method of *in situ* copper-salt reduction, which is also referred to in the literature as reaction soldering and the Littledale process.[41] The granules were positioned on the object with an organic glue mixed with a finely ground copper salt, for example malachite. The glue was burnt off, creating a reducing atmosphere in which the copper salt was reduced to metallic copper. This formed a liquid-phase alloy at the point of contact (Fig. 11.16). Many granules could be applied in one operation and further granules added by repeating the process. The temperature required for this reduction process was relatively low, around 800°C,[42] thus avoiding the risk of unsoldering the granules already in place. By this method the smallest granules could be positioned accurately, maintaining their shape without fusing together and joined to the goldwork by only a thin neck of metal.

A second method of granulation used conventional solder made of a metal alloy, rather than a metal salt, to fix the granules. Wolters (1981) reports numerous examples of granulation showing recognizable remnants of solder alloys. Soldering can be less satisfactory than using the copper-reduction method, as no matter how finely the solder is made, it always tends to fill the gaps between granules by surface tension.[43] This characteristic is used to distinguish conventional soldering of granules from copper-salt reduction: analytically it is impossible to distinguish between the two methods unless the solder alloy contains detectably higher amounts of silver than the granules.

A third method of granulation has been proposed, which relies on a phenomenon whereby the surface of the metal becomes liquid momentarily, at a point just below full melting temperature. The granules are first positioned with an organic glue but without any additional metal or metal salt, then the piece is heated until the granules fuse to the surface of the gold.[44] This technique obviously requires very tight control of the heating temperature but it has been demonstrated that it was possible with the simple charcoal hearth technology of antiquity.[45] Evidence for its use in the past is disputed and can only be of the negative variety: where there is no difference in composition at the join it may have been done by this method. Furthermore, the differences in composition created by the other techniques of granulation can be so small that they may be difficult to detect, especially when it is not possible to examine the joint in cross-section.

In the Americas the use of granulation was very localized. The La Tolita-Tumaco culture of the Pacific lowlands of South America on either side of the Ecuador-Colombia frontier used gold granules, sometimes combined with platinum components, to form decorative borders on small ornaments. Examples of these are in the collections of the Museo Nacional del Banco Central del Ecuador.[46] How this was done has not been studied. Beads, comprising clumps of spheres around a central hole for the suspension cord, are found in the Calima region of Colombia, and examples are in the collections of the Museo del Oro, Bogotá.[47] This type of bead has been reported by Bergsøe (1937) and examined in cross-section by Scott (1982). Scott found no evidence for an increase in copper content at the joint and concluded that the granules had been fused together by the third method of granulation discussed above, though the temperature control required would have been remarkable. Granulation on Vicús nose ornaments from northern Peru has been examined by Lechtman (1996), who found that the granules were attached with solder, perhaps in the form of tiny solid chips or very thin ribbons of metal, melted *in situ.*

In Central America granules were cast by the lost-wax process, as an integral part of the object. A Mixtec ring with feline head (Fig. 11.17) is an example of this 'false granulation' made by the lost-wax casting process. The ring comprises an openwork structure in which the granulation is not only decorative but also forms part of the ring's structure. The detail in Fig. 11.18 shows the granules are only 0.7 mm diameter; note also the very thin (0.1 mm) cast bridge between them.

The manufacture of thin gold sheet is another field in which there are two possible approaches:

11.17 (above) Mixtec ring with feline head, AD 1000–1521, showing the complex structure of the small cast ring with openwork 'granulation' (diam. 20 mm).

11.18 (right) SEM detail of the cast false filigree 'granulation' and 'wire' of the Mixtec ring in Fig. 11.17. The granules are about 0.7 mm in diameter. Note the very thin bridge of cast gold between granules, upper centre, and the open nature of the ring of granules around the 'wire' spiral. The original wax model was very finely made. (Scale marker 1.2 mm)

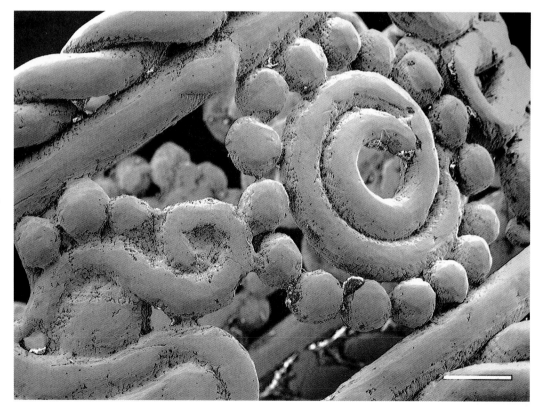

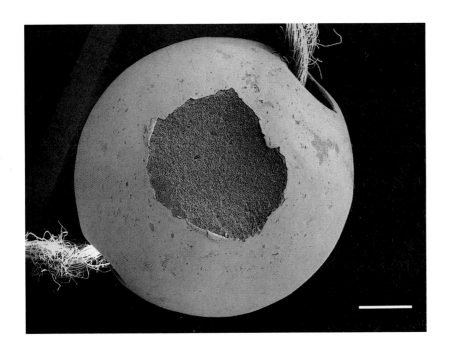

11.19 SEM detail of a hollow-cast bead from a burial mound at Tampacayal, Mexico, showing a region of damage that exposes the solid, fine-clay core. The gold is about 0.15 mm thick. This group has seventeen beads between 4.5 and 6.5 mm in diameter. (Scale marker 1.2 mm)

casting and working. The method of forming a sheet of gold adopted in the Old World and also amongst the metalworkers of northern Peru was to start with a cast billet of gold and hammer it until it spread and thinned to the required dimensions. The sheet could then be decorated by punching, stamping or working up from the back to produce a repoussé motif.[48] One advantage of this approach is that it is a quick method of producing a large number of thin metal objects with the same design motif, using a former or a die. The Muisca were adept at lost-wax casting and they cast the gold as thin sheet which needed no further working. By itself, direct lost-wax casting is not a practical technique for mass-producing identical objects: each time a mould is used it has to be broken up in order to extract the cast object. The Muisca successfully resolved this problem by using carved stone matrices (dies) to form the wax models for casting identical pendants.[49] To an Old World goldsmith this method would have seemed unnecessarily complex, especially as the cast gold pendants are extraordinarily thin (0.1 mm). Instead he might have used the matrix to impress the design directly onto thin, hammered gold sheet: the use of patterned punches for embossing repetitive patterns into gold dates back at least as early as second-millennium-BC Mycenae, and dies were widely used in the Classical world.[50] However, to a culture in which lost-wax casting was the usual means of manufacture, this technique must have been a logical solution to a requirement for multiple copies of the same design. A variation on this technique for producing thin sheet silver has been identified by Scott (1996) on a Sicán cer-

emonial *tumi* dated to c.AD 850–1050. He examined one of the thin sheet components (about 0.13 mm thick) and found that it had in fact been cast but, unlike the Muisca pendants, the decoration had been impressed into the cast metal sheet rather than into the wax model.

The manufacture of gold necklace beads is a related design problem. Large beads are often hollow for reasons of economy and wearable weight, and a number of identical beads may be required for one necklace. In the Old World sheet metal was made by hammering, and the usual solution was to work the sheet into a hollowed mould or doming block to form two identical hemispheres. These were soldered together to make a bead.[51] In areas of the Americas where lost-wax casting was the norm the solution was to form the wax over a sphere of clay, which acted as the core. The core could not be removed from the cast beads as the only openings are the narrow holes for the thread, so it was left inside the beads as a support for the thin gold shell (Fig. 11.19). In Peru, where hammering sheet metal was the usual method of manufacture, beads were made by soldering together two hollow hemispheres of metal, and similar technology was used by the Incas to make hollow figurines of sheet-metal components soldered together (Fig. 11.20).

Where there is gold, gilded metal is sure to be found. The driving force for developing a technology to transform the surface appearance of a base metal object into gold may be economic, aesthetic, fraudulent or, as argued by Reichel-Dolmatoff (1981) and Bray (1993), have more to do with cultural and symbolic values of the metals and alloys. Whatever the motivation, the technological problem was to provide a durable golden surface with no obvious joins in the gold covering. There are a number of possible approaches to producing a golden surface.

The mechanical approach, hammering out a thin covering of gold foil or leaf, is a logical step, especially given the unique properties of pure gold which allow it to be hammered extremely thin without cracking. It is a method found in all the goldworking traditions of the world. At the beginning of the third millennium BC foil was being used to gild silver and copper in the Middle East, and gold leaf (gold sheet which is thinner than 1μm) was certainly being used for gilding by the Hellenistic Greeks and the Romans (Oddy 1993). In several cultures of prehispanic South and Central America simple items like copper nose-rings were gilded with foil, though no true leaf has been identified.[52]

Gold foil can be applied by simply wrapping it

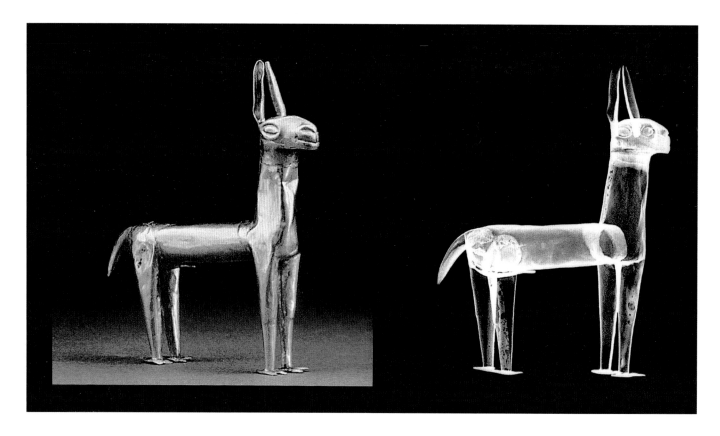

11.20 Inca sheet-gold llama (left), AD 1400–1500 (height 63mm), with radiograph (right), showing the multiple sheet components soldered together. The soldered joins appear white and porous in the photograph, for example at the top of the back legs and down the back of the neck.

around the base metal object or by burnishing it onto the surface, but a better bond can be created by heating to several hundred degrees, though well below the melting point, to promote limited solid-state diffusion between the gold and the metal beneath. This so-called diffusion-bonded gilding is known from an Elamite roundel from south west Iran, of the later second millennium BC.[53] In Ecuador diffusion bonding of gold foil has been recorded on a copper nose ornament from the Milagro-Quevedo phase urn burials at La Compañía.[54]

Fusion gilding, unlike diffusion bonding, requires the gilding layer to be molten, though how this molten gilding was applied is still not fully understood. It was originally identified by Bergsøe (1938) on objects from the La Tolita area on the Pacific coast of Ecuador, and fusion-gilded sheet-copper fragments from the Department of Nariño, Colombia, have been studied by David Scott (1986a and b). A cast Moche mace-head in the form of an owl's head (Fig. 11.21a) and two nose-rings from Ecuador, all in the collections of the British Museum, have also been found to have this type of gilding, which retains the cast microstructure of the molten gilding (Fig. 11.21b) and leaves traces of dendrites on the surface.[55] Two methods have been suggested for applying fusion gilding: dipping the copper object into a bath of molten gold alloy, or applying the molten alloy to

the heated copper ornament and allowing it to run over the surface. Neither of these methods would fully account for features seen on all of these gilded objects. There are practical problems with dipping a metal object into a molten bath of gold alloy, not least holding it securely and still coating it evenly. The Moche owl has strong relief decoration, which would have been eroded by dipping in molten metal or flooded by running molten metal over the surface. The gilding on this piece is, in fact, evenly distributed over the flat areas and in the channels, and the relief decoration is well preserved. A more practical method of fusion gilding would have been to coat the surface with fine particles of gold alloy in a paste, with a flux to prevent oxidation, and to heat until the gilding melted *in situ*, much like a soldering process.

It is possible that different methods of fusion gilding were used for different types of object. Scott has reported sheet-copper objects which have been fusion gilded on only one side, so could not possibly have been dipped in molten metal, but he did find evidence of dipping on a silvered copper nose-ring.[56] Whatever the techniques, fusion plating with either silver or gold is apparently not a common technique anywhere and in the Americas was largely confined to the coastal areas of Ecuador, reaching at its northern extent up into the Nariño area of Colombia and down as far as the Moche and Vicús regions of northern

11.21 Fusion-gilded copper owl mace-head (left), Moche, Peru AD 1–700 (height 65 mm), with SEM false-colour image (right) of a magnified cross-section through the fusion-gilt surface. Colour is used on these SEM images to accentuate composition differences between phases and across diffusion zones. The gilding layer (false orange) is 0.006 mm (6 μm) thick, and the gilding shows casting porosity. There has been some diffusion of gold into the copper body metal, now corroded (false blue) due to the heat from the gilding process.

Peru. Indeed, fusion gilding has not been identified anywhere else in the world, though tinning with molten metal was much used in the Old World,[57] the Celts and the Romans sometimes used molten silver alloy to plate copper,[58] and molten copper and its alloys were used to plate iron.[59] How far the current knowledge reflects the real limits of the use of fusion gilding, rather than the difficulty in distinguishing it from other types of gilding, remains to be seen.

The development of the technique of fire-gilding, also known as mercury gilding or amalgam gilding, was a significant step in plating technology in the Old World, where it was widely adopted because of its ability to economically gild the finest decorated surfaces without join marks and without marring the sharpness of the detail. Another major advantage of this method was that the gilding layer formed a close bond with the metal it plated, so it did not peel off like leaf or foil so often did. It could also be applied over selected portions of an artefact (parcel gilding) for sophisticated effects. Gold and mercury together form a pasty liquid amalgam which can be coated over other metals such as copper or silver. When heated to drive off the free mercury, a thin gold layer is left bonded to the surface. Further layers can be added and the surface burnished to produce a bright gold finish.[60] Some mercury remains, as a compound with gold, so it

is possible to identify this type of gilding by analysing the surface for traces of mercury. Fire-gilding appears first in China, in the Warring States period (428–221 BC). In Europe only a few examples of fire-gilding have been reported which date earlier than the Imperial Roman period, for example a gilt copper finger-ring from Naukratis is dated to about 300 BC,[61] but from the second century AD fire-gilding was widely used for gilding both silver and copper in Europe and Asia.[62] Fire-gilding continued in use until replaced in the nineteenth century by the mass-production techniques of modern electrolytic gilding tanks. However, in spite of the availability of mercury in South America, there is no evidence fire-gilding was used before the arrival of the Spanish.

In South and Central America other solutions were found to the problem of producing a thin, seamless surface layer of gold; the best known of these is depletion gilding, also known as *mise-en-couleur*.[63] The term gilding generally implies the addition of a layer of gold over a base metal such as copper, but depletion gilding entails the removal (or depletion) of base metal from the surface of a gold-alloy object, giving the finished appearance, after burnishing, of high purity gold. The prehispanic smiths deliberately removed copper from the surface of *tumbaga* alloys by heating in an open hearth until it oxidized. The black copper oxide scale was then dissolved in an acid solution, perhaps made from plant extracts.[64] This process of heating and pickling could be repeated to increase the thickness of the resulting gold-enriched surface layer, which was then burnished. The result was a thin (3 µm–10 µm) durable layer of much purer gold completely covering the *tumbaga*.

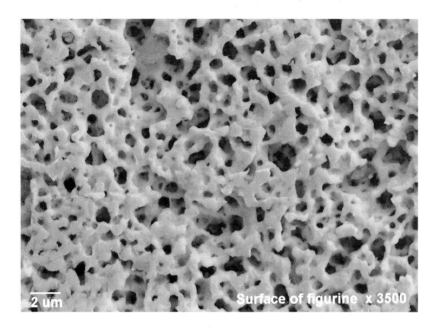

2 um   Surface of figurine x 3500

11.22 SEM detail of the surface of a depletion-gilt, *tumbaga*-alloy anthropomorphic figure from Panama at high magnification (x 3500) showing the depth of the characteristic porosity of the copper-depleted surface, in an unburnished area. (Scale marker 0.002 mm)

Depletion gilding can usually be distinguished from the loss of copper due to corrosion during burial because, unlike a naturally corroded surface, it has been burnished. Deliberate depletion gilding is also distinguishable at high magnification by the characteristic pitting of the surface in unburnished areas, caused by the accelerated removal of copper (Fig. 11.22).[65] Depletion gilding was equally applicable to cast and hammered sheet objects. Indeed the repeated hammering and annealing of *tumbaga* causes oxidation and the worked sheet would have to be pickled after each anneal to prevent oxide being hammered back into the surface. This process therefore enriches the gold concentration at the surface (frontispiece).

Where *tumbaga* alloys were used, the development of depletion gilding was a logical method of enhancing the golden colour, so it is not surprising that depletion gilding was widespread in South and Central America. Outside the American continent *tumbaga* alloys were rare and, although goldsmiths throughout the world have followed the practice of pickling a finished piece of goldwork in acidic solutions to clean it,[66] this has only a minor enrichment effect on already high-gold alloys. *Tumbaga*-type alloys are not, however,

entirely unique to prehispanic goldwork. Amongst the many gold items found in the third-millennium-BC grave of Queen Pu-abi at Ur were three chisels with golden surfaces but with body metal compositions of a base ternary alloy of gold, silver and copper.[67] A gold spear-head and another chisel from a roughly contemporary grave at the same site also showed evidence of depletion gilding. All these pieces had been burnished after the depletion process, and interestingly all showed significant losses of silver as well as copper from the surface layer.

Removal of silver from a gold alloy is not as simple as the depletion of copper described above. Silver can be parted from the gold in an alloy by two main methods. The first is a solid-state cementation process, which requires prolonged heating, usually in a sealed container, with active ions, for example, salt (sodium chloride) or alum (potassium aluminium sulphate), together with an absorbent medium such as clay or brick dust. The silver at the surface is corroded by a reaction with the salt and the corrosion products are absorbed by the brick dust.[68] Using experiments to replicate the thin gilding layer on silver-rich Chimú masks from northern Peru, Lechtman (1973) found that the cementation process removed silver throughout the thickness of the alloy sheets of moderate gold content (around 40% gold), and not just from the surface, as on the Chimú masks (and on the chisels from Ur).

The second method of removing silver is to attack the surface layer with solutions of a strongly corrosive medium applied as a poultice. Lechtman (1979) suggested that a corrosive mineral containing ferric sulphate, which occurs naturally in dessicated areas like coastal Peru, could have been used to produce similar results. This method was based on a description of a treatment for finishing gold objects in the sixteenth-century-AD manuscript of Sahagún, a Spaniard who collected contemporary accounts of the Aztecs.[69] Lechtman immersed the metal sheet in a cold, aqueous paste containing two parts ferric sulphate, two parts common salt and one part iron oxide. The black scale which formed on the surface was washed off in a hot strong saline solution, then the piece was heated and burnished to consolidate the gold-rich surface layer. She found this method most closely replicated the surface depletion of both silver and copper from the surface of the Chimú artefacts.

The relatively simple process of depletion gilding by oxidation of copper from the surface (of an alloy to which copper had been deliberately added) was probably more common in South and

Central America than the complex process of removing silver, which came as an accidental component with the placer gold from which the object was made. Scott (1983), who reviewed the ethnographic and ethnohistorical records for depletion gilding, suggested that in Colombia the practice was to use juices of plants of the *Oxalis* genus in solution with salt to oxidize and dissolve some of the copper content of the *tumbaga*-alloy surface. The extent to which silver-depletion technology was applied is not yet known: a database of the comparative compositions of gilded surfaces and body metal would be useful in determining this.

A unique solution to the problem of producing a thin, seamless surface layer of gold over copper appears to have been invented by the Vicús and Moche metalsmiths of northern Peru (*c*.100 BC–AD 600) and never to have been disseminated to other cultures. The technique, known as electrochemical replacement gilding, has been studied by Lechtman and co-workers (1979, 1982). They concluded after extensive experimental work that the minutely thin (0.5–2 μm) layer of gold could be deposited on copper sheet from solution. The analogous modern process of electroplating requires strong mineral acids to dissolve the gold, and potassium cyanide for the plating solution as well as an electrical current to drive the deposition reaction. None of these were available to the prehispanic goldsmith. Experiments by Lechtman *et al.* using corrosive minerals proved that sufficient gold could be dissolved to make a gilding solution, and the electrochemical reaction between the ions in solution and the copper sheet was sufficient to drive the plating reaction without the application of an external current. Gold was heated gently for two to five days in an aqueous solution of common salt (NaCl), saltpetre (KNO_3) and potash alum ($KAl(SO_4O_2).12H_2O$) until it dissolved. This acidic solution was neutralized with sodium bicarbonate ($NaHCO_3$) to a pH of 9 and heated to boiling point. When copper objects were immersed in the solution their surfaces became plated with a layer of gold closely resembling that seen on the metalwork from the site of Loma Negra in the Vicús region. A section through a gilded strip of copper from a plaque in the form of a feline (Fig. 11.23) illustrates the nature of this very thin, irregular plating. Recent work by Centeno and Schorsch (in press) has identified this technique for plating with silver and gold on objects from both the Moche and Vicús areas.

The exploitation of platinum in South America, centuries before it was utilized anywhere else in the world, is one of the most interesting metallurgical developments of the region. Platinum occurs in the Tumaco-Esmeraldas region of the Pacific coastal plains, on the border of present-day Colombia and Ecuador.[70] It is found as fine particles along with gold in the rivers of the region, and its working is closely linked with gold. It is easy to understand how the metal might have been first discovered, but as platinum melts at 1770°C, well above the temperatures which could be achieved by blowpipes, it might have been expected to be dismissed as an unusable impurity. This was certainly the reaction of Europeans to the intractable metal and it was only in the late eighteenth century that any real use was made of platinum outside the Americas. Even the much quoted example of a platinum inlay on an Egyptian box in the Louvre has now been discounted.[71] Scott, who has undertaken a survey of the known artefacts in South America, concluded that there were three major categories that deliberately incorporated platinum.[72] The first group comprises very few artefacts, hammered from native platinum nuggets. The largest group was made by sintering platinum-gold alloys: the particles of platinum were fused together by molten gold, and successive cycles of hammering and annealing caused partial dissolution of the platinum in the gold. The end result was a silver-coloured metal of variable homogeneity which was used to make small ornaments such as nose-rings, examples of which are in the Museo del Oro, Bogotá. The third group are gold or *tumbaga* items from the Esmeraldas region, clad on one or both sides with platinum,[73] examples of which are in the Museo Nacional del Banco Central del Ecuador, Quito.[74] Scott and Bray suggest this cladding was achieved by cycles of heating and hammering fine platinum particles onto gold.[75] Current research by Meeks, LaNiece and Estévez has found evidence for the manufacture of sintered platinum foil, which was plated onto sheet gold. Scott and Bray also examined the reason for the use of such a difficult metal in this one region: they noted that platinum was used only for decorative pieces, not for tools or other items where its hardness might be an advantage, and suggested that it was prized for its colour in a region where silver was not readily available.

The importance of the colour of metals is a recurring theme in studies of prehispanic metallurgy, whereas assessment of Eurasian metallurgy has concentrated more on the properties of metals, particularly in terms of improvement to tools and weapons. Whether or not this diver-

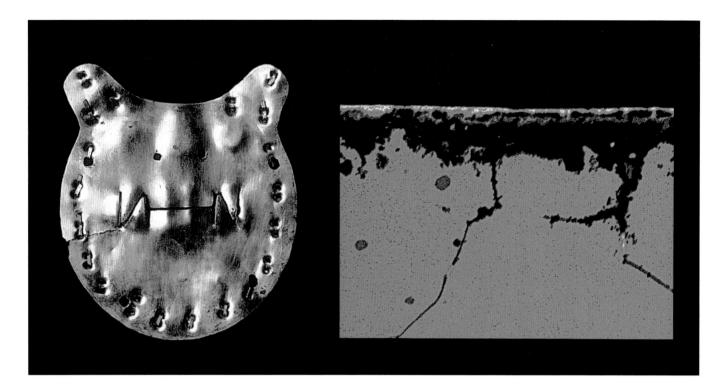

11.23 Electrochemically gilded Vicús copper-sheet plaque in the form of a feline head (left), Peru 100 BC–AD 600 (width 100 mm), with false-colour SEM image (right) of a magnified cross-section through the plaque, showing the thin electro-chemical gilding layer (false yellow). The gilding is only 0.0015mm (1.5 μm) thick. The copper body of the feline (false light blue) has corrosion under the gilding (false dark blue) and this penetrates along grain boundaries into the body metal.

gence in approach existed between the very earliest metalsmiths, by the time the first Europeans reached the Americas the difference in cultural attitude to metal, particularly to the alloying or refining of gold, was marked. Invention and development in metallurgy depends primarily on the availability of metals and relevant refractory technology, but beyond this the driving force must be a perceived need for metal, whether for utilitarian objects, for personal adornment, as a mark of social status or for ritual significance. The design of a metal artefact will be governed by cultural factors, which we might define as tradition, taste or fashion, as well as by practical factors, in other words, by what it is possible to make. Similarly the choices of methods of

making up the required design from metal have always been constrained not only by the practicalities associated with metalworking from raw metal to finished product but also by cultural influences, some of which will have been borrowed from existing material technologies such as ceramics, carpentry and textile manufacture. Outlined in this paper are some of these choices made by goldsmiths in Central and South America, independent of any outside metallurgical influences. It is interesting how many of the designs incorporate universal features, for example filigree, granulation, relief decoration, surface colouring. However, it is in the chosen manner of execution of these design features that the distinctive cultural influences are displayed.

Notes

1 Lechtman 1988; Bray 1985; Rehren and Temme 1994; West 1994; Burger and Gordon 1998.

2 Lechtman 1980: 275.

3 Shimada 1994: 44.

4 Craddock 1995: 97.

5 Muhly 1988.

6 Eluère 1989.

7 Lechtman 1988; Easby 1965; Patterson 1971.

8 Rodriguez 1986.

9 West 1994.

10 Newton Friend 1926.

11 Scott and Bray 1994.

12 McDonald and Hunt 1982: 15.

13 Rovira 1994.

14 Lucas and Harris 1962; Gale and Gale 1981.

15 Levey 1959a and b.

16 La Niece 1995.

17 Cowell et al. 1998; Craddock 1995: 115–19.

18 Bird 1979.

19 Hosler 1995; Bray 1985, in press; Reichel-Dolmatoff 1981; Lechtman 1984; Oliver, this volume.

20 Oddy 1977.

21 Williams and Ogden 1994: 231–4.

22 Scott 1991.

23 Easby 1956.

24 Meeks 1998.

25 Meeks, in press.

26 Oddy 1977; Ogden 1991.

27 Ogden and Schmidt 1990.

28 Williams 1974: 183.

29 Meeks 1998.

30 Ogden 1982: 58.

31 Higgins 1961; Williams and Ogden 1994.

32 Wolters 1983.

33 Wolters 1981.

34 Williams and Ogden 1994.

35 Bray 1978; Bergsøe 1937.

36 Lechtman 1996.

37 Bákula et al. 1994; Wolters 1983: 190, 222–24.

38 Untracht 1969: 203.

39 Sáenz Obregón and Cardale de Schrimpff 1989.

40 Duval et al. 1989; Wolters 1981; Carroll 1974; Nestler and Formigli 1993.

41 Littledale 1936: Untracht 1982: 351.

42 Duval et al. 1989; Higgins 1961: 20–21.

43 Untracht 1982: 350.

44 Duval et al. 1989; Baines 1988.

45 Carroll 1974.

46 Zapater 1995.

47 Plazas and Falchetti 1994.

48 Untracht 1982: 118.

49 Long 1989.

50 Ogden 1982: 37.

51 Untracht 1982: 114–16.

52 Bray 1993: 183–4

53 Oddy et al. 1981b.

54 Scott 1986a: 320.

55 La Niece, in press.

56 Scott 1986a: 322.

57 Meeks 1993.

58 La Niece 1993: 206.

59 Corfield 1993.

60 Oddy et al. 1981a.

61 Williams and Ogden 1994: no. 194.

62 Oddy 1993.

63 Lechtman 1973; del Solar and Grimwade 1982; Scott 1983.

64 Scott 1983.

65 Meeks, in press.

66 Untracht 1982: 417.

67 La Niece 1995.

68 Notton 1974; Craddock 1995.

69 Sahagún 1956.

70 Scott and Bray 1994.

71 Pers. comm., Christiane Eluère.

72 Scott 1982; Scott and Bray 1994.

73 Bergsøe 1937.

74 Estévez, in press.

75 Scott and Bray 1994: 307.

References

Baines, R.
1988 Technical antecedents of early Hellenistic disc and pendant ear ornaments. In *Art of the Greek Goldsmith*, ed. D. Williams, pp. 122–6, figs 17.3a, b, c. British Museum Press, London.

Bákula, C., M. Seledad Leiva and Clemencia Plazas
1994 *L'or des Dieux – l'or des Andes, Pérou, Equateur, Colombie*, exh. cat. Le Conseil Général de la Moselle, Metz.

Bergsøe, P.
1937 The metallurgy and technology of gold and platinum among the pre-Columbian Indians. *Ingenioervidenskabelige Skrifter* A44, Copenhagen.
1938 The gilding process and the metallurgy of copper and lead among the pre-Columbian Indians. *Ingenioervidenskabelige Skrifter* A46, Copenhagen.

Bird, J.
1979 Legacy of the stingless bee. *Natural History*, 88 (9): 49–51.

Bray, W.
1978 *The Gold of El Dorado*, exh. cat., Royal Academy of Arts. Times Books, London.
1985 Ancient American metallurgy: five hundred years of study. In *The Art of Pre-Columbian Gold: The Jan Mitchell Collection*, ed. J. Jones, pp. 76–84. Weidenfeld & Nicolson, London.
1993 Techniques of gilding and surface-enrichment in pre-Hispanic American metallurgy. In *Metal Plating & Patination: Cultural, Technical and Historical Developments*, ed. S. La Niece and P. Craddock, pp. 182–92. Butterworth Heinemann, Oxford.
In press Metallurgy and anthropology: two studies from prehispanic America. *Boletín Museo del Oro*.

Burger, R.L., and R.B. Gordon
1998 Early Central Andean metalworking from Mina Perdida, Peru. *Science* (282): 1108–11.

Carroll, D.L.
1974 A classification for granulation in ancient metalwork. *American Journal of Archaeology* 78 (1): 33–9, pl. 10.

Centeno, S.A., and D. Schorsch
In press The characterization of gold layers on copper artifacts from the Piura Valley (Peru) in the Early Intermediate period. In *Gilded Metals*, ed. T. Drayman-Weisser. Archetype Books, London.

Corfield, M.
1993 Copper plating on iron. In *Metal Plating and Patination: Cultural, Technical and Historical Developments*, ed. S. La Niece and P. Craddock, pp. 276–83. Butterworth Heinemann, Oxford.

Cowell, M.R., K. Hyne, N.D. Meeks and P.T. Craddock
1998 Analyses of the Lydian electrum, gold and silver coinages. In *Metallurgy in Numismatics 4*, ed. W.A. Oddy and M.R. Cowell, pp. 526–38.

Royal Numismatic Society special publication no. 30, London.

Craddock, P.T.
1995 *Early Mining and Metal Production*. Edinburgh University Press, 110–121.

Craddock, P.T., V.E. Chickwendu, A.C. Umeji, R.M. Farquhar and T. Shaw
1993 The technical origin of the Igbo bronzes. *West African Journal of Archaeology* (22): 191–201.

Del Solar, T., and Grimwade M.
1982 The art of depletion gilding. *Aurum* 12: 37–49.

Duval, A.R., C. Eluère, L.P. Hurtel and M. Menu
1989 The use of scanning electron microscopy in the study of gold granulation. In *Archaeometry, Proceedings of the 25th International Symposium*, ed. Y. Maniatis, pp. 325–33. Elsevier, Amsterdam.

Easby, D.T.
1956 Sahagún reviviscit in the gold collection of the University museum. *University Museum Bulletin* (20iii), pp. 3–15. University of Pennsylvania, Philadelphia.
1965 Pre-hispanic metallurgy and metalworking in the New World. *Proc. Amer. Phil. Soc.* 109(2): 89–98.

Eluère, C. (ed.)
1989 *Le Premier Or*. Editions de la Reunion des Musées Nationaux, Paris.

Gale, N.H., and Z.A. Gale
1981 Ancient Egyptian silver. *Journal of Egyptian Archaeology* 67: 103–15.

Higgins, R.A.
1961 *Greek and Roman Jewellery*. Methuen, London.

Hosler, D.
1995 Sound, color and meaning in the metallurgy of ancient west Mexico. *World Archaeology* 27(1): 100–115.

La Niece, S.
1993 Silvering. In *Metal Plating and Patination: Cultural, Technical and Historical Developments*, ed. S. La Niece and P. Craddock, pp. 201–10. Butterworth Heinemann, Oxford.
1995 Depletion gilding from third millennium BC Ur, *Iraq* LVII: 41–7.
In press. Metallurgical case studies from the British Museum's collections of pre-Hispanic gold. *Boletín Museo del Oro*.

Lechtman, H.N.
1973 The gilding of metals in pre-Columbian Peru. In *The Application of Science in Examination of Works of Art*, ed. W.J. Young, pp. 36–52. Museum of Fine Arts, Boston.
1979 A pre-columbian technique for electrochemical replacement plating of gold and silver on objects of copper. *Journal of Metals* 31: 154–60.
1980 The central Andes: metallurgy without iron. In T.A. Wertime and J.D. Muhly, *The Coming of the Age of Iron*, pp. 267–334. Yale University Press, Newhaven and London.

1984 Andean value systems and development of prehistoric metallurgy. *Technology and Culture* 25(1): 1–36.
1988 Traditions and styles in central Andean metalworking. In *The Beginning of the Use of Metals and Alloys*, ed. R. Maddin, 344–78. MIT Press, Cambridge, Massachusetts.
1996 Technical description. In *Andean Art at Dumbarton Oaks*, vol. 1, ed. E. Hill Boone, pp. 280–83. Dumbarton Oaks Research Library and Collection, Washington, DC.

Lechtman H., A. Erlij and E. Barry
1982 New perspectives on Moche metallurgy: techniques of gilding copper at Loma Negra, northern Peru. *American Antiquity* 47(1): 3–30.

Levey, M.
1959a The refining of gold in ancient Mesopotamia, *Chymia* 5: 31–6.
1959b *Chemistry and chemical technology in ancient Mesopotamia*, ch. 15. Elsevier, New York.

Littledale, H.A.P.
1936 *A new process for hard soldering and its possible connections with the methods used by the Ancient Greeks and Etruscans*. Lecture to the Worshipful Company of Goldsmiths, 24 February 1936, London (British Patent 415.181 applied for in 1933). Re-issued by University Microfilms International, 1981.

Long, S.
1989 Matrices de piedra y su uso en la metalurgia Muisca. *Boletín Museo del Oro* 25: 43–69.

Lucas, A., and J.R. Harris
1962 *Ancient Egyptian materials and industries*, pp. 490–92. 4th edition. Edward Arnold, London.

McDonald, D., and L.B. Hunt
1982 *A History of Platinum and its Allied Metals*. Johnson Matthey, London.

Meeks, N.D.
1993 Surface characterization of tinned bronze, high-tin bronze, tinned iron and arsenical bronze. In *Metal Plating and Patination: Cultural, Technical and Historical Developments*, ed. S. La Niece and P. Craddock, pp. 247–75. Butterworth Heinemann, Oxford.
1998 A Greek gold necklace: a case of dual identity. In *The Art of the Greek Goldsmith*, ed. D. Williams, pp. 127–38. British Museum Press, London.
In press. Pre-hispanic goldwork in the British Museum: some recent technological studies. *Boletín Museo del Oro*.

Muhly, J.D.
1988 The beginnings of metallurgy in the Old World. In *The Beginning of the Use of Metals and Alloys*, ed. R. Maddin, pp. 2–20. Massachusetts Institute of Technology.

Nestler, G., and E. Formigli
1993 *Etruskische Granulation: Eine Antike Goldschmiedetechnik*. Sienna.

Newton Friend, J.
1926 *Iron in Antiquity*, p. 11. Charles Griffin and Co. Ltd, London.

Notton, J.F.H.
1974 Ancient Egyptian gold refining. *Gold Bulletin* (7ii): 50–56.

Oddy, W.A.
1977 The production of gold wire in antiquity. *Gold Bulletin* (10iii): 79–87.
1993 Gilding of metals in the Old World. In *Metal Plating and Patination: Cultural, Technical and Historical Developments*, ed. S. La Niece and P. Craddock, pp. 171–81. Butterworth Heinemann, Oxford.

Oddy, W.A., M. Bimson and S. La Niece
1981a Gilding Himalayan images: history, tradition and modern techniques. In *Aspects of Tibetan Metallurgy*, ed. W.A. Oddy and W. Zwalf, pp. 87–101. British Museum Occasional Paper no. 15.

Oddy, W.A., W. La Niece, J.E. Curtis and N.D. Meeks
1981b Diffusion bonding as a method of gilding in Antiquity. *MASCA Journal* 1: 5–6.

Ogden, J.
1982 *Jewellery of the Ancient World*. Trefoil Books, London.
1991 Classical gold wire: some aspects of its manufacture and use. *Jewellery Studies* 5: 95–105.

Ogden, J., and S. Schmidt
1990 Late Antique jewellery: pierced work and hollow beaded wire. *Jewellery Studies* 4, 5–12.

Patterson, C.C.
1971 Native copper, silver and gold accessible to early metallurgists. *American Antiquity* 36(3): 286–321.

Plazas de Nieto, C., and A-M. Falchetti de Sáenz
1978 *El Dorado: Colombian Gold*. Exh. cat., Australian Art Exhibitions Corporation Ltd.
1994 *Museo del Oro* (catalogue), p. 142. Banco de la República, Santafé de Bogotá.

Rehren, T., and M. Temme
1994 Pre-Columbian gold processing at Putushio, South Ecuador: the archaeometallurgical evidence. In *Archaeometry of Pre-Columbian Sites and Artifacts*, ed. D.A. Scott and P. Meyers, pp. 267–84. J. Paul Getty Trust, Getty Conservation Institute.

Reichel-Dolmatoff, G.
1981 Things of Beauty Replete with Meaning – Metals and Crystals in Colombian Indian Cosmology. In *Sweat of the Sun, Tears of the Moon: Gold and Emerald Treasures of Colombia*, ed. D. Seligman, pp. 17–33, exh. cat., Natural History Museum of Los Angeles County. Terra Magazine Publications, Los Angeles.

Rodriguez, L.
1986 La Metalurgia precolombina de los Andes Meridionales. Una sintesis regional. In *Metalurgia de América Precolombina*, ed. C. Plazas de Nieto, pp. 379–417. Banco de la República, Bogotá.

Rovira, S.
1994 Pre-hispanic goldwork from the Museo de América, Madrid: a new set of analyses. In *Archaeometry of Pre-Columbian Sites and*

Artifacts, ed. D.A. Scott and P. Meyers, pp. 323–50. J.Paul Getty Trust, Getty Conservation Institute.

Sáenz Obregón, J., and M. Cardale de Schrimpff
1989 Un molde para fundir granulos de oro encontrado en Calima. *Boletín Museo del Oro* 24: 120–22.

Sahagún, B.
1956 *Historia general de las cosas de Nueva España (1558–1569)*. Editorial Porrúa, México.

Scott, D.A.
1982. Pre-hispanic Colombian Metallurgy: Studies of some Gold and Platinum Alloys. Doctoral thesis. University of London, Institute of Archaeology.
1983 Depletion gilding and surface treatment of gold alloys from the Nariño area of ancient Colombia. *Journal of the Historical Metallurgy Society*, 17(2): 99–115.
1986a Fusion gilding and foil gilding in pre-Hispanic Colombia and Ecuador. In *Metalurgia de América Precolombina*, ed. C. Plazas de Nieto, pp. 281–325. Banco de la República, Bogotá.
1986b Gold and silver alloy coatings over copper: an examination of some artifacts from Ecuador and Colombia. *Archaeometry* 28 (1): 33–50.
1991 Technical examination of some gold wire from pre-hispanic South America, *Studies in Conservation* 36: 65–75.
1996 Technical study of a ceremonial Sican tumi figurine. *Archaeometry* 38(2): 305–11.

Scott, D.A., and W. Bray
1994 Pre-hispanic platinum alloys: their composition and use in Ecuador and Colombia. In *Archaeometry of Pre-Columbian Sites and Artifacts*, ed. D.A. Scott and P. Meyers, pp. 285–322. J.Paul Getty Trust, Getty Conservation Institute.

Shimada, I.
1994 Pre-hispanic metallurgy and mining in the Andes: recent advances and future tasks. In *In Quest of Mineral Wealth: Aboriginal and Colonial Mining and Metallurgy in Spanish America*, ed. A.K. Craig and R.C. West, pp. 37–70. *Geoscience and Man* 33. Louisiana State University, Baton Rouge, LA.

Untracht, O.
1969 *Metal Techniques for Craftsmen*. Doubleday, New York.
1982 *Jewelry: Concepts and Technology*. Doubleday, New York.

West, R.C.
1994 Aboriginal metallurgy and metalworking in Spanish America: a brief overview. In *In Quest of Mineral Wealth: Aboriginal and Colonial Mining and Metallurgy in Spanish America*, ed. A.K. Craig and R.C. West, pp. 5–20. *Geoscience and Man* 33. Louisiana State University, Baton Rouge, LA.

Williams, D.
1974 *Icon and Image: A Study of Sacred and Secular Forms of African Classical Art*. Allen Lane, London.

Williams, D., and J. Ogden
1994 *Greek Gold Jewellery of the Classical World*, exh. cat. British Museum Press, London.

Wolters, J.
1981 The ancient craft of granulation: a re-assessment of established concepts. *Gold Bulletin* (14iii): 119–29.
1983 *Die Granulation: Geschichte und Technik einer alten Goldshmiedekunst*. Verlag George D.W. Callwey, München.

Zapater, I.I.
1995 *Catálogo de la Sala del Oro, Museo Nacional del Banco Central del Ecuador*. Quito.

Acknowledgements

We would like to thank Colin McEwan, Clara Bezanilla, Sheridan Bowman and Paul Craddock at the British Museum; Warwick Bray, Institute of Archaeology, University College London; Clemencia Plazas de Nieto and all the staff at the Museo del Oro, Bogotá; Patricia Estévez, Museo Nacional del Banco Central del Ecuador, Quito; Cecilia Bákula, Banco Central de Reserva del Peru; and all the many colleagues who have generously assisted in our research. The photographs of British Museum objects are by A. Milton, and micrographs are by the authors. For funding travel for research we thank The Royal Society of Great Britain and also The Historical Metallurgy Society.

Illustration Credits

Maps on pp. 10, 15, 93 and 153 were drawn by Robin Kiang. Unless otherwise indicated, the illustrations below are listed by figure number. Objects in the British Museum are shown by the following departmental abbreviations (photographs by the Museum Photographic Service unless stated otherwise):

Ethno   Ethnographic
GR   Greek and Roman Antiquities
PRB   Prehistoric and Romano-British Antiquities
MLA   Medieval and Later Antiquities

Frontispiece: Ethno 1904 10-31.1 (inset photo by A. Milton, S. La Niece and N. Meeks)

p. 11: Ethno 1938.7-6.1 (inset photo by N. Meeks)

1.1 Ethno 7820; photo by Saul Peckham

1.2 Ethno 7820; drawing by Hans Rashbrook

1.3–4 Private collection; drawings by Hans Rashbrook

1.5 Ethno 7819; drawing by Hans Rashbrook

1.6 Private collection; drawing by Hans Rashbrook

1.7 Ethno n/n; drawing by Hans Rashbrook

1.8 Private collection; drawing by Hans Rashbrook

1.9 Private collection; photo by Joerg Haberli

1.10 Institute of Andean Studies, Berkeley

1.11 Institute of Andean Studies, Berkeley

1.12 Brooklyn Museum, Brooklyn 41.428, Henry L. Batterman Fund

1.13 Staatliche Museen zu Berlin, Preussischer Kulturbesitz Museum für Völkerkunde, VA 28787

1.14 Museum für Völkerkunde, VA 31724; drawing by Hans Rashbrook

1.15 Private collection; drawing by Hans Rashbrook after Lapiner 1976, no. 563

2.1–2 The Gold of Peru Museum; photos by Y. Yoshii

2.3 Robin Kiang after I. Shimada

2.4 Drawing by E. Atalaya and I. Shimada.

2.5 Drawing by C. Samillán

2.6 Photo by Y. Yoshii

2.7 Drawing by I. Shimada

2.8–9 Drawings by I. Shimada and C. Samillán

2.10 Photo by I. Shimada

2.11 Drawing by I. Shimada and C. Samillán

2.12 Drawing by C. Samillán

2.13–14 Photos by Y. Yoshii

2.15 Drawing by S. Mueller and I. Shimada

2.16–17 Drawings by I. Shimada and C. Samillán

2.18–19 Drawings by C. Samillán

2.20 Photo by Y. Yoshii

2.21 Photo by I. Shimada

2.22 Drawing by P. Carcedo and I. Shimada

2.23–4 Drawings by C. Samillán

3.1 Metropolitan Museum of Art, Jan Mitchell and Sons Collection, Gift of Jan Mitchell, 1991 (1991.419.65-66)

3.2 Museo Arqueológico Rafael Larco Herrera, Lima, Perú

3.3 Neg. no. 334881, Dept. of Library Services, American Museum of Natural History

3.4 Drawing by Robin Kiang after Michael Moseley (enlargement by Michael Moseley and Chan Chan-Moche Valley Project)

3.5–6 Dumbarton Oaks Research Library and Collections, Washington, DC

3.7 The Textile Museum, Washington, DC, no. 91.729

3.8 The Metropolitan Museum of Art, Jan Mitchell and Sons Collection, Gift of Jan Mitchell, 1991 (1991.419.67–8)

3.9 Courtesy of the Michael C. Carlos Museum of Emory University (1992.15.261a, b)

3.10 Kate S. Buckingham Endowment Fund, 1955.1730; photograph copyright 1998, The Art Institute of Chicago, all rights reserved

4.1 Photographic Archives of the Anthropology Department at the Museo Nacional de Historia Natural, Santiago de Chile

4.2 The Board of Trustees of the National Museums & Galleries on Merseyside (65.77.2)

4.3 After Baessler 1904, pl. 37, fig. 543

4.4 From Guaman Poma de Ayala 1980: 379

4.5 Drawing by Robin Kiang after Penny Dransart

4.6 Ethno 1862 6-11.4

4.7 Ethno 1862 6-11.2

4.8 Museo Regional de Iquique, Chile; photo by Penny Dransart

4.9 Museo Nacional de Arqueología, Antropología e Historia del Perú

5.1 Private collections; drawing by Tessa Rickards

5.2–5 Private collection

5.6 George Ortiz collection; reproduced from Ortiz 1996, pl. 267 bis

5.7 Museo del Oro, Bogotá, and private collections; drawing by Tessa Rickards

5.8 Private collection; photo by Rudolf Schrimpf and Fidel Anzola

5.9–10 Private collection; drawings by Tessa Rickards

5.11 (a) Museo del Oro, Bogotá, no. 28443, (b) private collection; drawings by Tessa Rickards

5.12–15 Museo del Oro, Bogotá, nos: 33265 (5.12), 33272 (5.13), 33316 (5.14), 33312 (5.15); photos by Rudolf Schrimpf and Fidel Anzola

5.16 George Ortiz collection; drawing by Tessa Rickards

5.17 Museo del Oro, Bogotá, no. 33338-33339; photo by Rudolf Schrimpf and Fidel Anzola

5.18 Museo del Oro, Bogotá, nos: 32921 (a), 32924 (b), 32919 (c), 32923 (d), 32917 (e); drawings by Tessa Rickards

6.1, 6.3–13 Museo del Oro, Bogotá, nos: 141 (6.1), 1861 (6.3), 87 (6.5), 296 (6.10), 6755 (6.9), 11373 (6.6), 32866 (6.4), 33055 (6.7), 28513 (6.8), 6317 (6.12), 6914 (6.11), 11289 (6.13); photos by Rudolf Schrimpf, Jorge Mario Munera, Dirk Baker, Jorge Gamboa, Cristian Zitzmann

6.2 Ethno S.1321.

7.1 Drawings by Ana María Falchetti (c: after Balser 1966, d: after Lothrop 1952)

7.2 Robin Kiang after Ana María Falchetti

7.3 Museo del Oro, Bogotá, nos 33191 and 33192

7.4 Photo by Ana María Falchetti and Clemencia Plazas

7.5 Drawings by Ana María Falchetti

7.6 Museo del Oro, Bogotá, no. 7505

7.7–8 Dumbarton Oaks, Washington, nos: B-525.63 CG (7.7), B-526.63 CG (7.8)

7.9–10 Drawings by Ana María Falchetti

7.11 The University Museum of Archaeology and Anthropology, Philadelphia, Pennsylvania, no. SA 2703

7.12 Drawings by Ana María Falchetti

7.13–14 Museo del Oro, Bogotá, nos: CS 12766 (7.13), 25466 (7.14)

7.15 Drawing by Melba R. de León

7.16 Museo del Oro, Bogotá, no. 31725

7.17–18 Drawings by Ana María Falchetti

7.19 Ethno 1955 Am. 6-7

8.1 (a) Carl Hansen; (b–f) Richard Cooke; (g–i) Carl Hansen; (j) drawing by Luís Alberto Sánchez; (k–m) Richard Cooke

8.2 Redrawn from Ichon 1980

8.3 (a–f) Marcos Guerra, (g–h) Richard Cooke; all photos by Richard Cooke

8.4 Robin Kiang

8.5 (a) Luís Alberto Sánchez, (b) Koichi Udagawa, (c–d) Richard Cooke

8.6 Photos by Adrián Badilla, Richard Cooke, Luís Alberto Sánchez and Marcos Guerra

8.7 Photos by Richard Cooke

8.8 Drawings by Luís Alberto Sánchez

8.9 Photos by Richard Cooke

8.10 Drawings and photos by Richard Cooke

8.11 (a) courtesy of the Institute of Culture, Panama; (b–c) photos by Carl Hansen

8.12 Drawings and photos by Richard Cooke

9.1 Robin Kiang after Jeffrey Quilter

9.2 After MacCurdy 1911: 215

9.3 Photo by Jeffrey Quilter

9.4–5 Brooklyn Museum, Brooklyn (digitally manipulated)

9.6 American Museum of Natural History, New York; photo by Jeffrey Quilter

9.7–8 Brooklyn Museum, Brooklyn (9.8: digitally manipulated)

9.9 American Museum of Natural History, New York (K693); photo by Jeffrey Quilter

9.10–11 Brooklyn Museum

9.12 American Museum of Natural History, New York; photo by Jeffrey Quilter

10.1 Claudio Mari after Chanlatte Baik

10.2 Oviedo y Valdés 1944

10.3 Claudio Mari after Luis Chanlatte Baik

10.4 Claudio Mari after Vega 1979

10.5 Drawing by Tessa Rickards after Alonso 1950, p. 340, fig. 111

10.6 Drawing by Hans Rashbrook after Dacal and Rivero 1996, p. 124, pl. 102

10.7 Robin Kiang after Guarch 1996

10.8 Ethno 1949 Am. 22.118

10.9 Claudio Mari after José R. Oliver (item from Museo del Hombre Dominigano)

10.10 Photo by José R. Oliver

10.11 Ethno 1985 Am. 28.1a-b

10.12 Robin Kiang after José R. Oliver

10.13 Drawing by José R. Oliver

11.1–23 Photos by S. La Niece, N. Meeks and A. Milton

11.1 GR 1872.6-4.516

11.2 PRB 1974.12-1.342-6

11.3 Ethno W364

11.4–5 GR 1872.6-4.516

11.6 Ethno n/n

11.7 Ethno 1955 Am. 7.1

11.8 Ethno 1920.10-13.4a

11.9 Ethno 1936 RWB34

11.10 MLA AF332

11.11 Ethno 1900.4-27.28

11.12 GR 1872.6-4.651

11.13–14 Ethno +1669

11.15–16 GR BMCJ 1655

11.17–18 Ethno 1914.3-28.1

11.19 Ethno 1936 RWB57

11.20 Ethno 1921.7-21.1

11.21 Ethno 1949 Am. 22.217

11.23 Ethno 1966 Am. 6.5

Index